Porting UNIX Software

Porting UNIX Software

From Download to Debug

Greg Lehey

O'Reilly & Associates, Inc.
103 Morris Street, Suite A
Sebastopol, CA 95472

Porting UNIX Software: From Download to Debug
by Greg Lehey

Editor: Andy Oram

Production Editor: Nancy Crumpton

Printing History:

November 1995: First Edition.

This book is printed on acid-free paper with 85% recycled content, 15% post-consumer waste. O'Reilly & Associates is committed to using paper with the highest recycled content available consistent with high quality.

ISBN: 1-56592-126-7

Table of Contents

Tables

Preface

This book is about porting software between UNIX platforms—in other words, the process of taking a software package in source form and installing it on your machine. There's more to porting than meets the eye at first glance. You need to know how to get the software, how to unpack what you get, how to modify the package so that it will compile on your system, how to compile and install the software on your system, and how to deal with problems if they crop up.

Nevertheless, our topic doesn't involve anything that hasn't already been done to death in hundreds of well-written books. You can find out about getting software from the Internet in *The Whole Internet User's Guide and Catalog*, by Ed Krol. Unpacking software is basically a matter of using standard tools described in dozens of helpful introductory textbooks. Compiling programs is so simple that most C textbooks deal with it in passing. Installation is just a matter of copying software to where you want it. Programming is the meat of lots of books on UNIX programming. A fine example is *Advanced Programming in the UNIX Environment* by Richard Stevens.

So why yet another book?

Most textbooks give you an idealized view of programming: "This is the way to do it ("and it works"). They pay little attention to the ways things can go wrong. UNIX is famed for cryptic or misleading error messages, but not many books go into the details of why they appear or what they really mean. Even experienced programmers frequently give up when trying to port software. The probable advantage of completing the port just isn't worth the effort that it takes. In this book, I'd like to reduce that effort.

You'd have to find about three feet of shelf space to hold all the books I just mentioned. They're all good, but they contain information that you don't really want to know right now. (In fact, you're probably not sure if you ever want to know all of it.) Maybe you have a pressing requirement to get a debugger package, or maybe you finally want to get the latest version of *nethack*, complete with X11 support, up and running, and the last thing you want to do on the way is go through those three feet of books.

That's where this book comes in. It covers all steps of porting, from finding the software through porting and testing up to the final installation, in the sequence in which you perform them. It goes into a lot of detail comparing the features of many different UNIX systems and offers suggestions about how to emulate features not available on the platform to which you are porting. It views the problems from a practical rather than from a theoretical perspective. I hope that you'll find the approach more related to your immediate problems.

Audience

This book is intended for anybody who has to compile other people's software on a UNIX platform. It should be of particular interest to you if you're:

- A software developer porting software to a new platform
- A system administrator collecting software products for your system
- A computer hobbyist collecting software off the Internet

Whatever your interest, I expect that you know UNIX basics. If you're a real newcomer, you might like to refer to *Learning the UNIX Operating System* by Grace Todino, John Strang, and Jerry Peek. In addition, *UNIX in a Nutshell*, available in BSD and System V flavors, includes a lot of reference material that I have not included in this book.

The less you know, the more use this book is going to be to you. Nevertheless, even if you're an experienced programmer, you should find a number of tricks to make life easier.

Organization

One of the major problems in porting software is that you need to know everything first. While writing this book I had quite a problem deciding the order in which to present the material. In the end, I took a two-pronged approach, and divided this book into two major parts:

- In Part I, *The Story of a Port*, we'll look at the stages through which a typical port passes: getting the software, extracting the source archives, configuring the package, compiling the software, testing the results, and installing the completed package.
- In Part II, *UNIX Flavor Guide*, we'll take a look at the differences between different flavors of UNIX, how they can make life hard for you, and how we can solve the problems they cause.

Several appendixes list information that you'll find useful when you dig into unfamiliar source code or make files, and sources for software and information.

Operating System Versions

Nearly everything in this book is related to one version or another of UNIX,* and a lot of the text makes sense only in a UNIX context. Nevertheless, it should be of some use to users of other operating systems that use the C programming language and UNIX tools such as *make*.

As in any book about UNIX, it's difficult to give complete coverage to all flavors. The examples in this book were created with six different hardware/software platforms:

- SCO XENIX/386 on an Intel 386 architecture (version 2.3.2)
- UNIX System V.3 on an Intel 386 architecture (Interactive UNIX/386 version 2.2)
- UNIX System V.4.2 on an Intel 386 architecture (Consensys V4.2)
- BSD on an Intel 386 architecture (BSD/386† 1.1 and FreeBSD)
- SunOS on a Sparc architecture (SunOS 4.1.3)
- IRIX 5.3 on an SGI Indy workstation (mainly System V.4)

You may think this book has a strong bias toward Intel architectures. However, most problems are related more to the software platform than the hardware platform. The Intel platform is unique in offering almost every flavor of UNIX that is currently available, and it's easier to compare them if the hardware is invariant. These examples are representative of what you might find on other hardware.

The major difference in UNIX flavors is certainly between UNIX System V.3 and BSD, while System V.4 represents the logical sum of both of them. At a more detailed level, every system has its own peculiarities: there is hardly a system

---

* UNIX is, of course, a registered trademark of its current owner. In this context, I am referring to any operating system that presents a UNIX-like interface to the user and the programmer.

† Later versions of this operating system are called BSD/OS.

available that doesn't have its own quirks. These quirks turn out to be the biggest problem that you have to fight when porting software. Even software that ported just fine on the previous release of your operating system may suddenly turn into an error message generator.

Conventions Used in This Book

This book uses the following conventions:

Bold is used for the names of keys on the keyboard. We'll see more about this in the next section.

Italic is used for the names of UNIX utilities, programming functions, commands, directories, filenames, and options and to emphasize new terms and concepts when they are introduced.

`Constant Width` is used in examples to show the contents of files and the output from commands. It is also used for program variables, the actual values of keywords, and the names of *Usenet* newsgroups.

`Constant Width Italic` is used in examples to show variables for which context-specific substitutions should be made. For example, the variable *`filename`* would be replaced with an actual filename. In addition, *`Constant Width Italic`* is used for comments in code examples.

`Constant Width Bold` is used in examples to show commands or text that the user would type in literally.

Most examples assume the use of the Bourne shell or one of its descendants, such as the Korn shell or the Free Software Foundation's *bash*. The prompt is usually shown as the default `$`, unless it is an operation that requires the superuser, in which case the prompt is shown as `#`. When continuation lines are used, the prompt is the standard >. In cases where the command wouldn't work with the C shell, I present an alternative. In the C shell examples, the prompt is the default `%`.

It's important to distinguish the terms NULL (with two Ls) and NUL (with one L). Both terms refer to zero, but they are used in different ways by a C program. NULL is a pointer, while NUL is a single byte and is written in a program as `'\0'`.

I have tried to make the examples in this book as practical as possible, and most are from real-life sources. A book is not a monitor, however, and displays that look acceptable (well, recognizable) on a monitor can sometimes look really bad in print. In particular, the utilities used in porting sometimes print "lines" of several hundred characters. I have tried to modify such output in the examples so that the output fits on the page. For similar reasons, I have modified the line breaks in some literally quoted texts and have occasionally squeezed things like long directory listings.

Describing the Keyboard

It's surprising how many confusing terms exist to describe individual keys on the keyboard. My favorite is the **any** key ("Press any key to continue"). We won't be using the **any** key in this book, but the names of a number of other keys require explanation:

- I'll refer to the **Enter** or **Return** key as **RETURN**.
- Control characters are characters produced by holding down the **CTRL** key and pressing another key at the same time. These characters are frequently echoed on the screen as a caret (^) followed by the key entered. In keeping with other Nutshell books, I'll write **control-D** as **CTRL-D**.
- The **ALT** key, which Emacs aficionados call a **META** key, works like a second **CTRL** key but generates a different set of characters. These are sometimes abbreviated by prefixing the character with a tilde (~) or the characters **A-**. Since these abbreviations, although useful, can be confusing, I'll spell these out as **CTRL-X** and **ALT-D**, etc.
- **NL** is the *new line* character. In ASCII, it is **CTRL-J**, but UNIX systems generate it when you press the **RETURN** key.
- **CR** is the *carriage return* character, **CTRL-M** in ASCII. Most systems generate it with the **RETURN** key.
- **HT** is the *horizontal tab* character, **CTRL-I**. Most systems generate it when the **TAB** key is pressed.

Terminology

Any technical book uses jargon and technical terms that are not generally known. I've tried to recognize the ones used in this book and describe them when they occur. Apart from this, I will be particularly pedantic about the way I use the following terms in this book:

program

Everybody knows what a program is: a series of instructions to the computer that, when executed, cause a specific action to take place. Source files don't fit this category: a *source program* (a term you won't find again in this book) is really a *program source file* (a file that you canuse, under the correct circumstances, to create a program). Since a program may be interpreted, however, a shell script may qualify as a program. So may something like an Emacs macro, whether byte compiled or not (because Emacs can interpret uncompiled macros directly).

package

A package is a collection of software maintained in a source tree. At various stages in the build process, it includes the following types of files:

source

Files that are part of the distribution

auxiliary

Files such as configuration information and object files that are not part of the source distribution and are not installed

installable

Files that are used after the build process is complete. These files are usually copied outside the source tree so that the source tree can be removed, if necessary.

Some software does not require any conversion: you can simply install the sources straight out of the box. We won't argue whether this counts as a package. It certainly shouldn't give you any porting headaches.

I'll use two other terms as well: *building* and *porting*. It's difficult to come up with a hard-and-fast distinction between the two—we'll discuss the terms in Chapter 1, *Introduction*.

Acknowledgments

Without software developers all over the world, there would be nothing to write about. In particular, the Free Software Foundation and the Computer Sciences Research Group in Berkeley (now defunct) have given rise to an incredible quantity of freely available software. Special thanks go to the reviewers Larry Campbell and Matt Welsh, and particularly to James Cox, Jerry Dunham, and Jörg Micheel for their encouragement and meticulous criticism of what initially was just trying to be a book. Thanks also to Clive King of the University of Aberystwyth for notes on data types and alignment, Steve Hiebert with valuable information about HP-UX, and Henry Spencer and Jeffrey Friedl for help with regular expressions.

Thanks to Santa Cruz Operation, Inc. (SCO) for help with the source code from its header files.

At O'Reilly & Associates, Clairemarie Fisher O'Leary navigated the book through all the twists and turns of production, while Nancy Crumpton edited with a fine eye. Ellen Siever did conversions and formatting work, Kismet McDonough provided editorial back-up and quality checking, and Jane Ellin entered edits. Chris Reilley drew the figures and Edie Freedman put on a cover that stops everyone in their tracks. Seth Maislin edited and fine-tuned the index.

Finally, I can't finish this without mentioning Mike Loukides and Andy Oram at O'Reilly & Associates, who gently persuaded me to write a real book about porting, rather than just presenting the reader with a brain dump.

I

The Story of a Port

In This Chapter:
- *What Is Porting?*
- *How Long Does It Take?*
- *Why We Need to Port*
- *Where You Fit In*
- *But Can I Do It?*
- *How to Use This Book*
- *Preparations*

1

Introduction

One of the features that made UNIX successful was the ease with which it could be implemented on new architectures. This advantage has its down side, which is evident when you compare UNIX with a single-platform operating system such as MS-DOS: since UNIX runs on so many different architectures, it is not possible to write a program, distribute the binaries, and expect them to run on any machine. Instead, programs need to be distributed in source form, and installation involves compiling the programs for the target hardware. In many cases, getting the software to run may be significantly more involved than just typing `make`.

What Is Porting?

It's difficult to make a clear distinction between *porting* and *building*. In this book, I'll use three terms:

- *Building* a package is the planned process of creating an installable software package. This is essentially the content of Chapter 5, *Building the Package.*
- *Installation* is the planned process of putting an installable software package where users can use it. This is what we talk about in Chapter 9, *Installation.*
- Some people use the term *porting* to describe a software installation requiring undocumented changes to adapt it to a new environment. They don't include the process of configuration when it is intended to be part of the build process. Although this definition is useful, it contains an element of uncertainty: when you start, you don't know whether the process is going to be a build or a port. It's easier to call the whole process *porting*, whether you have to perform a simple build or make complicated modifications to the source. That's the way we'll use the term in this book.

The effort required to port a package can vary considerably. If you are running a SparcStation and receive software developed specifically for SparcStations, and the software does not offer much in the way of configuration options, you probably really *can* get it to run by reading the sources onto disk and typing `make` and `make install`. This is the exception, however, not the rule. Even with a SparcStation, you might find that the package is written for a different release of the operating system, and that this fact requires significant modifications. A more typical port might include getting the software, configuring the package, building the package, formatting and printing the documentation, testing the results, and installing files in the destination directories.

How Long Does It Take?

It is very difficult to gauge the length of time required to complete a port. If a port takes a long time, it's not usually because of the speed of the machine you use: few packages take more than a few hours to compile on a fast workstation. Even the complete X11R6 windowing system takes only about four hours on an 66 MHz Intel 486 PC.

The real time-consumers are the bugs you might encounter on the way: if you're unlucky, you can run into big trouble, and you may find yourself getting to know the package you're porting much more intimately than you wish, or even having to find and fix bugs.

Probably the easiest kind of program to port is free software, that is to say, software that is freely redistributable. As a result of the ease of redistribution, it tends to be ported more frequently and to more platforms, and configuration bugs get ironed out more evenly than in commercial software. Porting a product like *bison** from the Free Software Foundation usually involves just a matter of minutes:

```
$ configure
checking how to run the C preprocessor
... messages from configure
$ make
... messages from make
$ make install
```

On an Intel 486/66, *configure* runs for 15 seconds, *make* runs for about 85 seconds, and *make install* runs for about 5 seconds—all in all, less than two minutes. If everything were that simple, nobody would need this book.

On the other hand, this simple view omits a point or two. *bison* comes with typeset documentation. Like most products of the Free Software Foundation, it is written in *texinfo* format, which relies on TEX for formatting. It doesn't get formatted

* *bison* is a parser generator, compatible with *yacc*.

automatically. In fact, if you look for the target in the *Makefile*, you'll find that there isn't one: the *Makefile* ignores printed documentation. I consider this a bug in the *Makefile*. Never mind (you might think), it's easy enough to do it manually:

```
$ tex bison.texinfo
tex: not found
```

This occurrence is fairly typical when porting: in order to port a package, you first need to port three other, more complicated packages. In fact, most ports of *bison* are made in order to compile some other product, such as the GNU C compiler. In order to print the documentation, we first need to port TeX, which is appropriately depicted in its own printed documentation as a shaggy lion. Porting TeX is definitely nontrivial.

- TeX consists of dozens of different parts.
- The TeX source tree varies greatly depending on where you obtain it.
- The entire TeX program is written in Web (Donald Knuth's own private dialect of Pascal).
- Once you finally get TeX to run, you discover that the output (deliberately) does not print on any available printer and that you need a so-called "printer driver" to output it to your favorite laser printer—yet another port.

Under these circumstances, it wouldn't be surprising if you give up and rely on the online documentation supplied with *bison*. *bison* has two different online reference documents: a *man* page and something called *info*, a cross-linked documentation reader from the Free Software Foundation. The man page is two pages long, while info runs to over 200K in five files. You don't receive a prize for guessing where the real information is. But how do you run *info*? Simple: you port the GNU *texinfo* package. This time it's not quite as bad as porting TeX, but it's still more difficult than porting *bison*.

This scenario is fairly typical: you set out to port something simple, everything seems to be fine, and then you find that a minor part of the port can really consume lots of time. Typically, this is the point where most people give up and make do with what they have already achieved. This book is intended to help you go the whole distance.

Why We Need to Port

There are three main reasons why a port might be more than a simple recompilation:

Different operating system
: Depending on what features the operating system offers, the program may need to be modified. For example, when porting a program from UNIX to DOS, you definitely have to do something about filenaming conventions. If you port a System V.4 program to BSD, you may find you need to replace STREAMS calls with sockets calls.

Different hardware
: This barrier is obvious in the case of a display driver. If the driver you have is designed for a Sun workstation and you're porting it to a PC, you will be involved in some serious rewriting. Even in more mundane circumstances, such things as the kind of CPU involved might influence the program design.

Local choices
: These include installation pathnames and cooperation with other installed software. For example, if you use the *emacs* editor, you may choose to use the *etags* program to cross-reference your source files; if you use *vi*, you would probably prefer to use *ctags*. Depending on the C compiler, you may need to use different compilation options. Many local choices look like the differences you see when you have a different operating system, but you're much luckier when you have to deal with just local choices. You can change the C compiler or even the system library without changing the basic system.

UNIX Flavors

UNIX spent the first ten years of its existence as the object of computer science research. Developed at Bell Labs (which was part of AT&T), it was significantly extended at the University of California at Berkeley, which started releasing significant updates, the so-called Berkeley Software Distribution (BSD) in 1977. By the time AT&T decided to commercialize UNIX with System III in the early '80s, the fourth version of BSD was already available, and both System III and System V drew heavily from it. Nevertheless, the differences were significant, and despite the advent of System V.4, which basically added all features available in any UNIX dialect into one package, the differences remain. A good overview of the relationship between the UNIXes can be found in *The Design and the Implementation of the 4.3BSD UNIX Operating System* by Sam Leffler, Kirk McKusick, Mike Karels, and John Quarterman. In this book I will concentrate on the differences that can be of importance when porting from one flavor to another.

Research UNIX

Research UNIX is the original UNIX that has been developed at Bell Labs since 1969. The last version that became widely available was the Seventh Edition in 1978. This version can be considered the granddaddy of them all,* and is also frequently called Version 7. In this book, I'll make frequent references to this version. Work on Research UNIX continued until 1993, by which time it had reached the Tenth Edition. It's unlikely that you'll have much to do with it directly, but occasionally ideas from Research UNIX trickle into other flavors.

Berkeley UNIX (BSD)

The first Berkeley Software Distribution was derived from the Sixth Edition in 1977 and ran on PDP-11s only. 2BSD was the last PDP-11 version: 2.11BSD is still available for PDP-11s, if you have a need (and a UNIX source license). 3BSD was derived from 2BSD and the Seventh Edition—via a short-lived version called 32V—in 1979. Since then, BSD has evolved relatively free of outside borrowings. With the closure of the Computer Science Research Group in Berkeley in the autumn of 1993 and the release of 4.4BSD in early 1994, the original BSD line has died out, but the public release of the complete sources will ensure the continued availability of Berkeley UNIX for a long time to come.

Current BSD systems include BSD/OS (formerly called BSD/386), 386BSD, NetBSD, and FreeBSD. These were all originally ports of the BSD Net-2 tape, which was released in 1991, to the Intel 386 architecture. These ports are interesting because they are almost pure BSD and contain no AT&T licensed code. BSD/OS is a commercial system that costs money and supplies support; the other three are available free of charge. It is not clear how long all three free versions will continue to exist side by side. 386BSD may already be dead, and the difference between NetBSD and FreeBSD is difficult to recognize.

At the time of this writing, current versions of BSD/OS and FreeBSD are based on 4.4BSD, and NetBSD is planning to follow suit.

XENIX

XENIX is a version of UNIX developed by Microsoft for Intel architectures in the early '80s. It was based mainly on the System III versions available at the time, though some ideas from other versions were included and a significant amount of work was applied to making it an easier system to live with. Not much effort was put into making it compatible with other versions of UNIX, however, and so you

* In fact, a number of UNIX flavors, including System V and BSD, can trace their origins back to the Sixth Edition of 1976, but they all benefited from modifications made in the Seventh Edition.

can run into a few surprises with XENIX. SCO still markets it, but development appears to have stopped about 1989.

System V

System V was derived from the Sixth and Seventh editions via System III, with a certain amount borrowed from 4.0BSD. It has become the standard commercial UNIX and is currently the only flavor allowed to bear the UNIX trademark. It has evolved significantly since its introduction in 1982, with borrowings from Research UNIX and BSD at several points along the way. Currently available versions are V.3 (SCO Open Desktop) and V.4 (almost everybody else).

System V.3 lacked a number of features available in other UNIXes, with the result that almost all V.3 ports have borrowed significantly from other versions, mainly 4.2BSD. The result is that you can't really be sure what you have with System V.3—you need to consult the documentation for more information. In particular, vanilla System V.3 supports only the original UNIX file system, with the length of filenames limited to 14 characters and with no symbolic links. It also does not have a standard data communications interface, though both BSD sockets and System V STREAMS have been ported to it.

System V.3.2 is, as its name suggests, a version of System V.3. This version is compatible with XENIX system calls. As we saw earlier, XENIX went its own way for some time, resulting in incompatibilities with System V. These XENIX features should be supported by the kernel from System V.3.2 onward. SCO UNIX is version V.3.2 and includes STREAMS support.

System V.4 is the current version of System V. Previous versions of System V were often criticized for lacking features. This cannot be said of System V.4: it incorporates System V.3.2 (which already incorporates XENIX), 4.3BSD, and SunOS. The result is an enormous system that has three different ways to do many things. It also still has significant bugs.

Developing software under System V.4 is an interesting experience. Since the semantics of System V.3 and BSD differ in some areas, System V.4 supplies two separate sets of libraries, one with a System V personality and one with a BSD personality. You don't receive a prize for guessing which is more reliable: unless you really need to, you should use the System V libraries. When we discuss kernel and library differences in the second part of this book, the statement "This feature is supported by System V.4" means that the System V library interface supports it. The statement "This feature is supported by BSD" also implies that it should be supported by the BSD library interface of System V.4.

OSF/1

OSF/1 is a comparatively recent development in the UNIX market. It was developed by the Open Systems Foundation, an industry consortium formed as a result of dissatisfaction with AT&T's policy on UNIX. The kernel is based on CMU's Mach operating system, a so-called *microkernel*.* The original Mach operating system was styled on Berkeley UNIX. OSF/1 attempts to offer the same functionality as System V, though inevitably some incompatibilities exist.

POSIX.1

POSIX is a series of emerging IEEE standards that apply to operating systems, utilities, and programming languages. The relevant standard for operating systems is IEEE 1003.1-1990, commonly called POSIX.1. It has also been adopted by the International Standards Organization (ISO) as standard ISO/IEC 9945.1:1990.

POSIX.1 defines the interface between application programs and the operating system and makes no demands on the operating system except that it should supply the POSIX.1 interface. POSIX.1 looks very much like a subset of UNIX. In fact, most users wouldn't notice the difference. This makes it easy for UNIX operating systems to supply a POSIX.1 interface. Other operating systems might require more modification to become POSIX.1-compliant. From a UNIX viewpoint, since POSIX.1 does not supply as rich a set of functions as any of the commercially available UNIX flavors, programming to POSIX specifications can feel somewhat restrictive. This matter is discussed in the *POSIX Programmer's Guide* by Donald Lewine.

Despite these slight disadvantages, POSIX has a great influence on operating system development: all modern flavors of UNIX claim to be POSIX-compliant, although the degree of success varies somewhat, and other systems are also attempting to supply a POSIX.1 interface. The trend is clear: future UNIX-like operating systems will be POSIX-compliant, and if you stick to POSIX features, your porting problems will be over. And I have a supply of bridges for sale, first come, first served.

Linux

Linux is a UNIX clone for the Intel 386 architecture written by Linus Torvalds, a student in Helsinki. It has absolutely no direct connection with traditional UNIX flavors, which gives it the unique advantage among free UNIXes of not being a potential subject for litigation. Apart from that, it has a vaguely System V–like

* A microkernel operating system is an operating system that leaves significant operating system functionality to external components, usually processes. For example, device drivers and file systems are frequently implemented as separate processes. It does not imply that the complete system is any smaller or less functional than the monolithic UNIX kernel.

feeling about it. If you are porting to Linux, you should definitely subscribe to the very active network news groups *comp.os.linux.**.

Other flavors

It doesn't take much effort to add a new feature to a kernel, and people do it all the time. The result is a proliferation of systems that mix various features of the leading products and additional features of the developers. On top of that, the release of kernel sources to the Net has caused a proliferation of "free" operating systems. Systems that you might well run into include:

- AIX, IBM's name for its UNIX versions. Current versions are based on System V.3, but IBM has stated an intent to migrate to OSF/1. (IBM is a leading member of the OSF.) Compared to System V, AIX has a large number of extensions, some of which can cause significant pain to the unwary.
- HP-UX, Hewlett-Packard's UNIX system. It is based on System V.3 but contains a large number of so-called *BSD extensions*. Within HP, it is considered to be about 80 percent BSD-compliant.
- SunOS, the generic name of Sun Microsystems' operating systems. The original SunOS was derived from 4.2BSD and 4.3BSD, and until release 4.1 it was predominantly BSD-based with a significant System V influence. Starting with version 5.0, it is a somewhat modified version of System V.4. These later versions are frequently referred to as *Solaris*, though this term properly applies to the complete system environment, including the windowing system (OpenWindows), development tools, and such, and does not apply only to the System–V based versions. Solaris 1.x includes the BSD-based SunOS 4.1 as its kernel; Solaris 2.x includes the System V.4–based SunOS 5.x as its kernel.
- Ultrix is DEC's port of 4.1BSD and 4.2BSD to the VAX and MIPS-based workstations. It is now obsolete and has been replaced by OSF/1, marketed under the name Digital UNIX.

I would have liked to go into more detail about these versions of UNIX, but doing so would have increased the size of the book significantly. Even so, it wouldn't be possible to guarantee accuracy; most systems add functionality in the course of their evolution, and information that is valid for one release may not apply to an earlier or a later release. As a result, I've made a compromise: since nearly all UNIX features were introduced either in BSD or System V, I distinguish primarily between these two versions. Where significant differences exist in other operating systems—SunOS 4 is an example—I discuss them separately.

Where does this leave you with, say, NonStop UX version B30? NonStop UX version B is a version of UNIX System V.4 that runs on Tandem's Integrity series of fault-tolerant MIPS-based UNIX systems. It includes some additional functionality to manipulate the hardware, and some of the header files differ from the standard System V.4. In addition, it includes a minimal carryover of BSDisms from the System V.3 version. Obviously, you can start by treating it as an implementation of System V.4, but occasionally you will find things that don't quite seem to fit in. Since it's a MIPS-based system, you might consider it to be like SGI's IRIX operating system version 5, which is System V.4 for SGI's MIPS-based hardware. Indeed, most IRIX 5.x binaries also run unchanged on NonStop UX version B, but you will notice significant differences when you try to port packages that already run on IRIX 5.x.

These differences are typical of a port to just about every real-life system. Very few pure System V.4 or pure BSD systems are out there—everybody has added *something* to their ports. Ultimately, you need to examine each individual problem as it occurs. Here is a strategy you can use to untangle most problems on UNIX systems:

- Interpret the error messages to figure out what feature or function call is causing the problem. Typically, the error message comes from the compiler and points to a specific line in a specific file.
- Figure out how to achieve the same effect on your own system. Sometimes I recommend a change that you can make. After making the change, try running the program again. If you're not sure how your system works, you can probably find a manual page for the feature or call, and this book will help you interpret it.
- Reconfigure or change the code as necessary, and then try building again.

Where You Fit In

The effort involved in porting software depends a lot on the package and the way it is maintained. It doesn't make much difference whether the software is subject to a commercial license or is freely available on the Net: the people who write and maintain it can never hope to port it to more than a fraction of the platforms available. The result is that there will always be problems that they won't know about. There is also a very good chance that the well-known and well-used package you are about to port may never have been ported quite that way before. This can have some important consequences:

- You may run into bugs that nobody has ever seen before in a well-known and well-used package.

- The package that you ported in ten minutes last year and have been using ever since has been updated, and now you can't get the @&*(&@$ to compile or run.

This also means that if you do encounter problems porting a package, your feedback is important, whether or not you can supply a fix. If you do supply a fix, it should fit into the package structure so that it can be included in a subsequent release.

To reiterate: it makes very little difference whether we are talking about free or licensed software. The players involved are different, but the problems are not. In many ways, free software is easier, since there are fewer restrictions in talking about it (if you run into problems porting System V.4, you can't just send the code out on the net and ask for suggestions), and it's likely that more people will have ported it to more platforms already. Apart from that, few differences exist between free and licensed software.

But Can I Do It?

Of course, maybe your concern is whether you can do it at all. If you've never ported a program before, you might think that it is altogether too difficult. You might think you'll spend days and weeks of effort and confusion and in the end give it up because you don't understand what is going on, and that every time you solve a problem, two new ones spring up in its place.

I'd like to say "Don't worry, with *this* book nothing can go wrong," but unfortunately, that isn't always the case. On the other hand, it's easy to overestimate the things that can go wrong or how difficult a port might be.

Let's look at the bad news first. In most cases, you can assume that the worst that can happen when you try to port a package is that it won't work, but in some unfortunate cases, you may cause your system to panic, especially if you are porting kernel software such as device drivers. In addition, if you are porting system utilities and they don't work, you could find that you can no longer perform such essential system functions as starting or shutting down the system. These problems don't occur very often, though, and they should not cause any lasting damage if you religiously back up your system. (You *do* perform regular backups, don't you?)

Apart from such possible dangers, very little can go wrong. If you are building a package that has already had been ported to your platform, you should not run into any problems that this book can't help you solve, even if you have a negligible background in programming and none in porting.

How to Use This Book

Part One

The way you approach porting depends on how difficult it is. If it's a straightforward business, something that has been done dozens of times before, like our earlier example of porting *bison*, it's just a matter of following the individual steps. This is our approach in the first part of this book, in which we look at the following topics:

- *Getting the software*

  You might get the sources on tape or on CD-ROM or by copying them from the Internet. Getting them from one of these formats into a format you can use to compile them may not be as simple as you think. We'll look at this subject in Chapter 2, *Unpacking the Goodies*, and Chapter 3, *Care and Feeding of Source Trees*.

- *Configuring the package for building*

  Although UNIX is a relatively well-defined operating system, some features are less well defined. For example, there are a number of different ways to perform interprocess communication. Many packages contain alternative code for a number of operating systems, but you still need to choose the correct alternative. People often underestimate this step: it seems simple enough, but in many cases it can be more work than all the rest put together.

  Configuration is a complicated subject, and various methods have evolved. In Chapter 4, *Configuring the Package*, we'll look at manual configuration, shell scripts, and *imake*, the X11 configuration solution.

- *Building the package*

  This process is what most people understand as *porting*. We'll look at problems running *make* in Chapter 5, and problems running the C compiler in Chapter 6, *Running the Compiler*.

- *Formatting and printing the documentation*

  We'll investigate this topic in Chapter 7, *Documentation*.

- *Testing the results to make sure that they work*

  We'll look at this in Chapter 8, *Testing the Results*.

- *Installing correctly, accurately, and completely*

  We'll discuss how to do this in Chapter 9.

- *Tidying up after the build*

  In Chapter 10, *Where to Go from Here*, we'll look at what this entails.

Fortunately, almost no package gives you trouble all the way; but since it's interesting to follow a port through from getting the software to the finished installation, I'll draw my examples in these chapters from a few free software packages for electronic mail and Usenet news. Specifically, we'll consider Taylor *uucp*, the electronic mail reader *elm*, and C news. In addition, we'll look at the GNU C compiler *gcc*, because it is one of the most frequently ported packages. We'll port them to an Intel 486DX/2-66 machine running BSD/386 Version 1.1.*

Part Two

As long as things go smoothly, you can get through the kind of port described in the first part of this book with little or no programming knowledge. Unfortunately, things don't always go smoothly. If they don't, you may need to make possibly far-reaching changes to the sources. The first part of this book doesn't pay much attention to this kind of modification—that's the topic of the second part, which *does* expect an understanding of programming.

In Chapter 11, *Hardware Dependencies*, we'll look at problems caused by differences in the underlying hardware platforms. The biggest problem you'll probably have with configuration will be with the software platform. Even if you limit your scope to the various UNIX versions, 25 years of continuing (and mainly uncoordinated) evolution have left behind a plethora of marginally compatible versions. The only good aspect of the situation is that porting between UNIX versions is still an order of magnitude easier than porting to or from a non-UNIX environment.

It's easy to misjudge the effort required to port to a different platform. It helps to make clear distinctions between the following kinds of functionality:

- Functionality that relies on system calls (section two of the UNIX manual pages). These calls interface directly with the kernel. If the kernel doesn't supply the functionality, you may have serious difficulty in porting the product. Examples are the System V function `shmget`, which allocates an area of shared memory, or the BSD system call `symlink`, which creates a symbolic link.
- Functionality dependent on system library calls (section three of the UNIX man pages). If this kind of functionality does not rely on system calls, you may be able to port a corresponding call from another library. An example of this is the function `strcasecmp`, which compares strings ignoring case. This function is supplied with later versions of the BSD library and also with the GNU C

* BSD/OS, which was called BSD/386 in Version 1.1, already supplied *elm* and C news, so you would need to port them only if you wanted to modify them or use a new version.

library but not with System V libraries. If you don't have this function, it's trivial to port.

- Functionality contained totally *inside* the package, like math routines that don't call external libraries. This kind of functionality should work on any platform.

Some systems, such as OSF/1, have merged sections two and three of the manual pages. While that has some advantages (if you know a function name, you don't have to go to two different places to look for them), it *doesn't* mean that a difference no longer exists.

Kernel dependencies are significantly more difficult to handle than library dependencies because there's relatively little you can do about them. We'll look at kernel-related problems in Chapter 12, *Kernel Dependencies*, Chapter 13, *Signals*, Chapter 14, *File Systems*, Chapter 15, *Terminal Drivers*, and Chapter 16, *Timekeeping*. In Chapter 17, *Header Files*, we'll look at the surprising number of headaches caused by header files, and in Chapter 18, *Function Libraries*, we'll look at libraries.

In addition to these program dependencies, two tools can differ significantly: the *make* program and the C compiler. We'll look at these tools in Chapter 19, *make*, and Chapter 20, *Compilers*. Finally, in Chapter 21, *Object Files and Friends*, we'll look at some of the more esoteric aspects of object files.

The major difference between kernels and libraries is usually with System V and BSD, while other systems such as SunOS take a midfield position. System V.4 incorporates nearly everything in BSD. When programming, you have the choice between using the native System V development tools or the BSD tools. Some admixture is possible, but it can cause problems.

When using BSD development tools, everything that is supported by BSD should also be supported by System V.4. On the other hand, System V.4 includes some functionality that no other system provides. When, in the following chapters, I say that a function is supported by System V.4, I mean that it is supported by System V.4 using the standard development tools and libraries. If I state that it is supported by BSD, that implies that it is supported by System V.4 using the BSD libraries.

Appendixes and Bibliography

Finally, the five appendixes contain a good deal of reference material that you'll be glad to get your hands on in times of need.

Appendix A

Comparative Reference to UNIX Data Types describes the plethora of data types that have developed since the advent of ANSI C.

Appendix B

C Compiler Options gives you a comparative reference to the compiler flags of many common systems.

Appendix C

Assembler Directives and Options gives you a comparative reference to assembler directives and flags.

Appendix D

Linker Options provides a comparative reference to linker flags.

Appendix E

Where to Get Sources gives you information on where to find useful source files, including a number of the packages we discuss in this book.

The Bibliography lists the books mentioned in this book and additional ones you can consult for more information.

Preparations

You don't need much to port most packages. Usually everything you need—a C compiler, a C library, *make*, and some standard tools—should be available on your system. If you have a system that doesn't include some of these tools, such as a System V release in which every individual program seems to cost extra, or if the tools are so out of date that they are almost useless, such as XENIX, you may have problems.

If your tools are less than adequate, you should consider using the products of the Free Software Foundation. In particular, the GNU C compiler *gcc* is better than many proprietary compilers and is the standard compiler of the Open Software Foundation. You can get many packages directly from the Internet or on CD-ROM. If you are going to be doing any serious porting, I recommend that you get at least the GNU software packages, 4.4BSD Lite, and TEX, preferably on CD-ROM. In particular, the GNU software and 4.4BSD Lite contain the sources to many library functions that may be missing from your system. In addition, many of the GNU packages are available in precompiled binary form from a number of sources. I'll refer to these packages frequently in the text.

In This Chapter:
- *Getting the Sources*
- *Archives*

2

Unpacking the Goodies

Before you can start porting, you need to put the sources on disk. I use the term *source tree* to refer to the directory or hierarchy of directories in which the package is stored. Unpacking the archives may not be as trivial as it seems: software packages are supplied in many different formats, and it is not always easy to recognize the format. In this chapter, we'll look at how to extract the sources to create the source tree. In Chapter 3, *Care and Feeding of Source Trees*, we'll see how the source tree changes in the course of a port, and what you can do to keep it in good shape.

Getting the Sources

The standard way to get software sources is on some form of storage medium, such as CD-ROM or tape. Many packages are also available online via the Internet. The choice is not as simple as it seems.

Software from the Internet

If you have an Internet connection and if the software is available on the Net, it's tempting just to copy it across the Net with *ftp*. This may not be the best choice, however. Some packages are very big. The compressed sources of the GNU C compiler, for example, occupy about 6 MB. You can't rely on a typical 56 Kbps line to transfer more than about 2 kilobytes per second.* At this speed, it takes nearly an hour to copy the archives. If you're connected via a SLIP (Serial Line Internet Protocol), it could take several hours.

* Of course, it *should* approach 7 kilobytes per second, but network congestion can pull this figure down to a trickle.

Gaining access to the archive sites is not always trivial: many sites have a maximum number of users. In particular, `prep.ai.mit.edu`, the prime archive site for *gcc*, is frequently overloaded, and you may need several attempts to get in. Luckily, many other sites offer the same software, and you can find a list in the file named *FTP*.

In addition, copying software over the Net is not free. It may not cost you money, but somebody has to pay for the use of the telephone lines. And once you have the software, you need somewhere to store it, so you don't really save on archive media.

Choice of Archive Medium

If you do choose to get your software on some other medium, you have the choice between CD-ROM and tape. Many archive sites will send you tapes if you ask for them. This may seem like a slow and old-fashioned way to get the software, but the bandwidth is high.* Since DAT and Exabyte tapes can store 2 GB per tape, a single tape could easily contain as much software as you can duplicate in a week. In addition, you don't need to make a backup before you start.

Software on CD-ROM is not as up to date as that on a freshly copied tape, but it's easy to store and reasonably cheap. Many companies make frequent CD editions of the more widely known archive sites. For example, Walnut Creek CD-ROM has editions of most commonly known software, frequently preported, and Prime Time Freeware issues a pair of CD-ROMs twice a year with 5 GB of compressed software including lesser-known packages. These editions can be worthwhile just to find packages that you would otherwise not even have known about.

If you have already ported a previous version of the package, another alternative is to use *diffs* to bring the archive up to date. We'll look at this in the section called "Updating Old Archives" in Chapter 3.

Archives

You frequently get pure source trees on CD-ROM, but other media, and also many CD-ROMs, transform the source tree several times:

- A source tree is usually supplied in an *archive*, a file containing a number of other files. Like a paper bag around groceries, an archive puts a wrapper around the files so that you can handle them more easily.

* To quote a fortune from the *fortune* program: *Never underestimate the bandwidth of a station wagon full of tapes.*

- Archives make it easier to handle files, but they don't do anything to save space. Much of the information in files is redundant: each byte can have 256 different values, but typically 99% of an archive of text or program sources consists of the 96 printable ASCII characters, and a large proportion of these characters are blanks. It makes sense to encode them in a more efficient manner to save space. This is the purpose of *compression* programs. Modern compression programs such as *gzip* reduce the size of an archive by up to 90%.
- If you want to transfer archives by electronic mail, you may also need to *encode* them to comply with the allowable email character set.
- Large archives can become very unwieldy. We have already seen that it can take several hours to transfer *gcc*. If the connection to the Net drops in this time, you may find that you have to start transferring the file again. As a result, archives are frequently *split* into more manageable chunks.

The most common form of archive you'll find on the Internet or on CD-ROM is *gzipped tar*, a *tar* archive that has been compressed with *gzip*. A close second is *compressed tar*, a *tar* archive that has been compressed with *compress*. From time to time, you'll find a number of others. In the following sections we'll take a brief look at the programs that perform these tasks and recover the data.

Archive Programs

A number of archive programs are available:

- *tar*, the tape archive program, is the all-time favorite. The chances are about 95% that your archive will be in *tar* format, even if it has nothing to do with tape.
- *cpio* is a newer file format that once, years ago, was intended to replace *tar*. *cpio* archives suffer from compatibility problems, however, and you don't see them very often.
- *ar* is a disk archive program. Although it is occasionally used for source archives, nowadays it is almost always used for object file archives. Since the *ar* archive format has never been completely standardized, you get an *ar* archive from a different machine, you might have a lot of trouble extracting it. We'll look at *ar* formats again in the section called "Object Archive Formats" in Chapter 21, *Object Files and Friends*.
- *shar* is the shell archive program. It is unique among archive programs in never using nonprinting characters, so *shar* archives can be sent by mail. You can extract *shar* archives simply by feeding them to a (Bourne) shell, though it is safer to extract them using a program like *unshar*.

Living with tar

tar is a relatively easy program to use, but the consequences of mistakes can be far reaching. In the following sections, we'll look at how to use *tar* and how to avoid trouble.

Basic use

When it comes to unpacking software, one or two *tar* commands can meet all your needs. First, you often want to look at the contents before unpacking. Assuming that the archive is named *et1.3.tar*, the following command lists the files in the archive:

```
$ tar tf et1.3.tar
et1.3/
et1.3/bell.c
pet1.3/bltgraph.c
et1.3/BLURB
        .
        .
        .
```

The *t* option stands for table of contents. The *f* option means "use the next parameter in the command (*et1.3.tar*) as the archive to list."

To read in the files that were listed, use the command:

```
$ tar xfv et1.3.tar
et1.3/
et1.3/bell.c
pet1.3/bltgraph.c
et1.3/BLURB
        .
        .
        .
```

The list looks the same, but this time the command actually creates the directory *et1.3* if necessary, and then creates the contents. The *x* option stands for *extract*. The *f* option has the same meaning as before. The *v* option means "verbose" and is responsible for generating the list, which gives you the assurance that the command is actually doing something.

To bundle some files into an archive, use a command like:

```
$ tar cvf et1.3.tar et1.3
```

This command packs everything in the *et1.3* directory into an archive named *et1.3.tar* (which is where we started). The *c* option stands for "create" and the *v* option for "verbose." This time, the *f* means "use the next parameter in the command (*et1.3.tar*) as the archive to create."

Absolute pathnames

Many versions of *tar* have difficulties with absolute pathnames. If you specify */usr/bin* as the directory to back up, the user has to extract the contents of the archive into exactly this directory. It would be much more convenient if the user could create a new directory somewhere else and direct the contents of the archive there. (Imagine for instance, that the user is running a shell that resides in */usr/bin* and your archive replaces that shell—that leads to severe problems.) Some versions of *tar* have an option to ignore the leading */*, and others, such as GNU *tar*, ignore it unless you tell them otherwise.

Symbolic links

Many versions of *tar* back up a symbolic link as just the file containing a pointer, failing to include the file or directory to which it points. This backup method can be embarrassing if you send somebody a tape with what should be a complete software package, and it arrives with only a single symbolic link.

Tape block size

Many DDS (DAT) drives work better with high blocking factors, such as 65,536 bytes per block (128 "tape blocks"). You can change the blocking with the option `b` (block size):

```
$ tar cvfb /dev/tape 128 foo-dir
```

Unfortunately, this method can cause problems, too. Some DDS drives cannot read tapes with block sizes of more than 32,768 bytes, and some versions of *tar*, such as SGI IRIS 5.x, cannot handle tapes blocked larger than 20 tape blocks (10,240 bytes). It's not a show-stopper if you have a tape that is blocked at more than 20: you just won't be able to read it directly. You can solve this problem by installing GNU *tar* or piping the archive through *dd*:

```
$ dd if=/dev/rmt/ctape0 ibs=128b obs=2b | tar xvf -
```

Filenames

Most versions of *tar* perform filename matching based on the exact text as it appears on the tape. If you want to extract specific files, you must use the names by which they are known in the archive. For example, some versions of *tar* may end up writing absolute names with two leading slashes (*//usr/bin/sh*, for example). This doesn't worry the operating system, which treats multiple leading slashes the same as a single leading slash, but if you want to extract this file, you need to write:

```
$ tar x //usr/bin/sh
```

Filename sorting

A *tar* archive listing with *tar tv* deliberately looks very much like a listing done with *ls -l*. One major difference, however is that *ls -l* sorts the filenames by name before displaying them, whereas *tar*, being a serial archive program, displays the names in the order in which they occur in the archive. The list may look somewhat sorted, depending on how the archive was created, but you can't rely on it. This means that if you are looking for a filename in an archive, you should not be misled if it's not where you expect to find it: use tools like *grep* or *sort* to be sure.

Spurious "cannot create" messages

With System V systems, you may see messages like:

```
$ tar xvf shellutils-1.9.4.tar
tar: shellutils-1.9.4/ - cannot create
x shellutils-1.9.4/COPYING, 17982 bytes, 36 tape blocks
x shellutils-1.9.4/COPYING.LIB, 25263 bytes, 50 tape blocks
tar: shellutils-1.9.4/lib/ - cannot create
x shellutils-1.9.4/lib/Makefile.in, 2868 bytes, 6 tape blocks
x shellutils-1.9.4/lib/getopt.h, 4412 bytes, 9 tape blocks
```

This "bug" has been around so long that you might suspect it to be an insider joke. In fact, it is a benign compatibility problem. The POSIX.2 standard *tar* format allows archives to contain both directory and filenames, although the directory names are not really necessary: assuming it has permission, *tar* creates all directories necessary to extract a file. The only use of the directory names is to specify the modification time and permissions of the directory. Older versions of *tar*, including System V *tar*, do not include the directory names in the archive and don't understand them when they find them. In this example, we have extracted a POSIX.2 *tar* archive on a System V system, and it doesn't understand (or need) the directory information. The only effect is that the directories will not have the correct modification timestamps and possibly not the correct permissions.

Losing access to your files

Some versions of *tar*, notably System V versions, have another trick in store: they restore the original *owner* of the files, even if that owner does not exist. You can lose access to your files completely if they happen to have permissions like `rw-------`. You can avoid this by using the `o` option (restore ownership to current user).

It would be nice to be able to say "make a rule of always using the o option". Unfortunately, other versions of *tar* define this option differently—check your manual pages for details.

Multivolume archives

tar can also handle multivolume archives, in other words, archives that require more than one tape. The methods used are not completely portable: one version of *tar* may not be able to read multivolume archives written by a different version. Some versions of *tar* just stop writing data at the end of one tape and continue where they left off at the beginning of the next reel; others write header information on the second tape to indicate that it is a continuation volume. If possible, you should avoid writing multivolume archives unless you are sure that the destination system can read them. If you run into problems with multivolume archives you can't read, you might save the day with something like:

```
$ (dd if=$TAPE
++ echo 1>&2 Change tapes and press RET
++ read confirmation          the name of the variable isn't important
++ dd if=$TAPE
++ echo 1>&2 Change tapes and press RET
++ read confirmation
++ dd if=$TAPE) | tar xvf -
```

This uses *dd* to copy the first tape to *stdout*, then prints a message and waits for you to press **RETURN**, copies a second tape, prompts and waits again, and then copies a third tape. Since all the commands are in parentheses, the standard output of all three *dd* commands is piped into the *tar* waiting outside. The *echo* commands need to go to *stderr* (that's the 1>&2) to be displayed on the terminal—otherwise they would be piped into the *tar*, which would not appreciate it.

The script shown above works only if the version of *tar* you use doesn't put any header information (like reel number and a repeat of the file header) at the beginning of the subsequent reels. If it does and you can't find a compatible *tar* to extract it again, the following method may help. Assuming that a user of an SCO system has given you a large program *foo* spread over three diskettes, each of which contains header information that your *tar* doesn't understand, you might enter:

```
$ tar x foo        extract first part from first floppy
$ mv foo foo.0     save the first part
$ tar x foo        extract second part from second floppy
$ mv foo foo.1     save the second part
$ tar x foo        extract third part from third floppy
$ mv foo foo.2     save the third part
```

```
$ cat foo.* >foo      concatenate them
$ rm foo.*            and remove the intermediate files
```

Extracting an archive with tar

Using *tar* to extract a file is usually pretty straightforward. You can cause a lot of confusion, however, if you extract into a directory that contains other files you want to keep. Most archives contain the contents of a single directory as viewed from the parent directory—in other words, the name of the directory is the first part of all filenames. All GNU software follows this rule:

```
$ tar tvf groff-1.09.tar
drwxr-xr-x jjc/staff        0 Feb 19 14:15 1994 groff-1.09/
drwxr-xr-x jjc/staff        0 Feb 19 14:13 1994 groff-1.09/include/
-rw-r--r-- jjc/staff      607 Sep 21 12:03 1992 groff-1.09/include/Makefile.sub
-rw-r--r-- jjc/staff     1157 Oct 30 07:38 1993 groff-1.09/include/assert.h
-rw-r--r-- jjc/staff     1377 Aug  3 12:34 1992 groff-1.09/include/cmap.h
-rw-r--r-- jjc/staff     1769 Aug 10 15:48 1992 groff-1.09/include/cset.h
```

Others, however, show the files from the viewpoint of their own directory—the directory name is missing in the archive:

```
$ tar tvf blaster.tar
-rw-r--r-- 400/1         5666 Feb 14 01:44 1993 README
-rw-r--r-- 400/1         3638 Feb 14 01:44 1993 INSTALL
-r--r--r-- 400/1         2117 Feb 14 01:44 1993 LICENSE
-rw-r--r-- 400/1         2420 Feb 14 15:17 1993 Makefile
-rw-r--r-- 400/1         3408 Feb 14 01:44 1993 sb_asm.s
-rw------- 400/1        10247 Feb 14 01:44 1993 stream.c
-rw-r--r-- 400/1         1722 Feb 14 04:10 1993 apps/Makefile
```

If you have an archive like the first example, you want to be in the parent directory when you extract the archive; in the second case you need to first create the directory and then *cd* to it. If you extract the second archive while in the parent directory, you'll have a lot of cleaning up to do. In addition, since files with names like *README*, *INSTALL*, and *LICENSE* may already be present in that directory, extracting this archive would overwrite them.

There are a couple of ways to avoid these problems:

- Always look at the archive contents with *tar t* before extracting it. Once you have looked at the archive contents, you can change to the correct directory where you want to extract the archive. In the case of *groff* above, you might choose a directory name like *~/mysources.** In the case of *blaster*, you could create a directory *~/mysources/blaster* and extract into that directory.

---

* A number of shells use the shorthand notation ~/ to refer to your home directory.

- Alternatively, you can *always* create a subdirectory, extract there, and then rename the directory. In the first example, you might create a directory *~/mysources/temp.* After extraction, you might find that the files were in a directory *~/mysources/temp/groff-1.09*, so you could move them:

  ```
  $ mv groff-1.09 ..
  ```

  If they extract directly into *temp*, you can rename the directory:

  ```
  $ cd ..
  $ mv temp groff-1.09
  ```

  This method may seem easier, but in fact there are a couple of problems with it:

  – You need to choose a directory name that doesn't clash with the real name. That's why we used the name *temp* in this example; otherwise, it won't be possible to rename the directory in the first example because you would be trying to overwrite the directory with one of its own subdirectories.

  – Not all flavors of UNIX allow you to move directories.

The command to extract is almost identical to the command to list the archive—a clear case for a shell with command-line editing:

```
$ tar tvf groff-1.09.tar                List the archive
$ tar xvf groff-1.09.tar                Extract the archive
```

Frequently your *tar* archive is compressed in some way. You should know the different types of compression programs so you can use the right one.

Compression Programs

If the archive is compressed, you need to uncompress it before you can extract files from it. UNIX systems almost invariably use one of three compression formats:

- *Compressed* files are created with the *compress* program and extracted with *uncompress.* They can be up to 70% smaller than the original file. The *zcat* program uncompresses a compressed file to the standard output.
- *gzipped* files are created by *gzip* and extracted by *gunzip.* They can be up to 90% smaller than the original file. *gunzip* also uncompresses compressed or packed files.
- *Packed* files are obsolete, though you still occasionally see packed manual pages. They are created by the *pack* program and uncompressed by the *unpack* program. The *pcat* program uncompresses a packed file to the standard output.

Each of these programs is installed with three different names. The name determines the behavior. For example, *gzip* is also known as *gunzip* and *zcat*:

```
$ ls -li /opt/bin/gzip /opt/bin/gunzip /opt/bin/zcat
 13982 -rwxr-xr-x   3 grog     wheel        77824 Nov  5  1993 /opt/bin/gunzip
 13982 -rwxr-xr-x   3 grog     wheel        77824 Nov  5  1993 /opt/bin/gzip
 13982 -rwxr-xr-x   3 grog     wheel        77824 Nov  5  1993 /opt/bin/zcat
```

The *–i* option to *ls* tells it to list the inode number, which uniquely identifies the file. In this case, you see that all three names are linked to the same file (and that the link count field is 3 as a result). Notice that *gzip* has also been installed under the name *zcat*, replacing the name used by *compress*. This is not a problem because *gzcat* can do everything that *zcat* can do. It can, however, lead to confusion if you rely on it, and one day try to extract a *gzipped* file with the real *zcat*.

Encoded Files

Most archive programs and all compression programs produce output containing nonprintable characters. This can be a problem if you want to transfer the archive via electronic mail, which cannot handle all binary combinations. To solve this problem, the files can be *encoded*: they are transformed into a representation that contains only printable characters. Since this has the disadvantage of making the file significantly larger, it is used only when absolutely necessary. Two programs for encoding files are in common use:

- *uuencode* is by far the most common format. The companion program *uudecode* extracts the encoded file.
- *btoa* format is used more in Europe than in the U.S. The name means "binary to ASCII." It does not expand the file as much as *uuencode* (25% compared to 33% with *uuencode*) and is more resistant to errors. You decode the file with the *atob* program.

Split Archives

Many *ftp* sites split large archives into equal-sized chunks, typically between 256 KB and 1.44 MB (a floppy disk image). It's trivial to combine them back to the original archive: *cat* can do just that. For example, if you have a set of files *base09.000* through *base09.013* representing a *gzipped tar* archive, you can combine them with:

```
$ cat base09.* > base09.tar.gz
```

This requires twice the amount of storage, of course, and it takes time. It's easier to extract them directly:

```
$ cat base09.* | gunzip | tar xvf -
drwxr-xr-x root/wheel         0 Aug 23 06:22 1993 ./sbin/
-r-xr-xr-x bin/bin       106496 Aug 23 06:21 1993 ./sbin/chown
-r-xr-xr-x bin/bin        53248 Aug 23 06:21 1993 ./sbin/mount_mfs
... etc
```

cat pipes all archives in alphabetical order to *gunzip*. *gunzip* uncompresses the archive and pipes the uncompressed data to *tar*, which extracts the files.

Extracting a linked file

tar is clever enough to notice when it is backing up multiple copies of a file under different names—in other words, so-called *hard links*. When backing up, the first time it encounters a file, *tar* copies it to the archive, but if it encounters it again under another name, it simply creates an entry pointing to the first file. This saves space, but if you just try to extract the second file, *tar* fails: in order to extract the second name, you also need to extract the file under the first name that *tar* found. Most versions of *tar* tell you what the name was, but if you are creating archives, it helps to back up the most-used name first.

What's That Archive?

The preceding discussion assumes that you know the format of the archive. The fun begins when you don't. How do you extract it?

Your primary indication of the nature of the file is its filename. When archives are created, compressed and encoded, they usually receive a *filename suffix* to indicate the nature of the file. You may also have come across the term *extension*, which comes from the MS-DOS world. These suffixes accumulate as various steps proceed. A distribution of *gcc* might come in a file called *gcc-2.5.8.tar.gz.uue*. This name gives you the following information:

- The name of the package: *gcc*.
- The revision level: *–2.5.8*. You would expect the name of the root directory for this package to be *gcc-2.5.8*.
- The archive format: *.tar*. Since this is a GNU package, you can expect the name of the uncompressed archive to be *gcc-2.5.8.tar*.
- The compression format: *.gz* (*gzip* format). The name of the compressed archive would be *gcc-2.5.8.tar.gz*.
- The encoding format: *.uue* (encoded with *uuencode*).

Each format is nested within the next as shown in Figure 2-1. You have to extract files from the outside in.

Some operating systems, notably System V.3, still provide file systems that restrict filenames to 14 characters. Old file systems on Linux (before the Second Extended

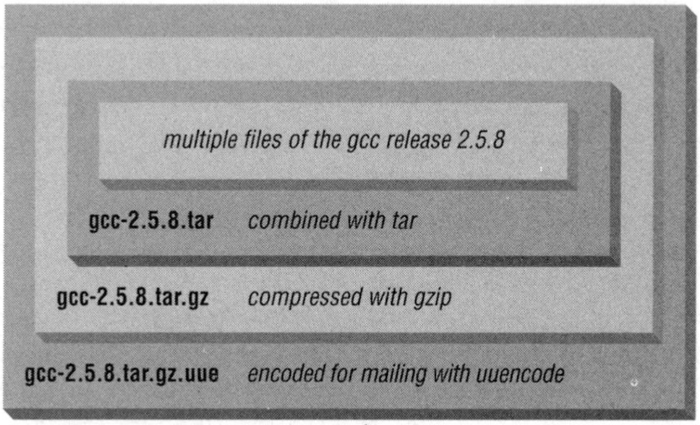

Figure 2-1: Transformations of files for archiving

File System was developed) also have this limitation. This can lead to several problems.* Archives distributed for these systems frequently use variants on these names designed to make them shorter; *gcc-2.5.8.tzue* might be an alternate name for the same package.

Table 2-1 gives you an overview of archive file suffixes you might encounter. We'll look at source file suffixes in the section called "Compiler Organization".

Table 2-1: Common Filename Suffixes

Name Suffix	Format
#	Alternate *patch* reject filename
~	Emacs backup files, also used by some versions of *patch*
,v	RCS file—created by *ci*, extracted by *co*
.a	*ar* format—created by and extracted with *ar*
.arc	Created by and extracted with *arc*
.arj	DOS *arj* format
.cpio	Created by and extracted with *cpio*
.diff	Difference file—created by *diff*, can be applied by *patch*
.gif	Graphics Interchange Format
.gz	*gzip* format—created by *gzip*, extracted with *gunzip*

* If you have a choice of file systems, you can save yourself a lot of trouble by installing one that allows long filenames.

Table 2-1: Common Filename Suffixes (continued)

Name Suffix	Format
.hqx	HQX (Apple Macintosh)
.jpg	JPEG (graphics format)
.lzh	LHa, LHarc, Larc
.orig	Original file after processing by *patch*
.rej	*patch* reject file
.shar	Shell archive—created by *shar*, extracted with any Bourne-compatible shell
.sit	Stuff-It (Apple Macintosh)
.tar	*tar* format—created by and extracted with *tar*
.uu	*uuencoded* file—created by *uuencode*, decoded with *uudecode*
.uue	Alternative for .uu
.Z	Compressed with *compress*, uncompressed with *uncompress*, *zcat*, or *gunzip*
.z	Two different formats—either *pack* format, compressed by *pack* and extracted with *pcat*, or old *gzip* format, compressed by *gzip* and extracted with *gunzip*
.zip	Zip format (compressed and extracted with either *zip/pkzip* and *unzip/pkunzip*)
.zoo	Zoo

Identifying Archives

Occasionally you'll get an archive whose name gives you no indication of the format. Under these circumstances, finding the kind of archive can be a matter of trial and error, particularly if it is compressed. This section contains a couple of ideas that might help.

file

The UNIX *file* command recognizes a lot of standard file types and prints a brief description of the format. Unfortunately, the file really needs to be a file: *file* performs some file system checks, so it can't read from standard input. For example,

```
$ file *
0install.txt:              English text
base09.000:                gzip compressed data - deflate method ,  original
file name ,  last modified: Mon Aug 23 07:53:21 1993 ,  max compression os:
Unix
base09.001:                data
...more of same
base09.011:                DOS executable (COM)
man-1.0.cpio:              cpio archive
```

```
tcl7.3.tar.gz:               empty
tex:                         directory
tk3.6.tar:                   POSIX tar archive
```

The information for base09.000 was one output line that wrapped around onto three output lines.

Most files have certain special values, so-called *magic numbers*, in specific locations in their headers. *file* uses a file, usually */etc/magic*, which describes these formats. Occasionally it makes a mistake. We can be reasonably sure that the file *base09.011* is not a DOS executable, but it has the right number in the right place, and thus fools *file*.

This version of *file* (from BSD/OS) recognizes *base09.000*—and none of the following pieces of the archive—as a *gzip* archive file and even extracts a lot of information. Not all versions of *file* do this. Frequently, it just tells you that the archive is data. In this case, the first assumption should be that the archive is compressed in a format that your version of *file* doesn't recognize. If the file is *packed*, *compressed*, or *gzipped*, *gzip* expands it; otherwise, it prints an error message. The next step might look something like:

```
$ unzip < mystery > /tmp/junk
$                                  aha! it didn't complain
$ file /tmp/junk
/tmp/junk:      POSIX tar archive
```

In this case, we have established that the file *mystery* is a compressed *tar* archive, though we don't know what kind of compression because *gzip* doesn't tell.

If *file* tells you that the file is ASCII or English text, then you can safely look at it with *more* or *less*:

```
$ more strange-file
Newsgroups: comp.sources.unix
From: clewis@ferret.ocunix.on.ca (Chris Lewis)
Subject: v26i014: psroff 3.0, Patch09
Sender: unix-sources-moderator@pa.dec.com
Approved: vixie@pa.dec.com

Submitted-By: clewis@ferret.ocunix.on.ca (Chris Lewis)
Posting-Number: Volume 26, Issue 14
Archive-Name: psroff3.0/patch9

    This is official patch 09 for Psroff 3.0.
...intervening lines skipped
        clewis@ferret.ocunix.on.ca (Chris Lewis)

./lib/lj3.fonts
./lib/psrofflib.S
./lib/lj3u.fonts
./lj.h
```

```
./README
./MISC
./defs.h
./lj.c

Patchwrapped: 920128230528

Index: ./lib/lj3.fonts
*** /tmp/PATCHold/./lib/lj3.fonts       Tue Jan 28 23:03:45 1992
--- ./lib/lj3.fonts     Tue Jan 28 23:03:46 1992
```

This is a plain text *patch* file: you can pass it straight through the *patch* program, since *patch* doesn't worry about junk at the beginning or the end of the file. We'll look at *patch* in depth in the section called "patch" in Chapter 3.

Here's another ASCII file:

```
Newsgroups: comp.sources.unix From: lm@Sunburn.Stanford.EDU (Larry McVoy)
Subject: v26i020: perfmon - interface to rstatd(8)
Sender: unix-sources-moderator@pa.dec.com
Approved: vixie@pa.dec.com
...more stuff omitted
#! /bin/sh
# This is a shell archive. Remove anything before this line,
# then unpack it by saving it into a file and typing "sh file".
```

As the text tells you, this is a shell archive. To extract it, you can remove all text up to the line starting with *#!/bin/sh* and extract it with the Bourne shell, or pass it through *unshar* as it is.

This kind of file is easy to recognize, once you've seen the format:

```
begin 666 magic.gz
M'XL("`_!NRT``V5A<W1E<@!-4KV.VS`,WO,4W'('N`;:\9:B+3)T.*1HT*DH
M<+3$V+I(HB'*2?/V)14W=YMED-\OGW8HE0K0.#[![V/A!'4B<(M4_>1C>ZTS
MNW&$:<D5>!`J9_(0\@:@C?SJ#SU@]I`P7V'&4L6V=TOAF?Y`[N%C#U\@D0B.
M!%/PGK+NV[)A\/!*KH)C3[:',!<>"R9`T<<KGZC3Z4K9*VUE&`B.O"C?H&Q4
MA+,8C`^"(I2&&/((7&`H?!'[;JX4O0?X]$Y)!\HR3\%U.FT(TE#I>#0YE$*M
MU$C>%#UPT>&L?WY\ZQKNU^_[`_S</S^N@1226061"15.!`K);DF4#4RHFD7'
M2;/R8BI/=)5:U*1TMG\W>C=O0PJF]N:(U[L45\B'*NIIGPDN%..'4^9+$T%8
MXA7>ZEWS"B;<\3+'%O3^0`(.%[%8)TK&<I/O6[6\!M>TPDM"U1+Y3%NXA#K!
M2^8*%RR?MZKA6:NWI5L?&&UM7I1>8,(S05K<!(D+`44<N&`E$R;OKD%#7!-P
M<?'66PQR.R73X>E,D0U_"QFUP@YFCJ$&IVST=^)2L0:-OH%(QNHF:MMI$>O8
I3#PH#VM<#H4>_]<O$)*>PYU)JPJE7>;*:>5!)4S]9O,/(PQ?IS4#``!I
`
end
```

This is a *uuencoded* file. The first line contains the word `begin`, the default security (which you can't change), and the name of the archive (*magic.gz*). The following lines usually have the same length and begin with the same letter (usually `M`)—this is the encoded length specification for the line. If they don't follow the rules, something has probably gone wrong in the transmission. The last data line is usually shorter and thus has a different first character. Finally, the archive contains two end lines: the first is usually the single character `, and the second is the word `end` on a line by itself.

To extract the file, first pass it through *uudecode*, which creates the file *magic.gz*, then *gunzip* it to create the file *magic*. Then you might need to use *file* to find out what it is.

```
$ uudecode < magic.uue
$ gunzip magic.gz
$ file magic
magic: English text
```

Don't confuse *uuencode* format with this:

```
xbtoa5 78 puzzle.gz Begin
+,^C1(V%L;!!?e@F*(u6!)69ODSn.:h/s&KF-$KGlWA8mP,0BTe$`Y<$qSODDdUZO:_0iqn&P/S%8H
[AX_&!0:k0$N^5WjWlkG?U*XLRJ6"1S^E;mJ.k'Ea#$EL9q3*Bb.c9J@t/K/'N>62BM=7Ujbp7$YHN
,m"%IZ93t15j%OV"_S#NMI4;GC_N'=%+k5LX,A*uli>IBE@i0T4cP/A#coB""`a]![8jgS1L=p6Kit
X9EU5N%+(>-N=YU4(aeoGoFH9SqM6#c1(r;;K<'aBE/aZRX/^:.cbh&9[r.^f3bpQJQ&fW:*S_7DW9
6No0QkC7@A0?=YtSYlAc@01eeX;bF/9%&4E627AA6GR!u]3?Zhke.14*T=U@TF9@1Gs4\jQPjbBm\H
K24N:$HKre7#7#jG"KFme^djs!<<*"N
xbtoa End N 331 14b E 5c S 75b7 R b506b514
```

This is a *btoa* encoded file, probably also *gzipped* like the previous example. Extract it with *atob* or *btoa -a*, and then proceed as with *uuencoded* files.

What's in That Archive?

Now you have discovered the format of the archive and can extract the files from it. There's a possibility, though, that you don't know what the archive is good for. This is frequently the case if you have a tape or a CD-ROM archive of an *ftp* server, and it contains some cryptic names that suggest the files might possibly be of interest. How do you find out what the package does?

README

By convention, many authors include a file *README* in the main directory of the package. *README* should tell you at least:

- The name of the package, and what it is intended to do
- The conditions under which you may use it

For example, the *README* file for GNU *termcap* reads:

```
This is the GNU termcap library -- a library of C functions that enable programs
to send control strings to terminals in a way independent of the terminal type.
Most of this package is also distributed with GNU Emacs, but it is available in
this separate distribution to make it easier to install as -ltermcap.
```

```
The GNU termcap library does not place an arbitrary limit on the size of termcap
entries, unlike most other termcap libraries.

See the file INSTALL for compilation and installation instructions.

Please report any bugs in this library to bug-gnu-emacs@prep.ai.mit.edu. You
can check which version of the library you have by using the RCS `ident' command
on libtermcap.a.
```

In some cases, however, there doesn't seem to be any file to tell you what the package does. Sometimes you may be lucky and find a good man page or even documentation intended to be printed as hard copy—see Chapter 7, *Documentation*, for more information. In many cases, though, you might be justified in deciding that the package is so badly documented that you give up.

There may also be files that have names such as *README.BSD*, *README.SYSV*, and *README.X11*. If present, these files usually give specific advice to people using these platforms.

INSTALL

The archive may contain a separate *INSTALL* file, or the information it should contain might be included in the *README* file. The information should tell you:

- A list of the platforms on which the package has been ported. This list may or may not include your system, but either way it should give you a first inkling of the effort that lies in store. If you're running System V.4, for example, and the software has already been ported to your hardware platform running System V.3, then porting the software should be easy. If the software has been ported to V.4, and you're running V.3, this can be a completely different matter.
- A description of how to configure the package (we'll look at this in Chapter 4, *Configuring the Package*).
- A description of how to build the package (see Chapter 4, and Chapter 19, *make*, for more details on this subject).

It may, in addition, offer suggestions on how to port to other platforms or architectures.

Other files

The package may include other information files as well. By convention, the names are written in uppercase or with an initial capital letter, so that they stand out in a directory listing. The GNU project software may include some or all of the following files:

- *ABOUT* is an alternative name used by some authors instead of *README*.
- *COPYING* and *COPYING.LIB* are legal texts describing the constraints under which you may use the software.
- *ChangeLog* is a list of changes to the software. Since this name is hard-coded into the Emacs editor macros, it's probable that a file with this name is an Emacs-style change log.
- *MANIFEST* may give you a list of the files intended to be in the package.
- *PROBLEMS* may help you if you run into problems.
- *SERVICE* is supplied by the Free Software Foundation to point you to companies and individuals who can help you if you run into trouble.

A good example of these files is the root directory of Taylor *uucp*:

```
$ gunzip </cd0/gnu/uucp/uucp-1.05.tar.gz |tar tvf -
drwxrwxr-x 269/15          0 May  6 06:10 1994 uucp-1.05/
-r--r--r-- 269/15      17976 May  6 05:23 1994 uucp-1.05/COPYING
-r--r--r-- 269/15     163997 May  6 05:24 1994 uucp-1.05/ChangeLog
^C$
```

This archive adheres to the GNU convention of including the name of the top-level directory in the archive. When we extract the archive, *tar* creates a new directory *uucp-1.05* and puts all the files in it. So we continue:

```
$ cd /porting/src                    The directory in which I do my porting
$ gunzip </cd0/gnu/uucp/uucp-1.05.tar.gz |tar xf -
$
```

After extraction, the resultant directory contains most of the "standard" files that we discussed previously:

```
$ cd uucp-1.05
$ ls -l
  total 1724
  drwxrwxr-x   7 grog     wheel       1536 May  6 06:10 .
  drwxrwxrwx  44 grog     wheel       3584 Aug 19 14:34 ..
  -r--r--r--   1 grog     wheel      17976 May  6 05:23 COPYING
  -r--r--r--   1 grog     wheel     163997 May  6 05:24 ChangeLog
  -r--r--r--   1 grog     wheel        499 May  6 05:24 MANIFEST
  -rw-r--r--   1 grog     wheel      14452 May  6 06:09 Makefile.in
  -r--r--r--   1 grog     wheel       4283 May  6 05:24 NEWS
  -r--r--r--   1 grog     wheel       7744 May  6 05:24 README
  -r--r--r--   1 grog     wheel      23563 May  6 05:24 TODO
  -r--r--r--   1 grog     wheel      32866 May  6 05:24 chat.c
  -r--r--r--   1 grog     wheel      19032 May  6 05:24 config.h.in
  -rwxrwxr-x   1 grog     wheel      87203 May  6 05:27 configure
  -r--r--r--   1 grog     wheel      11359 May  6 05:24 configure.in
...etc
```

In This Chapter:

- *Updating Old Archives*
- *Handling Trees on CD-ROM*
- *Tracking Changes to the Tree*
- *An Example–Updating an Existing Tree*

3

Care and Feeding of Source Trees

In Chapter 2, *Unpacking the Goodies*, we saw how to create an initial source tree. It won't stay in this form for long. During a port, the source tree is constantly changing:

- Before you can even start, you may apply *patches* to the tree to bring it up to date.
- After unpacking and possibly patching, you may find that you have to clean out junk left behind from a previous port.
- In order to get the software to compile in your environment, you perform some form of *configuration*, which modifies the tree to some extent. We'll look at package configuration in Chapter 4, *Configuring the Package*.
- During compilation, you add many new files to the tree. You may also create new subdirectories.
- After installation, you remove the unneeded files—for example, object files and possibly the final installed files.
- After cleaning up, you may decide to archive the tree again to save space on disk.

Modifying the source tree brings uncertainty with it: what is original, what have I modified, how do I remove the changes I have made and get back to a clean, well-defined starting point? In this chapter we'll look at how to get to a clean starting point. Usually you'll be at that point after you have extracted the source archive, but frequently you need to add patches or remove junk. We'll also look at how to build a tree with sources on CD-ROM, how to recognize the changes you have made, and how to maintain multiple versions of your software.

Updating Old Archives

You don't always need to get a complete package. You might already have an older version of the package, and if it is large—again, for example, the GNU C compiler—it might be better to get update the source tree using *patches*. Strictly speaking, a patch is any kind of modification to a source or object file. In UNIX parlance, it's almost always a *diff*, a file that describes how to modify a source file to produce a newer version. Diffs are almost always produced by the *diff* program, which we describe in Chapter 10, *Where to Go from Here*.

In our case study, we have *gcc* version 2.5.6 and want to update to 2.5.8. We discover the following files on the file server:

```
ftp> ls
200 PORT command successful.
150 Opening ASCII mode data connection for /bin/ls.
-rw-rw-r-- 1 117 1001   10753 Dec 12 19:15 gcc-2.5.6-2.5.7.diff.gz
-rw-rw-r-- 1 117 1001   14726 Jan 24 09:02 gcc-2.5.7-2.5.8.diff.gz
-rw-rw-r-- 1 117 1001 5955006 Dec 22 14:16 gcc-2.5.7.tar.gz
-rw-rw-r-- 1 117 1001 5997896 Jan 24 09:03 gcc-2.5.8.tar.gz
226 Transfer complete.
ftp>
```

In other words, we have two choices: copy the two *diff* files *gcc-2.5.6-2.5.7.diff.gz* and *gcc-2.5.7-2.5.8.diff.gz*, a total of 25 KB, and apply them to our source tree, or we can copy the complete 6 MB archive *gcc-2.5.8.tar.gz*.

patch

diff files are reasonably understandable, and you can apply the patches by hand if you want, but it's easier and safer to use a program, such as *patch*, to apply the changes. *patch* takes the output of the program *diff* and uses it to update one or more files.

To apply the patch, the *patch* program performs the following tasks:

1. *Looks for a file header*

   If it finds any junk before the file header, it skips it and prints a message to say that it has done so. It uses the file header to recognize the kind of *diff* to apply.

2. *Renames the old file by appending a string to its name*

   By default, the string is *.orig*, so *foo.c* would become *foo.c.orig*.

3. *Creates a new file with the name of the old file*

   patch then copies the old file to the new file, modifying it with the patches as it goes. Each set of changes is called a *hunk.*

Figure 3-1 illustrates the relationship between files and hunks of changes.

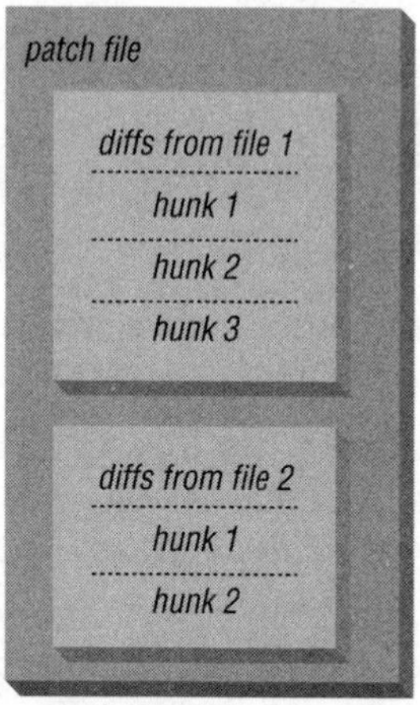

Figure 3-1: How changes are organized in the patch files

The way *patch* applies the patch depends on the format. The most dangerous kind are *ed* style diffs, because there is no way to be sure that the text is being replaced correctly. With context diffs, *patch* can check that the context is correct and looks a couple of lines in each direction if it doesn't find the old text where it expects to find it. You can set the number of lines it looks (the *fuzz factor*) with the *–F* option. It defaults to 2.

If the old version of the file does not correspond exactly to the old version used to make the diff, *patch* may not be able to find the correct place to insert the patch. Except for *ed* format diffs, it recognizes when this happens, prints an error message, and moves the corresponding hunk to a file with the suffix *.rej* (for reject).

A typical example are the patches for X11R5. You might start with the sources supplied on the companion CD-ROM to *X Window System Administrator's Guide* by Linda Mui and Eric Pearce. This CD-ROM includes the complete X11R5 sources to patch level 21. At the time of writing, five further patches to X11R5 have been released. To bring the source tree up to patch level 26, you would proceed as follows:

First, read the header of the patch file. As we have seen, *patch* allows text before the first file header, and the headers frequently contain useful information. Looking at patch 22, we see:

```
$ gunzip < /cd0/x11r5/fix22.gz | more
                       X11 R5 Public Patch #22
                          MIT X Consortium

To apply this patch:

cd to the top of the source tree (to the directory containing the
"mit" and "contrib" subdirectories) and do:

        patch -p -s < ThisFile

Patch works silently unless an error occurs. You are likely to get the
following warning messages, which you can ignore:
```

In this example we have used *gunzip* to look at the file directly; we could just as well have used GNU *zcat*. The patch header suggests the options *–s* and *–p*. The *–s* option to *patch* tells it to perform its work silently—otherwise, it prints lots of information about what it is doing and why. The *–p* option is one of the most complicated to use: it specifies the *pathname strip count*, how to treat the directory part of the filenames in the header. We'll look at it in more detail in the section called "Can't find file to patch".

Information from the header is important: *patch* is rather like a chainsaw without a guard, and if you start it without knowing what you are doing, you can make a real mess of its environment. In this case, we should find that the root of our source tree looks like:

```
$ cd /usr/x11r5
$ ls -FC mit
Imakefile     RELNOTES.ms   extensions/   rgb/
LABEL         bug-report    fonts/        server/
Makefile      clients/      hardcopy/     util/
Makefile.ini  config/       include/
RELNOTES.PS   demos/        lib/
RELNOTES.TXT  doc/          man/
... that looks OK, we're in the right place
$ gunzip < /cd0/x11r5/fix22.gz | patch -p -s
```

We've taken another liberty in this example: since the patch file was on CD-ROM in compressed form, we would have needed to extract it to disk in order to patch the way the file header suggests. Instead, we just *gunzip* directly into the *patch* program.

It's easy to make mistakes when patching. If you try to apply a patch twice, *patch* notices, but you can persuade it to reapply the patch anyway. In this section, we'll look at the havoc that can occur as a result. In addition, we'll disregard some of the advice in the patch header. This is the way I prefer to do it:

```
$ gunzip < /cd0/x11r5/fix23.gz | patch -p &> patch.log
```

This invocation allows *patch* to say what it has to say (no *-s* option), but copies both the standard output and the error output to the file *patch.log*, so nothing appears on the screen. You can, of course, pipe the output through the *tee* program, but in practice, the process happens so fast that any error message usually runs off the screen before you can read it. It certainly would have done so here: *patch.log* had a length of 930 lines. It starts with:

```
Hmm...  Looks like a new-style context diff to me...
The text leading up to this was:
--------------------------
|                        Release 5 Public Patch #23
|                             MIT X Consortium
... followed by the complete header
|Prereq: public-patch-22
```

This last line is one safeguard that *patch* offers to ensure that you are working with the correct source tree. If *patch* finds a `Prereq:` line in the file header, it checks that this text appears in the input file. For comparison, here's the header of *mit/bug-report*:

```
To: xbugs@expo.lcs.mit.edu
Subject: [area]: [synopsis]   [replace with actual area and short description]

VERSION:
    R5, public-patch-22
    [MIT public patches will edit this line to indicate the patch level]
```

In this case, *patch* finds the text. When it does, it prints out the corresponding message:

```
|
|*** /tmp/,RCSt1006225  Tue Mar  9 14:40:48 1993
|--- mit/bug-report     Tue Mar  9 14:37:04 1993
--------------------------
Good. This file appears to be the public-patch-22 version.
```

This message shows that it has found the text in *mit/bug-report*. The first hunk in any X11 *diff* changes this text (in this case to *public-patch-23*), so that it notices a repeated application of the patch. Let's continue:

```
Patching file mit/bug-report using Plan A...
Hunk #1 succeeded at 2.
Hmm...  The next patch looks like a new-style context diff to me...
The text leading up to this was:
```

```
--------------------------
|*** /tmp/,RCSt1005203  Tue Mar  9 13:45:42 1993
|--- mit/lib/X/Imakefile        Tue Mar  9 13:45:45 1993
--------------------------
Patching file mit/lib/X/Imakefile using Plan A...
Hunk #1 succeeded at 1.
Hunk #2 succeeded at 856.
Hunk #3 succeeded at 883.
Hunk #4 succeeded at 891.
Hunk #5 succeeded at 929.
Hunk #6 succeeded at 943.
Hunk #7 succeeded at 968.
Hunk #8 succeeded at 976.
Hmm...  The next patch looks like a new-style context diff to me...
```

This output goes on for hundreds of lines. What happens if you make a mistake and try again?

```
$ gunzip < /cd0/x11r5/fix23.gz | patch -p &> patch.log
This file doesn't appear to be the public-patch-22 version--patch anyway? [n] y
bad choice...
Reversed (or previously applied) patch detected! Assume -R? [y] RETURN pressed
Reversed (or previously applied) patch detected! Assume -R? [y] RETURN pressed
Reversed (or previously applied) patch detected! Assume -R? [y] ^C$
```

The first message is printed because *patch* didn't find the text public-patch-22 in the file (in the previous step, *patch* changed it to read public-patch-23). This message also appears in *patch.log*. Of course, in a normal application you should immediately stop and check what's gone wrong. In this case, I make the incorrect choice and go ahead with the patch. Worse still, I entered **RETURN** in response to the next two prompts. Finally, I came to my senses and hit **CTRL-C**, the interrupt character on my machine, to stop *patch*.

The result of this is that *patch* removed the patches in the first two files (the *–R* option tells *patch* to behave as if the files were reversed, which has the same effect as removing already applied patches). I now have the first two files patched to patch level 22, and the others patched to patch level 23. Clearly, I can't leave the files like this.

Two wrongs don't usually make a right, but in this case they do. We do it again, and what we get this time looks pretty much the same as the time before:

```
$ gunzip < /cd0/x11r5/fix23.gz | patch -p &> mit/patch.log
Reversed (or previously applied) patch detected! Assume -R? [y] ^C$
```

In fact, this time things went right, as we can see by looking at *patch.log*:

```
|*** /tmp/,RCSt1006225  Tue Mar  9 14:40:48 1993
|--- mit/bug-report     Tue Mar  9 14:37:04 1993
--------------------------
Good. This file appears to be the public-patch-22 version.
```

```
Patching file mit/bug-report using Plan A...
Hunk #1 succeeded at 2.
Hmm...  The next patch looks like a new-style context diff to me...
The text leading up to this was:
--------------------------
|*** /tmp/,RCSt1005203  Tue Mar  9 13:45:42 1993
|--- mit/lib/X/Imakefile        Tue Mar  9 13:45:45 1993
--------------------------
Patching file mit/lib/X/Imakefile using Plan A...
Hunk #1 succeeded at 1.
```
(lots of hunks succeed)
```
Hmm...  The next patch looks like a new-style context diff to me...
The text leading up to this was:
--------------------------
|*** /tmp/d03300         Tue Mar  9 09:16:46 1993
|--- mit/lib/X/Ximp/XimpLCUtil.c        Tue Mar  9 09:16:41 1993
--------------------------
Patching file mit/lib/X/Ximp/XimpLCUtil.c using Plan A...
Reversed (or previously applied) patch detected! Assume -R? [y]
```

This time the first two files have been patched back to patch level 23, and we stop before doing any further damage.

Hunk #3 failed

patch makes an implicit assumption that the patch was created from an identical source tree, which is not always the case. You may have changed something in the course of the port. The differences frequently don't cause problems if they are in an area unrelated to the patch.

In this example, we'll look at how things can go wrong. Let's consider the following situation: during a previous port of X11R5 pl 22,* you ran into some problems in *mit/lib/Xt/Selection.c* and fixed them. The original text read:

```
if (XtWindow(widget) == window)
  XtAddEventHandler(widget, mask, TRUE, proc, closure);
else {
  Widget w = XtWindowToWidget(dpy, window);
  RequestWindowRec *requestWindowRec;
  if (w != NULL && w != widget) widget = w;
  if (selectWindowContext == 0)
      selectWindowContext = XUniqueContext();
```

Since you had problems with this section, you commented out a couple of lines:

```
if (XtWindow(widget) == window)
    XtAddEventHandler(widget, mask, TRUE, proc, closure);
else {
/* This doesn't make any sense at all - ignore
 * Widget w = XtWindowToWidget(dpy, window); */
```

* The abbreviation *pl* is frequently used to mean *patch level.*

```
        RequestWindowRec *requestWindowRec;
        /* if (w != NULL && w != widget) widget = w; */
        if (selectWindowContext == 0)
            selectWindowContext = XUniqueContext();
```

Back in the present, you try to apply patch 24 to this file:

```
$ gunzip < /cd0/x11r5/fix24.gz | patch -p &> mit/patch.log
$
```

So far so good. But in *patch.log* we find:

```
|*** /tmp/da4854        Mon May 17 18:19:57 1993
|--- mit/lib/Xt/Selection.c      Mon May 17 18:19:56 1993
--------------------------
Patching file mit/lib/Xt/Selection.c using Plan A...
Hunk #1 succeeded at 1.
Hunk #2 succeeded at 70.
Hunk #3 failed at 361.
Hunk #4 succeeded at 1084.
Hunk #5 succeeded at 1199.
1 out of 5 hunks failed--saving rejects to mit/lib/Xt/Selection.c.rej
```

We have to look at the files concerned to find out what this means. In *fix24* we find:

```
*** /tmp/da4854 Mon May 17 18:19:57 1993
--- mit/lib/Xt/Selection.c      Mon May 17 18:19:56 1993
***************
*** 1,4 ****
this must be hunk 1
! /* $XConsortium: Selection.c,v 1.74 92/11/13 17:40:46 converse Exp $ */

  /**********************************************************
  Copyright 1987, 1988 by Digital Equipment Corporation, Maynard, Massachusetts,
--- 1,4 ----
! /* $XConsortium: Selection.c,v 1.78 93/05/13 11:09:15 converse Exp $ */

  /**********************************************************
  Copyright 1987, 1988 by Digital Equipment Corporation, Maynard, Massachusetts,
***************
*** 70,75 ****
--- 70,90 ----
this must be hunk 2
   Widget w;                    /* unused */
***************
*** 346,359 ****
and this must be hunk 3, the one that failed
  {
      Display *dpy = req->ctx->dpy;
      Window window = req->requestor;
!    Widget widget = req->widget;
... etc
***************
*** 1068,1073 ****
```

```
--- 1084,1096 ----
```
hunk 4
```
***************
*** 1176,1181 ****
--- 1199,1213 ----
```
and hunk 5—at least the count is correct

patch put the rejects in *Selection.c.rej*. Let's look at it:

```
***************
*** 346,359 ****
  {
      Display *dpy = req->ctx->dpy;
      Window window = req->requestor;
!    Widget widget = req->widget;

      if (XtWindow(widget) == window)
!       XtAddEventHandler(widget, mask, TRUE, proc, closure);
      else {
-       Widget w = XtWindowToWidget(dpy, window);
        RequestWindowRec *requestWindowRec;
-       if (w != NULL && w != widget) widget = w;
        if (selectWindowContext == 0)
            selectWindowContext = XUniqueContext();
        if (XFindContext(dpy, window, selectWindowContext,
--- 361,375 ----
  {
      Display *dpy = req->ctx->dpy;
      Window window = req->requestor;
!    Widget widget = XtWindowToWidget(dpy, window);

+     if (widget != NULL) req->widget = widget;
+     else widget = req->widget;
+
      if (XtWindow(widget) == window)
!       XtAddEventHandler(widget, mask, False, proc, closure);
      else {
        RequestWindowRec *requestWindowRec;
        if (selectWindowContext == 0)
            selectWindowContext = XUniqueContext();
        if (XFindContext(dpy, window, selectWindowContext,
```

The characters + and - at the beginning of the lines in this hunk identify it as a *unified context diff*. We'll look at them in more detail in the section called "unified context diffs" in Chapter 10. Not surprisingly, they are the contents of hunk 3. Because of our fix, *patch* couldn't find the old text and thus couldn't process this hunk. In this case, it's easiest to perform the fix by hand. To do so, we need to look at the partially fixed file that *patch* created, *mit/lib/Xt/Selection.c*. The line numbers have changed, of course, but since hunk 3 wasn't applied, we find exactly the same text that happened in *mit/lib/Xt/Selection.c.orig*, only now it starts at line 366. We can effectively replace it by the "after" text in *Selection.c.rej*, remembering, of course, to remove the indicator characters + and `!` in column 1.

Can't find file to patch

Sometimes you'll see a message like:

```
$ patch -p <hotstuff.diff &>patch.log
Enter name of file to patch:
```

One of the weaknesses of using a combination of *diff* and *patch* is that it's easy to get the filenames out of sync. What has probably happened here is that the filenames don't agree with the source tree, a discrepancy that can occur in a number of ways. The manner in which *patch* treats the filenames in diff headers depends on the *-p* option, the so-called *pathname strip count*:

- If you omit the *-p* option, *patch* strips all directory name information from the filenames and leaves just the filename part. Consider the following diff header:

  ```
  *** config/sunos4.h~   Wed Feb 29 07:13:57 1992
  --- config/sunos4.h    Mon May 17 18:19:56 1993
  ```

  Relative to the top of the source tree, the file is in the directory *config*. If you omit the *-p* option, *patch* looks for the file *sunos4.h*, not *config/sunos4.h*, and does not find it.

- If you specify *-p*, *patch* keeps the complete names in the headers.
- If you specify *-pn*, *patch* removes the first *n* directory name components in the pathname. This is useful when the diffs contain incorrect base pathnames. For example, you may find a diff header that looks like:

  ```
  *** /src/freesoft/gcc-patches/config/sunos4.h~  Wed Feb 29 07:13:57 1992
  --- /src/freesoft/gcc-patches/config/sunos4.h   Mon May 17 18:19:56 1993
  ```

  Unless your source tree also happens to be called */src/freesoft/gcc-patches*, *patch* won't be able to find the files if you use the *-p* option with no argument. Assuming that you are in the root directory of the package (in other words, the parent directory of *config*), you really don't want to know about the */src/freesoft/gcc-patches/* component. This pathname consists of four parts: the leading slash, which makes the pathname absolute; and the three directory names *src*, *freesoft*, and *gcc-patches*. In this case, you can enter:

  ```
  $ patch -p4 <hotstuff.diff &>patch.log
  ```

  The -p4 tells *patch* to ignore the first four pathname components, so it would read these filenames just as *config/sunos4.h~* and *config/sunos4.h*.

In addition to the problem of synchronizing the pathnames, you may run into broken diffs that don't specify pathnames, even though the files belong to different directories. For example, you may find that the diff headers look like:

```
*** sunos4.h~   Wed Feb 29 07:13:57 1992
--- sunos4.h    Mon May 17 18:19:56 1993
```

This kind of diff is a real nuisance: you at least need to search for the file *sunos4.h*, and if you're unlucky you'll find more than one and have to examine the patches to figure out which one is intended. Then you need to give this name to the prompt, and *patch* should perform the patches. Unfortunately, in a large collection of diffs, this can happen dozens of times.

I can't seem to find a patch in there

Sometimes you get what looks like a perfectly good unified context diff, but when you run *patch* against it, you get this message:

```
$ patch <diffs
Hmm...  I can't seem to find a patch in there anywhere.
$
```

Some versions of *patch* don't understand unified diffs, and since all versions skip anything they don't understand, this message could be the result. The only solution is to get a newer version of *patch*—see Appendix E for details.

Malformed patch

If *patch* finds the files and understands the headers, you could still run into problems. One of the most common is really a problem in making the diffs:

```
$ patch <diffs
Hmm...  Looks like a unified diff to me...
The text leading up to this was:
--------------------------
|--- real-programmers.ms~       Wed Dec  7 13:17:47 1994
|+++ real-programmers.ms        Wed Dec  7 14:53:19 1994
--------------------------
Patching file real-programmers.ms using Plan A...
Hunk #1 succeeded at 1.
Hunk #2 succeeded at 54.
patch: **** malformed patch at line 398: \ No newline at end of file
```

Well, it tells you what happened: *diff* prints this message if the last character in a file is not \n. Most versions of *patch* don't like the message. You need to edit the *diff* and remove the offending line.

Debris left behind by patch

At the end of a session, *patch* leaves behind a number of files. Files of the form *filename.orig* are the original versions of patched files. The corresponding *filenames* are the patched versions. The length of the suffix may be a problem if you are using a file system with a limited filename length; you can change it (perhaps to the Emacs standard suffix ~) with the *–b* option. In some versions of *patch*, ~ is the default.

If any patches failed, you also have files called *filename.rej* (for "rejected"). These contain the hunks that *patch* could not apply. Another common suffix for rejects is #. Again, you can change the suffix, this time with the *–r* flag. If you have any *.rej* files, you need to look at them and find out what went wrong. It's a good idea to keep the *.orig* files until you're sure that the patches have all worked as indicated.

Pruning the Tree

Making clean distribution directories is notoriously difficult, and the archive frequently contains irrelevant junk. For example, all Emacs distributions for at least the last six years have included a file *etc/COOKIES*. As you might guess from the name, this file is a recipe for cookies, based on a story that went round Usenet years ago. This file is not just present in the source tree: since the entire subdirectory *etc* gets installed when you install Emacs, you end up installing this recipe as well. This particular directory contains a surprising number of files, some of them quite amusing, which don't really have much to do with Emacs.

This example is a rather extreme case of a common problem. You don't need some of the files on the distribution, so you could delete them. As far as I know, Emacs works just as well without the cookie recipe, but in many cases, you can't be as sure. In addition, you might run into other problems: the GNU General Public License requires you to distribute the *complete* contents of the source tree if so requested. You may think that it's an accident that the cookie recipe is in the source tree, but in fact it's a political statement,* and you are *required* by the terms of the GNU General Public License to keep the file in order to give it to anybody who might want the Emacs distribution.

This is a rather extreme example, but you might find any of the following in overgrown trees:

- Old objects, editor backups, and core dumps from previous builds. They may or may not go away when you enter *make clean*.
- Test programs left behind by somebody trying to get the thing to work on his platform. These probably will not go away with a *make clean*.

---

* To quote the beginning of the file: "Someone sent this in from California, and we decided to extend our campaign against information-hoarding to recipes as well as software. (Recipes are the closest thing, not involving computers, to software.)"

- Formatted documentation. Although the *Makefile* should treat documents like objects when cleaning the tree, a surprising number of packages format and install documentation, and then forget about it when tidying up.
- Old mail messages, only possibly related to the package. I don't know why this is, but mail messages seem to be the last thing anybody wants to remove, and so they continue to exist for years in many trees. This problem seems to be worse in proprietary packages than in free packages.

The old objects are definitely the worst problem. Since *make* can't tell that they don't belong to this configuration, they prevent the correct version of the object being built. Depending on how different the architectures are, you may even find that the bogus objects fool the linker, too, and you run into bizarre problems when you try to execute.

Save the Cleaned Archive

If you had to go to any trouble (patches or cleanup) to get to a clean starting point for the port, *save the cleaned archive*. You won't need it again, of course, but Murphy's Law ensures that if you don't save it, you *will* need it again.

Handling Trees on CD-ROM

It's convenient to have your source tree on CD-ROM: you save disk space, and you can be sure that you don't accidentally change anything. Unfortunately, you also can't deliberately change anything. Since *Makefiles* expect to put their objects in the source tree, this complicates the build process significantly.

In the next two sections, we'll look at a couple of techniques that address this problem. Both use symbolic links.

Link Trees

You can simulate a writable tree on disk by creating symbolic links to the sources on CD-ROM. This way, the sources remain on the CD-ROM, but the objects get written to disk. From your viewpoint, it looks as if all the files are in the same directory. For example, suppose you have a CD-ROM with a directory */cd0/src/find* containing the sources to *find*:

```
$ ls -FC /cd0/src/find
COPYING         Makefile        config.status*  lib/
COPYING.LIB     Makefile.in     configure*      locate/
ChangeLog       NEWS            configure.in    man/
INSTALL         README          find/           xargs/
```

The forward slashes at the end of the filenames indicate that these files are directories; the asterisks indicate that they are executables. You could create a link tree with the following commands:

```
$ cd /home/mysrc/find          put the links here
$ for i in /cd0/src/find/*; do
>  ln -s $i .
> done
$ ls -l                        see what we got
total 16
lrwxrwxrwx COPYING -> /cd0/src/find/COPYING
lrwxrwxrwx COPYING.LIB -> /cd0/src/find/COPYING.LIB
lrwxrwxrwx ChangeLog -> /cd0/src/find/ChangeLog
lrwxrwxrwx INSTALL -> /cd0/src/find/INSTALL
lrwxrwxrwx Makefile -> /cd0/src/find/Makefile
lrwxrwxrwx Makefile.in -> /cd0/src/find/Makefile.in
lrwxrwxrwx NEWS -> /cd0/src/find/NEWS
lrwxrwxrwx README -> /cd0/src/find/README
lrwxrwxrwx config.status -> /cd0/src/find/config.status
lrwxrwxrwx configure -> /cd0/src/find/configure
lrwxrwxrwx configure.in -> /cd0/src/find/configure.in
lrwxrwxrwx find -> /cd0/src/find/find
lrwxrwxrwx lib -> /cd0/src/find/lib
lrwxrwxrwx locate -> /cd0/src/find/locate
lrwxrwxrwx man -> /cd0/src/find/man
lrwxrwxrwx xargs -> /cd0/src/find/xargs
```

I omitted most of the information that is printed by *ls -l* in order to fit the information on the page: what interests us here is that all the files, including the directories, are symbolic links. In some cases, we want symbolic links: we don't need to create copies of the directories on the hard disk when a single link to a directory on the CD-ROM does it just as well. In this case, unfortunately, that's not the case. Our sources are in the directory *find*, and that's where we have to write our objects. We need to do the entire process again for the subdirectory *find*:

```
$ cd ~mysource/find            change to the source directory on disk
$ rm find                      get rid of the directory symlink
$ mkdir find                   and make a directory
$ cd find                      and change to it
$ for i in /cd0/src/find/find/*; do
>  ln -s $i .
> done
$ ls -l
total 18
lrwxrwxrwx Makefile -> /cd0/src/find/find/Makefile
lrwxrwxrwx Makefile.in -> /cd0/src/find/find/Makefile.in
lrwxrwxrwx defs.h -> /cd0/src/find/find/defs.h
lrwxrwxrwx find -> /cd0/src/find/find/find
lrwxrwxrwx find.c -> /cd0/src/find/find/find.c
lrwxrwxrwx fstype.c -> /cd0/src/find/find/fstype.c
lrwxrwxrwx parser.c -> /cd0/src/find/find/parser.c
lrwxrwxrwx pred.c -> /cd0/src/find/find/pred.c
```

```
lrwxrwxrwx tree.c -> /cd0/src/find/find/tree.c
lrwxrwxrwx util.c -> /cd0/src/find/find/util.c
lrwxrwxrwx version.c -> /cd0/src/find/find/version.c
```

Yes, this tree really does have a directory called *find/find/find*, but we don't need to worry about it. Our sources and our *Makefile* are here. We should now be able to move back to the top-level directory and perform the *make*:

```
$ cd ..
$ make
```

This is a relatively simple example, but it shows two important aspects of the technique:

- You don't need to create a symlink (symbolic link) for every single file. Although symlinks are relatively small—in this case, less than 100 bytes—they occupy up to 1024 bytes of disk space per link, and you can easily find yourself taking up a megabyte of space just for the links.
- On the other hand, you *do* need to *make* all the directories where output from the build process is stored. You need to make symlinks to the existing files in these directories.

An additional problem with this technique is that many tools don't test whether they have succeeded in creating their output files. If they try to create files on CD-ROM and don't notice that they have failed, you may get some strange and misleading error messages later on.

Object Links on CD-ROM

Some CD-ROMs, notably those derived from the Berkeley Net/2 release, have a much better idea: the CD-ROM already contains a symlink to a directory where the object files are stored. For example, the FreeBSD 1.1 CD-ROM version of *find* is stored on */cd0/filesys/usr/src/usr.bin/find* and contains:

```
total 106
drwxrwxr-x   2 bin    2048 Oct 28  1993 .
drwxrwxr-x 153 bin   18432 Nov 15 23:28 ..
-rw-rw-r--   1 bin     168 Jul 29  1993 Makefile
-rw-rw-r--   1 bin    3157 Jul 29  1993 extern.h
-rw-rw-r--   1 bin   13620 Sep  7  1993 find.1
-rw-rw-r--   1 bin    5453 Jul 29  1993 find.c
-rw-rw-r--   1 bin    4183 Jul 29  1993 find.h
-rw-rw-r--   1 bin   20736 Sep  7  1993 function.c
-rw-rw-r--   1 bin    3756 Oct 17  1993 ls.c
-rw-rw-r--   1 bin    3555 Jul 29  1993 main.c
-rw-rw-r--   1 bin    3507 Jul 29  1993 misc.c
lrwxrwxr-x   1 root     21 Oct 28  1993 obj -> /usr/obj/usr.bin/find
-rw-rw-r--   1 bin    7766 Jul 29  1993 operator.c
```

```
-rw-rw-r--   1 bin    4657 Jul 29  1993 option.c
-rw-rw-r--   1 root   2975 Oct 28  1993 tags
```

All you have to do in this case is to create a directory called */usr/obj/usr.bin/find*. The *Makefiles* are set up to compile into that directory.

Tracking Changes to the Tree

The most obvious modification that you make to a source tree is the process of building: the compiler creates object files,* and the loader creates executables. Documentation formatters may produce formatted versions of the source documentation, and possibly other files are created as well. Whatever you do with these files, you need to recognize which ones you have created and which ones you have changed. We'll look at these aspects in the following sections.

Timestamps

It's easy enough to recognize files that have been added to the source tree since its creation. Since they are all newer than any file in the original source tree, the simple command *ls -lt* (probably piped into *more* or *less*) displays them in the reverse order in which they were created (newest first) and thus separates the new from the old.

Every UNIX file and directory has three timestamps. The file system represents timestamps in the `time_t` format, the number of seconds elapsed since January 1, 1970 UTC. See the section called "Differing Time Formats" in Chapter 16, *Timekeeping*, for more details. The timestamps are:

- The *last modification* timestamp, updated every time the file or directory is modified. This is what most users think of as *the* file timestamp. You can display it with the *ls -l* command.
- The *last access* timestamp, updated every time a data transfer is made to or from the file. You can display it with the *ls -lu* command. This timestamp can be useful in a number of different places.
- The *status change* timestamp (at least, that's what my header files call it). This is a sort of kludged† last modification timestamp for the inode, that part of a file which stores information about the file. The most frequent changes that don't affect the other timestamps are changes in the number of links or changes in the permissions, which normally isn't much use to anybody. On

* To be pedantic, usually the assembler creates the object files, not the compiler.

† A *kludge* is a programming shortcut, usually a nasty, untidy one. The *New Hacker's Dictionary* goes to a lot of detail to explain the term, including why it should be spelled *kluge* and not *kludge*.

the other hand, the inode also contains the other timestamps, so if this rule were enforced rigidly, a change to another timestamp would also change the status change timestamp. This would make it almost completely useless. As a result, most implementations suppress the change to the status change timestamp if the only change is to the other timestamps. If you want, you can display the status change timestamp with the *ls -lc* command.

Whichever timestamp you choose to display with *ls -l*, you can cause *ls* to sort by it with the *–t* option. Thus, *ls –lut* displays and sorts by the last access timestamp.

Of these three timestamps, the last modification timestamp is by far the most important. There are a number of reasons for this:

- *make* relies on the last modification timestamp to decide what it needs to compile. If you move the contents of a directory with *cp*, all the modification timestamps are changed to the time when the copy was performed. If you then run *make*, you will perform a significant amount of needless compilation.
- It's frequently important to establish if two files are in fact the same, in other words, if they have identical content. In the next section we'll see some programmatic tools that help us with this, but as a first approximation, we can assume that two files with the same name, size, and modification timestamp have an identical content, too. The modification timestamp is the most important of these three: you can change the name, but if the size and timestamp are the same, there's still a good chance it's the same file. If you change the timestamp, you can't rely on the two files being the same just because they have the same name and size.
- As we have seen earlier, the last modification timestamp is useful for sorting when you list directories. If you're looking for a file you made the week before last, it helps if it is dated accordingly.

Keeping timestamps straight

Unfortunately, it's not as easy to keep timestamps straight. Here are some of the things that can go wrong:

- If you copy the file somewhere else, traditional versions of *cp* always set the modification timestamp to the time of copying. *ln* does not, and neither does *mv* if it doesn't need to make a physical copy, so either of these are preferable. In addition, more modern versions of *cp* offer the option *–p* (preserve), which preserves the modification timestamp and the permissions.

- When extracting an archive, the default behavior of *cpio* is to set the modification timestamp to the time of extraction. You can avoid this with the *–m* to *cpio*.
- Editing the file changes the modification timestamp. You may frequently find that you make a modification to a file to see if it solves a problem. If it doesn't help, you edit the modification out, leaving the file exactly as it was, except for the modification timestamp, which points to the present time. A better strategy is to save the backup file, if the editor keeps one, or otherwise to rename the original file before making the modifications, then to rename it back to its original name if you decide not to keep the modifications.
- In a network, it's unusual for times to be exactly the same. UNIX machines are not very good at keeping the exact time, and some gain or lose as much as five minutes per day. This can cause problems if you are using NFS (Network File System). You edit your files on one machine, in which the clocks are behind, and compile on another, in which the clocks are ahead. The result can be that objects created before the last edit have a modification timestamp that is more recent, and *make* is fooled into believing that it doesn't need to recompile. Similar problems can occur when one system is running with an incorrect time zone setting.

cmp

A modification timestamp isn't infallible, of course: even if the size, timestamp, and name are identical, you can still have a lingering doubt as to whether the files really are identical. This doubt becomes more pronounced if you see something like:

```
$ ls -l
total 503
-rw-rw-rw-   1 grog     wheel       1326 May  1 01:00 a29k-pinsn.c
-rw-rw-rw-   1 grog     wheel      28871 May  1 01:00 a29k-tdep.c
-rw-rw-rw-   1 grog     wheel       4259 May  1 01:00 a68v-nat.c
-rw-rw-rw-   1 grog     wheel       4515 May  1 01:00 alpha-nat.c
-rw-rw-rw-   1 grog     wheel      33690 May  1 01:00 alpha-tdep.c
... etc
```

It's a fairly clear bet that somebody has done a *touch* on all the files, and their modification timestamps have all been set to midnight on May 1.* The *cmp* program can give you certainty:

---

* Midnight? That looks like 1 a.m. But remember that UNIX timestamps are all in UTC (Greenwich time), and that's 1 a.m. in my time zone. This example really *was* done with *touch*.

```
$ cmp foo.c ../orig/foo.c                  compare with the original
$ echo $?                                  show exit status
0                                          0: all OK
$ cmp bar.c ../orig/bar.c
bar.c ../orig/bar.c differ: char 1293, line 39
$ echo $?                                  show exit status
1                                          1: they differ
```

Remember that you can tell the shell to display the exit status of the previous command with the shell variable `$?`. In the C shell, the corresponding variable is called `$status`. If the contents of the files are identical, *cmp* says nothing and returns an exit status 0. If the contents are not identical, it tells you where they differ and returns 1. You can use the exit status in a shell script. For example, the following Bourne shell script (it doesn't work with *csh*) compares files that are in both the current tree (which is the current working directory) and the original tree (*../orig*) and makes a copy of the ones that have changed in the directory *../changed*:

```
$ for i in *; do                              check all files in the directory
>   if [ -f ../orig/$i ]; then                it is present in the orig tree
>     cmp $i ../orig/$i 2>&1 >/dev/null       compare them
>     if [ $? -ne 0 ]; then                   they're different
>       cp -p $i ../changed                   make a copy
>     fi
>   fi
> done
```

This example contains a couple of points to note:

- We're not interested in where the files differ or in even seeing the message. We just want to copy the files. As a result, we copy both *stdout* and *stderr* of *cmp* to */dev/null*, the UNIX bit bucket.
- When copying, we use *–p* to ensure that the timestamps don't get changed again.

An Example—Updating an Existing Tree

Chances are that before long you will have an old version of *gcc* on your system and that you will want to install a newer version. As we saw in the section called "Updating Old Archives", the *gzipped* archive for *gcc* is around 6 MB in size, whereas the patches run to 10 KB or 15 KB, so we opt to get *diffs* from `prep.ai.mit.edu` to update version 2.6.1 to 2.6.3. That's pretty straightforward if you have enough disk space: we can duplicate the complete source tree and patch it. Before doing so, we should check the disk space: the *gcc* source tree with all objects takes up 110 MB of disk space.

```
$ cd /porting/src            move to the parent directory
$ mkdir gcc-2.6.3            make a directory for the new tree
$ cd gcc-2.6.1               move to the old directory
$ tar cf - . | (cd ../gcc-2.6.3;tar xf -)          and copy all files*

$ cd ../gcc-2.6.3                    move to new directory
$ make clean                         and start off with a clean slate
$ gunzip < /C/incoming/gcc-2.6.1-2.6.2.tar.gz | patch -p | tee patch.log
Hmm...  Looks like a new-style context diff to me...
The text leading up to this was:
--------------------------
|Changes for GCC version 2.6.2 from version 2.6.1:
|
|Before applying these diffs, go to the directory gcc-2.6.1. Remove all
|files that are not part of the distribution with the command
|
|    make distclean
|
|Then use the command
|
|    patch -p1
|
|feeding it the following diffs as input. Then rename the directory to
|gcc-2.6.2, re-run the configure script, and rebuild the compiler.
|
|diff -rc2P -x c-parse.y -x c-parse.c -x c-parse.h -x c-gperf.h -x cexp.c -x
bi-parser.c -x objc-parse.y -x objc-parse.c
|-x TAGS -x gcc.?? -x gcc.??s -x gcc.aux -x gcc.info* -x cpp.?? -x cpp.??s -x
cpp.aux -x cpp.info* -x cp/parse.c -x cp/pa
|rse.h gcc-2.6.1/ChangeLog gcc-2.6.2/ChangeLog
|*** gcc-2.6.1/ChangeLog Tue Nov  1 21:32:40 1994
|--- gcc-2.6.2/ChangeLog Sat Nov 12 06:36:04 1994
--------------------------
File to patch:
```

Oops, these patches contain the directory name as well. As the diff header indicates, we can solve this problem by supplying the *–p1* option to *patch*. We can also solve the problem by moving up one level in the directory hierarchy, since we have stuck to the same directory names. This message also reminds us that *patch* is very verbose, so this time we enter:

```
$ gunzip < /C/incoming/gcc-2.6.1-2.6.2.tar.gz | patch -p1 -s | tee patch.log
1 out of 6 hunks failed--saving rejects to cccp.c.rej
$
```

* When moving directories with *tar*, it may not seem to be important whether you type `tar c .` or `tar c *`—but it is. If you type `*`, you miss any filenames starting with `.` (period).

What went wrong here? Let's take a look at *cccp.c.rej* and *cccp.c.orig*. According to the hunk, line 3281 should be

```
if (ip->macro != 0)
```

The hunk wants to change it to

```
if (output_marks)
```

However, line 3281 of *cccp.orig* is

```
if (output_marks)
```

In other words, we had already applied this change, probably from a message posted in `gnu.gcc.bugs`. Although the patch failed, we don't need to worry: all the changes had been applied.

Now we have a *gcc-2.6.2* source tree in our directory. To upgrade to 2.6.3, we need to apply the next patch:

```
$ gunzip < /C/incoming/gcc-2.6.2-2.6.3.diff.gz | patch -p1 -s | tee -a patch.log
```

We use the *–a* option to patch here to keep both logs—possibly overkill in this case. This time there are no errors.

After patching, a lot of original files are in the directory, along with the one *.rej* file. We need to decide when to delete the *.orig* files. If something goes wrong compiling one of the patched files, it's nice to have the original around to compare. In our case, though, we have a complete source tree of version 2.6.2 on the same disk, and it contains *all* the original files, so we can remove the *.orig* files:

```
$ find . -name "*.orig" -print | xargs rm
```

We use *xargs* instead of *-exec rm {} \;* because it's faster: *–exec rm* starts a *rm* process for every file, whereas *xargs* puts as many filenames onto the *rm* command line as possible. After cleaning up the tree, we *back it up*. It's taken us a while to create the tree, and if anything goes wrong, we'd like to be able to restore it to its initial condition as soon as possible.

In This Chapter:

- *Installation Paths*
- *Conveying Configuration Information*
- *What Do I Need to Change?*
- *Creating Configuration Information*
- *Multiple Makefile Targets*
- *Manual Configuration*
- *Configuration Scripts*
- *GNU Package Configuration*
- *imake program*

4

Configuring the Package

Programs don't run in a vacuum: they interface with the outside world. The view of this outside world differs from location to location: things like host names, system resources, and local conventions will be different. Theoretically, you could change the program sources every time you install a package on a new system, but besides being a pain, it's a very error-prone process. All modern packages supply a method of *configuration*, a simplified way of adapting the sources to the environment in which the program will run. In this chapter, we'll look at common configuration conventions.

We can divide system differences into three categories:

- The kind of hardware the package will run on. A compiler needs to generate the correct machine instructions, and an X server needs to know how to transfer data to the display hardware. Less well-written programs have hardware dependencies that could have been avoided with some forethought. We'll look at this in more detail in Chapter 11, *Hardware Dependencies*.
- The system software with which it will interact. Differences between UNIX systems are significant enough that you have to make certain decisions depending on the system flavor. For example, a communications program needs to

know what kind of network interface your system has. Programs that come from other systems may need significant rewriting to conform with UNIX library calls. We'll look at these dependencies in Part II of this book, from Chapter 12, *Kernel Dependencies* to Chapter 21, *Object Files and Friends.*

- The local configuration. This may include the obvious, such as the system name, aspects of program behavior, information about tools used locally, or local system conventions.

In this chapter, we'll look at what local configuration entails, and *how* we tell the package about our chosen configuration.

Installation Paths

Your system configuration may place constraints on where you can install the software. These constraints are not usually a problem for individual systems, but on a large, heterogeneous network, the system configuration could require more thought.

Traditionally, nonsystem software has been installed in the hierarchy */usr/local*. This is not an æsthetically pleasing location: the hierarchy can become quite large, and in a network many systems might share the directory.

One of the best thought-out descriptions of a modern file system structure is in the *UNIX System V Application Binary Interface*. The file system structure described there is similar to structures used by SunOS and the newer BSD variants. In brief, it specifies the following top-level directories:

/ The root directory.

/dev
: The directory tree containing device files.

/etc
: Directory for machine-specific configuration files.

/opt
: Directory for add-on software.

/usr
: This directory used to be *the* other file system on a UNIX machine. In the System V ABI it has lost most of its importance. The ABI states uses only for */usr/bin* and */usr/share* and specifies */usr* only as a location for system files that users may wish to access.

/usr/bin

This directory is intended for "utility programs and commands for the use of all applications and users." In practice, it's better to use this directory for system programs only.

/usr/share

The System V ABI states that */usr/share* is intended for "architecture-independent shareable files." In practice, those versions of System V that still have man pages put them in */usr/share/man*, and *terminfo* data is stored in */usr/share/lib/terminfo*. The rest of the directory may contain a few other odds and ends. These two subdirectories make up over 99% of the contents of */usr/share*. The choice of the location */usr/share* is not a happy choice. First, it is frequently a separate file system, but it must be mounted on a nonroot file system. Second, the man pages aren't really architecture independent. The choice makes more sense from the point of view of the Unix Systems Group, who are concerned only with pure System V: the man pages are mainly independent of hardware architecture. However, in a real-world network, you probably have two or three different operating systems, each with its own man pages.

/var

This directory contains files that are frequently modified. Typical subdirectories are */var/tmp* for temporary files and */var/spool* for printer output, *uucp*, and *news*.

The System V ABI does not specify where to store user files. The Seventh Edition typically stored them as a subdirectory of */usr*, but newer systems have tended to store them in a directory called */home*.

The */opt* hierarchy resembles that of */usr*. A typical structure is:

/opt/bin

The directory for executables.

/opt/man

The directory for man pages—not */opt/share/man*, unlike the structure in */usr*.

/opt/lib

The directory for additional files used by executables. In particular, this directory could contain library archives for compilers, as well as the individual passes of the compilers.

/opt/<pkg>
: The directory where the System V ABI places individual package data. Not many other systems follow this directory structure.

/opt/lib/<pkg>
: The directory where most packages place private data.

Using the */opt* hierarchy has one disadvantage: you may not want to have a separate file system. In modern systems, the solution is simple enough: place the directory where you want it, and create a symbolic link */opt* that points to it. Since this works only if your system has symbolic links, I have come to a compromise. I use */opt* on systems with symbolic links and */usr/local* on systems without symbolic links.

Many packages compile pathnames into the code, either because it's faster that way, or because it's easier. As a result, you should set the pathnames before compilation—don't put off this task until you're ready to install because you may run into problems in which the packages are all nicely installed in the correct place but look for data in the wrong directories.

Preferred Tools

Many of the most popular software packages are alternative tools. Free software such as *gcc*, Emacs, and *perl* have become so popular that they are frequently supplied with proprietary system releases, and many other systems have ported them and use them as standard tools. If you want to use such programs, you need to tell the configuration routines about them.

Depending on the tools you use, you may also need to change the flags that you pass to them. For example, if you compile with *gcc*, you may choose to include additional compiler flags such as *–fstrength-reduce*, which is specific to *gcc*.

Conveying Configuration Information

The goal of configuration is to supply the configuration information to the program sources. A good configuration mechanism hides this from you, but it's helpful to understand what it's doing. In this section, we'll look under the covers.

You can use configuration information in a number of possible ways: for example, the package may have separate communication modules for STREAMS and sockets, and the configuration routines may decide which of the two modules to compile. More typically, however, the configuration routines convey configuration information to the package by defining preprocessor variables indicating the presence or absence of a specific feature. Many packages provide this information in the *make* variable CFLAGS—for example, when you make *bash*, the GNU Bourne Again Shell, you see things like:

```
$ make
gcc  -DOS_NAME='"FreeBSD"' -DProgram=bash          -DSYSTEM_NAME='"i386"'  \
-DMAINTAINER='"bug-bash@prep.ai.mit.edu"'  -O -g -DHAVE_SETLINEBUF \
-DHAVE_VFPRINTF  -DHAVE_UNISTD_H -DHAVE_STDLIB_H -DHAVE_LIMITS_H          \
-DHAVE_GETGROUPS  -DHAVE_RESOURCE -DHAVE_SYS_PARAM -DVOID_SIGHANDLER \
-DOPENDIR_NOT_ROBUST  -DINT_GROUPS_ARRAY -DHAVE_WAIT_H        -DHAVE_GETWD \
-DHAVE_DUP2 -DHAVE_STRERROR  -DHAVE_DIRENT -DHAVE_DIRENT_H  -DHAVE_STRING_H \
-DHAVE_VARARGS_H -DHAVE_STRCHR  -DHAVE_STRCASECMP -DHAVE_DEV_FD          \
-D"i386" -D"FreeBSD" -DSHELL -DHAVE_ALLOCA \
-I. -I. -I././lib/ -c shell.c
```

The *–D* arguments, which come from CFLAGS, pass preprocessor variables that define the configuration information.

An alternative method is to put this information in a file with a name like *config.h*. Taylor *uucp* does it this way: in *config.h* you find things like:

```
/* If your compiler supports prototypes, set HAVE_PROTOTYPES to 1. */
#define HAVE_PROTOTYPES 1

/* Set ECHO_PROGRAM to a program which echoes its arguments; if echo
   is a shell builtin you can just use "echo". */
#define ECHO_PROGRAM "echo"

/* The following macros indicate what header files you have. Set the
   macro to 1 if you have the corresponding header file, or 0 if you
   do not. */
#define HAVE_STDDEF_H 1 /* <stddef.h> */
#define HAVE_STDARG_H 1 /* <stdarg.h> */
#define HAVE_STRING_H 1 /* <string.h> */
```

I prefer this approach because you have all the configuration information in one place, it is documented, and it's more reliable. Assuming that the *Makefile* dependencies are correct, any change to *config.h* causes the programs to be recompiled on the next *make*. As we will see in the section called "No dependency on Makefile" in Chapter 5, *Building the Package*, this usually doesn't happen if you modify the *Makefile*.

Typically, configuration information is based on the kind of operating system you run and the kind of hardware you use. For example, if you compile for a Sparc II running SunOS 4.1.3, you might define sparc to indicate the processor architecture used and sunos4 to indicate the operating system. Since SunOS 4 is basically UNIX, you might also need to define unix. On an Intel 486 running UnixWare you might need to define i386 for the processor architecture* and SVR4 to indicate the operating system. This information is then used in the source files as arguments to preprocessor #ifdef commands. For example, the beginning of each source file, or a general configuration file, might contain:

```
#ifdef i386
#include "m/i386.h"
#endif
#ifdef sparc
#include "m/sparc.h"
#endif

#ifdef sunos4
#include "s/sunos4.h"
#endif
#ifdef SVR4
#include "s/usg-4.0.h"
#endif
```

You can get yourself into real trouble if you define more than one machine architecture or more than one operating system. Since configuration is usually automated to some extent, the likelihood of this is not very great. If you end up with lots of double definitions when compiling, however, one possible reason is that you defined more than one architecture or operating system.

Configuration through the preprocessor works nicely if the hardware and software both exactly match the expectations of the person who wrote the code. Often this is not the case: looking at the previous example, note that the file included for SVR4 is *s/usg-4.0.h*, which suggests that it is intended for UNIX System V release 4.0. UnixWare is System V release 4.2. Will this work? Maybe. It could be that the configuration mechanism was last revised before System V.4.2 came out. If you find a file *s/usg-4.2.h*, it's a good idea to use it instead, but otherwise, it's a matter of trial and error.

Most software uses #ifdef commands, although this approach has a number of significant drawbacks:

- The choices are not very detailed: for example, most packages don't distinguish between Intel 386 and Intel 486, although the latter has a floating point coprocessor and the former doesn't.
- There is no general consensus on what abbreviations to use. For UnixWare, you may find that the correct operating system information is determined by

* Why not i486? The processor is an Intel 486, but the architecture is called the i386 architecture. You also use i386 when compiling for a Pentium.

USG (USG is the Unix Systems Group, which, with some interruption,* is responsible for System V), SYSV, SVR4, SYSV_4, SYSV_4_2 or even SVR3. This last can happen when the configuration needed to be updated from System V.2 to System V.3, but not again for System V.4.

- The choice of operating system is usually determined by just a couple of differences. For example, base System V.3 does not have the system call `rename`, but most versions of System V.3 that you find today have it. System V.4 does have `rename`. A software writer may use `#ifdef SVR4` only to determine whether or not the system has the `rename` system call. If you are porting this package to a version of System V.3.2 with `rename`, it might be a better idea to define SVR4, and not SVR3.
- Many aspects attributed to the kernel are in fact properties of the system library. As we will see in the introduction to Part II of this book, there is a major difference between kernel functionality and library functionality. The assumption is that a specific kernel uses the library with which it is supplied. The situation is changing, though: many companies sell systems without software development tools, and alternative libraries, such as the GNU C library, are becoming available. Making assumptions about the library based on the kernel was never a good idea—now it's completely untenable. For example, the GNU C library supplies a function `rename` where needed, so our previous example would fail even on a System V.3 kernel without a `rename` system call if it uses the GNU C library. As you can imagine, many packages break when compiled with the GNU C library, through their own fault, not that of the library.

In the previous example, it would make a whole lot more sense to define a macro HAS_RENAME that can be set if the `rename` function is present. Some packages use this method, and the GNU project is gradually working toward it. The majority of packages, however, base their decisions primarily on the combination of machine architecture and operating system.

The results of incorrect configuration can be far reaching and subtle. In many cases, a bug is in the package and instead of reconfiguring, you can find yourself making significant changes to the source. This can cause the package to work for the environment in which it is compiled, but to break for anything else.

* The first USG was part of AT&T and was superseded by UNIX Systems Laboratories (USL). After the sale of USL to Novell, USL became Novell's UNIX Systems Group.

What Do I Need to Change?

A good configuration mechanism should be able to decide the hardware and software dependencies that interest the package, but only you can tell it about the local preferences. For example, which compiler do you use? Where do you want to install the executables? If you don't know the answers to these questions, you'll probably be happy with the defaults chosen by the configuration routines. On the other hand, you may want to use *gcc* to compile the package and to install the package in the */opt* hierarchy. In all probability, you will have to tell the configuration routines about this. Some configuration routines look for *gcc* explicitly and use it if they find it. In this case, you may have a reason to tell the configuration routines *not* to use *gcc*.

Some packages have a number of local preferences: for example, do you want the package to run with X11 (and possibly fail if X isn't running)? This sort of information should be in the *README* file.

Creating Configuration Information

A number of configuration methods exist, none of them perfect. In most cases you don't get a choice: you use the method that the author of the package decided upon. The first significant problem can arise at this point: *what* method does she use? This is not always easy to figure out—it should be described in a file called *README* or *INSTALL* or some such, but occasionally you just find cryptic comments in the *Makefile*.

In the rest of this chapter we'll look at configuration via multiple *Makefile* targets, manual configuration, shell scripts, and *imake*, the X11 configuration mechanism. In addition, the new BSD *make* system includes a system of automatic configuration. Once it is set up, you don't have to do anything, assuming you already have a suitable *Makefile*. We'll look at this method in more detail in the section called "BSD make" in Chapter 19, *make*.

Multiple Makefile Targets

Some packages anticipate every possibility for you and supply a customized *Makefile*. For example, when building *unzip*, a free decompression utility compatible with the DOS package *pkzip*, you would find:

```
$ make
If you're not sure about the characteristics of your system, try typing "make
generic". If the compiler barfs and says something unpleasant about "timezone
redefined," try typing "make clean" followed by "make generic2". One of these
actions should produce a working copy of unzip on most Unix systems. If you
know a bit more about the machine on which you work, you might try "make list"
```

```
for a list of the specific systems supported herein. And as a last resort, feel
free to read the numerous comments within the Makefile itself. Note that to
compile the decryption version of UnZip, you must obtain the full versions of
crypt.c and crypt.h (see the "Where" file for ftp and mail-server sites). Have
an excruciatingly pleasant day.
```

As the comments suggest, typing `make generic` should work most of the time. If it doesn't, the *Makefile* contains a whole host of targets for a number of combined hardware/software platforms. If one of them works for you and you can find which one, this might be an easy way to go. If none does, you might find yourself faced with some serious *Makefile* rewriting. This method has an additional disadvantage: it might compile with no problems but then run into subtle problems when you try to execute it. For example, if the program expects System V `sigpause` and your system supplies BSD `sigpause`,* the build process may complete without detecting any problems, but the program won't run correctly, and you might have a lot of trouble finding out why.

Manual Configuration

Modifying the *Makefile* or *config.h* manually is a better approach than trying multiple *Makefile* targets. This seemingly arduous method has a number of advantages:

- You get to see what is being changed. If you have problems with the resultant build, it's usually relatively easy to pinpoint them.
- Assuming that the meanings of the parameters are well documented, it can be easier to modify them manually than run an automated procedure that hides much of what it is doing.
- If you find you *do* need to change something, you can usually do it fairly quickly. With an automated script, you may need to go through the entire script to change a single minor parameter.

On the down side, manual configuration requires that you understand the issues involved: you can't configure manually if you don't understand the build process. In addition, you may need to repeat the manual configuration every time you get an update of the package, and repeating it is susceptible to error.

* See the section called "BSD Signal Functions" in Chapter 1, *Signals*, for further information.

Configuration Scripts

Neither multiple *Makefile* targets nor manual modification of the *Makefile* leave you with the warm, fuzzy feeling that everything is going to work correctly. It would be nice to have a more mechanized method to ensure that the package gets the correct information about the environment in which it is to be built. One way to do this is to condense the decisions you need to make in manual configuration into a shell script. Some of these scripts work very well. A whole family of configuration scripts has grown up in the area of electronic mail and news. Here's part of the configuration script for C news, which for some reason is called *build*:

```
$ cd conf
$ build
This interactive command will build shell files named doit.root,
doit.bin, doit.news, and again.root to do all the work. It will not
actually do anything itself, so feel free to abort and start again.

C News wants to keep most of its files under a uid which preferably
should be all its own. Its programs, however, can and probably should
be owned by another user, typically the same one who owns most of the
rest of the system. (Note that on a system running NFS, any program
not owned by "root" is a gaping security hole.)
What user id should be used for news files [news]? RETURN pressed
What group id should be used for news files [news]? RETURN pressed
What user id should be used for news programs [bin]? RETURN pressed
What group id should be used for news programs [bin]? RETURN pressed
Do the C News sources belong to bin [yes]? no
You may need to do some of the installation procedures by hand
after the software is built; doit.bin assumes that it has the
power to create files in the source directories and to update
the news programs.

It would appear that your system is among the victims of the
4.4BSD / SVR4 directory reorganization, with (e.g.) shared
data in /usr/share. Is this correct [yes]? RETURN pressed
This will affect where C News directories go. We recommend
making the directories wherever they have to go and then making
symbolic links to them under the standard names that are used
as defaults in the following questions. Should such links
be made [yes]? no
```

We chose not to use the symbolic links: the script doesn't say why this method is recommended, they don't buy us anything, and symbolic links mean increased access time.

The configuration script continues with many more questions such as those in the example. We'll pick the script up at various places in the book.

The flexibility of a shell script is an advantage when checking for system features that are immediately apparent, but most of them require that you go through the entire process from start to finish if you need to modify anything. This can take up to 10 minutes on each occasion. Since the shell scripts are often interactive, you can't just go away and let the script do its thing.

GNU Package Configuration

Most GNU project packages supply another variety of configuration script. GNU configuration scripts sometimes expect you to know the machine architecture and the operating system, but they often attempt to guess if you don't tell them. The main intention of the configuration utility is to figure out which features are present in your particular operating system port, thus avoiding the problems with functions like *rename*, such as those discussed in the section called "Conveying Configuration Information". Taylor *uucp* uses this method:

```
$ sh configure
checking how to run the C preprocessor
checking whether -traditional is needed see the section called "Choosing a Compiler" in
                                        Chapter 20, Compilers
checking for install                    the install program, see the section called "install"
                                        in Chapter 9
checking for ranlib
checking for POSIXized ISC              Interactive POSIX extensions?
checking for minix/config.h             MINIX specific
checking for AIX                        IBM UNIX
checking for -lseq                      libseq.a needed?
checking for -lsun                      libsun.a?
checking whether cross-compiling
checking for lack of working const      see the section called "UNIX C" in Chapter 20
checking for prototypes                 does the compiler understand function prototypes?
checking if `#!' works in shell scripts
checking for echo program               is echo a program or a builtin?
checking for ln -s                      do we have symbolic links? (see
                                        the section called "symlink") in Chapter 14
```

This method makes life a whole lot easier if the package has already been ported to your particular platform and if you are prepared to accept the default assumptions that it makes. It can be a real pain if not:

- You may end up having to modify the configuration scripts, which can turn into a complicated job.
- It's not always easy to configure things you want. In the previous example, we accepted the default compiler flags. If you want maximum optimization and the executables should be installed in */opt/bin* instead of being installed in the

default */usr/local/bin*, running *configure* becomes significantly more complicated:*

```
$ CFLAGS="-O3 -g" sh configure --prefix=/opt
```

- The scripts aren't perfect. You should really check the resultant *Makefiles*, and you may often find that you need to modify them. For example, the configuration scripts of many packages, including the GNU debugger, *gdb*, do not allow you to override the preset value of CFLAGS.

  In other cases, you can run into a lot of trouble if you do things that the script didn't expect. I once spent a couple of hours trying to figure out the behavior of the GNU *make* configuration script when porting to Solaris 2.4. I noticed a problem in last line of the following output:

```
$ CFLAGS="O3 -g" configure --prefix=/opt
creating cache ./config.cache
checking for gcc...gcc
checking whether we are using GNU C...yes
checking how to run the C preprocessor...gcc -E
checking whether cross-compiling...yes
```

  Although this was a normal port, the configuration script claimed I was trying to cross-compile. After a lot of experimentation, I discovered that the script checks for cross-compilation by compiling a simple program. If this compilation fails for any reason, the script assumes that it should set up a cross-compilation environment. In this case, I had mistakenly set my CFLAGS to `O3 -g` (note that the string doesn't start with a hyphen). Of course, I had meant to write `-O3 -g` with an initial hyphen. The compiler looked for a file *O3* and couldn't find one, so it failed. The configuration script saw this failure and assumed I was cross-compiling.

- In most cases, you need to rerun the configuration script every time a package is updated. If the script runs correctly, this is not a problem, but if you need to modify the *Makefile* manually, it can be a pain. For example, *gdb* creates 12 *Makefiles*. If you want to change the CFLAGS, you need to modify each of them every time you run *configure*.

- Like all configuration scripts, the GNU scripts have the disadvantage of only configuring things they know about. If your *man* program requires pre-formatted man pages, you may find that you can't configure the package to do what you want, and you end up modifying the *Makefile* after you have built it.

* This example uses the feature of modern shells, which enables you to specify environment variables at the beginning of the command. The program being run is *sh*, and the definition of CFLAGS is exported only to the program being started.

Modifying automatically built *Makefiles* is a pain. An alternative is to modify *Makefile.in*, the raw *Makefile* used by *configure*. That way, you won't have to redo the modifications after each run of *configure*.

imake program

imake is the X11 solution to package configuration. It uses the C preprocessor to convert a number of configuration files into a *Makefile*. Here are the standard files for X11R6:

- *Imake.tmpl* is the main configuration file that is passed to the C preprocessor. It is responsible for including all the other configuration files via the preprocessor `#include` directive.
- *Imake.cf* determines the kind of system upon which *imake* is running. This may be based on preprocessor variables supplied by default to the preprocessor or on variables compiled in to *imake*.
- *site.def* describes local preferences. This is one of the few files that you should normally consider modifying.
- As its name implies, *<vendor>.cf* has a different name for each platform. *Imake.tmpl* decides which file to include based on the information returned by *Imake.cf*. For example, on BSD/OS, the file *bsdi.cf* is included, whereas under SunOS 4 or Solaris 2, the file *sun.cf* is included.
- *Imake.rules* contains preprocessor macros used to define the individual *Makefile* targets.
- *Imakefile* is part of the package, not the *imake* configuration, and describes the package to *imake*.

You don't usually run *imake* directly, because it needs a couple of pathname parameters. Instead you have two possibilities:

- Run *xmkmf*, which is a one-line script that supplies the parameters to *imake*.
- Run *make Makefile*. This assumes that some kind of functional *Makefile* is present in the package.

Strangely, the *imake* documentation recommends running *make Makefile* to create a new *Makefile*. I don't agree. One of the most frequent reasons to make a new *Makefile* is because the old one doesn't work, or because it just plain isn't there. If your *imake* configuration is messed up, you can easily remove all traces of a functional *Makefile* and have to restore the original version from tape. *xmkmf* always works, and anyway, it's less effort to type.

Once you have a *Makefile*, you may not be finished with configuration. If your package contains subdirectories, you may need to create *Makefiles* in the subdirectories as well. In general, the following sequence builds most packages:

```
$ xmkmf              run imake against the Imakefile
$ make Makefiles     create subordinate Makefiles
$ make depend        run makedepend against all Makefiles
$ make               make the packages
$ make install       install the packages
```

These commands include no package-dependent parameters—the whole sequence can be run as a shell script. Well, yes, there are minor variations: *make Makefiles* fails if no subordinate *Makefiles* are to be made, and sometimes you have targets like a *make World* instead of *make* or *make all*. In general, however, it's very straightforward.

If your *imake* configuration files are set up correctly and the package that you are porting contains no obscenities, we've just covered almost everything you need to know about *imake*. Otherwise, check the Nutshell Handbook *Software Portability with imake*, by Paul DuBois, for the gory details.

In This Chapter:
- *Preparation*
- *Standard Targets*
- *Problems Running make*
- *Modifying Makefiles*

5

Building the Package

Now we have configured our package, and we're ready to build. This is the Big Moment: at the end of the build process we should have a complete, functioning software product in our source tree. In this chapter, we'll look at the surprises that *make* can have in store for you. You can find the corresponding theoretical material in Chapter 19, *make*.

Preparation

If you're unlucky, a port can go seriously wrong. The first time that error messages appear thick and fast and scroll off the screen before you can read them, you could get the impression that the packages were built this way deliberately to annoy you.

A little bit of preparation can go a long way toward keeping you in control of what's going on. The following sections offer some suggestions.

Be Sure You Have Enough Space

One of the most frequent reasons a build fails is that the file system fills up. If possible, ensure that you have enough space before you start. The trouble is knowing how much is enough. Hardly any package tells you how much space you need, and if it does, it's probably wrong because the size depends greatly on the platform. If you are short on space, consider compiling without debugging symbols (which take up a lot of space). If you do run out of space in the middle of a build, you might be able to save the day by *stripping* the objects with *strip*—in other words, removing the symbols from the file.

Use a Windowing System

The sheer size of a complicated port can be a problem. Like program development, porting tends to be an iterative activity. You edit a file, compile, link, test, go back to edit the file, and so on. It's not uncommon to find yourself having to compare and modify up to 20 different files in five different directories, not to mention running *make* and the debugger. In adddition, a single line of output from *make* can easily be 5,000 or 10,000 characters long, many times the screen capacity of a conventional terminal.

All of these facts speak in favor of a windowing system such as X11, preferably with a high-resolution monitor. You can keep your editor (or editors, if they don't easily handle multiple files) open all the time and run the compiler and debugger in other windows. If multiple directories are involved, it's easier to maintain multiple *xterms*, one per directory, than to continually change directories. A correctly set up *xterm* allows you to scroll back as far as you want—I find that 250 lines is adequate.

Keep a Log File

Sooner or later, you're going to run into a bug that you can't fix immediately: you will have to experiment a bit before you can fix the problem. Like finding your way through a labyrinth, the first time through you will probably not take the most direct route, and it's nice to be able to find your way back again. In the original Labyrinth, Theseus used a ball of string to find his way out. The log file, a text file describing what you've done, is the computer equivalent of the ball of string. If you're running an editor like Emacs, which can handle multiple files at a time, you can keep the log in the editor buffer and remove the notes when you back out the changes.

In addition to helping you find your way out of the labyrinth, the log can also be of use later when you install an updated version of the software. To be of use in this situation, it helps to keep additional information. For example, here are some extracts from a log file for *gcc*:

```
Platform:       SCO UNIX System V.3.2.2.0
Revision:       2.6.0
Date ported:    25 August 1994
Ported by:      Greg Lehey, LEMIS
Compiler used: rcc, gcc-2.6.0
Library:               SCO


0. configure i386-unknown-sco --prefix=/opt. It sets local_prefix to
   /usr/local anyway, and won't listen to --local_prefix. For some
   reason, config decides that it should be cross-compiling.
```

1. function.c fails to compile with the message function.c: 59: no space. Compile this function with ISC gcc-2.5.8.

2. libgcc.a was not built because config decided to cross-compile. Re-run config with configure i386-*-sco --prefix=/opt, and do an explicit make libgcc.a.

3. crtbegin.o and crtend.o were not built. Fix configure:

```
--- configure~  Tue Jul 12 01:25:53 1994
+++ configure   Sat Aug 27 13:09:27 1994
@@ -742,6 +742,7 @@
                else
                        tm_file=i386/sco.h
                        tmake_file=i386/t-sco
+                       extra_parts="crtbegin.o crtend.o"
                fi
                truncate_target=yes
                ;;
```

Keeping notes about problems you have with older versions helps a lot. This example represents the results of considerable time spent debugging the *make* procedure. If you didn't have the log, you'd risk tripping over this problem every time.

Save make Output

Typically, to build a package after you have configured it, you simply type the following:

```
$ make
```

Then the fireworks start. You can sit and watch, but watching a package compile for hours on end gets rather boring. You can usually leave it alone once you have a reasonable expectation that the process won't die as soon as you turn your back. The problem is, of course, that you may come back and find a lot of gobbledegook on the screen, such as:

```
make[5]: execve: ../../config/makedepend/makedepend: No such file or directory
make[5]: *** [depend] Error 127
make[5]: Leaving directory `/cdcopy/SOURCE/X11/X11R6/xc/programs/xsetroot'
depending in programs/xstdcmap...
make[5]: Entering directory `/cdcopy/SOURCE/X11/X11R6/xc/programs/xstdcmap'
checking ../../config/makedepend/makedepend over in ../../config/makedepend first
make[6]: Entering directory `/cdcopy/SOURCE/X11/X11R6/xc/config/makedepend'
gcc -DNO_ASM -fstrength-reduce -fpcc-struct-return -fwritable-strings -O   \\
-I../../config/imake  -I../.. OSDefines -DSYSV -DSYSV386        -c include.c
gcc: OSDefines: No such file or directory
In file included from include.c:30:
def.h:133: conflicting types for `getline'
/opt/include/stdio.h:505: previous declaration of `getline'
Broken pipe
```

This output is from a real-life attempt to compile X11R6, usually a fairly docile port. The target *makedepend* failed to compile, but the reason has long since scrolled off the screen.* You can have your cake and eat it too if you use *tee* to save your output:

```
$ make 2>&1 | tee -a Make.log
```

This command performs the following actions:

- It copies error output (file descriptor 2) to standard output (file descriptor 1) with the expression `2>&1`.
- It pipes the combined standard output to the program *tee*, which echos it to its standard output and also copies it to the file *Make.log*.
- The *–a* option tells *tee* to append to any existing *Make.log*. If you don't supply this flag, *tee* erases any previous contents.

If you're not sure what your *make* is going to do and especially if the *Makefile* is complicated, consider using the *–n* option. This option tells *make* to perform a "dry run": it prints out the commands that it would execute but doesn't actually execute them.

These comparatively simple conventions can save a lot of pain. I use a primitive script called *Make* that contains just the single line:

```
make 2>&1 $* | tee -a Make.log
```

Always use the same name for the log files so that you can find them easily.

Standard Targets

Building packages consists of more than just compiling and linking, and by convention many *Makefiles* contain a number of targets with specific meanings. In the following sections we'll look at some of the most common ones.

make depend

make depend creates a list of dependencies for your source tree and usually appends it to the *Makefile*. Most often it performs this task with *make depend*, but sometimes you may see a `depend` target that uses *gcc* with the *–M* option or *cpp*. `depend` should be the first target to run, since it influences which other commands

* Well, there *is* a clue, but it's very difficult to see unless you have been hacking X11 configurations longer than is good for your health. `OSDefines` is a symbol used in X11 configuration. It should have been replaced by a series of compiler flags used to define the operating system to the package. In this case, the X11 configuration was messed up, and nothing defined `OSDefines`, so it found its way to the surface.

need to be executed. Unfortunately, most *Makefiles* don't have a depend target. It's not difficult to write one, and it pays off in the reduction of strange, unaccountable bugs after a rebuild of the package. Here's a starting point:

```
depend:
        makedepend *.[ch]
```

This target works most of the time, but to do it correctly you need to analyze the structure of the package. It might contain files from other languages, or some files might be created by shell scripts or special configuration programs. Hopefully, if the package is this complicated, it will also include a depend target.

Even if you have a depend target, it does not always work as well as you would hope. If you make some really far-reaching changes and things don't work the way you expect, it's worth starting from scratch with a *make clean* to be sure that the make still works.

make all

make all is the usual way to perform the build. Frequently, it is the default target (the first target in the *Makefile*), and you just need to enter make. This target typically rebuilds the package but does not install it.

make install

make install installs the compiled package into the local system environment. The usage varies considerably; we'll look at this target in more detail in the section called "make install" in Chapter 9, *Installation*.

make clean

make clean usually removes everything that *make all* has made—the objects, executables and possibly auxiliary files. You use it after deciding to change a compiler, for example, or to save space after you have finished an installation. Be careful with *make clean*: there is no complete agreement about exactly what it removes, and frequently you will find that it doesn't remove everything it should or removes lots of things it shouldn't. Look at the *rm* commands under the target in the *Makefile*. *make clean* should remove everything that *make all* can make again—the intermediate and installable files but not the configuration information that you may have taken days to get right.

make stamp-halfway with an Empty File

Occasionally you see a target like `make stamp-halfway`. The commands perform a lot of other tasks and, at the end, just create an empty file called *stamp-halfway*. This is a shortcut to save lots of complicated dependency checking. The presence of this file is intended to indicate that the first half of the build is complete and that a restart of *make* can proceed directly to the second half. Good examples of this technique can be found in the *Makefile* for the GNU C compiler and in the X11 source tree, which uses the name *DONE* for the stamp file.

Problems Running make

Ideally, running *make* should be simple:

```
$ make all
lots of good messages from make
```

make doesn't always run this smoothly. You may encounter a number of problems:

- You may not be able to find a *Makefile*, or the targets don't work the way you expect.
- *make* may not be able to make any sense of the *Makefile*.
- The *Makefile* may refer to nonexistent files or directories.
- *make* seems to run, but it doesn't rebuild things it should, or it rebuilds things it shouldn't.
- You can't find anything that's wrong, but *make* still produces obscure error messages.

In the following sections we'll look at each of these problems.

Missing Makefile or Targets

Sometimes *make* won't even let you in the door—it prints a message like:

```
$ make all
Don't know how to make all. Stop.
```

When you receive this message, first check whether a *Makefile* exists. If you don't find *Makefile* or *makefile*, check for one under a different name. If one exists under a different name, the author should have documented where the *Makefile* comes from. Check the *README* files and other documentation that came with the package. You may find that the package uses separate *Makefiles* for different architectures. For example, *Makefile* may be correct only if you are compiling in a BSD environment. If you want to compile for a System V machine, you may need to specify a different *Makefile*:

```
$ make -f Makefile.sysv
```

This is a pain because it's so easy to make a mistake. In extreme cases the compiler successfully creates objects, but they fail to link.

Other possibilities include:

- The *Makefile* is created by the configuration process, and you haven't configured yet. This would be the case if you find an *Imakefile* (from which you create a *Makefile* with *xmkmf*—see the section called "imake program" in Chapter 4, *Configuring the Package*)—or *Makefile.in* (GNU *configure*—see the section called "GNU Package Configuration" in Chapter 4).
- The directory you are looking at doesn't need a *Makefile*. The *Makefile* in the parent directory, also part of the source tree, could contain rules like:

  ```
  foo/foo:        foo/*.c
          ${CC} foo/*.c -o foo/foo
  ```

  In other words, the executable is made automatically when you execute *make foo/foo* in the parent directory. As a rule, you start building in the root directory of a package and perform explicit builds in subdirectories only if something is obviously wrong.
- The author of the package doesn't believe in *Makefiles* and has provided a shell script instead. You often encounter this with programs that originated on platforms that don't have a *make* program.
- There is really nothing to build the package: the author is used to doing the compilation manually. In this case, your best bet is to write a *Makefile* from scratch. The skeleton in the following example will get you a surprisingly long way. The empty targets are to remind you what you need to fill in:

  ```
  SRCS =                      list of C source files
  OBJS = ${SRCS:.c=.o}        corresponding object files
  CC=gcc                      filename of compiler
  CFLAGS=-g -O3               flags for compiler
  LDFLAGS=-g                  flags for linker
  , BINDIR=/opt/bin
  LIBDIR=/opt/lib
  MANDIR=/opt/man
  MAN1DIR=man1
  INFODIR=/opt/info
  PROGRAM=                    name of finished program

  all:    $(PROGRAM)
          ${CC} ${LDFLAGS} -o ${PROGRAM} ${OBJS}
  ```

```
man:

doc:

install: all

depend:
        makedepend ${SRCS}

clean:
        rm -f \#* *~ core $(PROGRAM) *.o
```

Missing targets

Another obvious reason for the error message might be that the target `all` doesn't exist. Some *Makefiles* have a different target name for each kind of system to which the *Makefile* has been adapted. The *README* file should tell you if this is the case. One of the more unusual examples is *gnuplot*. You need to enter:

```
$ make All
$ make x11 TARGET=Install
```

The better packages at least warn you—see the section called "Multiple Makefile Targets" in Chapter 4 for an example. I personally don't like these solutions: it's so much easier to add the following line at the top of the *Makefile*:

```
BUILD-TARGET = build-bsd
```

The first target would then be:

```
all:    ${BUILD-TARGET}
```

If you then want to build the package for another architecture, you need only change the single line defining `BUILD-TARGET`.

make Doesn't Understand the Makefile

Sometimes *make* produces messages that make no sense at all. The compiler tries to compile the same file multiple times, each time giving it a different object name, or it claims not to be able to find files that exist. One possible explanation is that various flavors of *make* have somewhat different understandings of default rules. In particular, as we will see in Chapter 19, a number of incompatibilities exist between BSD *make* and GNU *make*.

Alternatively, *make* may not even be trying to interpret the *Makefile*. Somebody could have hidden a file called *makefile* in the source tree. Most people today use the name *Makefile* for *make*'s description file, probably because it's easier to see in an *ls* listing, but *make* always looks for a file called *makefile* (with a lowercase *m*) first. GNU *make* first looks for a file called *GNUmakefile* before checking for *makefile* and *Makefile.*

make Refers to Nonexistent Files

In the process of building a package, *make* refers to a large number of files, and one of the most frequent sources of confusion is a file that can't be found. There are various flavors of this problem. Occasionally the opposite happens, and you have trouble with a file that *make* finds, but *you* can't find.

To analyze this kind of problem, it's helpful to know how *make* is referring to a file. Here are some possibilities:

- *make* may be looking for a dependent file but can't find it, and it can't find a rule to build it. In this case you get a message like:

  ```
  $ make
  make: *** No rule to make target `config.h'. Stop.
  ```

- *make* may not be able to locate a program specified in a command. You get a message like:

  ```
  $ make foo.o
  /bin/cc -c foo.o -o foo.c
  make: execve: /bin/cc: No such file or directory
  make: *** [foo.o] Error 127
  ```

- The compilers and other programs started by *make* also access files specified in the source. If they don't find them, you'll see a message like:

  ```
  $ make foo.o
  gcc    -c foo.c -o foo.o
  foo.c:1: bar.h: No such file or directory
  make: *** [foo.o] Error 1
  ```

No matter where the file is missing, the most frequent reasons why it is not found are:

- The package has been configured incorrectly. This is particularly likely if you find that the package is missing a file like *config.h.*
- The search paths are incorrect. This could be because you configured incorrectly, but it also could be that the configuration programs don't understand your environment. For example, it's quite common to find *Makefiles* with contents like:

  ```
  AR = /bin/ar
  AS = /bin/as
  CC = /bin/cc
  LD = /bin/cc
  ```

Some older versions of *make* need this, since they don't look at the PATH environment variable. Since most modern versions of *make* do look at PATH, the easiest way to fix such a *Makefile* is to remove the directory component of the definitions:

Problems with Subordinate makes

While building, the compiler occasionally complains about a file that doesn't seem to exist. This can occur because the make is running in a subdirectory: large projects are frequently split into multiple subdirectories, and all the top-level *Makefile* does is to run a number of subordinate *makes*. If it is friendly, it also echos some indication of where it is at the moment, and if it dies you can find the file. Newer versions of GNU *make* print messages on entering and leaving a directory, for example:

```
make[1]: Entering directory `/cdcopy/SOURCE/Core/glibc-1.08.8/assert'
make[1]: Nothing to be done for `subdir_lib'.
make[1]: Leaving directory `/cdcopy/SOURCE/Core/glibc-1.08.8/assert'
```

If neither of these methods work, you have the option of searching for the file:

```
$ find . -name foo.c -print
```

Or you can modify the *Makefile* to tell you what's going on.

make Doesn't Rebuild Correctly

One of the most insidious problems in rebuilding programs occurs when *make* doesn't rebuild programs correctly. There's no easy way to know that a module has been omitted, and the results can be far reaching and time consuming. Let's look at some possible causes of this kind of problem.

Incorrect dependencies

One weakness of *make* is that you have to tell it the interdependencies between the source files. Unfortunately, the dependency specifications are *very* frequently incorrect. Even if they were correct in the source tree as delivered, changing configuration flags frequently causes other header files to be included, and as a result, the dependencies change. Make it a matter of course to run a *make depend* after reconfiguring if the depend target is supplied. (See the section called "make depend" for details on how to create one.)

No dependency on Makefile

What happens if you change the *Makefile*? Changing a rule, for example, could require recompilation of a program. To put it in *make* terms: all generated files depend on the *Makefile*. The *Makefile* itself is not typically included in the dependency list. It really should be, but that would mean rebuilding everything every time you change the *Makefile*, and in most cases, it's not needed. On the other hand, if you do change your *Makefile* in the course of a port, it's a good idea to save your files, do a *make clean*, and start all over again. If everything is okay, it will build correctly without intervention.

Other Errors from make

The categories we have previously describe account for a large proportion of the error messages you will see from *make*, but there are many others as well. In this section, we'll look at other frequent problems.

Trailing blanks in variables

You define a *make* variable with the syntax:

```
NAME = Definition      # optional comment
```

The exact definition starts at the first nonspace character after the equal sign and continues to the end of the line or the start of the comment, if there is one. You can occasionally run into problems with things like:

```
MAKE = /opt/bin/make     # in case something else is in the path
```

When starting subsidiary *make*s, *make* uses the value of the variable `MAKE` as the name of the program to start. In this case, it is "*/opt/bin/make*   "—it has trailing blanks, and the *exec* call fails. If you're lucky, you get:

```
$ make
make: don't know how to make make     . stop.
```

This message provides a clue to what the problem is: there shouldn't be any white space between the name of the target and the following period. On the other hand, GNU *make* is "friendly" and tidies up trailing blanks, so it says:

```
$ make
/opt/bin/make           subdir       note the space before the target name "subdir"
make: execve: /opt/bin/make: No such file or directory
make: *** [suball] Error 127
```

The only clue you have here is the length of the space on the first line.

It's relatively easy to avoid this sort of problem by not adding comments at the end of definition lines.

Comments in command lists

Some versions of *make*, notably XENIX, can't handle rules of the form:

```
doc.dvi:        doc.tex
        tex doc.tex
# do it again to get the references right
        tex doc.tex     # same thing again
```

The first comment causes *make* to think that the rule is completed, and it stops. When you fix this problem by removing the comment, you run into a second one: *make* doesn't understand the second comment either, and this time it produces an error message. Again, you need to remove the comment.

make forgets the current directory

Occasionally, it looks as if *make* has forgotten what you tell it. Consider the following rule:

```
docs:
        cd doc
        ${ROFF} ${RFLAGS} doc.ms > doc.ps
```

When you run it, you get:

```
$ make docs
cd doc
groff -ms doc.ms >doc.ps
gtroff: fatal error: can't open `doc.ms': No such file or directory
make: *** [docs] Error 1
```

So you look for *doc.ms* in *doc*, and it's there. What's going on? Each command is run by a new shell. The first one executes the *cd doc* and then exits. The second one tries to execute the *groff* command. Since the *cd* command doesn't affect the parent environment, it has no further effect, and you're still in the original directory. To do this correctly, you need to write the rule as:

```
docs:
        cd doc; \
        ${ROFF} ${RFLAGS} doc.ms > doc.ps
```

This causes *make* to consider both lines as a single line, which is then passed to a single shell. The semicolon after the *cd* is necessary, because the shell sees the command as a single line.

Missing separator - stop

This strange message is usually made more complicated because it refers to a line that looks perfectly normal. In all probability it is trying to tell you that you have put leading spaces instead of a tab on a command line. BSD *make* expects tabs, too, but it recovers from the problem, and the message it prints if they are missing is much more intelligible:

```
"Makefile", line 21: warning: Shell command needs a leading tab
```

Commands commence before first target

This message, from System V *make*, is trying to tell you that you have used a tab character instead of spaces at the beginning of the definition of a variable. GNU *make* does not have a problem with this—it doesn't even mention the fact—so you might see this in a *Makefile* written for GNU *make* when you try to run it with System V *make*. BSD *make* cannot handle tabs at the beginning of definitions either and produces the message:

```
"Makefile", line 3: Unassociated shell command "CC=gcc"
Fatal errors encountered -- cannot continue
```

Syntax errors from the shell

Many *Makefiles* contain relatively complicated shell script fragments. As we have seen, these are constrained to be on one line, and most shells have rather strange relationships between newline characters and semicolons. Here's a typical example:

```
if test -d $(texpooldir); then exit 0; else mkdir -p $(texpooldir); fi
```

This example is all on one line, but you can break it *anywhere* if you end each partial line with a backslash (\). The placement of the semicolons is important: a rule of thumb is to put a semicolon where you would otherwise put a newline, but *not* after `then` or `else`. For more details, check your shell documentation.

Circular dependency dropped

This message comes from GNU *make*. In System V *make*, it is even more obscure:

```
$! nulled, predecessor circle
```

BSD *make* isn't much more help:

```
Graph cycles through docs
```

In each case, the message is trying to tell you that your dependencies are looping. This particular example was caused by the dependencies:

```
docs:  man-pages

man-pages: docs
```

In order to resolve the dependency `docs`, *make* first needs to resolve `man-pages`. But in order to resolve `man-pages`, it first needs to resolve `docs`—a Catch 22 situation. Real-life loops are, of course, usually more complex.

Nonsensical targets

Sometimes the first target in the *Makefile* does nothing useful: you need to explicitly enter `make all` in order to make the package. There is no good reason for this, and every reason to fix it—send the mods back to the original author if possible (and be polite).

Unable to stop make

Some *Makefiles* start a number of second- and third-level *Makefiles* with the *-k* option, which tells *make* to continue if the subsidiary *Makefile* dies. This is quite convenient if you want to leave it running overnight and collect all the information about numerous failures the next morning. It also makes it almost impossible to stop the make if you want to: hitting the **QUIT** key (**CTRL-C** or **DEL** on most systems) kills the currently running *make*, but the top-level *make* just starts the next subsidiary *make*. All you can do here is to identify the top-level *make* and stop it first, which is not easy to do if you have only a single screen.

Problems with make clean

make clean is supposed to put you back to square one with a build. It should remove all the files you created since you first typed `make`. Frequently, it doesn't achieve this result very accurately:

- It goes back further than that and removes files that the *Makefile* doesn't know how to make.*
- Other *Makefiles* remove configuration information when you do a *make clean*. This isn't quite as catastrophic, but you still won't appreciate it if this happens to you after you have spent 20 minutes answering configuration questions and fixing incorrect assumptions on the part of the configuration script. Either way,

* If this does happen to you, don't despair too soon. Check first whether this occurred because of simple-mindedness on the part of the *Makefile*. Maybe there is a relatively simple way to recreate the files. If not and you forgot to make a backup of your source tree before you started, *then* you can despair.

before running a *make clean* for the first time, be sure that you have a backup.

- *make clean* can also start off by doing just the opposite. In early versions of the GNU C library, for example, it first compiled some things in order to determine what to clean up. This may work most of the time but is still a Bad Idea. *make clean* is frequently used to clean up after some catastrophic mess or when restarting the port on a different platform, and it should not be able to rely on being able to compile anything.
- Yet another problem with *make clean* is that some *Makefiles* have varying degrees of cleanliness, from *clean* via *realclean* all the way to *squeakyclean*. There may be a need to distinguish the various degrees of cleanliness, but it's confusing for casual users.

Subordinate makes

Some subordinate *makes* use a different target name for the subsidiary *makes*. You might write `make all`, but *make* might start the subsidiary *makes* with *make subdirs*. Although this cannot always be avoided, it makes it difficult to debug the *Makefile*. When modifying *Makefiles*, you may frequently come across a situation where you need to modify the behavior of only one subsidiary *make*. For example, in many versions of System V, the man pages need to be formatted before installation. It's easy to tell if this applies to your system: if you install BSD-style unformatted man pages, the *man* program just displays a lot of hard-to-read *nroff* source.

Frequently, fixing the *Makefile* is more work than you expect. A typical *Makefile* may contain a target `install` that looks like:

```
install:
H        for dir in ${SUBDIRS}; do \
          echo making $@ in $$dir; \
          cd $$dir; ${MAKE} ${MDEFINES} $@; \
          cd ..; \
        done
```

`make $@` expands to `make install`. One of these subdirectories is the subdirectory *doc*, which contains the documentation and requires special treatment for the *catman* pages: they need to be formatted before installation, whereas the man pages are not formatted until the first time they are referenced. (See the section called "Man Pages" in Chapter 7, *Documentation*, for further information.) To offer a choice between *catman* and raw man pages, the simplest solution is a different target that singles out the *doc* and creates a different target, say `install-catman`. This is untidy and requires some modifications to the variable `SUBDIRS` to exclude *doc*. A simpler way is to create a new target, `install-catman`, and modify *all* *Makefiles* to recognize it:

```
install-catman install-manman:
        for dir in ${SUBDIRS}; do \
          echo making $@ in $$dir; \
          cd $$dir; ${MAKE} ${MDEFINES} $@; \
          cd ..; \
        done
```

In the *Makefiles* in the subdirectories, you might then find targets like

```
install-catman: ${MANPAGES}
        for i in $<; do ${NROFF} -man $$i > ${CATMAN}/$i; done

install-manman: ${MANPAGES}
        for i in $<; do cp $$i > ${MANMAN}/$i; done
```

The rule in the top-level *Makefile* is the same for both targets: you just need to know the name to invoke it with. In this example we have also renamed the original `install` target so that it doesn't get invoked accidentally. By removing the `install` target altogether, you need to make a conscious decision about what kind of man pages that your system wants.

We're not finished yet. We now have exactly the situation we were complaining about in the section called "Missing targets": it is still a nuisance to have to remember *make install-catman* or *make install-manman*. We can get round this problem, too, with:

```
INSTALL_TYPE=install-catman

install: ${INSTALL_TYPE}
```

After this, you can just enter `make install`, and the target `install` performs the type of installation specified in the variable `INSTALL_TYPE`. This variable needs to be modified from time to time, but it makes it easier to avoid mistakes while porting.

Incorrect continuation lines

Makefiles frequently contain numerous continuation lines ending with a backslash (\). This works only if it is the very last character on the line. A blank or a tab following the backslash is invisible to you, but it really confuses *make*.

Alternatively, you might continue something you don't want to. Consider the following *Makefile* fragment, taken from an early version of the *Makefile* for this book:

```
PART1 = part1.ms config.ms imake.ms make.ms tools.ms compiler.ms obj.ms \
        documentation.ms testing.ms install.ms epilogue.ms
```

At some point I decided to change the sequence of chapters and removed the file *tools.ms*. I was not completely sure I wanted to do this, so rather than just changing the *Makefile*, I commented out the first line and repeated it in the new form:

```
# PART1 =        part1.ms config.ms imake.ms make.ms tools.ms compiler.ms obj.ms \
PART1 = part1.ms config.ms imake.ms make.ms compiler.ms obj.ms \
        documentation.ms testing.ms install.ms epilogue.ms
```

This change works just fine—at first. In fact, it turns out that *make* treats all three lines as a comment, because the comment finished with a backslash character. As a result, the variable PART1 remained undefined. If you comment out a line that ends with a backslash, you should also remove the backslash.

Prompts in Makefiles

If you do the Right Thing and copy your *make* output to a log file, you may find that *make* just hangs. The following kind of *Makefile* can cause this problem:

```
all:    checkclean prog

checkclean:
        @echo -n "Make clean first? "
        @read reply; if [ "$$reply" = 'y' ]; then make clean; fi
```

If you run *make* interactively, you see:

```
$ make
Make clean first?
```

If you copy the output to a file, of course, you don't see the prompt, and it looks as if *make* is hanging. This doesn't mean it's a bad idea to save your *make* output; it's generally a bad idea to put prompts in *Makefiles*. There are some exceptions, of course. The Linux configuration program is a *Makefile*, and to interactively configure the system, you enter *make config*.

Arg list too long

Sometimes *make* fails with this message, especially if you are running a System V system. Many versions of System V limit the argument list to 5120 bytes—we'll look at this in more detail in the section called "exec" in Chapter 12, *Kernel Dependencies*. Modern versions of System V allow you to rebuild the kernel with a larger parameter list: modify the tuneable parameter ARG_MAX to a value in the order of 20000. If you can't do this, a couple of workarounds are possible:

- The total storage requirement is the sum of the length of the argument strings and the environment strings. It's very possible that you have environment variables that aren't needed in this particular situation. (In fact, if you're like me, you probably have environment variables that you will never need again.) If you remove some of these environment variables from your shell startup file, you may get below the limit.

- You might be able to simplify expressions. For example, your *Makefile* may contain a line like:

  ```
  clean:
          rm -rf *.o *.a *.depend *~ core ${INTERMEDIATES}
  ```

  You can split this line into:

  ```
  clean:
          rm -rf *.o
          rm -rf *.a *.depend *~ core ${INTERMEDIATES}
  ```

  In most large trees, since the **.o* filenames constitute the majority of the arguments, you don't need more than two lines.

- Even after trying the solution given in the previous example, you might find that the length of the **.o* parameters is too long. In this case, you could try naming the objects explicitly:

  ```
  clean:
          rm -rf [a-f]*.o
          rm -rf [g-p]*.o
          rm -rf [r-z]*.o
          rm -rf *.a *.depend *~ core ${INTERMEDIATES}
  ```

- Alternatively, you could specify the names explicitly in the *Makefile*:

  ```
  OBJ1S = absalom.o arthur.o ...  fernand.o
  OBJ2S = gerard.o guillaume.o ...  pierre.o
  OBJ3S = rene.o roland.o ...  zygyszmund.o
  OBJS = ${OBJ1S} ${OBJ2S} ${OBJ3S}

  clean:
          rm -rf ${OBJ1S}
          rm -rf ${OBJ2S}
          rm -rf ${OBJ3S}
  ```

- Yet another method involves the use of the *xargs* program, which has the advantage of not breaking after new files have been added to the lists:

  ```
  clean:
          find . -name "*.o" -print | xargs rm -f
  ```

  This chops the parameter list into chunks that won't overflow the system limits.

Creating executable files The *xargs* method is not much help if you want to build an executable file. If the command that fails looks like the following, you can try other possible solutions:

```
${PROG}:
        ${CC} ${ALLOBJS} -o ${PROG}
```

You might be able to shorten the pathnames. If you are building in a directory */next-release/SOURCE/sysv/SCO/gcc-2.6.0* and every filename in `ALLOBJS` is absolute, it's much easier to exceed the limit than if the directory name was, say, */S*. You *could* use a symbolic link to solve this problem, but most systems that don't support `ARG_MAX` also don't have symbolic links.*

If this doesn't work, you could place the files in a library, possibly using *xargs*:

```
${PROG}:
        rm libkludge.a
        echo ${ALLOBJS} | xargs ar cruv libkludge.a
        ${CC} libkludge.a -o ${PROG}
```

Since there's no object file, this looks strange, but it works. By the time it finds the name *libkludge.a*, the linker has already loaded the object file *crt0.o* (see the section called "The Linker" in Chapter 21, *Object Files and Friends*) and is looking for a symbol `main`. It doesn't care whether it finds it in an object file or a library file.

Modifying Makefiles

Frequently enough, you find that the *Makefile* is inadequate. Targets are missing, or some error occurs that is almost untraceable: you need to fix the *Makefile*. Before you do so, you should check whether you are changing the correct *Makefile*. Some packages build a new *Makefile* every time you run *make*. In particular, you frequently see *Makefiles* that start with text like

```
# Makefile generated by imake - do not edit!
```

Depending on what you're doing, you may decide to follow this advice or not. If you are just trying to figure out what the *Makefile* is trying (and presumably failing) to do, it's nice to know that you can subsequently delete your modified *Makefile* and have it automatically remade.

After you find out why the *Makefile* is doing what it is, you need to fix the source of the *Makefile*, which is not usually too difficult. The input files to the *Makefile* generation phase typically don't look too different from the finished *Makefile*. For example, *Makefile.in* in the GNU packages is a skeleton that is processed by *m4*, and except for the *m4* parameters, *Makefile.in* looks very similar to the finished *Makefile*. Finding the way back to the *Imakefile* from the *Makefile* requires a little more understanding of the *imake* process, but with a little practice, it's not that difficult.

* If you are on a network with other machines with more modern file systems, you could work around this problem by placing the files on the other system and accessing them via NFS.

In This Chapter:
- *Compiler Warnings*
- *Compiler Errors*

6

Running the Compiler

In the previous chapter, we looked at the use of *make* in the build process. The other central program in the build process is the compiler, which in UNIX is almost always a C compiler. Like *make*, the compiler can discover a surprising number of problems in ostensibly debugged source code. In this chapter, we'll look at these problems and how to solve them. In Chapter 20, *Compilers*, we'll look at how the compiler works and how the various flavors of C differ. Although we restrict our attention to the C compiler, much of what we discuss relates to other compilers as well, particularly, of course, to C++. This chapter expects a certain understanding of the C language but don't be discouraged if you're still a beginner. This is more about living with C than writing it.

You'll encounter information from the compiler in a number of forms:

- The compiler may issue *warnings*, which are informational messages intended to draw attention to possible program errors. Their reliability and their value vary significantly. Some are a sure-fire indication that something is wrong, while others should be taken with a pinch of salt.
- The compiler may issue *error* messages, indicating its conviction that it cannot produce a valid output module. An error message also usually means that the compiler won't create any output files, but you can't always rely on this.
- The compiler may fail completely, either because of an internal bug or because it realizes that it no longer understands the input sufficiently to continue.

Compiler Warnings

It's easy to make mistakes when writing programs, but it used to be even easier: nowadays, even the worst compilers attempt to catch dubious constructs and warn you about them. In this section, we'll look at what compilers can and can't do.

Before compilers worried about coding quality, the program *lint* performed this task. *lint* is still around, but hardly anybody uses it any more because it doesn't always match the compiler being used. This is a pity, because *lint* can catch a number of dubious situations that evade most compilers.

Modern compilers can recognize two kinds of potential problems:

- Problems related to suspicious program text, like the following:

  ```
  if (a = 1)
    return;
  ```

  The first line of this example is almost superfluous: if I allocate the value `1` to `a`, I don't need an `if` to tell me what the result is. This is probably a typo, and the text should have been as follows:

  ```
  if (a == 1)
    return;
  ```

- Problems related to program flow, which are detected by the flow analysis pass of the optimizer. For example:

  ```
  int a;
  b = a;
  ```

  The second line uses the value of `a` before it has been assigned a value. The optimizer notices this omission and may print a warning.

In the following sections, we'll examine typical warning messages, how they are detected, and how reliable they are. I'll base the sections on the warning messages from the GNU C compiler, because it has a particularly large choice of warning messages and is also widely used. Other compilers warn you about the same kind of problems, but the messages may be different.

Implicit Return Type

K&R C allowed programs such as the following:

```
main ()
  {
  printf ("Hello, World!\n");
  }
```

ANSI C has two problems with this program:

- The function named `main` does not specify a return type. It defaults to `int`.
- Since `main` is implicitly an `int` function, it should return a value. This one does not.

Both of these situations can be caught by specifying the *–Wreturn-type* option to *gcc*. This causes the following messages:

```
$ gcc -c hello.c -Wreturn-type
hello.c:2: warning: return-type defaults to `int'
hello.c: In function `main':
hello.c:4: warning: control reaches end of non-void function
```

Inconsistent Function Returns

The following function does not always return a defined value:

```
foo (int x)
  {
  if (x > 3)
    return x - 1;
  }
```

If `x` is greater than `3`, this function returns `x - 1`. Otherwise it returns with some uninitialized value, since there is no explicit `return` statement for this case. This problem is particularly insidious, since the return value is the same for every invocation on a particular architecture (possibly the value of `x`). This is a by-product of the way the compiler works and may be completely different if you use a different compiler or compile on some other architecture.

Uninitialized Variables

Consider the following code:

```
void foo (int x)
  {
  int a;
  if (x > 5)
    a = x - 3;
  bar (a);
  ... etc
```

Depending on the value of `x`, `a` may or may not be initialized when you call `bar`. If you select the *–Wuninitialized* compiler option, the compiler warns you when this situation occurs. Some compilers, including current versions of *gcc*, place some limitations on this test.

Signed Comparisons of Unsigned Values

Occasionally you see code in the form:

```
int foo (unsigned x)
  {
  if (x >= 0)
... etc
```

Since `x` is unsigned, its value is *always* >= 0, so the `if` is superfluous. This kind of problem is surprisingly common. System header files may differ in opinion as to whether a value is signed or unsigned. The *–W* option causes the compiler to issue warnings for this and a whole lot of other situations.

Character Subscripts to Arrays

Sometimes, the subscript to an array is a character. Consider the following code:

```
char iso_translate [256] =     /* translate table for ISO 8859-1 to LaserJet */
{
 codes for the first 160 characters
  0xa0, 0xa1, 0xa2, 0xa3, 0xa4, 0xa5, 0xa6, 0xa7,
  0xa8, 0xa9, 0xaa, 0xab, 0xac, 0xad, 0xae, 0xaf,
 ... etc
  };

#define xlate(x) iso_translate [x];

char *s;                       /* pointer in buf */
for (*s = buf; *s; s++)
  *s = xlate (*s);
```

The intention of `xlate` is to translate text to a form used by older model HP LaserJet printers. This code works only if the `char *s` is unsigned. By default, the C `char` type is a signed value, and so the characters `0x80` to `0xff` represent a negative array offset, and the program attempts (maybe successfully) to access a byte outside the table `iso_translate`. *gcc* warns about this if you set the option *–Wchar-subscripts*.

Dequalifying Types

The following code fragment can cause problems:

```
char *profane;
void foo (const char *holy)
  {
  profane = holy;
```

The assignment of holy to profane loses the qualifier const, and the compiler complains about the fact. On the other hand, this is valid:

```
profane = (char *) holy;
```

Being valid doesn't make it a better idea: holy is supposed to be unchangeable, and in this statement, you are removing this qualifier. If you specify the *-Wcast-qual* option to *gcc*, it complains when you use a cast to remove a type qualifier such as *const*.

Increasing Alignment Requirements

Many processors require that specific data types be aligned on specific boundaries, and the results can be spectacular if they are not—see the section called "Data Alignment" in Chapter 11, *Hardware Dependencies*, for more details. We can easily outsmart the C compiler with code like:

```
void foo (char *x)
  {
  int *ip = (int *) x;
```

In this case, there is a good chance that the int * pointer ip requires a specific alignment and is not allowed to point at any address in memory the way the char pointer x is allowed to. If you specify the *-Wcast-align* option to *gcc*, it warns you of such assignments.

Implicit Conversions Between enums

One of the advantages of *enums* is that they make type checking easier—we'll look at that in more detail in the section called "UNIX C" in Chapter 20. If you specify the *-Wenum-clash* option to *gcc*, and you're compiling C++, the compiler warns about the sloppy use of *enums*.

Incomplete Switch Statements

A frequent cause of error in a switch statement is that the index variable (the variable that decides which case is chosen) may assume a value for which no case has been specified. If the index variable is an int of some kind, there is not much you can do except include a default clause. If the index variable is an enum, the compiler can check that case clauses exist for all the possible values of the variable, and warns if they do not. It also warns if case clauses exist for values that are not defined for the type of the index variable. Specify the *-Wswitch* option for these warnings.

long Indices for switch

In some dialects of pre-ANSI C, you could write code like:

```
foo (x)
long x;
  {
  switch (x)
    {
...  etc
```

This is no longer allowed in ANSI C: indices for `switch` must evaluate to an `int`, even if `int` and `long` have the same length. *gcc* issues a warning about `long` indices in `switch` unless you specify the *–traditional* option.

Changing Nonvolatile Automatic Variables

Under certain circumstances, a signal handler might modify a local automatic variable if the function has called `setjmp`—see the section called "setjmp and longjmp" in Chapter 13, *Signals*, for more details. *gcc* considers this situation a warning if you specify the *–W* option. The value of the warning is limited because potential problems are recognized only when you compile with optimization. This is because the optimizer is the part of the compiler that can deduce the problem and recognizes the keyword `volatile`. However, the optimizer cannot recognize when a `longjmp` could be performed because this depends on semantics outside the scope of the optimizer. As a result, it could issue this warning when there is, in fact, no danger.

Invalid Keyword Sequences in Declarations

Currently, it is permissible to write declarations like:

```
int static bad_usage;
```

Here the storage class specifier `static` comes after the type specifier `int`. The ANSI standard still permits this, but declares the usage to be obsolete. *gcc* issues a warning when it encounters this and the *–W* option has been set.

Trigraphs

Trigraphs (see the section called "Differences in the ANSI C Preprocessor" in Chapter 20) are no error, at least according to the ANSI standard. The Free Software Foundation makes no bones about their opinion of them, and so *gcc* supplies the option *–Wtrigraphs*, which prints a warning if any trigraphs occur in the source code. Since this works only if the option *–trigraphs* is used to enable them, it is not clear that this is of any real use.

Nested Comments

Occasionally you see code like:

```
void foo (int x)
  {
  int y;                    /* state information
  y = bar ();               /* initialize y */
  if (y == 4)
... etc
```

The code looks reasonable, and it is syntactically correct C. In fact, however, the comment after the declaration of y is not terminated, so it includes the whole of the next line, which is almost certainly not the intention. *gcc* recognizes this when it finds the sequence /* in a comment and warns of this situation if you specify the *–Wcomment* option.

Missing Parentheses

What value does the following code return?

```
int a = 11 << 4 & 7 << 2 > 4;
```

The result is 0, but the real question is: in what order does the compiler evaluate the expression? You can find the real answer in K&R, but you don't want to do that all the time. We can rewrite the code as:

```
int a = (11 << 4) & ((7 << 2) > 4);
```

This rewrite clarifies what is intended. *gcc* warns about what it considers to be missing parentheses if you select the *–Wparentheses* option. By its nature, this option is subjective, and you may find that it complains about code that looks fine.

Functions with Embedded Extern Definitions

K&R C allowed you to write code like:

```
int datafile;
foo (x)
  {
  extern open ();
  datafile = open ("foo", 0777);
  }
```

The extern declaration was then valid until the end of the source file. In ANSI C, the scope of open would be the scope of foo: outside of foo, it would no longer be known. *gcc* issues a warning about extern statements inside a function definition unless you supply the *–traditional* option. If you are using *–traditional* and want these messages, you can supply the *–Wnested-externs* option as well.

Compiler Errors

You also frequently see error messages from the compiler. They are the usual reason for a build to fail. In this section, we'll look at some of the more common ones.

Undefined Symbols

During porting, this compiler error message is one of the most frequent ones you see during porting. At first sight, it seems strange that the compiler should find undefined symbols in a program that has been installed on another platform: if the program contains such primitive code, how could it have worked?

In almost every case, you will find one of the following problems:

- The definition you need may have been `#ifdefed` out. For example, in a manually configured package, if you forget to specify a processor architecture, the package may try to compile with no processor definitions, which is sure to give rise to this kind of problem.
- The symbol may have been defined in a header file on the system where it was developed. If this header file is different on your system, the symbol you need may never be defined.
- You may be looking at the wrong header files. Some versions of *gcc* install "fixed" copies of the system header files in their own private directory. For example, under BSD/386 version 1.1, *gcc* version 2.6.3 creates a version of *unistd.h* and hides it in a private directory. This file omits a number of definitions supplied in the BSDI version of *unistd.h*. You can confirm which header files have been included by running *gcc* with the *–H* option. In addition, in the section called "Conflicts Between Preprocessor and Compiler Variables" we look at a way to check exactly what the preprocessor did.

The second problem is surprisingly common, even on supposedly identical systems. For example, in most versions of UNIX System V.4.2, the system header file *link.h* defines information and structures used by debuggers. In UnixWare 1.0, it defines information used by some Novell-specific communications protocols. If you try to compile *gdb* under UnixWare 1.0, you will have problems as a result: the system simply does not contain the definitions you need.

Similar problems occur on newer System V systems with POSIX.1 compatibility. A program that seems formally correct may fail to compile with an undefined symbol `O_NDELAY`. `O_NDELAY` is an option to `open`, which specifies that the call to `open` should not wait for completion of the request. This can be very useful, for example, when the open is on a serial line and will not complete until an incoming call occurs. The option is supported by almost all modern UNIX ports, but it is not defined in POSIX.1. The result is that the definition is carefully removed if you compile defining *-D_POSIX_SOURCE.*

You might think that this isn't a problem and that you can replace O_NDELAY with the POSIX.1 option O_NONBLOCK. Unfortunately, the semantics of O_NONBLOCK vary from those of O_NDELAY: if no data is available, O_NONBLOCK returns –1, and O_NDELAY returns 0. You can make the change, of course, but this requires more modifications to the program. A straighforward alternative is available: #undef _POSIX_SOURCE. If you do this, you may find that suddenly other macros are undefined, for example, O_NOCTTY. System V.4 defines this variable only if _POSIX_SOURCE is set.

There's no simple solution to this problem. It is caused by messy programming style: the programmer has mixed symbols defined only by POSIX.1 with those that are not defined in POSIX.1. The program may run on your current system but may stop doing so at the next release.

Conflicts Between Preprocessor and Compiler Variables

Occasionally you'll see things that seem to make absolutely no sense at all. For example, porting *gcc*, I once ran into this problem:

```
gcc -c  -DIN_GCC    -g -O3      -I. -I. -I./config \
          -DGCC_INCLUDE_DIR=\"/opt/lib/gcc-lib/i386--sysv/2.6.0/include\" \
  -DGPLUSPLUS_INCLUDE_DIR=\"/opt/lib/g++-include\" \
          -DCROSS_INCLUDE_DIR=\"/opt/lib/gcc-lib/i386--sysv/2.6.0/sys-include\" \
  -DTOOL_INCLUDE_DIR=\"/opt/i386--sysv/include\" \
  -DLOCAL_INCLUDE_DIR=\"/usr/local/include\" \
  -DSTD_PROTO_DIR=\"/opt/lib/gcc-lib/i386--sysv/2.6.0\" \
  ./protoize.c
./protoize.c:156: macro `puts' used without args
```

Looking at this part of *protoize.c*, I found lots of external definitions:

```
extern int fflush ();
extern int atoi ();
extern int puts ();
extern int fputs ();
extern int fputc ();
extern int link ();
extern int unlink ();
```

Line 156 is, not surprisingly, the definition of puts. But this is a definition, not a call, and certainly not a macro. And why didn't it complain about all the other definitions? There were many more than the ones shown here.

In cases like this, it's helpful to understand the way the compiler works—we'll look at this in more detail in the section called "Compiler Organization" in Chapter 20. At the moment, we just need to recall that programs are compiled in two stages: first, the preprocessor expands all preprocessor definitions and macros, and then the compiler itself compiles the resultant output, which can look quite different.

If you encounter this kind of problem, there's a good chance that the compiler is not seeing what you expect it to see. You can frequently solve this kind of riddle by examining the view of the source that the compiler sees, the output of the preprocessor. In this section, we'll look at the technique I used to solve this particular problem.

All compilers allow you to run the preprocessor separately from the compiler, usually by specifying the *-E* option—see your compiler documentation for more details. In this case, I was running the compiler in *xterm*,* so I was able to cut and paste the complete eight-line compiler invocation as a command to the shell, and all I needed to type was the text shown in boldface:

```
$ gcc -c  -DIN_GCC   -g -O3      -I. -I. -I./config \
          -DGCC_INCLUDE_DIR=\"/opt/lib/gcc-lib/i386--sysv/2.6.0/include\" \
  -DGPLUSPLUS_INCLUDE_DIR=\"/opt/lib/g++-include\" \
          -DCROSS_INCLUDE_DIR=\"/opt/lib/gcc-lib/i386--sysv/2.6.0/sys-include\" \
  -DTOOL_INCLUDE_DIR=\"/opt/i386--sysv/include\" \
  -DLOCAL_INCLUDE_DIR=\"/usr/local/include\" \
  -DSTD_PROTO_DIR=\"/opt/lib/gcc-lib/i386--sysv/2.6.0\" \
  ./protoize.c -E -o junk.c
$
```

If you don't have *xterm*, you can do the same by editing the *make* log (see the section called "Keep a Log File" in Chapter 5, *Building the Package*), which contains the invocation as well.

junk.c starts with:

```
# 1 "./config.h" 1


# 1 "./config/i386/xm-i386.h" 1
40 empty lines
# 1 "./tm.h" 1
19 empty lines
# 1 "./config/i386/gas.h" 1
22 empty lines
```

* *xterm* is a terminal emulator program that runs under X11. If you don't use X11, you should—for example, it makes this particular technique much easier.

This file seems to consist mainly of empty lines, and the lines that aren't empty don't seem to be C! In fact, the `#` lines *are* C (see the `line` directive in the section called "Differences in the ANSI C Preprocessor" in Chapter 20), except that in this case the keyword `line` has been omitted. The empty lines are where comments and preprocessor directives used to be. Since the error message referred to line 156 of *protoize.c*, I searched for lines with `protoize.c` on them. I found a number of them:

```
$ grep protoize.c junk.c
# 1 "./protoize.c"
# 39 "./protoize.c" 2
# 59 "./protoize.c" 2
# 62 "./protoize.c" 2
# 63 "./protoize.c" 2
... etc
# 78 "./protoize.c" 2
# 222 "./protoize.c"
```

Clearly, the text was between lines 78 and 222. I positioned my cursor on the line *after* the marker for line 78 and moved down (156 – 78) or 78 lines. There I found:

```
extern int fflush ();
extern int atoi ();
extern int ((fputs(( ), stdout) || (( stdout )->_\/_bufp <
( stdout )->_\/_put_limit ? (int) (unsigned char) (*( stdout )->_\/_bufp++ =
(unsigned char) ( '\n' )) :_\/_flshfp (( stdout ), (unsigned char) ( '\n' )))
== (-1) ) ? (-1) : 0) ;
extern int fputs ();
extern int fputc ();
extern int link ();
extern int unlink ();
```

Well, at any rate this made it clear why the compiler was complaining. But figuring out where this junk came from can be difficult. With *gcc* you can use the *–dD* option to keep the preprocessor definitions—unfortunately, the compiler still removes the other preprocessor directives. I used *–dD* and found in *junk.c*:

```
# 491 "/opt/include/stdio.h" 2
25 lines missing
extern int fputs  (_\/_const char *_\/_s, FILE *_\/_stream)  ;
/* Write a string, followed by a newline, to stdout. */
extern int puts  (_\/_const char *_\/_s)  ;

#define puts(s) ((fputs((s), stdout) || _\/_putc('\n', stdout) == EOF) ? EOF : 0)
```

This looks strange: first it declares *puts* as an external function, then it defines it as a macro. Looking at the original source of *stdio.h*, I found:

```
/* Write a string, followed by a newline, to stdout. */
extern int puts _\/_P ((_\/_const char *_\/_s));

#ifdef  _\/_OPTIMIZE_\/_
#define puts(s) ((fputs((s), stdout) || _\/_putc('\n', stdout) == EOF) ? EOF : 0)
#endif /* Optimizing. */
```

No, this doesn't make sense—it's a real live bug in the header file. At the very least, the declaration of *puts* should have been in an `#else` clause. But that's not the real problem: it doesn't worry the preprocessor, and the compiler doesn't see it. The real problem is that *protoize.c* is trying to do the work of the header files and define *puts* again. There are many programs that try to out-guess header files. This kind of definition breaks them all.

There are at least two ways to fix this problem, both of them simple. The real question is, what is the Right Thing? System or library header files should be allowed to define macros instead of functions if they want, and an application program has no business trying to do the work of the header files, so it would make sense to fix *protoize.c* by removing all these external definitions. Apart from this problem, external definitions are also incompatible with ANSI C, because they don't describe the parameters. In fact, I chose to remove the definition from the header file, since that way I only had to do the work once, and in any case, it's not clear that the definition really would run any faster.

Preprocessor output usually looks even more illegible than this, particularly if lots of clever nested `#defines` have been performed. In addition, you'll frequently see references to non-existent line numbers. Here are a couple of ways to make output more legible:

- Use an editor to put comments around all the `#line` directives in the preprocessor output, and then recompile. This will make it easier to find the line in the preprocessor output to which the compiler or debugger is referring; then you can use the comments to follow it back to the original source.
- Run the preprocessor output through a program like *indent*, which improves legibility considerably. This is especially useful if you find yourself in the unenviable position of having to modify the generated sources. *indent* is not guaranteed to maintain the same number of lines, so after indenting you should recompile.

Other Preprocessors

In many other cases, the source file you use is not the source file that the compiler gets. For example, *yacc* and *bison* take a grammar file and make a (more or less illegible) *.c* file out of it. Other examples are database preprocessors like Informix ESQL, which takes C source with embedded SQL statements and converts it into a form that the C compiler can compile. The preprocessor's output is intended to be read by a compiler, not by humans.

All of these preprocessors use lines beginning with # to insert information about the original line numbers and source files into their output. Not all of them do it correctly. If the preprocessor inserts extra lines into the source, they can become ambiguous, and you can run into problems when using symbolic debuggers, in which you normally specify code locations by line number.

Syntax Errors

Syntax errors in previously functional programs usually have the same causes as undefined symbols, but they show their faces in a different way. A favorite one results from omitting */usr/include/sys/types.h*. For example, consider the following *bar.c*:

```
#include <stdio.h>
#ifdef USG
#include <sys/types.h>
#endif

ushort num;
int main (int argc, char *argv [])
{
  num = atoi (argv [1]);
  printf ("First argument: %d\n", num);
  }
```

If you compile this under BSD/OS, you get:

```
$ gcc -o bar bar.c
bar.c:6: parse error before `num'
bar.c:6: warning: data definition has no type or storage class
```

There's an error because ushort hasn't been defined. The compiler expected a type specifier, so it reported a syntax error, not an undefined symbol. To fix it, you need to define the type specified—see Appendix A for a list of the more common type specifiers.

Virtual Memory Exhausted

You occasionally see this message, particularly when you're using *gcc*, which has a hunger for memory. This message may be due to unrealistically low virtual memory limits for your system. By default, some systems limit total virtual memory per process to 6 MB. *gcc* frequently requires 16 or 20 MB of memory space, and on occasion it can use up to 32 MB for a single compilation. If your system has less than this amount available, increase the limit accordingly. Don't forget to ensure that you have enough swap space! Modern systems can require over 100 MB of swap space.

Sometimes increasing the amount of memory space doesn't help. *gcc* seems to have particular difficulties with large data definitions; bitmap definitions in X11 programs are the sort of things that cause problems. *xphoon*, which displays a picture of the current phase of the moon on the root window, is a good example of a *gcc*-breaker.

Compiler Limits Exceeded

Some compilers have difficulties with complicated expressions. This can cause *cc1*, the compiler itself, to fail with messages like "expression too complicated" or "out of tree space." Fixing such problems can be tricky. Straightforward code shouldn't give the compiler indigestion, but some nested `#defines` can cause remarkable increases in the complexity of expressions. In some cases, a single line can expand to over 16K of text. One way to get around the problem is to preprocess the code and then break the preprocessed code into simpler expressions. The *indent* program is invaluable here: preprocessor output is not intended to be human-readable, and most of the time it isn't. *indent* makes a pretty printout of a program.

Running Compiler Passes Individually

Typical compilers run four distinct passes to compile and link a program—see the section called "Compiler Organization" in Chapter 20 for more details. Sometimes running the passes separately can be useful for debugging a compilation:

- If you find yourself with header files that confuse your preprocessor, you can run a different preprocessor, collect the output, and feed it to your compiler. Since the output of the preprocessor is not machine-dependent, you could even do this on a different machine with different architecture, as long as you ensure that you use the correct system header files. By convention, the preprocessor output for *foo.c* would be called *foo.i*, but you can call it *foo.c* and pass it through the preprocessor again, because there should no longer be anything for the second preprocessor to do.

- If you want to report a compiler bug, you should supply the preprocessor output. The bug might be dependent on some header file conflict that doesn't exist on the system on which the compiler development takes place.
- If you suspect the compiler of generating incorrect code, you can stop compilation after the compiler pass and collect the generated assembler output.

Incorrect Code from Compiler

Compilers sometimes generate incorrect code. Incorrect code is frequently difficult to debug because the source code looks (and might be) perfect. For example, a compiler might generate an instruction with an incorrect operand address, or it might assign two variables to a single location. All you can do in these situations is to analyze the assembler output.

One kind of compiler bug is immediately apparent: if the code is so bad that the assembler can't assemble it, you get messages from the assembler. Unfortunately, the message doesn't usually tell you that it comes from the assembler, but the line numbers change between the compiler and the assembler. If the line number seems completely improbable, either because it is larger than the number of lines in your source file, or because it seems to have nothing to do with the context of that line, the assembler may have produced the message. There are various ways to confirm which pass of the compiler produced the message. If you're using *gcc*, the simplest one is to use the *–v* option for the compiler, which "announces" each pass of compilation as it starts, together with the version numbers and parameters passed to the pass. This makes it relatively easy to figure out which pass is printing the error messages. Otherwise you can run the passes individually.

In This Chapter:
- *Preformatted Documentation*
- *roff and Friends*
- *Man Pages*
- *TEX*
- *GNU info and texinfo*
- *The World Wide Web*

7

Documentation

Ask any real guru a question, so the saying goes, and he will reply with a cryptic "RTFM."* Cynics claim this is even the answer to the question, "Where can I find the manual?" All too often, programmers consider documentation a necessary (or even unnecessary) evil, and if the documentation is completed at all, it's usually the last thing to be done. This is particularly evident when you look at the quality of documentation supplied with some free software packages. (Many free packages, however, such as most of those from the Free Software Foundation, are very well documented.) The quality and kind of documentation in source packages varies wildly. In Chapter 2, *Unpacking the Goodies*, we looked at the documentation that *should* be automatically supplied with the package to describe what it is and how to install it. In this chapter, we'll look at documentation that is intended for use after you have installed the package.

The documentation you obtain with a package is usually in one of the following formats:

- Manual pages, the traditional online documentation for UNIX, which are formatted with *nroff*
- *info* files, used with the GNU project's *info* online documentation reader
- Unformatted *roff*, TEX, or *texinfo* hard copy documentation
- Preformatted documentation in PostScript or *.dvi* format or, occasionally, in other formats such as HP LaserJet

We know where we want to get to—the formatted documentation—but we don't always know where to start, so it's easier to look at documentation in reverse

* "Read The Manual"—the F is usually silent.

order. First, we'll look at the end result, then at the formatters, and finally at the input files.

Preformatted Documentation

Occasionally you get documentation that has been formatted so that you can print it on just about any printer, but this doesn't happen very often. In order to print documentation on any printer, the text must be free of frills and formatted so that any typewriter can print it. Nearly any printer nowadays is capable of better results, so preformatted files are usually supplied in a format that can produce high-quality printouts on a laser printer. The following three formats are about the only ones you will come across:

- *PostScript* is a specialized programming language for printers, and the printed data is in fact embedded in the program. This makes it an extremely flexible format.
- *.dvi* is the format that is output by TEX. In order to print it, you need a TEX driver.
- Unlike PostScript and *.dvi*, the *Hewlett-Packard LaserJet* format is not portable: you need a LaserJet-compatible printer to print it. The LaserJet format is obsolete. Even many LaserJet printers made today also support PostScript, and since there are programmatic ways to print PostScript on other laser printers, there is little motivation for using the much more restrictive LaserJet format.

PostScript

PostScript is the current format of choice. Because it is a programming language, it is much more flexible than conventional data formats. For example, it is easily scalable. You can take a file intended for a phototypesetter with a resolution of 2540 bpi, print it on a laser printer, and it will print correctly.* In addition, better quality printers perform the formatting themselves, resulting in a considerable load reduction for the computer. A large number of printers and all modern phototypesetters can process PostScript directly.

If your printer doesn't handle PostScript, you can use programs like *ghostscript*, which interpret PostScript programs and output in a multitude of other formats, including LaserJet. Even if you have a LaserJet, it can be a better idea to use PostScript format. *ghostscript* is distributed by the Free Software Foundation—see Appendix E. *ghostscript* can also display PostScript files on X displays.

---

* You may have to wait a while before a few megabytes of font information are transferred and processed, but eventually you get your document.

Most PostScript files are encoded in plain ASCII without any control characters except newline (though that doesn't make them easy to read). Even when you include special characters in your text, they appear in the PostScript document as plain ASCII sequences. It's usually pretty easy to recognize PostScript, even without the *file* program. Here's the start of a draft version of this chapter:

```
%!PS-Adobe-3.0
%%Creator: groff version 1.09
%%CreationDate: Thu Aug 18 17:34:24 1994
%%DocumentNeededResources: font Times-Bold
```

The data itself is embedded in parentheses between the commands. Looking at a draft of this text, we see:

```
(It')79.8 273.6 Q 2.613(su)-.55 G .113
(sually pretty easy to recognize a PostScript program, e)-2.613 F -.15
(ve)-.25 G 2.614(nw).15 G .114(ithout the)-2.614 F F2(\2141e)2.614 E F1
(program--here')79.8 285.6 Q 2.5(st)-.55 G(he start of a draft v)-2.5 E
```

Problems with PostScript

PostScript doesn't pose too many problems, but occasionally you might encounter one of the problems discussed in this section.

Missing fonts

PostScript documents include information about the fonts they require. Many fonts are built into printers and PostScript display software, but if the fonts are not present, the system chooses a default value that may have little in common with the font that the document requested. The default font is typically Courier, which is `fixed width`, and the results look terrible. You can find the list of required fonts with the following command:

```
$ grep '%%.* font ' mumble.ps
%%DocumentNeededResources: font Garamond-BookItalic
%%+ font Times-Roman
%%+ font Garamond-Light
%%+ font Garamond-LightItalic
%%+ font Courier
%%+ font Garamond-Book
%%+ font Courier-Bold
%%IncludeResource: font Garamond-BookItalic
%%IncludeResource: font Times-Roman
%%IncludeResource: font Garamond-Light
%%IncludeResource: font Garamond-LightItalic
%%IncludeResource: font Courier
%%IncludeResource: font Garamond-Book
%%IncludeResource: font Courier-Bold
(%%DocumentNeededResources: font Times-Bold)131.711 327.378 S F1 1.281
```

This command extracts the font requests from the PostScript file. In this case, the document requires Times Roman, Courier, and Garamond fonts. Just about every printer and software package supplies Times Roman and Courier, but Garamond (the font in which this book is written) is less common. In addition, most fonts are copyrighted, so you probably won't be able to find them on the Internet. If you have a document that requires the Garamond font in PostScript format, your choices are:

- Reformat it with a different font if you have the source.
- Get the Garamond fonts.
- Edit the file, and change the name of the font to a font with similar metrics (in other words, with similar size characters). The results won't be as good as if you had used Garamond, but if the font you find is similar enough, the results might be acceptable. For example, you might change the text *Garamond* to *Times Roman.*

Wrong font type

Most PostScript fonts are in plain ASCII. You may also come across *Type 2 PostScript* and *display PostScript,* both of which include binary data. Many printers can't understand the binary format, and they may react to it in an unfriendly way. For example, my National KX-P 4455 printer hangs if I copy display PostScript to it. See the section "Format Conversion" for ways to solve this dilemma.

.dvi Format

One of the goals of TEX was to be able to create output for just about any printer. As we will see, old versions of *troff,* the main competitor, were able to produce output only for a very limited number of phototypesetters. Even if you have one of them in your office, it's unlikely that you will want to use it for printing a draft of a 30-page paper.

The TEX solution, which was later adopted by *troff* in *ditroff* (device- independent *troff*), was to output the formatted data in a *device-independent* format, *.dvi,* and leave it to another program, a so-called *driver,* to format the files in a format appropriate to the output device. Unlike PostScript, *.dvi* contains large numbers of control characters and characters with the sign bit set and is not even remotely legible. Most versions of *file* know about *.dvi* format.

Format Conversion

Not so long ago your choice of documentation software determined your output format. For example, if you used TeX, you would get *.dvi* output, and you needed a TeX driver to print it. Nowadays, it's becoming easier to handle file formats. GNU *troff* outputs in *.dvi* format and programs are available to convert from *.dvi* to PostScript. Here's a list of conversions you might like to perform—see Appendix E for information on how to get software to perform them.

- A number of programs convert from *.dvi* to PostScript—for example, *dvips.*
- Since there's no good reason to want to convert from PostScript to *.dvi,* no programs are available to make the conversion. *.dvi* is not much use in itself—it needs to be transformed to a final printer form, and if you have PostScript output, you can go directly to the printer form with *ghostscript* (see below) without going via *.dvi.*
- To display *.dvi* files on an X display, use *SeeTeX.*
- To convert from *.dvi* to a printer output format, use one of the *dvi2xxx* programs.
- To convert from PostScript to a printer format, use *ghostscript.*
- To display PostScript on an X display, you can also use *ghostscript,* but *ghostview* gives you a better interface.
- To convert PostScript with binary data into ASCII, use *t1ascii.*

roff and Friends

The original UNIX formatting program was called *roff* (for *run-off*). It is now completely obsolete, but it has a number of descendents:

- *nroff* is a comparatively simple formatter designed to produce output for plain ASCII displays and printers.
- *troff* is a more sophisticated formatter designed to produce output for phototypesetters. Many versions create output only for the obsolete APS-5 phototypesetter, and you need postprocessing software to convert this output to a format that modern typesetters or laser printers understand. Fortunately, versions of *troff* that produce PostScript output are now available.
- *ditroff* (device-independent *troff*) is a newer version of *troff* that produces output in a device-independent intermediate form that can then be converted into the final form by a conversion program. This moves the problem of correct output format from *troff* to the conversion program. Despite the terminology, this device-independent format is not the same as *.dvi* format.

- *groff* is the GNU project *troff* and *nroff* replacement. In *troff* mode *groff* can produce output in PostScript and *.dvi* format.

All versions of *roff* share the same source file syntax, though *nroff* is more restricted in its functionality than *troff*. If you have a usable version of *troff*, you can use it to produce properly formatted hard copy versions of the man pages, for example. This is also what *xman* (the X11 manual browser) does.

Formatting with nroff or troff

troff input bears a certain resemblance to the traces left behind when a fly falls into an inkwell and then walks across a desk. The first time you run *troff* against a file intended for *troff*, the results may be less than heartening. For example, consider the following passage from the documentation of the Revision Control System (RCS). When correctly formatted, the output is:

> Besides the operations *ci* and *co*, RCS provides the following commands:
>
> | | |
> |---|---|
> | ident | extract identification markers |
> | rcs | change RCS file attributes |
> | rcsclean | remove unchanged working files (optional) |
> | rcsdiff | compare revisions |
> | rcsfreeze | record a configuration (optional) |
> | rcsmerge | merge revisions |
> | rlog | read log messages and other information in RCS files |
>
> A synopsis of these commands appears in the Appendix.
>
> **2.1 Automatic Identification**
>
> RCS can stamp source and object code with special identification strings, similar to product and serial numbers. To obtain such identification, place the marker
>
> *Id*
>
> into the text of a revision, for instance inside a comment. The check-out operation will replace this marker with a string of the form
>
> *$Id: filename revisionnumber date time author state locker $*

To format it, you can try:

```
$ troff rcs.ms >rcs.ps
```

This command assumes the use of *groff* or another flavor of *troff* that creates PostScript output (thus the name *rcs.ps* for the output file). If you do this, you get output that looks like:

> Besides the operations *ci* and *co*, RCS provides the following commands: tab(%); li l. ident%extract identification markers rcs%change RCS file attributes rcsclean%remove unchanged working files (optional) rcsdiff%compare revisions rcsfreeze%record a configuration (optional) rcsmerge%merge revisions rlog%read log messages and other information in RCS files A synopsis of these commands appears in the Appendix. Automatic Identification RCS can stamp source and object code with special identification strings, similar to product and serial numbers. To obtain such identification, place the marker Id into the text of a revision, for instance inside a comment. The check-out operation will replace this marker with a string of the form Id: filename revisionnumber date time author state locker

Most of the text seems to be there, but it hasn't been formatted at all (well, it *has* been justified). What happened?

Almost every *troff* or *roff* input document uses some set of *macros*. You can define your own macros in the source, of course, but over time a number of standard macro packages have evolved. They are stored in a directory called *tmac*. In the days of no confusion, this was */usr/lib/tmac*, but nowadays it might as equally well be */usr/share/tmac* (for systems close to the System V.4 ABI—see the section called "Installation Paths" in Chapter 4, *Configuring the Package*, for more details) or */usr/local/groff/tmac* for GNU *roff*. The name is known to *troff* either by environment variables or by instinct (the pathname is compiled into the program). *troff* loads specific macros if you specify the name of the file as an argument to the *-m* option. For example, to specify the man page macros */usr/lib/tmac/an*, you would supply *troff* with the parameter *-man*. Since *man* makes more sense than *an*, these macros are called the *man* macros. The names of other macro packages also usually grow an *m* at the beginning. Some systems change the base name of the macros from, say, */usr/lib/tmac/an* to */usr/lib/tmac/tmac.an*.

Most versions of *troff* supply the following macro packages:

- The *man* (*tmac/an*) and *mandoc* (*tmac/andoc*) packages are used to format man pages.
- The *mdoc* (*tmac/doc*) package is used to format hard copy documents, including some man pages.
- The *mm* (*tmac/m*) macros, the so-called *memorandum* macros, are described in the documentation as macros to "format letters, reports, memoranda, papers, manuals and books." The documentation doesn't describe what you shouldn't use these macros for.
- The *ms* (*tmac/s*) macros were the original macros supplied with the Seventh Edition. They are now supposedly obsolete, but you will see them again and again. Many books by O'Reilly & Associates were formatted with a modified version of the *ms* macros.

- The *me* (*tmac/e*) macros are another, more recent set of macros that originated in Berkeley.

There is no sure-fire way to tell which macros a file needs. Here are a couple of possibilities:

- The filename suffix might provide a hint. For example, our file is called *rcs.ms*, so there is a very good chance that it wants to be formatted with *–ms*.
- The program *grog*, which is part of *groff*, examines the source and guesses the kind of macro set. It is frequently wrong.
- The only other way is trial and error. Since there aren't that many different macro sets, this might be a good solution.

In our example, the filename suggests that the file should be formatted with the *ms* macros. Let's try that:

```
$ troff -ms rcs.ms >rcs.ps
```

Now we get:

> Besides the operations *ci* and *co*, RCS provides the following commands: tab(%); li l. ident%extract identification markers rcs%change RCS file attributes rcsclean%remove unchanged working files (optional) rcsdiff%compare revisions rcsfreeze%record a configuration (optional) rcsmerge%merge revisions rlog%read log messages and other information in RCS files A synopsis of these commands appears in the Appendix.
>
> **2.1 Automatic Identification**
>
> RCS can stamp source and object code with special identification strings, similar to product and serial numbers. To obtain such identification, place the marker
>
> *Id*
>
> into the text of a revision, for instance inside a comment. The check-out operation will replace this marker with a string of the form
>
> *$Id: filename revisionnumber date time author state locker $*

Well, it doesn't look quite as bad, but it's still not where we want to be. What happened to that list of program names?

troff does not do all the work by itself. The tabular layout of the program names in this example is done by the preprocessor *tbl*, which handles tables. Before we let *troff* at the document, we need to pass it through *tbl*, which replaces the following code with a couple of hundred lines of complicated and illegible *troff* instructions to build the table.

```
.TS
tab(%);
li l.
ident%extract identification markers
rcs%change RCS file attributes
rcsclean%remove unchanged working files (optional)
rcsdiff%compare revisions
rcsfreeze%record a configuration (optional)
rcsmerge%merge revisions
rlog%read log messages and other information in RCS files
.TE
```

To get the desired results, we need to enter:

```
$ tbl rcs.ms | troff -ms >rcs.ps
```

nroff, *troff*, and *groff* use a number of preprocessors to perform special functions. They are:

- *soelim* replaces *.so* statements (which correspond to C *#include* statements) with the contents of the file to which the line refers. The *roff* programs do this too, of course, but the other preprocessors don't. Thus, if the contents of one of the files is of interest to another preprocessor, you need to run *soelim* first.
- *refer* processes references.
- *pic* draws simple pictures.
- *tbl* formats data in tabular form.
- *eqn* formats equations.

Unless you *know* that the document you're formatting doesn't use any of these preprocessors or if formatting takes a very long time, it's easier to use all the preprocessors. There are two possible ways to do this:

- You can pipe from one processor to the next. This is the standard way:

  ```
  $ soelim rcs.ms | refer | pic | tbl | eqn | troff -ms
  ```

  The *soelim* preprocessor reads in the document and replaces any *.so* commands with the contents of the file to which they refer. It then passes the output to *refer*, which processes any textual references and passes it to *pic*, which processes any pictures it may find, and passes the result to *tbl*. *tbl* processes any tables and passes its result to *eqn*, which processes any equations before passing the result to *troff*.

- Some versions of *troff* invoke the preprocessors themselves if passed appropriate options. For example, Table 7-1 lists the options that invoke the preprocessors in *groff*.

Table 7–1: Starting Preprocessors from groff

Option	Preprocessor
-e	*eqn*
-t	*tbl*
-p	*pic*
-s	*soelim*
-R	*refer*

Starting the preprocessors from *troff* not only has the advantage of involving less typing, it also ensures that the preprocessors are started in the correct sequence. Problems can arise when you run *eqn* before *tbl*, for example, if tables contain equations. See *Typesetting Tables with tbl* by Henry McGilton and Mary McNabb for further details.

Other roff-Related Programs

As you can see, the *troff* system uses a large number of programs. Once they were relatively small, which was the UNIX way. Now the programs are large, but there are still a lot of them. Apart from the programs we have already seen, you could encounter the GNU variants, which can optionally be installed with a name beginning in *g*. For example, GNU *eqn* may be installed as *geqn* if the system already has a different version of *eqn*. *indxbib* and *lookbib* (sometimes called *lkbib)* process bibliographic references and are available in the *groff* package. *groff* also includes a number of other programs, such as *grops* and *grotty*, which you don't usually need to invoke directly.

Man Pages

Almost from its beginning, UNIX had an *online manual*, traditionally called *man pages*. You can peruse man pages with the *man* program, or you can print them as hard copy documentation.

Traditionally, man pages are cryptic and formalized. They were introduced when disk storage was expensive, so they are short, and they were intended as a reference for people who already understood the product. More and more, unfortunately, they are taking on the responsibility of being the sole source of documentation. They don't perform this task very well.

man History

The UNIX *man* facility has had a long and varying history, and knowing it helps you understand some of the reasons for its strange nature. The Seventh Edition of the *UNIX Programmer's Manual* was divided into nine sections. Section 9, which contained the quick reference cards, has since atrophied. Traditionally, you refer to man pages by the name of the item to which they refer, followed by the section number in parentheses. The man page for the C compiler would be called *cc(1)*. BSD systems have substantially retained the Seventh Edition structure, but System V has reorganized them. There are also differences of opinion about where individual man pages belong, so Table 7-2 can only be a guide.

Table 7-2: UNIX Manual Sections

Seventh Edition Section	Contents	System V Section
1	Commands (programs)	1
2	System Calls (direct kernel interface)	2
3	Subroutines (library functions in user space)	3
4	Special Files	7, 4
5	File Formats and Conventions	4, 5
6	Games	6
7	Macro Packages and Language Conventions	7
8	Maintenance	1m
9	Quick Reference Cards	

What distinguished the UNIX manual from that of other systems was that it was designed to be kept online. Each of the sections listed in Table 7-2, except for the quick reference cards, was stored in *nroff* format in a directory called */usr/man/man<section>*, where *<section>* was the section number. Each entry was (and is) called a *man page*, although nowadays some can run on for 100 pages or more.

The manual was stored in *nroff* format in order to be independent of the display hardware and because formatting the entire manual took such a long time. For these reasons, pages were formatted on an individual basis when they were accessed, which slowed access to the manual.

The speed problem was solved by saving the formatted copy of the man page in a second directory hierarchy, */usr/man/cat<section>*, the first time that the page was formatted. Subsequent requests for the man pages would access the formatted page and display it more quickly.

This basic process has survived more or less intact to the present day. People have, of course, thought of ways to confuse it:

- As the manual got larger, it seemed reasonable to subdivide it further. Most users weren't interested in system administration functions, so some systems put them into a separate directory, such as */usr/man/cat1m*. Some systems gave them a filename suffix such as *m*, so that the manual page for the *shutdown* function might end up being called */usr/man/cat1/shutdown.1m* or */usr/man/man1m/shutdown.1m* or a similar name.
- Various commercial implementations reorganized the sequence of the sections in the printed manual and reorganized the directories to coincide. For example, in System V the description of the file */etc/group* is in Section 4, but in the Seventh Edition and BSD it is in Section 5.
- Even without the uncertainty of which section to search for a command, it was evident that section numbers were not very informative. Some implementations, such as XENIX and some versions of System V, chose to replace the uninformative numbers with uninformative letters. For example, *ls(1)* becomes *ls(C)* in XENIX.
- Some *man* programs have lost the ability to format the man pages, so you need to format them before installation. You'll find this problem on systems where *nroff* is an add-on component.
- There is no longer a single directory where you can expect to put man pages: some System V versions put formatted man pages for users in a directory */usr/catman/u_man* and man pages for programmers in */usr/catman/p_man*. Since most programmers are users and the distinction between the use of the man pages is not always clear, *man* has to search two separate directory hierarchies for the man pages.
- As we saw in the section called "Installation Paths" in Chapter 4, System V.4 puts its man pages in */usr/share/man*. Many System V.4 systems require formatted man pages, and some, such as UnixWare, don't provide a *man* program at all.
- Many *man* programs accept compressed input, either formatted or nonformatted. For some reason, the *pack* program still survives, but other versions of *man* also understand man pages compressed with *compress* or *gzip*. We looked at all of these programs in Chapter 2.
- Different *man* programs place different interpretations on the suffix of the man page filename. They seldom document the meanings of the suffix.

- To keep up the tradition of incompatible man pages, BSD has changed the default macro set from *man* to *mdoc*. This means that older man page readers can't make any sense of unformatted BSD man pages.

This combination of affairs makes life difficult. For example, I have a number of different man pages in different directories on my system. The filenames for the man pages for *printf*, which is both a command and a library function, are:

```
BSD printf command, formatted:
        /usr/share/man/cat1/printf.0
Solaris printf command, nroff:
        /pub/man/solaris-2.2/man1/printf.1
SVR4.2 printf command, formatted, compressed:
        /pub/man/svr4.2/cat1/printf.1.Z
BSD printf function, formatted:
        /usr/share/man/cat3/printf.0
Solaris 2.2 printf function, nroff, standard:
        /pub/man/solaris-2.2/man3/printf.3s
Solaris 2.2 printf function, nroff, BSD version:
        /pub/man/solaris-2.2/man3/printf.3b
SunOS 4.1.3 printf function, nroff:
        /pub/man/sunos-4.1.3/man3/printf.3v
SVR3 printf function, formatted, packed:
        /pub/man/catman/p_man/man3/printf.3s.z
SVR4.2 printf function, formatted, compressed:
        /pub/man/svr4.2/cat3/printf.3s.Z
SVR4.2 printf function, formatted, compressed, BSD version:
        /pub/man/svr4.2/cat3/printf.3b.Z
XENIX printf function, nroff, packed:
        /pub/man/xenix-2.3.2/man.S/printf.S.z
```

Most packages assume that unformatted man pages will be installed in */usr/man*. They usually accept that the path may be different, and some allow you to change only the subdirectory and the filename suffix.

This lack of standardization can cause such problems that many people just give up and don't bother to install the man pages, which is a pity. Instead, why not install a *man* program that isn't as fussy? A number of alternatives are available, including one for System V.4 from Walnut Creek and a number on various Linux distributions.

TEX

TEX is Donald Knuth's monument to the triumph of logic over convention. To quote Knuth's *The TEXbook*,

> Insiders pronounce the X of TEX as a Greek chi, not as an "x", so that TEX rhymes with the word blecchhh. It's the "ch" sound in Scottish words like *loch* or German words like *ach*; it's a Spanish "j" and a Russian "kh". When you say it correctly to your computer, the terminal may become slightly moist.

This is one of the more informative parts of *The TeXbook*. It is, unfortunately, not a manual but a textbook, and most of the essential parts are hidden in exercises flagged "very difficult." If you just want to figure out how to format a TeX document, the Nutshell Handbook *Making TeX Work*, by Norman Walsh, is a much better option.

Here's part of the file *plain.tex*, which defines some of what any TeX macro package should be able to do:

```
\def\cases#1{\left\{\,\vcenter{\normalbaselines\m@th
    \ialign{$##\hfil$&\quad##\hfil\crcr#1\crcr}}\right.}
\def\matrix#1{\null\,\vcenter{\normalbaselines\m@th
    \ialign{\hfil$##$\hfil&&\quad\hfil$##$\hfil\crcr
      \mathstrut\crcr\noalign{\kern-\baselineskip}
      #1\crcr\mathstrut\crcr\noalign{\kern-\baselineskip}}}\,}
```

More than anywhere else in porting, it is good for your state of mind to steer clear of TeX internals. The assumptions on which the syntax is based differ markedly from those of other programming languages. For example, identifiers may not contain digits, and spaces are required only when the meaning would otherwise be ambiguous (to TeX, not to you). The sequence `fontsize300` is in fact the identifier `fontsize` followed by the number `300`. On the other hand, since it is almost impossible to find any solid helpful information in the documentation, you could spend hours trying to solve a minor problem. I have been using TeX frequently for years, and I still find it the most frustrating program I have ever seen.*

Along with TeX, a couple of macro packages have become so important that they are almost text processors in their own right:

- LaTeX is a macro package that is not quite as painful as plain TeX but also not as powerful. It is usually built as a separate program when installing TeX, using a technique of dumping a running program to an object file. (We will examine this technique in the section called "Dumping to Object Files" in Chapter 21, *Object Files and Friends*.)
- BibTeX is an auxiliary program that, in conjunction with LaTeX, creates bibliographic references. Read all about it in *Making TeX Work*. It usually takes three runs through the source files to create the correct auxiliary files and format the document correctly.
- *texinfo* is a GNU package that supplies both online and hard copy documentation. It uses TeX to format the hard copy documentation. We'll look at it along with GNU *info* in the next section.

* When I wrote this sentence, I wondered if I wasn't overstating the case. Mike Loukides, the author of *Programming with GNU Software*, reviewed the final draft and added a single word: *Amen*.

GNU info and texinfo

It's unlikely that you'll break out in storms of enthusiasm about the documentation techniques we've looked at so far. The GNU project didn't, either, when they started, though their concerns were somewhat different:

- Man pages are straightforward, but the *man* program is relatively primitive. In particular, *man* does not provide a way to follow up on references in the man page.
- Man pages are intended to be stored online and thus tend to be cryptic, which makes them unsuited to being hard copy documentation. Increasing the length of the man pages and adding more detailed information would make them less suited for online documentation.
- There is almost no link between man pages and the hard copy documentation, unless they happen to be the same for a particular package.
- Maintaining man pages *and* hard copy documentation is double the work and opens you to the danger of omissions in one or the other document.

As in other areas, the GNU project started from scratch and came up with a third solution, *info*. This is a system of online and hard copy documentation. Both forms of documentation are contained in the source file: you use the *makeinfo* program to create *info* documents, which you read with the online browser *info*, and you use TEX and the *texinfo* macro set to format the documentation for printing.

info is a menu-driven, tree-structured online browser. You can follow in-text references and then return to the original text. *info* is available both as a standalone program and as an Emacs macro.

If you have a package that supplies documentation in *info* format, you should use it. Even if some GNU programs, such as *gcc* and Emacs, have both *info* and man pages, the *info* is much more detailed.

Running *texinfo* is straightforward: run TEX. The document reads in the file *texinfo.tex*, and you are likely to encounter a problem only if *texinfo* doesn't find this file.

The World Wide Web

The World Wide Web (WWW) is not primarily a program documentation system, but it has a number of properties that make it suitable as a manual browser. As a result of the growth of the Internet, WWW is well known and generally available, it supplies a transparent cross-reference system, and the user interface is easy to use and understand. It's likely that it will gain importance in the years to come. I hope it will do so without causing as much confusion as the documentation systems discussed in this chapter.

In This Chapter:
- *A Strategy for Testing*
- *Symbolic Debuggers*
- *Libraries and Debugging Information*
- *Tracing System Calls*

8

Testing the Results

Finally *make* has run through to the end and has not reported errors. Your source tree now contains all the objects and executables. You're done!

After a brief moment of euphoria, you sit down at the keyboard and start the program:

```
$ xterm
Segmentation fault - core dumped
```

Well, maybe you're not quite done after all. Occasionally the program doesn't work as advertised. What you do now depends on how much programming experience you have. If you are a complete beginner, you could be in trouble. All you can do (apart from asking somebody else for help) is to check that you really did configure the package correctly.

On the other hand, if you have even a slight understanding of programming, you should try to analyze the cause of the error—it's easier than you think. Hold on, and try not to look down.

There are thousands of possible reasons for the problems you encounter when you try to run a buggy executable, and lots of good books explain debugging techniques. In this chapter, we will touch only on aspects of debugging that relate to porting. First we'll attack a typical, if somewhat involved, real-life bug and solve it, discussing the pros and cons on the way. Then we'll look at alternatives to traditional debuggers: kernel and network tracing.

Before you even start your program, of course, you should check if any test programs are available. Some packages include their own tests, and separate test suites are available for others. For other packages there may be test suites that were not designed for the package but that can be used with it. If there are any tests, you should obviously run them. You might also consider writing some tests and including them as a target `test` in the *Makefile*.

Ported programs don't usually fail for the same reasons as programs under development. A program under development still has bugs that prevent it from running correctly on any platform, while a ported program has already run reasonably well on some other platform. If it doesn't run on your platform, the reasons are usually the following:

- A latent bug has found more fertile feeding ground. For example, a program may read from a null pointer, which frequently doesn't get noticed if the data at address 0 doesn't cause the program to do anything unusual. On the other hand, if the new platform does not have any memory mapped at address 0, a segmentation violation or a bus error occurs.
- Differences in the implementation of library functions or kernel functionality cause the program to behave differently in the new environment. For example, the function `setpgrp` has completely different semantics under System V and under BSD. See the section called "setpgrp" in Chapter 12, *Kernel Dependencies*, for more details.
- The configuration scripts have never been adequately tested for your platform. As a result, the program contains bugs that were not in the original versions.

A Strategy for Testing

When you write your own program with its own bugs, it helps you understand exactly what the program is trying to do, and if you think about it, you can usually shorten the debugging process. When debugging software that you have just ported, the situation is different. You *don't* understand the package, and learning its internals could take months. You need to find a way to track down the bug without getting bogged down with the specifics of how the package works.

You can overdo this approach, of course. It still helps to know what the program is trying to do. For example, when *xterm* dies, it's nice to know roughly how *xterm* works: it opens a window on an X server and emulates a terminal in this window. Knowing something about the internals of X11 will also be of use to you. But it's not time effective to try to fight your way through the source code of *xterm*.

In the rest of this chapter, we'll use this bug (yes, it was a real live bug in X11R6) to look at various techniques that you can employ to localize and finally pinpoint the problem. We'll use the old GIGO principle—garbage in, garbage out. We'll subdivide the program into pieces that we can conveniently observe and check which of them does not produce the expected output. After we find the piece with the error, we'll subdivide it further and repeat the process until we find the bug. The emphasis in this method is on *convenient*: it doesn't necessarily have to make sense. As long as you can continue to divide your problem area into between two and five parts and localize the problem in one of the parts, it won't take long to find the bug.

So what's a convenient way to look at the problems? That depends on the tools you have at your disposal:

- If you have a symbolic debugger, you can divide your problem into the individual functions and examine what goes in and what goes out.
- If you have a system call trace program, such as *ktrace* or *truss*, you can monitor what the program says to the system and what the system replies.
- If you have a communications line trace program, you can divide your program into pieces that communicate across this line, so you can see what they are saying to each other.

Of course, I have all these programs. In the following sections we'll look at each of these programs in more detail.

Symbolic Debuggers

If you don't have a symbolic debugger, get one. Now. Many people still claim to be able to get by without a debugger, and it's horrifying how many people don't even know how to use one. Of course you can debug just about anything without a symbolic debugger. Historians tell us that you can build pyramids without wheels—that's comparable to testing without a debugger. The GNU debugger, *gdb*, is available on just about every platform you're likely to encounter, and though it's not perfect, it runs rings around techniques like putting *printf* statements in your programs.

In UNIX, a debugger is a process that takes control of the execution of another process. Most versions of UNIX allow only one way for the debugger to take control: it must start the process that it debugs. Some versions, notably SunOS 4, but not Solaris 2, also allow the debugger to *attach* to a running process.

Whichever debugger you use, you will need a surprisingly small number of commands. In the following discussion, we'll look at the command set of *gdb*, since it is widely used. The commands for other symbolic debuggers vary considerably, but they usually have similar purposes.

- A *stack trace* command answers the question, "Where am I, and how did I get here?" and is almost the most useful of all commands. It's certainly the first command you should execute when examining a core dump or after getting a signal while debugging the program. *gdb* implements this function with the *backtrace* command.
- *Displaying data* is the most obvious requirement: what is the current value of the variable `bar`? In *gdb*, you do this with the *print* command.
- *Displaying register contents* is really the same thing as displaying program data. In *gdb*, you display individual registers with the *print* command or all registers with the *info registers* command.
- *Modifying data and register contents* is an obvious way of modifying program execution. In *gdb*, you do this with the *set* command.
- *Breakpoints* stop execution of the process when it attempts to execute an instruction at a certain address. *gdb* sets breakpoints with the *break* command.
- Many modern machines support hardware for more sophisticated breakpoint mechanisms. For example, the i386 architecture can support four hardware breakpoints on instruction fetch (in other words, traditional breakpoints), memory read, or memory write. These features are invaluable in systems that support them; unfortunately, UNIX usually does not. *gdb* simulates this kind of breakpoint with a so-called *watchpoint*. When watchpoints are set, *gdb* simulates program execution by single-stepping through the program. When the condition (for example, writing to the global variable `foo`) is fulfilled, the debugger stops the program. This slows down the execution speed by several orders of magnitude, whereas a real hardware breakpoint has no impact on the execution speed.*
- *Jumping* (changing the address from which the next instruction will be read) is really a special case of modifying register contents, in this case the *program counter* (the register that contains the address of the next instruction). This register is also sometimes called the *instruction pointer*, which makes more sense. In *gdb*, use the *jump* command to do this. Use this instruction with care: if the compiler expects the stack to look different at the source and at the destination, this command can easily cause incorrect execution.
- *Single-stepping* in its original form is supported in hardware by many architectures: after executing a single instruction, the machine automatically generates a hardware interrupt that ultimately causes a `SIGTRAP` signal to the debugger. *gdb* performs this function with the *stepi* command.

---

* Some architectures slow the overall execution speed slightly in order to test the hardware registers. This effect is negligible.

- You won't want to execute individual machine instructions until you are in deep trouble. Instead, execute a *single line* instruction, which effectively single-steps until you leave the current line of source code. To add to the confusion, this is also frequently called *single-stepping*. This command comes in two flavors, depending on how it treats function calls. One form executes the function and stops the program at the next line after the call. The other, more thorough, form stops execution at the first executable line of the function. It's important to notice the difference between these two functions: both are extremely useful, but for different purposes. *gdb* performs single line execution omitting calls with the *next* command and includes calls with the *step* command.

There are two possible approaches when using a debugger. The easier one is to wait until something goes wrong, then find out where it happened. This approach is appropriate when the process gets a signal and does not overwrite the stack: the *backtrace* command shows you how it got there.

Sometimes this method doesn't work well: the process may end up in no-man's-land, and you see something like:

```
Program received signal SIGSEGV, Segmentation fault.
0x0 in ?? ()
(gdb) bt                          abbreviation for backtrace
#0  0x0 in ?? ()                  nowhere
(gdb)
```

Before dying, the process has mutilated itself beyond recognition. Clearly, the first approach won't work here. In this case, we can start by conceptually dividing the program into a number of parts. Initially we take the function `main` and the set of functions that `main` calls. By single-stepping over the function calls until something blows up, we can localize the function in which the problem occurs. Then we can restart the program and single-step through this function until we find what it calls before dying. This iterative approach sounds slow and tedious, but in fact it works surprisingly well.

Libraries and Debugging Information

Let's return to our *xterm* program, and use *gdb* to figure out what is going on. We could, of course, look at the core dump, but since, in this case, we can repeat the problem at will, we're better off looking at the live program. We enter:

```
$ gdb xterm
(political statement for the FSF omitted)
(gdb) r -display allegro:0        run the program
Starting program: /X/X11/X11R6/xc/programs/xterm/xterm -display allegro:0
```

```
Program received signal SIGBUS, Bus error.
0x3b0bc in _XtMemmove ()
(gdb) bt                          look back down the stack
#0  0x3b0bc in _XtMemmove ()      all these functions come from the X toolkit
#1  0x34dcd in XtScreenDatabase ()
#2  0x35107 in _XtPreparseCommandLine ()
#3  0x4e2ef in XtOpenDisplay ()
#4  0x4e4a1 in _XtAppInit ()
#5  0x35700 in XtOpenApplication ()
#6  0x357b5 in XtAppInitialize ()
#7  0x535 in main ()
(gdb)
```

The stack trace shows that the main program called `XtAppInitialize`, and the rest of the stack shows the program deep in the X Toolkit, one of the central X11 libraries. If this were a program that you had just written, you could expect the bug to lie in some function you have written. In this case, where we have just built the complete X11 core system, there's also every possibility that it is a library bug. As usual, the library was compiled without debug information, and without that you hardly have a hope of finding it.

Apart from size constraints, there is no reason why you can't include debugging information in a library. The object files in libraries are just the same as any others—we discuss them in detail in the section called "Function Libraries" in Chapter 21, *Object Files and Friends*. If you want, you can build libraries with debugging information, or you can take individual library routines and compile them separately.

Unfortunately, the size constraints are significant: without debugging information, the file *libXt.a* is about 330 KB and contains 53 object files. With debugging information, it might easily reach 20 MB, since all the myriad X11 global symbols would be included with each object file in the archive. It's not just a question of disk space. You also need virtual memory during the link phase to accommodate all these symbols. Most of these files don't interest us anyway. The first one that does is the one that contains `_XtMemmove`, the function that *gbd* showed to be on top of the stack when the core dump occurred. So we find where it is, and compile it separately with debugging information.

That's not as simple as it sounds. First we need to find the source file, and to do that we need to find the source directory. We could read the documentation, but to do that we need to know that the *Xt* functions are in fact the X Toolkit. If we're using GNU *make* or if our *Makefile* documents directory changes, an alternative would be to go back to our *make* log and look for the text *Xt*. If we do this, we quickly find:

```
make[4]: Leaving directory `/X/X11R6/xc/lib/Xext'
making Makefiles in lib/Xt...
        mv Makefile Makefile.bak
make[4]: Entering directory `/X/X11R6/xc/lib/Xt'
make[4]: Nothing to be done for `Makefiles'.
make[4]: Leaving directory `/X/X11R6/xc/lib/Xt'
```

So the directory is */X/X11R6/xc/lib/Xt*. The next step is to find the file that contains `_XtMemmove`. It may be called *XtMemmove.c*, but in this case, there is no such file. We'll have to *grep* for it. Some versions of *grep* have an option to descend recursively into subdirectories, which can be very useful if you have one available. Another useful tool is *cscope*, which is supplied with System V.

```
$ grep XtMemmove *.c
Alloc.c:void _XtMemmove(dst, src, length)
Convert.c:      XtMemmove(&p->from.addr, from->addr, from->size);
...many more references to XtMemmove
```

So `_XtMemmove` is in *Alloc.c*. By the same method, we look for the other functions mentioned in the stack trace and discover that we also need to recompile *Initialize.c* and *Display.c*.

In order to compile debugging information, we add the compiler option *–g*. At the same time, we remove *–O*. *gcc* doesn't require this, but it's usually easier to debug an nonoptimized program. We have three choices of how to set the options:

- We can modify the *Makefile*. (*make World*, the main *make* target for X11, rebuilds the *Makefiles* from the corresponding *Imakefiles*, so modifying the *Makefile* is not overly dangerous.)
- If we have a working version of *xterm*, we can use its facilities. First we start the compilation with *make*, but we don't need to wait for the compilation to complete. As soon as the compiler invocation appears on the screen, we abort the build with **CTRL-C**. Using the *xterm* copy function, we copy the compiler invocation to the command line and add the options we want:

```
$ rm Alloc.o Initialize.o Display.o      remove the old objects
$ make                                   and start make normally
rm -f Alloc.o
gcc -DNO_ASM -fstrength-reduce -fpcc-struct-return -c      -I../.. \
-DNO_AF_UNIX -DSYSV -DSYSV386      -DUSE_POLL  Alloc.c
^C                                       interrupt make with CTRL-C
make: *** [Alloc.o] Interrupt
copy the invocation lines above with the mouse, and paste below, then
modify as shown in bold print
$ gcc -DNO_ASM -fstrength-reduce -fpcc-struct-return -c      -I../.. \
-DNO_AF_UNIX -DSYSV -DSYSV386      -DUSE_POLL  Alloc.c -g
```

You can also type make -n, which just shows the commands that *make* would execute, rather than aborting the *make*, but you frequently find that make -n prints a whole lot you don't expect. When you have made *Alloc.o*, you can repeat the process for the other two object files.

- We could change CFLAGS from the *make* command line. Our first attempt doesn't work too well, though. If you compare the following line with the previous invocation, you'll see that a whole lot of options are missing. They were all in CFLAGS; by redefining CFLAGS, we lose them all:

  ```
  $ make CFLAGS=-g
  rm -f Alloc.o
  gcc -DNO_ASM -fstrength-reduce -fpcc-struct-return -c -g  Alloc.c
  ```

  Since CFLAGS included all the compiler options starting from *–I/../..*, we need to write:

  ```
  $ make CFLAGS='-g -c -I../.. -DNO_AF_UNIX -DSYSV -DSYSV386 -DUSE_POLL'
  ```

When we have created all three new object files, we can let *make* complete the library for us. It will not try to remake the object files we built by hand just now, because they are newer than any of their dependencies:

```
$ make                                          run make to build a new library
rm -f libXt.a
ar clq libXt.a ActionHook.o Alloc.o ArgList.o Callback.o ClickTime.o Composite.o \
Constraint.o Convert.o Converters.o Core.o Create.o Destroy.o Display.o Error.o \
Event.o EventUtil.o Functions.o GCManager.o Geometry.o GetActKey.o GetResList.o \
GetValues.o HookObj.o Hooks.o Initialize.o Intrinsic.o Keyboard.o Manage.o \
NextEvent.o Object.o PassivGrab.o Pointer.o Popup.o PopupCB.o RectObj.o \
Resources.o Selection.o SetSens.o SetValues.o SetWMCW.o Shell.o StringDefs.o \
Threads.o TMaction.o TMgrab.o TMkey.o TMparse.o TMprint.o TMstate.o VarCreate.o \
VarGet.o Varargs.o Vendor.o
ranlib libXt.a
rm -f ../../usrlib/libXt.a
cd ../../usrlib; ln ../lib/Xt/libXt.a .
$
```

Now we have a copy of the X Toolkit in which these three files have been compiled with symbols. Next, we need to rebuild *xterm*. That's straightforward enough:

```
$ cd ../../programs/xterm/
$ pwd
/X/X11R6/xc/programs/xterm
$ make
rm -f xterm
gcc -DNO_ASM -fstrength-reduce -fpcc-struct-return -fwritable-strings -o xterm \
-L../../usrlib main.o input.o charproc.o cursor.o util.o tabs.o screen.o \
scrollbar.o button.o Tekproc.o misc.o VTPrsTbl.o TekPrsTbl.o data.o menu.o -lXaw \
-lXmu -lXt -lSM -lICE -lXext -lX11 -L/usr/X11R6/lib -lpt -ltermlib
```

Finally, we try again. Since the library is not in the current directory, we use the *dir* command to tell *gdb* where to find the sources. Now we get:

```
$ gdb xterm
(gdb) dir ../../lib/X11        set source paths
Source directories searched:
/X/X11/X11R6/xc/programs/xterm/../../lib/X11:$cdir:$cwd
(gdb) dir ../../lib/Xt
Source directories searched:
/X/X11/X11R6/xc/programs/xterm/../../lib/Xt/X/X11/X11R6/xc/programs/xterm/../..\
/lib/X11:$cdir:$cwd
(gdb) r                            and run the program
Starting program: /X/X11/X11R6/xc/programs/xterm/xterm

Program received signal SIGBUS, Bus error.
0x3ced6 in _XtMemmove (dst=0x342d8 "\(-DE 03", src=0x41c800 "", length=383) \
at Alloc.c:101
101                 *dst++ = *src++;
(gdb)
```

This shows a typical byte-for-byte memory move. About the only thing that could cause a bus error on that statement would be an invalid address, but the parameters show that the addresses appear to be valid.

There are two possible gotchas here:

- The debugger may be lying. The parameters it shows are the parameters on the stack. If the code has been optimized, the source and destination addresses may be stored in registers, and thus the value of `dst` on the stack is not up to date.
- The destination address may be in the text segment, in which case an attempt to write to it will cause some kind of error. Depending on the system, the error could be a segmentation violation or a bus error.

The most reliable way to find out what is really going on is to look at the machine instructions being executed. First we tell the debugger to look at the current instruction and the following five instructions:

```
(gdb) x/6i $eip              list the next 6 instructions
0x3ced6 <_XtMemmove+74>:      movb   %al,(%edx)
0x3ced8 <_XtMemmove+76>:      incl   0xc(%ebp)
0x3cedb <_XtMemmove+79>:      incl   0x8(%ebp)
0x3cede <_XtMemmove+82>:      jmp    0x3cec2 <_XtMemmove+54>
0x3cee0 <_XtMemmove+84>:      leave
0x3cee1 <_XtMemmove+85>:      ret
```

The first instruction is a byte move, from register al to the address stored in register edx. Let's look at the address in edx:

```
(gdb) p/x $edx
$9 = 0x342d8
```

Well, this is our dst address all right—why can't it store there? It would be nice to try to set values in memory and see if the debugger can do it:

```
(gdb) set *dst = 'X'b
(gdb) p *dst
$13 = 88 'X'
```

That looks writable enough. Unfortunately, you can't rely on the debugger to tell the truth. Debuggers must be able to write to the text segment. If the write had failed, you could have been sure that the address was not writable, but if the write succeeds, you can't be sure the address is writable. What we need to know are the exact segment limits. Some debuggers show you the segment limits, but current versions of *gdb* do not. An alternative is the *size* command:

```
$ size xterm
text    data    bss     dec     hex     filename
846204  56680   23844   926728  e2408   xterm
```

Since the text segment is 846,204 decimal bytes long (0xce97c), and on this system (SCO UNIX) it starts at address 0, the address is, indeed, in the text segment. But where did it come from? To find an answer to that question, we need to look at the calling function. In *gdb*, we do this with the *frame* command:

```
(gdb) f 1                    look at the calling function (frame 1)
#1  0x35129 in _MergeOptionTables (src1=0x342d8, num_src1=24,
    src2=0x400ffe, num_src2=64, dst=0x7ffff9c0, num_dst=0x7ffff9bc)
    at Initialize.c:602
602         (void) memmove(table, src1, sizeof(XrmOptionDescRec) * num_src1 );
```

That's funny—last time it died, the function was called from XtScreenDatabase,* not from _MergeOptionTables. Why? At the moment it's difficult to say for sure, but this difference may have happened because we removed optimization. In any case, since we still have a problem, we should fix this one first. We can then go back and look for the other one if solving this problem isn't enough.

In this case, the *frame* command doesn't help much, but it does tell us that the destination variable is called table and, implicitly, that memmove has been defined as _XtMemmove in this source file. We could now look at the source file in an editor in a different X window, but it's easier to list the instructions around the current line with the *list* command:

---

* See frame 1 in the stack trace on the section called "Libraries and Debugging Information".

```
(gdb) l
597         enum {Check, NotSorted, IsSorted} sort_order = Check;
598
599         *dst = table = (XrmOptionDescRec*)
600             XtMalloc( sizeof(XrmOptionDescRec) * (num_src1 + num_src2) );
601
602         (void) memmove(table, src1, sizeof(XrmOptionDescRec) * num_src1 );
603         if (num_src2 == 0) {
604             *num_dst = num_src1;
605             return;
606         }
```

So, the address is returned by the function `XtMalloc`—it seems to be allocating storage in the text segment. At this point, we could examine it more carefully, but let's first be sure that we're looking at the right problem. The address in `table` should be the same as the address in the parameter `dst` of `_XtMemmove`. We're currently examining the environment of `_MergeOptionTables`, so we can look at it directly:

```
(gdb) p table
$29 = (XrmOptionDescRec *) 0x41c800
```

That looks just fine. Where did this strange `dst` address come from? Let's set a breakpoint on the call to `memmove` on line 602, and then restart the program.

```
(gdb) b 602
Breakpoint 8 at 0x35111: file Initialize.c, line 602.
(gdb) r
The program being debugged has been started already.
Start it from the beginning? (y or n) y
Starting program: /X/X11/X11R6/xc/programs/xterm/xterm

Breakpoint 8, _MergeOptionTables (src1=0x342d8, num_src1=24,
    src2=0x400ffe, num_src2=64, dst=0x7ffff9c0, num_dst=0x7ffff9bc)
    at Initialize.c:602
602         (void) memmove(table, src1, sizeof(XrmOptionDe
(gdb) p table                          look again, to be sure
$31 = (XrmOptionDescRec *) 0x41c800
(gdb) s                                single step into memmove
_XtMemmove (dst=0x342d8 "\(-DE 03", src=0x41c800 "", length=384)
    at Alloc.c:94
94          if (src < dst) {
```

This is really strange! `table` has a valid address in the data segment, but the address we pass to `_XtMemmove` is in the text segment and seems unrelated. It's not clear what we should look at next:

- The source of the function calls `memmove`, but after preprocessing it ends up calling `_XtMemmove`. `memmove` might simply be defined as `_XtMemmove`, but it might also be defined with parameters, in which case some subtle type conversions might result in our problem.

- If you understand the assembler of the system, it might be instructive to look at the actual instructions that the compiler produces.

It's definitely quicker to look at the assembler instructions than to fight your way through the thick undergrowth in the X11 source tree:

```
(gdb) x/8i $eip                        look at the next 8 instructions
0x35111 <_MergeOptionTables+63>:        movl   0xc(%ebp),%edx
0x35114 <_MergeOptionTables+66>:        movl   %edx,0xffffffd8(%ebp)
0x35117 <_MergeOptionTables+69>:        movl   0xffffffd8(%ebp),%edx
0x3511a <_MergeOptionTables+72>:        shll   $0x4,%edx
0x3511d <_MergeOptionTables+75>:        pushl  %edx
0x3511e <_MergeOptionTables+76>:        pushl  0xfffffffc(%ebp)
0x35121 <_MergeOptionTables+79>:        pushl  0x8(%ebp)
0x35124 <_MergeOptionTables+82>:        call   0x3ce8c <_XtMemmove>
```

This isn't easy stuff to handle, but since it's worth understanding, we'll pull it apart, instruction by instruction. This discussion is easier to understand if you refer to the diagram of stack structure shown in the section called "Stack Frames" in Chapter 21.

- `movl 0xc(%ebp),%edx` takes the content of the stack word offset 12 in the current stack frame and places it in register `edx`. As we have seen, this is `num_src1`, the second parameter passed to `_MergeOptionTables`.
- `movl %edx,0xffffffd8(%ebp)` stores the value of `edx` at offset -40 in the current stack frame. This is for temporary storage.
- `movl 0xffffffd8(%ebp),%edx` does *exactly* the opposite: it loads register `edx` from the location where it just stored it. These two instructions are completely redundant. They are also a sure sign that the function was compiled without optimization.
- `shll $0x4,%edx` shifts the contents of register `edx` left by 4 bits, multiplying it by 16. If we compare this to the source, it's evident that the value of `XrmOptionDescRec` is 16, and that the compiler has taken a short cut to evaluate the third parameter of the call.
- `pushl %edx` pushes the contents of `edx` onto the stack.
- `pushl 0xfffffffc(%ebp)` pushes the value of the word at offset -4 in the current stack frame onto the stack. This is the value of `table`, as we can confirm by looking at the instructions generated for the previous line.
- `pushl 0x8(%ebp)` pushes the value of the first parameter, `src1`, onto the stack.
- Finally, `call 0x3ce8c <_XtMemmove` calls the function. Expressed in C, we now know that it calls

```
memmove (src1, table,  num_src1 << 4);
```

This is, of course, wrong: the parameter sequence of source and destination has been reversed. Let's look at `_XtMemmove` more carefully:

```
(gdb) l _XtMemmove
89      #ifdef _XNEEDBCOPYFUNC
90      void _XtMemmove(dst, src, length)
91          char *dst, *src;
92          int length;
93      {
94          if (src < dst) {
95              dst += length;
96              src += length;
97              while (length--)
98                  *--dst = *--src;
99          } else {
100             while (length--)
101                 *dst++ = *src++;
102         }
103     }
104     #endif
```

Clearly the function parameters are the same as those of `memmove`, but the calling sequence has reversed them. We've found the problem, but we haven't found what's causing it.

Debugging is not an exact science. We've found our problem, but we still don't know what's causing it. But looking back a couple pages where we set a breakpoint and ran the program, we see that the address for `src` on entering `_XtMemmove` was the same as the address of `table`. That tells us as much as analyzing the machine code did. This happens again and again: after you find a problem, you discover you did it the hard way.

Next we need to figure out why the compiler reversed the sequence of the parameters. Can this be a compiler bug? Theoretically, yes, but it's very unlikely that such a primitive bug would go undiscovered up to now.

Remember that the compiler does not compile the sources you see. It compiles whatever the preprocessor hands to it. It makes a lot of sense to look at the preprocessor output. To do this, we go back to the library directory. Since we used *pushd*, this is easy—just enter *pushd* again. In the library, we use the same trick as before in order to run the compiler with different options, only this time we use the options *–E* (stop after running the preprocessor), *–dD* (retain the text of the definitions in the preprocessor output), and *–C* (retain comments in the preprocessor output). In addition, we output to a file *junk.c*:

```
$ pushd
$ rm Initialize.o
$ make Initialize.o
```

```
rm -f Initialize.o
gcc -DNO_ASM -fstrength-reduce -fpcc-struct-return -c -g     -I../.. \\
   -D_SVID -DNO_AF_UNIX -DSYSV -DSYSV386     -DUSE_POLL  Initialize.c
make: *** [Initialize.o] Interrupt                     hit CTRL-C
... copy the command into the command line, and extend:
$ gcc -DNO_ASM -fstrength-reduce -fpcc-struct-return -c -g -I../.. \\
 -D_SVID -DNO_AF_UNIX -DSYSV -DSYSV386     -DUSE_POLL  Initialize.c \\
  -E -dD -C >junk.c
$
```

As you might have guessed, we now look at the file *junk.c* with an editor. We're looking for `memmove`, of course. We find a definition in */usr/include/string.h*, then later on we find, in */X/X11/X11R6/xc/X11/Xfuncs.h*:

```
#define memmove(dst,src,len) bcopy((char *)(src),(char *)(dst),(int)(len))


#define memmove(dst,src,len) _XBCOPYFUNC((char *)(src),(char *)(dst),(int)(len))
#define _XNEEDBCOPYFUNC
```

For some reason, the configuration files have decided that `memmove` is not defined on this system and have replaced it with `bcopy` (which is really not defined on this system). Then they replace it with the substitute function `_XBCOPYFUNC`, almost certainly a preprocessor definition. It also defines the preprocessor variable `_XNEEDBCOPYFUNC` to indicate that `_XtMemmove` should be compiled.

Unfortunately, we don't see what happens with `_XNEEDBCOPYFUNC`. The preprocessor discards all `#ifdef` lines. It does include `#defines`, however, so we can look for where `_XBCOPYFUNC` is defined—it's in *IntrinsicI.h*, as the last `#line` directive before the definition indicates.

```
#define _XBCOPYFUNC _XtMemmove
```

IntrinsicI.h also contains a number of definitions for `_XtMemmove`, none of which are used in the current environment, but all of which have the parameter sequence `(dst, src, count)`. `bcopy` has the parameter sequence (`src`, `dst`, `count`). Clearly, somebody has confused something in this header file, and under certain rare circumstances, the call is defined with the incorrect parameter sequence.

Somewhere in this example is a lesson to be learned. This is a real bug that occurred in X11R6, patch level 3, one of the most reliable and most portable software packages available, yet containing a really primitive bug. The problem lies in the configuration mechanism: automated configuration can save a lot of time in normal circumstances, but it can also cause lots of pain if it makes incorrect assumptions. In this case, the environment was unusual: the kernel platform was SCO UNIX, which has an old-fashioned library, but the library was GNU *libc*. This caused the assumptions of the configuration mechanism to break down.

Let's look more carefully at the part of *Xfuncs.h* where we found the definitions:

```
/* the new Xfuncs.h */

#if !defined(X_NOT_STDC_ENV) && (!defined(sun) || defined(SVR4))
/* the ANSI C way */
#ifndef _XFUNCS_H_INCLUDED_STRING_H
#include <string.h>
#endif
#undef bzero
#define bzero(b,len) memset(b,0,len)
#else /* else X_NOT_STDC_ENV or SunOS 4 */
#if defined(SYSV) || defined(luna) || defined(sun) || defined(__sxg__)
#include <memory.h>
#define memmove(dst,src,len) bcopy((char *)(src),(char *)(dst),(int)(len))
#if defined(SYSV) && defined(_XBCOPYFUNC)
#undef memmove
#define memmove(dst,src,len) _XBCOPYFUNC((char *)(src),(char *)(dst),(int)(len))
#define _XNEEDBCOPYFUNC
#endif
#else /* else vanilla BSD */
#define memmove(dst,src,len) bcopy((char *)(src),(char *)(dst),(int)(len))
#define memcpy(dst,src,len) bcopy((char *)(src),(char *)(dst),(int)(len))
#define memcmp(b1,b2,len) bcmp((char *)(b1),(char *)(b2),(int)(len))
#endif /* SYSV else */
#endif /* ! X_NOT_STDC_ENV else */
```

This is hairy (and incorrect) stuff. *Xfuncs.h* makes its decisions based on the variables `X_NOT_STDC_ENV`, `sun`, `SVR4`, `SYSV`, `luna`, `__sxg__`, and `_XBCOPYFUNC`. These are the decisions:

- If the variable is *not* defined, it assumes ANSI C, unless this is a pre-SVR4 Sun machine.
- Otherwise, it checks the variables `SYSV` (for System V.3), `luna`, `sun`, or `__sxg__`. If any of these are set, it includes the file *memory.h* and defines `memmove` in terms of `bcopy`. If `_XBCOPYFUNC` is defined, it redefines `memmove` as `_XBCOPYFUNC`, reversing the parameters as it goes.
- If none of these conditions apply, it assumes a vanilla BSD machine and defines the functions `memmove`, `memcpy`, and `memcmp` in terms of the BSD functions `bcopy` and `bcmp`.

There are two errors here:

- The only way that `_XBCOPYFUNC` is ever defined is as `_XtMemmove`, which does *not* have the same parameter sequence as `bcopy`. Instead, it has the same parameter sequence as `memmove`. We can fix this part of the header by changing the definition line to:

```
#define memmove(dst,src,len) _XBCOPYFUNC((char *)(dst),(char *)(src),(int)(len))
```

We could even change it to:

```
#define memmove _XBCOPYFUNC
```

- There is no reason to assume that this system does not use ANSI C. It's using *gcc* and GNU *libc.a*, both of them very much standard compliant. We need to examine this point in more detail.

Going back to our *junk.c*, we search for `X_NOT_STDC_ENV` and find it defined at line 85 of */X/X11/X11R6/xc/X11/Xosdefs.h*:

```
#ifdef SYSV386
#ifdef SYSV
#define X_NOT_POSIX
#define X_NOT_STDC_ENV
#endif
#endif
```

In other words, this bug is likely to occur only with System V.3 implementations on Intel architecture. This is a fairly typical way to make decisions about the system, but it is wrong: `X_NOT_STDC_ENV` relates to a compiler, not an operating system, but both `SYSV386` and `SYSV` define operating system characteristics. At first sight it would seem logical to modify the definitions like this:

```
#ifdef SYSV386
#ifdef SYSV
#ifndef __GNU_LIBRARY__
#define X_NOT_POSIX
#endif
#ifndef __GNUC__
#define X_NOT_STDC_ENV
#endif
#endif
#endif
```

This would define the variables only if the library is not GNU *libc* or the compiler is not *gcc*. This is still not correct: the relationship between `__GNUC__` and `X_NOT_STDC_ENV` or `__GNU_LIBRARY__` and `X_NOT_POSIX` is not related to System V or the Intel architecture. Instead, it makes more sense to backtrack at the end of the file:

```
#ifdef __GNU_LIBRARY__
#undef X_NOT_POSIX
#endif
#ifdef __GNUC__
#undef X_NOT_STDC_ENV
#endif
```

Whichever way we look at it, this is a mess. We're applying cosmetic patches to a configuration mechanism based in incorrect assumptions. Until some better configuration mechanism comes along, unfortunately, we're stuck with this situation.

Limitations of Debuggers

Debuggers are useful tools, but they have their limitations. This section describes a couple that could cause you problems.

Can't breakpoint beyond fork

UNIX packages frequently start multiple processes to do the work on hand. Frequently enough, the program that you start does nothing more than spawn a number of other processes and wait for them to stop. Unfortunately, the *ptrace* interface that debuggers use requires the process to be started by the debugger. Even in SunOS 4, in which you can attach the debugger to a process that is already running, there is no way to monitor it from the start. Other systems don't offer even this facility. In some cases you can determine how the process was started and start it with the debugger in the same manner. This is not always possible—for example, many child processes communicate with their parent.

Terminal logs out

The debugger usually shares a terminal with the program being tested. If the program changes the driver configuration, the debugger should change it back again when it gains control (for example, on hitting a breakpoint), and set it back to the way the program set it before continuing. In some cases, however, it can't: if the process has taken ownership of the terminal with a system call like *setsid* (see the section called "setsid" in Chapter 12), it will no longer have access to the terminal. Under these circumstances, most debuggers crawl into a corner and die. Then the shell in control of the terminal awakes and dies too. If you're running in *xterm*, the *xterm* then stops; if you're running on a glass tty, you are logged out.

The best way out of this dilemma is to start the child process on a different terminal, if your debugger and your hardware configuration support it. To do this with *xterm* requires starting a program that just sleeps, so that the window stays open until you can start your test program:

```
$ xterm -e sleep 100000&
[1] 27013
$ ps aux|grep sleep
grog  27025  3.0  0.0   264  132 p6  S+  1:13PM  0:00.03 grep sleep
root  27013  0.0  0.0  1144  740 p6  I   1:12PM  0:00.37 xterm -e sleep 100000
grog  27014  0.0  0.0   100   36 p8  Is+ 1:12PM  0:00.06 sleep 100000
$ gdb myprog
(gdb) r < /dev/ttyp8 > /dev/ttyp8
```

This example was created on a BSD machine. On a System V machine you need to use *ps -ef* instead of *ps aux*. First, you start *xterm* with *sleep* in the controlling shell (so that it stays there). With *ps* you *grep* for the controlling terminal of the *sleep* process (the third line in the example), and then you start your program with *stdin* and *stdout* redirected to this terminal.

Can't interrupt process

The *ptrace* interface uses the signal `SIGTRAP` to communicate with the process being debugged. What happens if you block this signal or ignore it? Nothing—the debugger doesn't work any more. It's bad practice to block `SIGTRAP`, of course, but it can be done. More frequently, though, you'll encounter this problem when a process gets stuck in a signal processing loop and doesn't get around to processing the `SIGTRAP`—precisely one of the times when you would want to interrupt it. My favorite is the program that had a `SIGSEGV` handler that went and retried the instruction. Unfortunately, the only signal to which a process in this state still responds is `SIGKILL`, which doesn't help you much in finding out what's going on.

Tracing System Calls

An alternative approach is to divide the program between system code and user code. Most systems have the ability to trace the parameters supplied to each system call and the results that they return. This approach is not nearly as good as using a debugger, but it works with all object files, even if they don't have symbols. It can be very useful when you're trying to figure out why a program doesn't open a specific file.

Tracing is a very system-dependent function, and a number of different programs can do it: *truss* runs on System V.4, *ktrace* runs on BSD NET/2 and 4.4BSD derived systems, and *trace* runs on SunOS 4. They vary significantly in their features. We'll look briefly at each. Other systems supply still other programs. For example, SGI's IRIX operating system supplies the program *par*, which offers similar functionality.

trace

trace is a relatively primitive tool supplied with SunOS 4 systems. It can either start a process or attach to an existing process, and it can print summary information or a detailed trace. In particular, it *cannot* trace the child of a `fork` call, which is a great disadvantage. Here's an example of *trace* output with a possibly recognizable program:

```
$ trace hello
open ("/usr/lib/ld.so", 0, 040250) = 3
read (3, "".., 32) = 32
mmap (0, 40960, 0x5, 0x80000002, 3, 0) = 0xf77e0000
```

```
mmap (0xf77e8000, 8192, 0x7, 0x80000012, 3, 32768) = 0xf77e8000
open ("/dev/zero", 0, 07) = 4
getrlimit (3, 0xf7fff488) = 0
mmap (0xf7800000, 8192, 0x3, 0x80000012, 4, 0) = 0xf7800000
close (3) = 0
getuid () = 1004
getgid () = 1000
open ("/etc/ld.so.cache", 0, 05000100021) = 3
fstat (3, 0xf7fff328) = 0
mmap (0, 4096, 0x1, 0x80000001, 3, 0) = 0xf77c0000
close (3) = 0
open ("/opt/lib/gcc-lib/sparc-sun-sunos".., 0, 01010525) = 3
fstat (3, 0xf7fff328) = 0
getdents (3, 0xf7800108, 4096) = 212
getdents (3, 0xf7800108, 4096) = 0
close (3) = 0
open ("/opt/lib", 0, 056) = 3
getdents (3, 0xf7800108, 4096) = 264
getdents (3, 0xf7800108, 4096) = 0
close (3) = 0
open ("/usr/lib/libc.so.1.9", 0, 023170) = 3
read (3, "".., 32) = 32
mmap (0, 458764, 0x5, 0x80000002, 3, 0) = 0xf7730000
mmap (0xf779c000, 16384, 0x7, 0x80000012, 3, 442368) = 0xf779c000
close (3) = 0
open ("/usr/lib/libdl.so.1.0", 0, 023210) = 3
read (3, "".., 32) = 32
mmap (0, 16396, 0x5, 0x80000002, 3, 0) = 0xf7710000
mmap (0xf7712000, 8192, 0x7, 0x80000012, 3, 8192) = 0xf7712000
close (3) = 0
close (4) = 0
getpagesize () = 4096
brk (0x60d8) = 0
brk (0x70d8) = 0
ioctl (1, 0x40125401, 0xf7ffea8c) = 0
write (1, "Hello, World!\n", 14) = Hello, World!
14
close (0) = 0
close (1) = 0
close (2) = 0
exit (1) = ?
```

What's all this output? All we did was a simple write, but we have performed a total of 43 system calls. This example shows in some detail how much the viewpoint of the world differs when you're on the other side of the system library. This program, which was run on a SparcStation 2 with SunOS 4.1.3, first sets up the shared libraries (the sequences of `open`, `read`, `mmap`, and `close`), then initializes the `stdio` library (the calls to `getpagesize`, `brk`, `ioctl`, and `fstat`), and finally writes to *stdout* and exits. It also looks strange that it closed *stdin* before writing the output text. Again, this is a matter of perspective. The `stdio` routines buffer the text, and it didn't actually get written until the process exited, just before closing *stdout*.

ktrace

ktrace is supplied with newer BSD systems. Unlike the other trace programs, it writes unformatted data to a log file (by default, *ktrace.out*), and you need to run another program, *kdump*, to display the log file. It has the following options:

- It can trace the descendents of the process it is tracing. This is particularly useful when the bug occurs in large complexes of processes, and you don't even know which process is causing the problem.
- It can attach to processes that are already running. Optionally, it can also attach to existing children of the processes to which it attaches.
- It can specify broad subsets of system calls to trace: system calls, `namei` translations (translation of a filename to inode number), I/O, and signal processing.

Here's an example of *ktrace* running against the same program:

```
$ ktrace hello
Hello, World!
$ kdump
 20748 ktrace   RET   ktrace 0
 20748 ktrace   CALL  getpagesize
 20748 ktrace   RET   getpagesize 4096/0x1000
 20748 ktrace   CALL  break(0xadfc)
 20748 ktrace   RET   break 0
 20748 ktrace   CALL  break(0xaffc)
 20748 ktrace   RET   break 0
 20748 ktrace   CALL  break(0xbffc)
 20748 ktrace   RET   break 0
 20748 ktrace   CALL  execve(0xefbfd148,0xefbfd5a8,0xefbfd5b0)
 20748 ktrace   NAMI  "./hello"
 20748 hello    RET   execve 0
 20748 hello    CALL  fstat(0x1,0xefbfd2a4)
 20748 hello    RET   fstat 0
 20748 hello    CALL  getpagesize
 20748 hello    RET   getpagesize 4096/0x1000
 20748 hello    CALL  break(0x7de4)
 20748 hello    RET   break 0
 20748 hello    CALL  break(0x7ffc)
 20748 hello    RET   break 0
 20748 hello    CALL  break(0xaffc)
 20748 hello    RET   break 0
 20748 hello    CALL  ioctl(0x1,TIOCGETA,0xefbfd2e0)
 20748 hello    RET   ioctl 0
 20748 hello    CALL  write(0x1,0x8000,0xe)
 20748 hello    GIO   fd 1 wrote 14 bytes
       "Hello, World!
       "
 20748 hello    RET   write 14/0xe
 20748 hello    CALL  exit(0xe)
```

This display contains the following information in columnar format:

1. The process ID of the process.
2. The name of the program from which the process was started. We can see that the name changes after the call to `execve`.
3. The kind of event. `CALL` is a system call, `RET` is a return value from a system call, `NAMI` is a system internal call to the function `namei`, which determines the inode number for a pathname, and `GIO` is a system internal I/O call.
4. The parameters to the call.

In this trace, run on an Intel 486 with BSD/OS 1.1, we can see a significant difference from the trace run on SunOS: there are no shared libraries. Even though each system call produces two lines of output (the call and the return value), the output is much shorter.

truss

truss, the System V.4 trace facility, offers the most features:

- It can print statistical information instead of a trace.
- It can display the argument and environment strings passed to each call to `exec`.
- It can trace the descendants of the process it is tracing.
- Like *ktrace*, it can attach to processes that are already running and optionally attach to existing children of the processes to which it attaches.
- It can trace specific system calls, signals, and interrupts (called *faults* in System V terminology). This is a very useful feature: as we saw in the *ktrace* example previously, the C library may issue a surprising number of system calls.

Here's an example of *truss* output:

```
$ truss -f hello
511:    execve("./hello", 0x08047834, 0x0804783C)  argc = 1
511:    getuid()                                  = 1004  [ 1004 ]
511:    getuid()                                  = 1004  [ 1004 ]
511:    getgid()                                  = 1000  [ 1000 ]
511:    getgid()                                  = 1000  [ 1000 ]
511:    sysi86(SI86FPHW, 0x80036058, 0x80035424, 0x8000E255) = 0x00000000
511:    ioctl(1, TCGETA, 0x08046262)              = 0
Hello, World!
511:    write(1, " H e l l o ,   W o r l d".., 14)      = 14
511:    _exit(14)
```

truss offers a lot of choice in the amount of detail it can display. For example, you can select a verbose parameter display of individual system calls. If we're interested in the parameters to the `ioctl` call, we can enter:

```
$ truss -f -v ioctl hello
...
516:   ioctl(1, TCGETA, 0x08046262)                        = 0
516:           iflag=0004402 oflag=0000005 cflag=0002675 lflag=0000073 line=0
516:               cc: 177 003 010 030 004 000 000 000
```

In this case, *truss* shows the contents of the `termio` structure associated with the `TCGETA` request. See Chapter 15, *Terminal Drivers*, for the interpretation of this information.

Tracing Through fork

We've seen that *ktrace* and *truss* can both trace the child of a `fork` system call. This is invaluable: as we saw in the *trace* example earlier, debuggers can't do this.

Unfortunately, SunOS *trace* doesn't support tracing through *fork*. *truss* does it better than *ktrace*. In extreme cases (like debugging a program of this nature on SunOS 4, which doesn't support *trace* through `fork`), you might find it an advantage to port to a different machine running an operating system such as Solaris 2 in order to be able to test with *truss*. Of course, Murphy's law says that the bug won't show up under Solaris 2.

Tracing Network Traffic

Another place where we can trace is at the network interface. Many processes communicate across the network, and if we have tools to look at this communication, they may help us isolate the part of the package that is causing the problem.

Two programs trace message flow across a network:

- On BSD systems, *tcpdump* and the *Berkeley Packet Filter* provide a flexible means of tracing traffic across Internet domain sockets. See Appendix E for availability.
- *trpt* prints a trace from a socket marked for debugging. This function is available on System V.4 as well. It is not clear, however, what use it is under these circumstances, since System V.4 emulates sockets in a library module. On BSD systems, it comes in a poor second to *tcpdump*.

Tracing net traffic is an unusual approach, and we won't consider it here. In certain circumstances, it is an invaluable tool. You can find all you need to know about *tcpdump* in *TCP/IP Illustrated*, vol. 1, by Richard Stevens.

In This Chapter:

- *make install*
- *Installing the Correct Files*
- *install*
- *Installing Documentation*
- *Removing Installed Software*
- *Keeping Track of Installed Software*

9

Installation

Finally you have built and tested the package, and it works. Up to this point, everything in the package has been in the private source tree where it was built. Most packages are not intended to be executed from the source directory: before we can use them, we need to move the component parts to their intended directories. In particular:

- We need to put executables where a normal PATH environment variable can find them.
- We need to place online documentation in the correct directories in a form that the document browser understands.
- The installed software needs to be given the correct permissions to do what it has to do: all executables need to have their execute permissions set, and some programs may need *setuid* or *setgid* bits set (see the section called "Real and Effective User IDs" in Chapter 12, *Kernel Dependencies*). In addition, software is frequently installed in directories to which regular users have no access. In these cases, the install must be done by *root.*
- Library routines and configuration files need to be installed where the package expects them: the location could be compiled into the programs, or an environment variable could point to the location.
- If the package uses environment variables, you may also need to update *.profile* and *.cshrc* files to add or modify environment variables.
- Many packages—for example, news transfer programs—create data in specific directories. Although initially there may be no data to install, the install process may need to create the directories.

- At some future date, you may want to remove the package again or to install an updated version. The installation routines should make some provision for removing the package when you no longer want it.

Real-life packages differ significantly in their abilities to perform these tasks. Some *Makefiles* consider that their job is done when the package has been compiled and leave it to you to install the files manually. In some cases, as when there is only a single program, this is no hardship, but it does require that you understand exactly what you need to install. On the other hand, very few packages supply an `uninstall` target.

In this chapter, we'll look at the following subjects:

- The way *Makefiles* typically install software.
- Alternatives if the *Makefile* doesn't do everything it should do.
- How to install documentation.
- How to keep track of installed software.
- How to remove installed software.

Installation is an untidy process. At the end of this chapter, you'll probably be left with a feeling of dissatisfaction—this area has been sadly neglected, and there just aren't enough good answers.

make install

The traditional way to install a precompiled package is with *make install*. Typically, *make install* performs the following functions:

- Creates the necessary directories if they don't exist.
- Copies all necessary files to their run-time locations.
- Sets the permissions of the files to their correct values. This frequently requires you to be *root* when you install the package. If you don't have root access, you should at least arrange for access to the directories into which you want to install.
- May strip debug information from executables.

Some other aspects of *make install* are less unified:

- *make install* may imply a *make all*: you can't install until you have made the package, and you'll frequently see an install target that starts with

```
install: all
        installation commands
```

- On the other hand, *make install* may not only expect the *make all* to be completed—and fail if it is not—but remove the executables after installation. Sometimes this is due to the use of BSD *install* without the *-c* option—see the section on the *install* program later in this chapter—but it means that if you want to make a change to the program after installation, you effectively have to repeat the whole build. Removing files from the tree should be left to *make clean*. (See the section called "make clean" in Chapter 5, *Building the Package*.)
- Some install targets install man pages or other online documentation, others leave it to a separate target with a name like `install-man`, and yet other *Makefiles* completely ignore online documentation, even if the package supplies it.

Configuring the Installed Package

Some packages have run-time configuration files that need to be set up before the package can run. Also, it's not always enough just to install the files in the correct place and with the correct permissions: you may need to modify the individual user's environment before she can use the package. Here are some examples:

- *sendmail*, the Internet mail transport agent, has an extremely complicated configuration file *sendmail.cf*, which needs to be set up to reflect your network topology. A description of how to set up this file takes up hundreds of pages in *sendmail*, by Bryan Costales, Eric Allman, and Neil Rickert.
- Many X11 clients have supplementary files that define *application defaults*, which may or may not be suitable for your environment. They are intended to be installed in a directory like */usr/X11/lib/X11/app-defaults*. Not all *Imakefiles* perform this task.
- The path where the executables are installed should be in your `PATH` environment variable.
- If you install man pages, the path should be in your `MANPATH` environment variable.
- Many packages define their own environment variables. For example, TEX defines the environment variables `TEXCONFIG`, `TEXFONTS`, `TEXFORMATS`, `TEXINPUTS`, and `TEXPOOL` to locate its data files.
- Some programs require a setup file in the home directory of each user who uses the program. Others do not require it but read it if it is present.
- Some programs create links with other names. For example, if you install *pax*, the portable archive exchange program, you have the opportunity of creating links called *tar* and *cpio*. This is really a configuration option, but the *Makefile* for *pax* does not account for it.

Typical *Makefiles* are content with moving the files to where they belong and leave such details to the user. We'll see an alternative in the section called "System V pkgadd".

Installing the Correct Files

At first, installation seems straightforward enough: you copy the files to where they belong, and that's that. In practice, a number of subtle problems can occur. There's no hard and fast solutions to them, but if you run into trouble it helps to understand the problem.

To Replace or Not to Replace?

Throughout the build process, we have used *make* to decide whether to rebuild a target or not: if the target exists and is newer than any of its dependencies, it is not rebuilt. Traditionally, installation is different. The files are installed anyway, even if newer files are already present in the destination directory.

The reasons for this behavior are shrouded in time but may be related to the fact that both *install* (which we will discuss later in this chapter) and *cp* traditionally modify the timestamps of the files, so that the following scenario could occur:

1. Build version 1 of a package, and install it.
2. Start building version 2, but don't complete it.
3. Make a modification to version 1, and re-install it.
4. Complete version 2, and install it. Some of the files in version 2 were compiled before version 1 was re-installed and are thus older than the installed files. As a result, they are not installed, and the installed software is inconsistent.

It's obviously safer to replace everything. But is that enough? We'll look at the opposite problem in the next section.

Updating

Frequently you install several versions of software over a period of time, as the package evolves. Simply installing the new version on top of the old version works cleanly only if you can be sure that you install a new version of every file that was present in the old version; otherwise, some files from the old version remain after installation. For example, version 1.07.6 of the GNU *libc* included a file *include/sys/bitypes.h*, which is no longer present in version 1.08.6. After installing version 1.08.6, *include/sys/bitypes.h* is still present from the earlier installation.

The correct way to handle this problem is to *uninstall* the old package before installation. For reasons we will investigate in the section called "Removing Installed Software", too many people omit this step.

install

install is a program that is used in installing software. It performs the tasks of creating any necessary directories, copying files, stripping executables, and setting permissions.

install originated in Berkeley, and older System V systems don't support it. It's a fairly trivial program, of course, and many packages supply a script with a name like *install.sh* that performs substantially the same functions. The source is available in the 4.4BSD Lite distribution—see Appendix E.

Although *install* is a relatively simple program, it seems that implementors have done their best to make it differ from one system to the next. The result is a whole lot of incompatible and just downright confusing options. System V.4 even supplies two different versions with conflicting options, a BSD compatible one and a native one—the one you get depends on your PATH environment variable.

System V.4 native *install* is sufficiently different from the others that we need to look at it separately—it can install only a single file. The syntax is:

```
install options file [dir dir ...]
```

If the *dirs* are specified, they are appended to the fixed list of directories */bin*, */usr/bin*, */etc*, */lib*, and */usr/lib*. *install* searches the resultant list of directories sequentially for a file with the name *file*. If it finds one, it replaces it and prints a message stating in which directory it has installed the file. The *-i* option tells *install* to omit the standard directories and take only the list specified on the command line.

Other versions of *install* have a syntax similar to *mv* and *cp*, except that they take a number of supplementary options:

```
install options file1 file2
install options file1 ...  fileN dir
```

The first form installs *file1* as *file2*, the second form installs *file1* through *fileN* in the directory *dir*.

Table 9-1 contains an overview of *install* options.

Table 9-1: install Options

Option	Purpose
`-c`	In BSD, copy the file. If this option is not specified, the file is moved (the original file is deleted after copying). In GNU and System V.4 (BSD compatibility), this option is ignored. Files are always copied.
`-c` *dir*	System V.4 native: install the file in directory *dir* only if the file does not already exist. If the file exists already, exit with an error message.
`-d`	In GNU and SunOS, create all necessary directories if the target directory does not exist. Not available in BSD. This option lets you create the directory with the command: `install -d [-g group] [-m perm] [-o owner] dir`
`-f` *flags*	In 4.4BSD, specify the target's file flags. This relates to the *chflags* program introduced with 4.4BSD—see the man page *usr.bin/chflags/chflags.1* in the 4.4BSD Lite distribution.
`-f` *dir*	System V.4 native: force the file to be installed in *dir*. This is the default for other versions.
`-g` *group*	Set the group ownership to *group*.
`-i`	System V.4 native: ignore the default directory list (see below). This is not applicable with the `-c` or `-f` options.
`-m` *perm*	Set the file permissions to perm. perm may be in octal or symbolic form, as defined for chmod(1). By default, perm is 0755 (rwxr-xr-x).
`-n` *dir*	System V.4 native: if *file* is not found in any of the directories, install it in dir.
`-o`	System V.4 native: if file is already present at the destination, rename the old version by prepending the letters *OLD* to the filename. The old file remains in the same directory.
`-o` *owner*	All except System V.4 native: change the owner to *owner*.
`-s`	System V.4 native: suppress error messages.
`-s`	All except System V.4 native: strip the final binary.
`-u` *owner*	System V.4 native: change the owner to owner.

Other points to note are:

- *install* attempts to prevent you from moving a file onto itself.
- Installing */dev/null* creates an empty file.
- *install* exits with a return code of 0 if successful and 1 if unsuccessful.

System V.4 install is definitely the odd man out: if you can avoid it, do. Even Solaris 2 supplies only the BSD version of *install*. On the other hand, pure BSD *install* also has its problems, since it requires the *-c* option to avoid removing the original files.

Installing Documentation

Installing man pages would seem to be a trivial exercise, but in fact, a number of problems can occur. In this section, we'll look at problems you might encounter installing man pages and GNU *info*.

man Pages

As we saw in the section called "Man Pages" in Chapter 7, *Documentation*, there is not much agreement about naming or placing or the format of man pages. In order to install man pages correctly you need to know the following:

- The name of the man directory.
- The naming convention for man files. As we saw, the naming conventions are many and varied.
- Whether the man pages should be formatted or not.
- If the man pages should be formatted, which formatter should be used? Which macros should be used? This may seem like a decision to be made when building the package, but many *Makefiles* delay this operation to the install phase.
- Whether the man pages should be packed, compressed, or zipped.

Typically, this information is supplied in the *Makefile*, as in this example from the electronic mail reader *elm*, which is one of the better ones:

```
FORMATTER       =       /usr/ucb/nroff
MAN             =       /opt/man/man1
MANEXT          =       .1
CATMAN          =       /opt/man/cat1
CATMANEXT       =       .1
TBL             =       /usr/ucb/tbl
MANROFF         =       /usr/ucb/nroff
SUFFIX          =       .Z
PACKED          =       y
PACKER          =       /bin/compress

# List of installed man pages (except for wnemail.1 - handled differently)
MAN_LIST        =       $(MAN)/answer$(MANEXT)                  \
                        $(MAN)/autoreply$(MANEXT)               \
...etc
# List of installed catman pages (except for wnemail.1 - handled differently)
CATMAN_LIST     =       $(CATMAN)/answer$(CATMANEXT)$(SUFFIX)      \
                        $(CATMAN)/autoreply$(CATMANEXT)$(SUFFIX)    \
...etc

# List of formatted pages for catman
FORMATTED_PAGES_LIST =  catman/answer$(CATMANEXT)$(SUFFIX)         \
                        catman/autoreply$(CATMANEXT)$(SUFFIX)     \
```

```
...etc

# Targets
all:
        @if $(TEST) '$(CATMAN)' != none; then $(MAKE) formatted_pages ; \
          else true ; fi

formatted_pages: catman $(FORMATTED_PAGES_LIST)

catman:
        mkdir catman

install: $(LIB_LIST)
        @if $(TEST) '$(MAN)' != none; then $(MAKE) install_man ; \
           else true ;  fi
        @if $(TEST) '$(CATMAN)' != none; then $(MAKE) install_catman ; \
           else true ;  fi

install_man: $(MAN_LIST) $(MAN)/wnewmail$(MANEXT)

install_catman: $(CATMAN_LIST) $(CATMAN)/wnewmail$(CATMANEXT)$(SUFFIX)

#       Dependencies and rules for installing man pages and lib files
$(MAN)/answer$(MANEXT): answer.1
                                  $(CP) $? $@
                                  $(CHMOD) u=rw,go=r $@

$(MAN)/autoreply$(MANEXT):       autoreply.1
                                  $(CP) $? $@
                                  $(CHMOD) u=rw,go=r $@
```

This *Makefile* is in the subdirectory *doc*, which is concerned only with documentation, so all the targets relate to the man pages. The target `all` makes the decision whether to format the pages based on the value of the make variable `CATMAN`. If `CATMAN` is set to the special value `none`, the *Makefile* does not format the pages.

The target `install` uses the same technique to decide which man pages to install: if the variable `MAN` is not set to `none`, the sources of the man pages are copied there, and if `CATMAN` is not set to `none`, the formatted pages are installed there. This *Makefile* does not use *install*: it performs the operations with *cp* and *chmod* instead.

GNU info

Installing GNU *info* is somewhat more straightforward, but it is also not as clean as it could be:

- *info* is always formatted, so you need the formatter, a program called *makeinfo*, which is part of the *texinfo* package. Before you can run *makeinfo*, you need to port *texinfo*. It's not that big a job, but it needs to be done. Of course, in order to completely install *texinfo*, you need to format the documentation with *makeinfo*—a vicious circle. The solution is to port the *texinfo* executables, then port *makeinfo*, and then format the *texinfo* documentation.

- All *info* files are stored in a single directory with an index file called *dir*. This looks like:

```
-*- Text -*-
This is the file /opt/info/dir, which contains the topmost node of the
Info hierarchy. The first time you invoke Info you start off
looking at that node, which is (dir)Top.

File: dir       Node: Top       This is the top of the INFO tree
  This (the Directory node) gives a menu of major topics.
  Typing "d" returns here, "q" exits, "?" lists all INFO commands, "h"
  gives a primer for first-timers, "mTexinfo<Return>" visits Texinfo topic,
  etc.

  Note that the presence of a name in this list does not necessarily
  mean that the documentation is available. It is installed with the
  package in question. If you get error messages when trying to access
  documentation, make sure that the package has been installed.
  --- PLEASE ADD DOCUMENTATION TO THIS TREE. (See INFO topic first.) ---

* Menu: The list of major topics begins on the next line.

* Bash: (bash).          The GNU Bourne Again SHell.
* Bfd: (bfd).            The Binary File Descriptor Library.
* Bison: (bison).        The Bison parser generator.
* CL: (cl).              Partial Common Lisp support for Emacs Lisp.
...etc
```

The lines at the bottom of the example are menu entries for each package. They have a syntax that isn't immediately apparent—in particular, the sequence `* item:` has a special significance in Emacs *info* mode. Programs that supply *info* documentation *should* supply such an entry, but many of them do not, and none of them install the line in *dir*—you need to do this by hand.

Removing Installed Software

For a number of reasons, you may want to remove software that you have already installed:

- You may decide you don't need the software.
- You may want to replace it with a newer version, and you want to be sure that the old version is gone.

- You may want to install it in a different tree.

If you look for a `remove` or `uninstall` target in the *Makefile*, chances are that you won't find one. Packages that supply a `remove` target are very rare. If you want to remove software, and you didn't take any precautions when you installed it, you have to do it manually with the computer equivalent of an axe and a spear: *ls* and *rm*.

Removing Software Manually

In fact, it's frequently not *that* difficult to remove software manually. The modification timestamps of all components are usually within a minute or two of each other, so *ls* with the *–lt* options lists them all together. For example, let's consider the removal of *ghostscript*.

The first step is to go back to the *Makefile* and see what it installed:

```
prefix = /opt
exec_prefix = $(prefix)
bindir = $(exec_prefix)/bin
datadir = $(prefix)/lib
gsdatadir = $(datadir)/ghostscript
mandir = $(prefix)/man/man1
...skipping
install: $(GS)
        -mkdir $(bindir)
        for f in $(GS) gsbj gsdj gslj gslp gsnd bdftops font2c \
           ps2ascii ps2epsi; \
        do $(INSTALL_PROGRAM) $$f $(bindir)/$$f ; done
        -mkdir $(datadir)
        -mkdir $(gsdatadir)

        for f in README gslp.ps gs_init.ps gs_dps1.ps gs_fonts.ps gs_lev2.ps \
        gs_statd.ps gs_type0.ps gs_dbt_e.ps gs_sym_e.ps quit.ps Fontmap \
        uglyr.gsf bdftops.ps decrypt.ps font2c.ps impath.ps landscap.ps \
        level1.ps prfont.ps ps2ascii.ps ps2epsi.ps ps2image.ps pstoppm.ps\
        showpage.ps type1ops.ps wrfont.ps ; \
          do $(INSTALL_DATA) $$f $(gsdatadir)/$$f ; done

        -mkdir $(docdir)
        for f in NEWS devices.doc drivers.doc fonts.doc hershey.doc \
        history.doc humor.doc language.doc lib.doc make.doc ps2epsi.doc \
        psfiles.doc readme.doc use.doc xfonts.doc ; \
          do $(INSTALL_DATA) $$f $(docdir)/$$f ; done
        -mkdir $(mandir)
        for f in ansi2knr.1 gs.1 ; do $(INSTALL_DATA) $$f $(mandir)/$$f ; done
        -mkdir $(exdir)
        for f in chess.ps cheq.ps colorcir.ps golfer.ps escher.ps \
        snowflak.ps tiger.ps ; \
          do $(INSTALL_DATA) $$f $(exdir)/$$f ; done
```

One alternative is to make a `remove` target for this *Makefile*, which isn't too difficult:

1. Copy the `install` target and call it `remove`.
2. Move the *mkdir* lines to the bottom, and change them to *rmdir*. You'll notice that this *Makefile* accepts that *mkdir* can fail because the directory already exists (the - in front of *mkdir*). We'll do the same with *rmdir*: if the directory isn't empty, *rmdir* fails, but that's okay.
3. Replace `$(INSTALL_PROGRAM) $$f` and `$(INSTALL_DATA) $$f` with `rm -f`.

The result looks like:

```
remove: $(GS)
        for f in $(GS) gsbj gsdj gslj gslp gsnd bdftops font2c \
           ps2ascii ps2epsi; \
        do rm -f $(bindir)/$$f ; done

        for f in README gslp.ps gs_init.ps gs_dps1.ps gs_fonts.ps gs_lev2.ps \
        gs_statd.ps gs_type0.ps gs_dbt_e.ps gs_sym_e.ps quit.ps Fontmap \
        uglyr.gsf bdftops.ps decrypt.ps font2c.ps impath.ps landscap.ps \
        level1.ps prfont.ps ps2ascii.ps ps2epsi.ps ps2image.ps pstoppm.ps\
        showpage.ps type1ops.ps wrfont.ps ; \
          do rm -f $(gsdatadir)/$$f ; done

        for f in NEWS devices.doc drivers.doc fonts.doc hershey.doc \
        history.doc humor.doc language.doc lib.doc make.doc ps2epsi.doc \
        psfiles.doc readme.doc use.doc xfonts.doc ; \
          do rm -f $(docdir)/$$f ; done
        for f in ansi2knr.1 gs.1 ; do $(INSTALL_DATA) $$f $(mandir)/$$f ; done
        for f in chess.ps cheq.ps colorcir.ps golfer.ps escher.ps \
        snowflak.ps tiger.ps ;
          do rm -f $(exdir)/$$f ; done
        -rmdir $(bindir)
        -rmdir $(datadir)
        -rmdir $(gsdatadir)
        -rmdir $(docdir)
        -rmdir $(mandir)
        -rmdir $(exdir)
```

More frequently, however, you can't use this approach: the *Makefile* isn't as easy to find, or you have long since discarded the source tree. In this case, you'll have to do it differently. First, you find the directory where the executable *gs*, the main *ghostscript* program, is stored:

```
$ which gs
/opt/bin/gs
```

Then look at the last modification timestamp of */opt/bin/gs*:

```
$ ls -l /opt/bin/gs
-rwxrwxr-x   1 root     wheel     3168884 Jun 18 14:29 /opt/bin/gs
```

This timestamp helps you know where to look in the next step: you list the directory */opt/bin* sorted by modification timestamp. It's a lot easier to find what you're looking for if you know the date. If you don't have *which*, or possibly even if you do, you can use the following script, called *wh*:

```
for j in $*; do
  for i in `echo $PATH|sed 's/:/ /g'`; do
    if [ -f $i/$j ]; then
      ls -l $i/$j
    fi
  done
done
```

wh searches the directories in the current environment variable PATH for a specific file and lists all occurrences in the order in which they appear in PATH in *ls -l* format, so you could also have entered:

```
$ wh gs
-rwxrwxr-x   1 root     wheel     3168884 Jun 18 14:29 /opt/bin/gs
```

Once you know the date you're looking for, it's easy to list the directory, page it through *more*, and find the time frame you're looking for.

```
$ ls -lt /opt/bin|more
total 51068
-rw-------   1 root     bin        294912 Sep  6 15:08 trn.old
-rwxr-xr-x   1 grog     lemis      106496 Sep  6 15:08 man
...skipping lots of stuff
-rw-rw-rw-   1 grog     bin           370 Jun 21 17:24 prab~
-rw-rw-rw-   1 grog     bin           370 Jun 21 17:22 parb
-rw-rw-rw-   1 grog     bin           196 Jun 21 17:22 parb~
-rwxrwxrwx   1 grog     wheel         469 Jun 18 15:19 tep
-rwxrwxr-x   1 root     wheel          52 Jun 18 14:29 font2c
-rwxrwxr-x   1 root     wheel         807 Jun 18 14:29 ps2epsi
-rwxrwxr-x   1 root     wheel          35 Jun 18 14:29 bdftops
-rwxrwxr-x   1 root     wheel         563 Jun 18 14:29 ps2ascii
-rwxrwxr-x   1 root     wheel          50 Jun 18 14:29 gslp
-rwxrwxr-x   1 root     wheel     3168884 Jun 18 14:29 gs
-rwxrwxr-x   1 root     wheel          53 Jun 18 14:29 gsdj
-rwxrwxr-x   1 root     wheel          51 Jun 18 14:29 gsbj
-rwxrwxr-x   1 root     wheel          18 Jun 18 14:29 gsnd
-rwxrwxr-x   1 root     wheel          54 Jun 18 14:29 gslj
-rwxr-xr-x   1 root     bin         81165 Jun 18 12:41 faxaddmodem
-r-xr-xr-x   1 bin      bin        249856 Jun 17 17:18 faxinfo
-r-xr-xr-x   1 bin      bin        106496 Jun 17 15:50 dialtest
...more stuff follows
```

It's easy to recognize the programs in this format: they were all installed in the same minute, and the next older file (*faxaddmodem*) is more than 90 minutes older, the next newer file (*tep*) is 50 minutes newer. The files you want to remove are, in sequence, *font2c, ps2epsi, bdftops, ps2ascii, gslp, gs, gsdj, gsbj, gsnd*, and *gslj*.

We're not done yet, of course. *ghostscript* also installs a lot of fonts and PostScript files, as we saw in the *Makefile*. How do we find and remove them? It helps, of course, to have the *Makefile*, from which we can see that the files are installed in the directories */opt/bin*, */opt/lib/ghostscript* and */opt/man/man1* (see the *Makefile* excerpt in the section called "Removing Software Manually"). If you don't have the *Makefile*, all is not lost, but process gets a little more complicated. You can search the complete directory tree for files modified between Jun 18 14:00 and Jun 18 14:59 with:

```
$ find /opt -follow -type f -print|xargs ls -l|grep "Jun 18 14:"

-rwxrwxr-x  1 root  wheel     35 Jun 18 14:29 /opt/bin/bdftops
...etc
-rw-rw-r--  1 root  wheel    910 Jun 18 14:29 /opt/man/man1/ansi2knr.1
-rw-rw-r--  1 root  wheel  10005 Jun 18 14:29 /opt/man/man1/gs.1
-rw-rw-r--  1 root  wheel  11272 Jun 18 14:29 /opt/lib/ghostscript/Fontmap
-rw-rw-r--  1 root  wheel  22789 Jun 18 14:29 /opt/lib/ghostscript/bdftops.ps
-rw-rw-r--  1 root  wheel    295 Jun 18 14:29 /opt/lib/ghostscript/decrypt.ps
-rw-rw-r--  1 root  wheel  74791 Jun 18 14:29 /opt/lib/ghostscript/doc/NEWS
-rw-rw-r--  1 root  wheel  13974 Jun 18 14:29 /opt/lib/ghostscript/doc/devices.doc
...many more files
```

Note the following points:

- We used GNU *find*, which uses the *–follow* option to follow symbolic links. If your */opt* hierarchy contains symbolic links, *find* would otherwise not search the subdirectories. Other versions of *find* may require different options.
- You can't use *ls -lR* here because *ls -lR* does not show the full pathnames: you would find the files, but the name at the end of the line would just be the name of the file, and you wouldn't know the name of the directory.
- If the file is more than six months old, *ls -l* lists it in the form:

  ```
  -rwxrwxrwx   1 grog     wheel          22 Feb 10  1994 xyzzy
  ```

  This may be enough to differentiate between the files, but it's less certain. GNU *ls* (in the fileutils package) includes an option *--full-time* (note the two leading hyphens). This always prints the full time, regardless of the age of the file. With this option, the file above lists as:

  ```
  $ ls --full-time -l xyzzy
  -rwxrwxrwx   1 grog     wheel          22 Thu Feb 10 16:00:24 1994 xyzzy
  ```

Removing Too Much

None of these methods for removing installed software can handle one remaining serious problem: some programs install a modified version of a standard program, and if you remove the package, you remove all trace of this standard program. For example, GNU *tar* and GNU *cpio* both include the remote tape protocol program *rmt*. If you install both of these packages and then decide to remove *cpio*, *tar* does not work properly either. It's not always enough to keep track of which packages depend on which programs. In some cases, a modified version of a program is installed by a package, and if you remove the package, you need to re-install the old version of the program.

Keeping Track of Installed Software

All the methods we've seen so far smell strongly of kludge:

- They involve significant manual intervention, which is prone to error.
- The *remove* or *uninstall* targets of a *Makefile* are based on names, not contents. If you stop using a package, install a new one with some names that duplicate the names of the old package, and then remove the old package, the files from your new package will go too.
- The manual method based on the dates does not discover configuration or data files—if you remove net news from a system, you have to remember to remove the news spool area as well, because that certainly won't have the same modification timestamp as the installed software.
- It's almost impossible to safely and automatically remove modifications to environment variables in *.cshrc* and *.profile* files.

We can come closer to our goal if we have a method to keep track of the files that were actually installed. This requires the maintenance of some kind of database with information about the relationship between packages and files. Ideally,

- It would contain a list of the files installed, including their sizes and modification timestamps.
- It would prevent modification to the package except by well-defined procedures.
- It would contain a list of the files that were modified, including *diffs* to be able to reverse them.

- It would keep track of the modifications to the package as time went by: which files were created by the package, which files were modified.

This database method is an ideal, but the System V.4 *pkgadd* system comes reasonably close, and the concept is simple enough that we can represent the most important features as shell scripts. We'll look at it in the next section.

System V pkgadd

UNIX System V.4 is supplied as a number of binary *packages*[*] can choose which to install and which not to install. You can even choose whether or not to install such seemingly essential components as networking support and man pages.

Packages can be created in two formats: *stream format* for installation from serial data media like tapes, and *file system* format for installation from file systems. In many cases, such as diskettes, either form may be used. The program *pkgtrans* transforms one format into the other. In the following discussion, we'll assume file system format.

The package tools offer a bewildering number of options, most of which are not very useful. We'll limit our discussion to standard cases: in particular, we won't discuss *classes* and multipart packages. If you are using System V.4 and want to use other features, you should read the documentation supplied with the system. In the following sections we'll look at the individual components of the packages.

pkginfo

The file *pkginfo*, in the root directory of the package, contains general information about the package, some of the information may be used to decide whether or not to install the package. For example, the *pkginfo* file for an installable Emacs package might look like:

```
ARCH=i386                              the architecture for which the package is intended
PKG=emacs                              the name of the package
VERSION=19.22                          the version number
NAME=Emacs text editor                 a brief description
CATEGORY=utilities                     the kind of package
CLASSES=none                           class information
VENDOR=Free Software Foundation        the name of the owner
HOTLINE=LEMIS, +49-6637-919123, Fax +49-6637-919122    who to call if you have trouble
EMAIL=lemis@lemis.de                   mail for HOTLINE
```

This information is displayed by *pkgadd* as information to the user before installation.

---

* As used here, the term *package* is a collection of precompiled programs and data and information necessary to install them. This meaning of *package* isn't the same as the meaning we have been talking about in the rest of this book.

pkgmap

The file *pkgmap* is also in the root directory of the package. It contains information about the destination of the individual files. For example, here's information from the same Emacs package:

```
: 1 37986
1 d none /opt 0755 bin bin
1 d none /opt/README 0755 bin bin
1 f none /opt/README/emacs-19.22 0644 root sys 1518 59165 760094611
1 d none /opt/bin 0755 bin bin
1 f none /opt/bin/emacs 0755 root sys 1452488 11331 760577316
1 f none /opt/bin/etags 0755 root sys 37200 20417 760577318
1 d none /opt/info 0755 bin bin
1 f none /opt/info/cl.info 0644 root sys 3019 62141 760094526
1 f none /opt/info/dir 0644 root sys 2847 23009 760559075
1 f none /opt/info/emacs 0644 root sys 10616 65512 760094528
1 d none /opt/lib 0755 bin bin
1 d none /opt/lib/emacs 0755 bin bin
1 d none /opt/lib/emacs/19.22 0755 bin bin
1 d none /opt/lib/emacs/19.22/etc 0755 bin bin
1 f none /opt/lib/emacs/19.22/etc/3B-MAXMEM 0644 root sys 1913 18744 574746032
```

The first line specifies that the package consists of a single part and that it contains 37,986 512-byte blocks. The other lines describe files or directories:

- The first parameter is the part to which the file belongs.
- The next parameter specifies whether the file is a plain file (`f`), a directory (`d`), a link (`l`) or a symbolic link (`s`). A number of other abbreviations are also used.
- The next parameter is the *class* of the file. Like most packages, this package does not use classes, so the class is always set to `none`.
- The following four parameters specify the name of the installed object, its permissions, the owner, and the group.
- After this come the size of the file, a checksum, and the modification time in naked `time_t` format. The checksum ensures that the package is relatively protected against data corruption or deliberate modification.

Package subdirectories

In addition to the files in the main directory, packages contain two subdirectories *root* and *install*:

- *root* contains the files that are to be installed. All the files described in *pkgmap* are present under the same names in *root*. For example, */opt/bin/emacs* is called *root/opt/bin/emacs* in the package.

- The file *install/copyright* contains a brief copyright notice that is displayed on installation. Since *pkgadd* does not wait for you to read this, the notice should be really brief.
- Optionally, there may be scripts with names like *install/preinstall* and *install/postinstall*, which are executed before and after copying the files, respectively. *preinstall* might, for example, set up the directory structure */opt* if it does not already exist. *postinstall* might update *.cshrc* and *.profile* files. In some cases, it may need to do more. For example, the ISO 9660 directory standard for CD-ROMs limits allows only eight nested directories (in other words, the directory */a/b/c/d/e/f/g/h/i* is nested too deeply). *gcc* on a CD-ROM would violate this limitation, so some of the package has to be stored as a *tar* file, and the *postinstall* script extracts it to the correct position.

pkgadd

With this structure, adding a package is almost child's play. You just have to enter:

```
$ pkgadd emacs
```

Well, almost. The name *emacs* is the name of the package and not a filename. By default, *pkgadd* expects to find it in */var/spool/pkg*. If your package is elsewhere, you can't tell *pkgadd* simply by prepending the name—instead, you need to specify it with the *–d* option:

```
$ pkgadd -d /cdrom emacs
```

This command line installs Emacs from the directory *cdrom*.

Removing packages

One really nice feature of the System V.4 package system is the ease with which you can remove a package. Assuming that you have decided that *vi* is a better choice than Emacs or that you just don't have the 19 MB that the Emacs package takes up, you just have to type:

```
$ pkgrm emacs
```

All the files are then removed.

Making installable packages

The discussion of *pkgadd* assumes that you already have an installable package. This is appropriate for System V.4, but if you have just ported a software package, you first need to create an installable binary package from it. This is the purpose of *pkgmk*. It takes a number of input files, the most important of which is *prototype*, which describes which files should be installed. It is almost identical in format to the *pkgmap* file we discussed previously. For example, the *prototype* file for the Emacs example in the section called "pkgmap" looks like:

```
# Prototype file created by /cdcopy/ETC/tools/mkmkpk on Wed Jan 19 18:24:41 WET
i pkginfo
i preinstall
i postinstall
i copyright
# Required directories
d none /opt 755 bin bin
d none /opt/bin 755 bin bin
d none /opt/README 755 bin bin
d none /opt/man 755 bin bin
d none /opt/lib 755 bin bin
d none /opt/lib/emacs 755 bin bin
d none /opt/lib/emacs/19.22 755 bin bin
d none /opt/lib/emacs/19.22/etc 755 bin bin
d none /opt/info 755 bin bin
# Required files
f none /opt/lib/emacs/19.22/etc/3B-MAXMEM 644 root sys
f none /opt/bin/emacs 755 root sys
f none /opt/info/emacs 644 root sys
f none /opt/info/dir 644 root sys
```

This looks rather different from *pkgmap*:

- Comment lines start with `#`. The first line indicates that this file was created by a script. Later on we'll see the kind of function *mkmkpk* might perform.
- The first column (part number) and the last three columns (size, checksum and modification timestamp) are missing.
- Some lines start with the keyletter `i`. These describe installation files: you should recognize the names from the previous discussion. *pkgmk* copies these files into the directory tree as discussed previously. What is not so immediately obvious is that *pkginfo* is placed in the main directory of the package, and the others are placed in the subdirectory *install*. It is also not obvious that some of these files are required: if they are not specified, *pkgmk* dies.

Making a prototype file

There's still a gap between the original *make install* and building an installable package. We need a *prototype* file, but *make install* just installs software. The packaging tools include a program called *pkgproto* that purports to build *prototype* files. It searches a directory recursively and creates *prototype* entries for every file it finds. If you have just installed Emacs, say, in your */opt* directory, *pkgproto* gives you a prototype including every file in */opt*, including all the packages that are already installed there—not what you want. A number of alternatives can solve this problem:

- You can install into a different directory. *pkgproto* supports this idea: you can invoke it with:

  ```
  $ pkgproto /tmp-opt=/opt
  ```

  This tells it to search the directory */tmp-opt* and generate entries for */opt*. The disadvantage of this approach is that you may end up building programs with the path */tmp-opt* hard-coded into the executables, and though it may test just fine on your system, the executable files won't work on the target system—definitely a situation to avoid.

- You rename */opt* temporarily and install Emacs in a new directory, which you can then rename. This virtually requires you to be the only user on the system.

- Before installing Emacs, you create a dummy file *stamp-emacs* just about anywhere on the system. Then you install Emacs and make a list of the files you have just installed:

  ```
  $ find /opt -follow  -cnewer stamp-emacs -type f -print | xargs ls -l >info
  ```

  This requires you to be the only person on the system who can write to the directory at the time, which is not as simple as you might think. Mail and news can come in even if nobody else is using the system. Of course, they won't usually write in the same directories that you're looking in. Nevertheless, you should be prepared for a few surprises. For example, you might find a file like this in your list:

  ```
  /opt/lib/emacs/lock/!cdcopy!SOURCE!Core!glibc-1.07!version.c
  ```

  This is an Emacs lock file: it is created by Emacs when somebody modifies a buffer (in this case, a file called */cdcopy/SOURCE/Core/glibc-1.07/version.c*: Emacs replaces the slashes in the filename with exclamation marks) and causes another Emacs to warn the user before it, too, tries to modify the same file. It contains the pid of the Emacs process that has the modified buffer. Obviously you don't want to include this file in your installable package.

  Once you have tidied up your list of files, you can generate a *prototype* file with the aid of a shell script or an editor.

Running pkgmk

Once you have a *prototype* file, you're nearly home. All you have to do is run *pkgmk*. We encounter terminology problems here. Throughout this book, we have been using the term *package* to refer to the software we are building—more properly, this is the *software package*. *pkgmk* refers to its output as a package, too. In this context, we'll refer to it as the *installable package*.

Unfortunately, *pkgmk* handles some pathnames strangely. You can read the man page (preferably several times) or use this method, which works:

- Before building the installable package, change to the root directory of the software package.
- Ignore path specifications in the *prototype* file, and specify the *root path* as the root file system: *–r /*.
- Specify the *base directory* as the root directory of the package: since that's the directory we're in, just add *–b 'pwd'*.
- Choose to overwrite any existing package: *–o*.
- Specify the destination path explicitly: *–d /usr/pkg*. *pkgmk* creates packages as subdirectories in the directory you specify: in this case, the package *gcc* would create a directory hierarchy */usr/pkg/gcc*.

The resultant call doesn't change from one package to the next. It is:

```
pkgmk -r / -b `pwd` -o -d /usr/pkg
```

There is a whole lot more to using *pkgmk*, of course, but if you have *pkgmk*, you will also have the man pages. The man pages are the best source of further information.

In This Chapter:
- *Reporting Modifications*
- *Saving the Archive*
- *Not Done After All?*

10

Where to Go from Here

Finally it's all over. The package is ported, you've installed the software, and it really *does* work. This time, we're done!

Well, we said that once before, before we started testing, and we were wrong. We're wrong here, too. You may have a task or two more to complete.

- In the course of the port, you may find a bug or a misfeature and fix it. If you do so, you have effectively created a new version of the package. You should send information about these changes to the author. If this is a popular package, you might consider reporting the changes to the Usenet group that exists for the package.
- You no longer need the space on disk, so you can clean up the archive and write it to tape. It's a good idea to maintain enough documentation to be able to retrieve it again.
- Sometime, maybe very soon, somebody will come out with a fix for a bug that will probably bite you eventually or with a feature that could really be of use to you. Your experience with this port will help you to port the new version.

None of these tasks is much work now, and completing them will save you grief later on. Let's look at them in a little more detail.

Reporting Modifications

Once you have the software running, you should report any changes to the author or maintainer of the software. In order for this to be of any use, you need to supply the following information:

- A description of the problems you ran into. Don't spare details here. Remember the pain you endured to figure out what was going wrong, and you had an interest in solving the problem. If you're the first person to run into the problem, it probably hasn't hurt anybody else, least of all the author. He probably gets lots of mail saying "*xfoo* is broke," and he may not believe what you have to say until you prove it to him.
- How you fixed them. Again, supply lots of detail. The author probably understands the package better than you do. If you explain the problem properly, she may come up with a better fix.
- The fixes themselves. *diffs*, lists of differences between the previous version and your versions, are the method of choice. We'll look at them in the rest of this section.

diff

diff is a program that compares two related source files and outputs information about how to create the second file from the first. You typically use it after making modifications to a file in order to describe how the modified file differs from the original. The resultant output file is also called a *diff*. We saw the application of *diff*s in the section called "Updating Old Archives" in Chapter 3, *Care and Feeding of Source Trees*. In this chapter, we'll look at how to make them.

It's useful to recognize and understand diff formats, since you occasionally have to apply them manually. *diff* compares two source files and attempts to output a reasonably succinct list of the differences between them. In *diff* terminology, the output is grouped into *hunks*, information about relatively local groups of differences.

Like most useful programs, *diff* has grown in the course of time, and modern versions can output in a bewildering number of formats. Fortunately, almost all diffs nowadays use the *context* format. We'll look at some other formats so that you can recognize them.

In the following examples, we compare the files *eden.1*:

```
        A doctor, an architect, and a computer scientist
were arguing about whose profession was the oldest. In the
course of their arguments, they got all the way back to the
Garden of Eden, whereupon the doctor said, "The medical
profession is clearly the oldest, because Eve was made from
Adam's rib, as the story goes, and that was a simply
incredible surgical feat."
        The architect did not agree. He said, "But if you
look at the Garden itself, in the beginning there was chaos
and void, and out of that, the Garden and the world were
created. So God must have been an architect."
```

```
        The computer scientist, who had listened to all of
this said, "Yes, but where do you think the chaos came
from?"
```

and *eden.2*:

```
        A doctor, an architect, and a computer scientist
were arguing about whose profession was the oldest. In the
course of their arguments, they came to discuss the Garden
of Eden, whereupon the doctor said, "The medical profession
is clearly the oldest, because Eve was made from Adam's rib,
as the story goes, and that was a simply incredible surgical
feat."
        The architect did not agree. He said, "But if you
look at the Garden itself, in the beginning there was chaos
and void, and out of that, the Garden and the world were
created. So God must have been an architect."
        The computer scientist, who had listened to all of
this, said, "Yes, but where do you think the chaos came
from?"
```

normal format diffs

As the name implies, the *normal* format is the default. You don't need to specify any format flags:

```
$ diff eden.1 eden.2
3,7c3,7
< course of their arguments, they got all the way back to the
< Garden of Eden, whereupon the doctor said, "The medical
< profession is clearly the oldest, because Eve was made from
< Adam's rib, as the story goes, and that was a simply
< incredible surgical feat."
---
> course of their arguments, they came to discuss the Garden
> of Eden, whereupon the doctor said, "The medical profession
> is clearly the oldest, because Eve was made from Adam's rib,
> as the story goes, and that was a simply incredible surgical
> feat."
13c13
< this said, "Yes, but where do you think the chaos came
---
> this, said, "Yes, but where do you think the chaos came
```

The first line of each hunk specifies the line range: `3,7c3,7` means "lines 3 to 7 of the first file, lines 3 to 7 of the second file". `13c13` means "line 13 of the first file, line 13 of the second file, has changed (c)". Instead of `c` you will also see `d` (lines deleted) and `a` (lines added).

After this header line come the lines of the first file, with a leading < character, then a divider (---), and the lines of the second file with a leading > character. This example has two hunks.

ed format diffs

ed format diffs have the dubious advantage that the program *ed* can process them. You can create them with the *–e* option. In this example, we also use shell syntax to shorten the input line. Writing `eden.[12]` is completely equivalent to writing `eden.1 eden.2`.

```
$ diff -e eden.[12]
13c
this, said, "Yes, but where do you think the chaos came
.
3,7c
course of their arguments, they came to discuss the Garden
of Eden, whereupon the doctor said, "The medical profession
is clearly the oldest, because Eve was made from Adam's rib,
as the story goes, and that was a simply incredible surgical
feat."
.
```

Just about everybody who has *diff* also has *patch*, and nowadays not everybody has *ed*. In addition, this format is extremely dangerous, since there is no information about the old content of the file: you can't be sure if the patch will be applied in the right place. As a result, you almost never see this form.

context diffs

You select a context diff with the *–c* option:

```
$ diff -c eden.[12]
*** eden.1      Tue May 10 14:21:47 1994
--- eden.2      Tue May 10 14:22:38 1994
***************
*** 1,14 ****
        A doctor, an architect, and a computer scientist
  were arguing about whose profession was the oldest. In the
! course of their arguments, they got all the way back to the
! Garden of Eden, whereupon the doctor said, "The medical
! profession is clearly the oldest, because Eve was made from
! Adam's rib, as the story goes, and that was a simply
! incredible surgical feat."
        The architect did not agree. He said, "But if you
  look at the Garden itself, in the beginning there was chaos
  and void, and out of that, the Garden and the world were
  created. So God must have been an architect."
        The computer scientist, who had listened to all of
! this said, "Yes, but where do you think the chaos came
  from?"
--- 1,14 ----
        A doctor, an architect, and a computer scientist
  were arguing about whose profession was the oldest. In the
! course of their arguments, they came to discuss the Garden
! of Eden, whereupon the doctor said, "The medical profession
```

```
! is clearly the oldest, because Eve was made from Adam's rib,
! as the story goes, and that was a simply incredible surgical
! feat."
        The architect did not agree. He said, "But if you
  look at the Garden itself, in the beginning there was chaos
  and void, and out of that, the Garden and the world were
  created. So God must have been an architect."
        The computer scientist, who had listened to all of
! this, said, "Yes, but where do you think the chaos came
```

The output here gives us significantly more information. The first two lines give the name and modification timestamp of the files. Then the hunks start, with a row of asterisks as a leader. The next line is line number information for the first file (lines 1 to 14), after which come the lines themselves, surrounded by a number of lines of *context*, unchanged information. You can specify the number of lines of context, but by default *diff* includes two lines either side of the changes. The lines that have been modified are flagged with an exclamation point (`!`) at the beginning of the line. In this case, the file is so small that the two modifications have been merged into one large one, and the whole file gets repeated. In a larger file, *diff* would include only the information immediately surrounding the changes. This format is more reliable than normal diffs: if the original source file has changed since the diff, the context information helps establish the correct location to apply the patch.

unified context diffs

unified diffs are similar to normal context diffs. They are created with the *-u* option:

```
$ diff -u eden.[12]
--- eden.1      Tue May 10 14:21:47 1994
+++ eden.2      Tue May 10 14:22:38 1994
@@ -1,14 +1,14 @@
        A doctor, an architect, and a computer scientist
 were arguing about whose profession was the oldest. In the
-course of their arguments, they got all the way back to the
-Garden of Eden, whereupon the doctor said, "The medical
-profession is clearly the oldest, because Eve was made from
-Adam's rib, as the story goes, and that was a simply
-incredible surgical feat."
+course of their arguments, they came to discuss the Garden
+of Eden, whereupon the doctor said, "The medical profession
+is clearly the oldest, because Eve was made from Adam's rib,
+as the story goes, and that was a simply incredible surgical
+feat."
        The architect did not agree. He said, "But if you
 look at the Garden itself, in the beginning there was chaos
 and void, and out of that, the Garden and the world were
 created. So God must have been an architect."
```

```
        The computer scientist, who had listened to all of
-this said, "Yes, but where do you think the chaos came
+this, said, "Yes, but where do you think the chaos came
 from?"
```

As with context diffs, there is a header with information about the two files, followed by a hunk header specifying the line number range in each of the two files. Unlike a normal context diff, the following hunk contains the old text mingled with the new text. The lines prefixed with a minus sign (–) belong to the first file, those prefixed with a plus sign (+) belong to the second file. In other words, to convert the old file to the new file you remove the lines prefixed with minus signs and insert the lines prefixed with plus signs.

Various flavors of *diff* offer still other formats, but these are the only important ones.

What kind of diff?

As we've seen, *ed* style diffs are out of the question. You still have the choice between regular diffs, context diffs, and unified context diffs. It's not that important which kind of diff you choose, but context diffs are easier to apply manually. Unified context diffs take up less space than regular context diffs, but versions of *patch* are still out there that don't understand unified diffs. Until that changes, it's probably best to settle for regular context diffs. You may have noticed that all the examples in Chapter 3 were regular context diffs.

Living with diff

diff is a straightforward enough program, but you might run into a couple of problems:

- After a large port, it makes sense to make diffs of the whole directory hierarchy. This requires that you have copies of all the original files. You can use *rcsdiff*, part of the RCS package, but it does diffs only one file at a time. I find it easier to maintain a copy of the complete original source tree and then run *diff* with the option *–r* (descend recursively into directories):

  ```
  $ diff -ru /S/SCO/Base/gcc-2.6.3 /S/Base/Core/gcc-2.6.3 >SCO.diffs
  ```

  This command creates a single file with all the diffs and a list of files that only exist in the first directory. This can be important if you have added files, but it also means that you should do a *make clean* before running *diff*, or you will have entries of this kind for all the object files you create.

- Another problem that may occur is that one of the files does not have a newline character at the end of the last line. This does not normally worry compilers, but *diff* sees fit to complain. This is insidious, because *patch* doesn't like the message, and it causes *patch* to fail.

Saving the Archive

Most of us have had the message *Don't forget to make backups* drummed into us since we were in elementary school, but nowhere does it make more sense than at the end of a port. Don't forget where you put it! After archiving your port of *xfoo*, you may not look at it again for three years. When the new version comes out, you try to port it, but all sorts of things go wrong. That's the time to get out the old version and read your notes—but where is it?

It's beyond the scope of this book to go into backup strategies, but you should think about the subject. One good idea is to keep separate tapes (DAT or Exabyte) of old ports and just add additional archives at the end. That way you don't have to worry about overwriting them accidentally: the tapes are small and cheap enough that you can afford to keep their contents almost indefinitely. If you don't choose this method (maybe because the media don't fit into your QIC-150 tape drive), you need to think carefully about how to track the archives and when they are no longer needed.

Not Done After All?

Of course, it may be that this optimistic finish is completely out of place. After what seems like months of frustration, you finally decide that you are never going to get this &%%$@# to work, and you give up. You can never rule out this possibility. As I said in Chapter 1, *Introduction*, I hope this book made porting easier, but it's not a magic scroll.

Even if you *do* give up, you have some tidying up to do: you obviously can't send the author your bug fixes, but you can at least report the bugs. What he does with them depends on his interest and contractual obligations, but even with free software, which is free of obligations of this nature, the author may be interested enough to fix the problem. One way or another, you should go to the trouble to report problems you experience, even if you can't fix them and there is no support obligation.

A final word: if you give up on a port after getting this far, this book has failed for you. I don't want that to happen. Please contact me, too (`grog@lemis.de` or via O'Reilly & Associates), and explain the problem. Like the authors of the software, I don't guarantee I'll do anything about it, but I might, and your experience might help to make the next edition of this book more useful.

II

UNIX Flavor Guide

In This Chapter:
- Data Types
- Pointer Size
- Address Space
- Character Order
- Data Alignment

11 Hardware Dependencies

The days are gone when moving a package from one hardware platform to another meant rewriting the package, but a number of points still cause you problems. In this chapter, we'll look at the most common causes.

Data Types

All computers have at least two basic data types, characters and integers. While European languages can get by with a character width of 8 bits, integers must be at least 16 bits wide to be of any use, and most UNIX systems use 32-bit integers, as much storage as four characters. Problems can obviously arise if you port a package to a system whose `int` size is less than the author of the package expected.

Integer Sizes

Data sizes aren't the problem they used to be—times were when a machine word could be 8, 12, 16, 18, 24, 30, 32, 36, 48, 60, 64, or 72 bits long, and so were the primary integer data objects. Nowadays you can expect nearly every machine to have an `int` of 16, 32, or 64 bits, and the vast majority of these have a 32-bit `int`. Still, one of the biggest problems in ANSI C is the lack of an exact definition of data sizes. `int` is the most used simple data type, but depending on implementation, it can vary between 16 and 64 bits long. `short` and `long` can be the same size as `int`, or they can be shorter or longer, respectively. There are advantages to this approach: the C compiler usually chooses an `int` that results in the fastest processing time for the processor on which the program runs. This is not always the smallest data size: most 32-bit machines handle 32-bit arithmetic operations faster than 16-bit operations. Problems don't arise until the choice of `int` is too small to hold the data that the program tries to store in it. If this situation arises, you have a number of options:

- You can go through the sources with an editor and replace all occurrences of the word `int` with `long` (and possibly `short` with `int`*).
- You can simplify this process a little by inserting the following definition in a common header file:

  ```
  #define int long
  ```

  This method has the disadvantage that you can't define `short` as `int`, because preprocessor macros are recursive, and you will end up with both `int` and `short` defined as `long`.
- Some compilers, particularly those with 16-bit native `int`s, offer compiler flags to generate longer standard `int`s.

All these "solutions" have the problem that they do not affect library functions. If your system library expects 16-bit integers, and you write the following code, the library routine `printf` still assumes that the parameter `x` is 16 bits long and prints the value as a single 16-bit value (–7616), not what you want.

```
int x = 123456;
printf ("x is %d\n", x);
```

To get it to work, you need to either specify an alternate library or change the format specification to `printf`:

```
int x = 123456;
printf ("x is %l\n", x);
```

There are a few other points to note about the size of an `int`:

- Portable software doesn't usually rely on the size of an `int`. The software from the Free Software Foundation is an exception: one of the explicit design goals is a 32-bit target machine.
- The only 64-bit machine that is currently of any significance is the DEC Alpha. You don't need to expect too many problems there.
- Sixteen-bit machines—including the 8086 architecture, which is still in use under MS-DOS—are a different matter, and you may experience significant pain porting, say, a GNU program to MS-DOS. If you really want to do this kind

* If you do this, be sure to check that you don't replace `short int` with `int int`!

of port, you should look at the way *gcc* has been adapted to MS-DOS: it continues to run in 32-bit protected mode and has a library wrapper[*] to allow it to run under MS-DOS.

Floating-Point Types

Floating-point data types have the same problems that integer types do: they can be of different lengths, and they can be big-endian or little-endian. I don't know of any system in which `int` is big-endian and `float` is little-endian, or vice-versa. (The terms *big-endian* and *little-endian* are defined in the section called "Character Order" later in this chapter.)

Apart from these problems, floats have a number of different structures, which are as good as completely incompatible. Fortunately, you don't usually need to look under the covers: as long as a `float` handles roughly the same range of values as the system for which the program was written, you shouldn't have any problems. You do need to look more carefully, for example, if the programmer was making assumptions, say, about the position of the sign bit of the mantissa, then you should prepare for some serious rewriting.

Pointer Size

For years, people assumed that pointers and `int`s were the same size. The lax syntax of early C compilers didn't even raise an eyebrow when people assigned `int`s to pointers or vice-versa. Nowadays, a number of machines have pointers that are not the same size as `int`s. If you are using such a machine, you should pay particular attention to compiler warnings that `int`s are assigned to pointers without a cast. For example, if you have 16-bit `int`s and 32-bit pointers, sloppy pointer arithmetic can result in the loss of the high-order bits of the address, with obvious consequences.

Address Space

All modern UNIX variants offer *virtual memory*, though the exact terminology varies. If you read the documentation for System V.4, you discover that it offers virtual memory, whereas System V.3 offered only *demand paging*. This is more marketspeak than technology: System V.2, System V.3, and System V.4 each have very different memory management, but we can define *virtual memory* to mean any kind of addressing scheme in which a process address space can be larger than real memory (the hardware memory installed in the system). According to

---

* A *library wrapper* is a library that insulates the program (in this case, a UNIX-like application) from the harsh realities of the outside world (in this case, MS-DOS).

this definition, all versions of System V and all the other versions of UNIX you are likely to come across have virtual memory.

With virtual memory you're a lot less dependent on the actual size of physical memory. The software from the Free Software Foundation makes liberal use of the fact: programs from the GNU project make no attempt to economize on memory usage. Linking the *gcc* C++ compiler *cc1plus* with GNU *ld* uses about 23 MB of virtual address space on System V.3 on an Intel architecture. This works with just about any memory configuration, as long as the following conditions are met:

- Your processes are allowed as much address space as they need. (If you run into trouble, you should reconfigure your kernel for at least 32 MB maximum process address space, and more if the system allows it.)
- You have enough swap space.
- You can wait for the virtual memory manager to do its thing.

From a configuration viewpoint, we have different worries:

- Is the address space large enough for the program to run?
- How long are pointers? A 16-bit pointer can address only 64 kilobytes, while a 32-bit pointer can address 4 GB.
- How do we address memory? Machines with 16-bit pointers need some kind of additional hardware support to access more than 64 kilobytes. 32-bit pointers are adequate for a "flat" addressing scheme, in which the address contained in the pointer can address the entire virtual address space.

Modern UNIX systems run on hardware with 32-bit pointers, even if some machines have `int`s with only 16 bits, so you don't need to worry much about these problems. Operating systems such MS-DOS, which runs on machines with 16-bit pointers, have significant problems as a result, and porting 32-bit software to them can be an adventure. We'll touch on these problems in the section called "Intel 8086 Memory Models" in Chapter 20, *Compilers*.

Character Order

The biggest headache you are likely to encounter in the field of hardware dependencies is the differing relationship between `int` and character strings from one architecture to the next. Nowadays, all machines have integers large enough to hold more than one character. In the old days, characters in memory weren't directly addressable, and various tricks were employed to access individual characters. The concept of byte addressing, introduced with the IBM System/360, solved that problem but introduced another: two different ways of looking at bytes within a word arose. One camp decided to number the bytes in a register or a machine word from left to right, the other from right to left. For hardware reasons, text was always stored from low byte address to high byte address.

A couple of examples will make character order more intelligible. As we said, text is always stored low byte to high byte, so in any architecture, the text "UNIX" would be stored as:

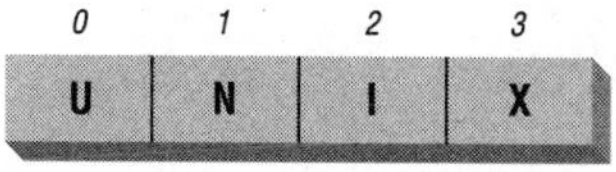

Some architectures, such as Sparc and Motorola 68000, number the bytes in a binary data word from left to right. This arrangement is called *big-endian*. On a big-endian machine, the bytes are numbered from left to right, so the number 0×12345678 would be stored as:

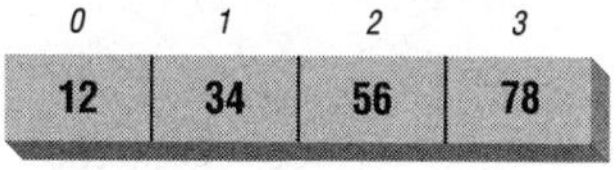

Others, notably older Digital Equipment machines and all Intel machines, number the bytes the other way round: byte 0 in a binary data word is on the right, byte 3 is on the left. This arrangement is called *little-endian*.* The same example on a little-endian machine would look like:

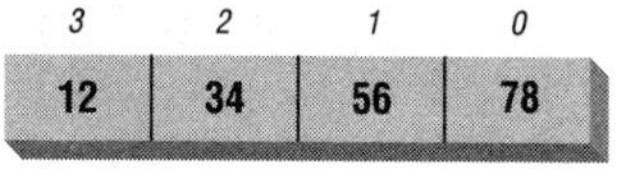

This may look just the same as before, but the byte numbers are now numbered from right to left, so the text now reads:

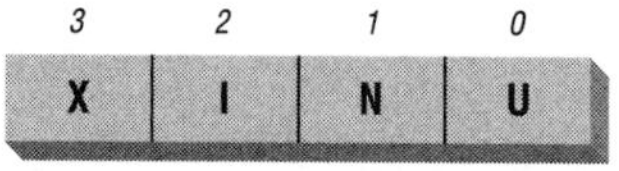

* The names *big-endian* and *little-endian* are derived from Jonathan Swift's *Gulliver's Travels*, in which they are a satirical reference to the conflicts between the Catholics and the Church of England in the 18th century.

As a result, this phenomenon is sometimes called the *NUXI*[*] syndrome. This is only one way to look at it, of course. From a memory point of view, where the bytes are numbered left to right, it looks like:

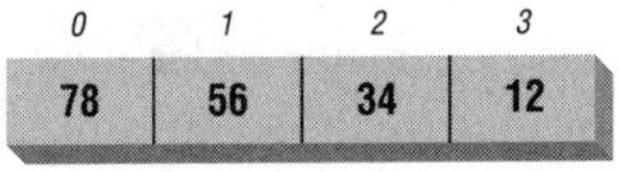

and

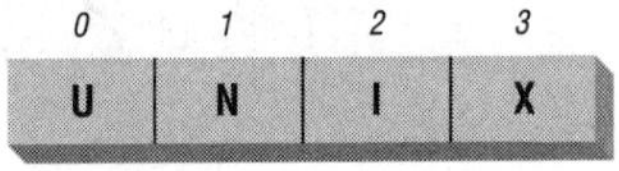

Since it's rather confusing to look at the number 0×12345678 as 78563412, the NUXI (or XINU) view predominates. It's easier to grasp the concepts if you remember that this is all a matter of the mapping between bytes and words and that text is *always* stored correctly from low byte to high byte.

An alternative term for *big-endian* and *little-endian* is *byte sex*. To make matters even more confusing, machines based on the MIPS chips are veritable hermaphrodites—all have configurable byte sex, and the newer machines can even run different processes with different byte sex.

The problem of byte sex may seem like a storm in a teacup, but it crops up in the most unlikely situation. Consider the following code, originally written on a VAX, a little-endian machine:

```
int c = 0;

read (fd, &c, 1);
if (c == 'q')
  exit (0);
```

On a little-endian machine, the single character is input to the low-order byte of the word, so the comparison is correct, and entering the character `q` causes the program to stop. On a 32-bit big-endian machine, entering the character `q` sets `c` to the value 0×71000000, not the same value as the character `q`. Any good or even mediocre compiler will, of course, warn you if you hand the address of an `int` to

---

* Why not *XINU*? Because the term arose when words were 16 bits long. The PDP-11, for example, stored `ints` (16-bit quantities) in a little-endian format, so pairs of bytes were swapped. The PDP-11 also had 32-bit `long` quantities that were stored with their component words in a big-endian format. This arrangement has been called *mixed-endian*, just to add to the general confusion.

`read`, but only if you remember to include the correct header files: it happens anyway.

This discussion has concentrated on how characters are ordered within words, but the same considerations also affect bit fields within a word. Most hardware platforms don't support bit fields directly: they're an idea in the mind of the compiler. Nonetheless, all architectures define a bit order: some number from left to right, some from right to left. Well-written programs don't rely on the order of bit fields in `ints`, but occasionally you see register definitions as bit fields. For example, the 4.4BSD sources for the HP300 include the following definition:

```
struct ac_restatdb
  {
  short ac_eaddr;                    /* element address */
  u_int ac_res1:2,
        ac_ie:1,                     /* import enabled (IEE only) */
        ac_ee:1,                     /* export enabled (IEE only) */
        ac_acc:1,                    /* accessible from MTE */
        ac_exc:1,                    /* element in abnormal state */
        ac_imp:1,                    /* 1 == user inserted medium (IEE only) */
        ac_full:1;                   /* element contains media */
  };
```

This definition defines individual bits in a hardware register. If the board in question fits in machines that number the bits differently, then the code needs to be modified to suit that scheme.

Data Alignment

Most architectures address memory at the byte level, but that doesn't mean that the underlying hardware treats all bytes the same. In the interests of efficiency, the processor accesses memory several bytes at a time. A 32-bit machine, for example, usually accesses data 4 bytes at a time—this is one of the most frequent meanings of the term "32-bit machine." It's the combined responsibility of the hardware and the software to make it look as if every byte is accessed in the same way.

Conflicts can arise as soon as you access more than a byte at a time. If you access two bytes starting in the last byte of a machine word, you are effectively asking the machine to fetch a word from memory, throw away all of it except the last byte, then fetch another word, throw away all except the first, and make a 16-bit value out of the 2 remaining bytes. This is obviously a lot more work than accessing 2 bytes at an even address. The hardware can hide a lot of this overhead, but in most architectures the two memory accesses can't be avoided if the address spans two bus words.

Hardware designers have followed various philosophies in addressing data alignment. Some machines, such as the Intel 486, allow unaligned access, but performance is reduced. Others, typically RISC machines, were designed to consider this to be a Bad Thing and don't even try: if you attempt to access unaligned data, the processor generates a trap. It's then up to the software to decide whether to signal a bus error or simulate the transfer—in either case it's undesirable.

Compilers know about alignment problems and "solve" them by moving data to the next address that matches the machine's data access restrictions, leaving empty space, so-called *padding*, in between. Since the C language doesn't have any provision for specifying alignment information, you're usually stuck with the solution supplied by the compiler writer: the compiler automatically aligns data of specific types to certain boundaries. This doesn't do much harm with scalars but can be a real pain with *struct*s when you transfer them to disk. Consider the following program excerpt:

```
struct emmental
  {
  char flag;
  int count;
  short choice;
  int date;
  short weekday;
  double amount;
  }
emmental;
read_disk (struct emmental *rec)
  {
  if (read (disk, rec, sizeof (rec)) < sizeof (rec))
    report_bad_error (disk);
  }
```

On just about any system, `emmental` looks like a Swiss cheese. On an i386 architecture, for instance, `shorts` need to be on a 2-byte boundary and `ints` and `doubles` need to be on a 4-byte boundary. Figure 11-1 shows the offsets that end up in your data.

As if this weren't bad enough, on a Sparc `doubles` must be on an 8-byte boundary, so on a Sparc we have 6 bytes of empty space after `weekday`, to bring the offset up to 24. As a result, `emmental` has 21 useful bytes of information and up to 13 of wasted space.

This is, of course, a contrived example, and good programmers would take care to lay out the `struct` better. There are still valid reasons why you encounter this kind of alignment problem:

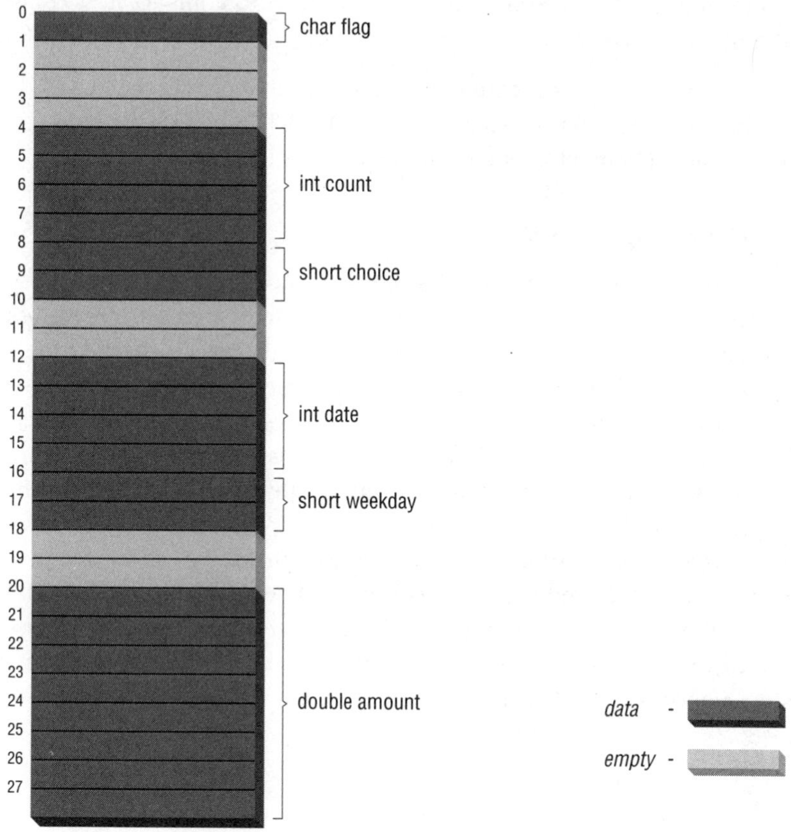

Figure 11-1: Structure with padding (empty bytes)

- If `flag`, `count`, and `choice` are a key in a database record, they need to be stored in this sequence.
- A few years ago, even most good programmers didn't expect to have to align a `double` on an 8-byte boundary.
- A lot of the software you get looks as if it has never seen a good programmer.

Apart from the waste of space, alignment introduces a host of other problems. If the first three fields really are a database key, somebody (probably the database manager) has to ensure that the gaps are set to a known value. If this database is shared between different machines, our `read_disk` routine is going to be in trouble. If you write the record on an i386, it is 28 bytes long. If you try to read it in on a Sparc, `read_disk` expects 32 bytes and fails. Even if you fix that, `amount` is in the wrong place.

A further problem in this example is that Sparcs are big-endian and i386s are little-endian: after reading the record, you don't just need to compact it, you also need to flip the bytes in the `shorts`, `ints`, and `doubles`.

Good portable software has accounted for these problems, of course. On the other hand, if your program compiles just fine and then falls flat on its face when you try to run it, data alignment is one of the first things to check.

Instruction Alignment

The part of the processor that performs memory access usually doesn't distinguish between fetching instructions from memory and fetching data from memory. The only difference is what happens to the information after it has reached the CPU. As a result, instruction alignment is subject to the same considerations as data alignment. Some CPUs require all instructions to be on a 32-bit boundary, which is typically the case for RISC CPUs. It implies that all instructions should be the same length. Other CPUs allow instructions to start at any address, which is virtually a requirement for machines with variable length instructions.* As with data access, being *allowed* to make this kind of access doesn't make it a good idea. For example, the Intel 486 and Pentium processors execute instructions aligned on any address, but they run significantly faster if the target address of a jump instruction is aligned at the beginning of a processor word—the alignment of other instructions is not important. Many compilers take a flag to tell them to align instructions for the i486.

---

* Some machines with variable length instructions *do* have a requirement that an instruction fit in a single machine word. This was the case with the Control Data 6600 and successors, which had a 60-bit word and 15- or 30-bit instructions. If a 30-bit instruction would have started at the 45-bit position inside a word, it had to be moved to the next word, and the last 15 bits of the previous instruction word were filled with a *nop*, a "no-operation" instruction.

In This Chapter:
- *Interprocess Communication*
- *Miscellaneous System Functionality*

12

Kernel Dependencies

The biggest single problem in porting software is the operating system. The operating system services play a large part in determining how a program must be written. UNIX versions differ enough in some areas to require significant modifications to programs to adapt them to a different version. In this and the following chapters, we'll look at what has happened to UNIX since it was essentially a single system, around the time of the Seventh Edition.

Many books have been written on the internals of the various UNIX flavors, for example *The Design of the UNIX System* by Maurice Bach for System V.2; *The Design and the Implementation of the 4.3BSD UNIX Operating System* by Sam Leffler, Kirk McKusick, Mike Karels, and John Quarterman for 4.3BSD; and *The Magic Garden Explained: The Internals of UNIX System V Release 4* by Berny Goodheart and James Cox for System V.4. In addition, a number of books have been written about programming in these environments—*Advanced Programming in the UNIX Environment* by Richard Stevens gives an excellent introduction to System V.4 and "4.3+BSD"* for programmers. In this chapter and the ones following it, we'll restrict our view to brief descriptions of aspects that can cause problems when porting software from one UNIX platform to another. We'll look at specific areas in this chapter; Chapter 1, *Signals*; Chapter 14, *File Systems*; and Chapter 15, *Terminal Drivers*.

* 4.3BSD was released in 1987, 4.4BSD in 1994. In the time in between, releases had names like *4.3BSD Tahoe*, *4.3BSD Reno*, and *NET/2*. For want of a better term, Stevens refers to systems roughly corresponding to NET/2 as *4.3+BSD*.

In the rest of this chapter, we'll look at:

- Interprocess communication
- Nonblocking I/O
- Miscellaneous aspects of kernel functionality

The descriptions are not sufficient to help you use the functionality in writing programs. They are intended to help you understand existing programs and rewrite them in terms of functions available to you. If you need more information, you may find it in the 4.4BSD man pages (see Appendix E) or in *Advanced Programming in the UNIX Environment*, by Richard Stevens.

Interprocess Communication

Interprocess communication (frequently written as the abbreviation *IPC*), the ability to transfer data between processes, was one of the important original concepts of UNIX. The original methods were what you might expect of a concept that, at the time, was revolutionary and still under development: there were more than a few limitations. Even today there is no agreement on how interprocess communication should take place.

In this section we'll look very briefly at the various kinds of interprocess communication and what to do if the package you are porting uses a method your kernel doesn't support. To start with the bad news: if you find your kernel doesn't support the IPC model that the package expects, you will probably need to make significant modifications to adapt it to a different model.

Interprocess communication was originally limited to a single processor, but of course network communication is also a form of interprocess communication. We'll touch briefly on network communication in the following discussion.

UNIX systems offer a bewildering number of different forms of interprocess communication:

Pipes
: The original form of communication and are found in all versions of UNIX. They have the disadvantages that they transfer data in one direction only and that they can connect only two processes that have a common ancestor.

Sockets
: The BSD interprocess communication mechanism. They are by far the most powerful mechanism, offering unidirectional, bidirectional, and network communication. In BSD systems, they are even used to implement the `pipe` system call.

*STREAMS**
: A generalized I/O concept available in newer System V systems and their derivatives. It was originally intended to replace character device drivers, but its flexibility makes it useful for interprocess communication as well. Like sockets, it can be used both for local and remote communication. *UNIX Network Programming*, by Richard Stevens, describes STREAMS in some detail, and *The Magic Garden Explained*, by Berny Goodheart and James Cox, describes the implementation. We won't consider them further here.

Stream pipes
: These differ from regular pipes by being able to transfer data in both directions. They have no particular connection with STREAMS.

FIFOs
: Also called *named pipes*, FIFOs are like pipes, but they have a name in the file system hierarchy.

Named stream pipes
: Not surprisingly, these are stream pipes with names. They bear the same relationship to stream pipes that FIFOs do to regular pipes.

System V IPC
: A bundle that offers *message queues*, yet another form of message passing; *shared memory*, which enables processes to pass data directly; and *semaphores*, which synchronize processes.

In the following sections, we'll look at these features in a little more detail.

Pipes

The original UNIX interprocess communication facility was *pipes*. Pipes are created by the *pipe* function call:

```
#include <unistd.h>

int pipe (int *fildes);
```

This call creates a pipe with two file descriptors, a read descriptor and a write descriptor. It returns the value of the read descriptor to `fildes [0]` and the value of the write descriptor to `fildes [1]`. At this point, only the creating process can use the pipe, which is not very useful. After calling `fork`, however, both of the resultant processes can use the pipe. Depending on their purpose, the processes may decide to close one direction of the pipe. For example, if you write output to

* Why the shouting? STREAMS was derived from the Eighth Edition *Streams* concept (see *A Stream Input-Output System* by Dennis Ritchie). System V always spells it in uppercase, so this is a convenient way of distinguishing between the implementations.

the *more* program, you don't expect any reply from *more*, so you can close the read file descriptor.

A fair amount of code is involved in opening a pipe, starting a new process with `fork` and `exec`, and possibly waiting for it terminate with `wait`. The standard library functions `popen` and `pclose` make this job easier:

```
#include <stdio.h>

FILE *popen(const char *command, const char *type);
int pclose(FILE *stream);
```

`popen` creates a pipe, then forks and execs a shell with `command` as its parameter. `type` specifies whether the pipe should be open for reading ("`r`") or writing ("`w`"). Since pipes are unidirectional, they cannot be opened both for reading and for writing.

After opening the command, you can write to the process with regular `write` commands. On completion, `pclose` waits for the child process to terminate and closes the file descriptors.

Sockets

Sockets were originally developed at Berkeley as part of the TCP/IP networking implementation introduced with 4.2BSD, but they are in fact a general interprocess communication facility. In BSD systems, the other interprocess communication facilities are based on sockets.

Most of the features of sockets are related to networking, which we don't discuss here. The call is:

```
#include <sys/types.h>
#include <sys/socket.h>

int socket (int domain, int type, int protocol);
```

`domain`
: Specifies the communications domain. Common domains are `AF_UNIX` (UNIX domain),* used for local communication, `AF_INET` (Internet domain), and `AF_ISO` (ISO protocol domain).

* Not all UNIX implementations support UNIX domain sockets. In particular, some System V systems support only the Internet domain. People with a System V background often place the emphasis on the word "domain," and some even refer to UNIX domain sockets as "domain sockets." As you can see from the above, this is incorrect.

`type`

Specifies the type of socket. For local interprocess communication, you would use *SOCK_STREAM*, which supplies a reliable two-way communication channel.

`protocol`

Specifies the communications protocol to use. In the UNIX domain, this parameter is not used and should be set to 0.

As we shall see in the next section, the way that pipes are implemented means that you need two sockets to simulate a pipe. You can do this with the *socketpair* system call, which creates a pair of file descriptors with identical properties.

```
#include <sys/types.h>
#include <sys/socket.h>

int socketpair (int domain, int type, int protocol, int *sv);
```

Currently, `socketpair` works only in the UNIX domain, so you don't have much choice in the parameters: `domain` must be `AF_UNIX`, `type` must be `SOCK_STREAM`, and `protocol` is meaningless in the UNIX domain. The only important parameter is `sv`, which is where the socket descriptors are returned—exactly the same as the `fildes` parameter to `pipe`.

Most systems have some kind of socket support, but sometimes it is just an emulation library that omits significant functionality, such as the UNIX domain and the `socketpair` call. Many older System V sockets emulation libraries also have a bad reputation regarding performance and reliability. On the other hand, many System V.3 ports included the original Berkeley socket implementation in the kernel.

Other Kinds of Pipes

Pipes have two main restrictions:

- They are unidirectional: you write to one descriptor, you read from the other. It would be a nice idea to be able to read from and write to the same descriptor.
- They are anonymous: you don't open an existing pipe, you create a new one, and only you and your descendants can use it. It would be nice to be able to use pipes like regular files.

In fact, you can get all combinations of these properties. We've seen regular pipes—the others are *stream pipes*, *FIFOs*, and *named stream pipes*. We'll look at them in the following sections.

Stream pipes

Most systems allow you to create bidirectional pipes. For some reason, they're generally called *stream pipes*, which is not a good name at all.

- In System V.4, regular pipes are bidirectional, so you don't need to do anything special.
- In 4.4BSD, the *socketpair* system call, which we have already seen, creates stream pipes, so you'd expect regular pipes to be bidirectional in 4.4BSD as well. In fact, before returning, the library function *pipe* closes one descriptor in each direction, so 4.4BSD pipes really are unidirectional. If you want a stream pipe, just use the `socketpair` system call.
- In System V.3 systems with STREAMS, bidirectional pipes are possible, too, but things are more difficult. You have to connect two streams back to back. See *UNIX Network Programming* for a discussion of how to do this.

FIFOs

FIFOs are pipes with filenames, which allow unrelated processes to communicate with each other. To create a FIFO, you use the function `mkfifo`:

```
#include <sys/stat.h>

int mkfifo (const char *path, mode_t mode);
```

This call corresponds exactly to `mkdir`, except that it creates a FIFO instead of a directory. BSD implements `mkfifo` as a system call, while System V.4 implements it as a library function that calls `mknod` to do the work. System V.3 systems frequently implemented it as a system call. Once you have created a FIFO, you can use it just like a file: typically, one process, the *listener process*, opens the FIFO for reading, and one or more open it for writing to the listener process.

Named stream pipes

Stream pipes are bidirectional, but they don't normally have names. FIFOs have names, but they're usually not bidirectional. To get both of these properties, we need a new kind of connection, a *named stream pipe*. In 4.4BSD, this can be done by binding a name to a stream socket—see the man pages for `bind` for further details. In System V.4, you can create a named stream pipe with the `connld` STREAMS module. See *Advanced Programming in the UNIX Environment* for more details.

System V IPC

System V supplies an alternative form of interprocess communication consisting of three features: *shared memory*, *message queues*, and *semaphores*. SunOS 4 also supports System V IPC, but pure BSD systems do not. In the industry there is a significant amount of aversion to this implementation, which is sometimes called the *Three Ugly Sisters*.

System V IPC is overly complicated and sensitive to programming bugs, which are two of the main reasons why it has not been implemented on other systems. Converting programs written for System V IPC to other methods of interprocess communication is nontrivial. If you have a BSD system with kernel sources, it might be easier to implement Daniel Boulet's free software implementation (see Appendix E).

Shared memory

An alternative form of interprocess communication involves sharing data between processes. Instead of sending a message, you just write it into a buffer that is also mapped into the address space of the other process. You may encounter two forms of shared memory on UNIX systems—System V shared memory and `mmap`, which is more commonly used for mapping files to memory. We'll look at `mmap` in the section called "Memory-Mapped Files" in Chapter 14.

System V shared memory is implemented with four system calls:

```
#include <sys/types.h>
#include <sys/ipc.h>
#include <sys/shm.h>

int shmget (key_t key, int size, int shmflg);
int shmctl (int shmid, int cmd, ...      /* struct shmid_ds *buf */);
void *shmat (int shmid, void *shmaddr, int shmflg);
int shmdt (void *shmaddr);
```

- `shmget` allocates a shared memory segment or adds the process to the list of processes sharing the segment. The shared memory segment identifier is conceptually like a filename or an identifier, but for some reason the identifiers are called *keys* when talking about System V shared memory. `shmget` returns a segment identifier, conceptually like a file number.
- `shmctl` performs control operations on shared memory segments. It can set ownerships and permissions, retrieve status information, or remove shared memory segments. Like files, shared memory segments remain on the system until explicitly removed, even if they are currently not assigned to any process.

- shmat attaches the shared memory segment shmid to the calling process.
- shmdt detaches a shared memory segment from the calling process.

With some limitations, you can use mmap to replace System V shared memory. The limitations are that mmap on non-System V platforms normally maintains separate data pages for each process, so if you write to a page in one process, other processes will not see the new data. You need to call msync in order to update the segments used by other processes. Between the time when you modify the segment and when you call msync, the data is inconsistent. msync is not a fast call, so this could also cripple performance.

Message queues

As if there weren't enough ways of passing data between processes already, System V IPC includes *message queues*. Message queues are rather like FIFOs, but there are two differences:

- A FIFO transmits a byte stream, but a message queue is record oriented.
- Messages can have different priorities, which determine the sequence in which they are received, if the receiving process allows them to queue up.

The system calls to handle message queues are analogous to the shared memory calls:

```
#include <sys/types.h>
#include <sys/ipc.h>
#include <sys/msg.h>

int msgget (key_t key, int msgflg);
int msgsnd (int msqid, const void *msgp, size_t msgsz, int msgflg);
int msgrcv (int msqid, void *msgp, size_t msgsz, long msgtyp, int msgflg);
int msgctl (int msqid, int cmd, .../* struct msqid_ds *buf */);
```

- msgget opens an existing queue or creates a new queue.
- messaging msgsnd sends a message.
- msgrcv receives a message.
- msgctl performs control functions on message queues.

Message queues were originally intended to offer fast interprocess communication. Nowadays they have little to offer that a FIFO couldn't handle. If you run into problems with message queues, you might prefer to replace them with FIFOs.

Semaphores

One disadvantage with shared memory implementations is that one process doesn't know when another process has done something. This can have a number of consequences:

- Two processes may modify the same area at the same time.
- One process may be waiting for the other process to do something and needs to know when it has finished.

There are two possible solutions: send a signal, or use *semaphores.*

A semaphore is a means of voluntary process synchronization, similar to advisory locking. To use the facility, a process requests access to the semaphore. If access is currently not possible, the process blocks until access is permitted. Unlike locking, semaphores allow more than one process access to the semaphore at any one point. They do this by maintaining a counter, a small positive integer, in the semaphore. When a process accesses the semaphore, it decrements the counter. If the value of the counter is still non-negative, the process has access; otherwise, it is blocked. This could be used to gain access to a limited number of resources.

System V semaphores look superficially similar to System V shared memory. There are three functions:

```
int semctl (int semid, int semnum, int cmd, ... /* union semun arg */);
int semget (key_t key, int nsems, int semflg);
int semop (int semid, struct sembuf *sops, size_t nsops);
```

The implementation is less than perfect. In particular, it is overly complex, and it almost encourages deadlocks, situations where no process can continue:

- Instead of a single counter, a System V semaphore declares an array of counters. The size of the array is determined by the `nsems` parameter of the `semget` system call.
- It takes two calls (`semget` and `semctl`) to create and initialize a semaphore. Theoretically, this creates an opportunity for another process to initialize the semaphore differently.
- It's possible for semaphores to remain locked after a process ends, which means that a reboot is necessary to unlock the semaphore again. A flag is provided to specify that a semaphore should be removed on exit, but you can't rely upon it completely.
- The implementation is not very fast.

Miscellaneous System Functionality

The rest of this chapter describes miscellaneous system calls that can occasionally cause problems when porting.

exec

Since exec is one of the original system calls at the heart of the UNIX system, it may come as a surprise to discover that exec is no longer a system call on modern systems. Instead, it is implemented as a library function that uses new system calls such as execve. Even the Seventh Edition man pages stated, "Plain exec is obsoleted by exece, but remains for historical reasons."

Nowadays, a large number of alternatives are available. Your system probably has most of the following calls:

```
#include <unistd.h>
extern char **environ;

int exec    (char *path, char *argv []);
int exece   (char *path, char *argv [], char *envp []);
int execl   (char *path, char *arg, ..., NULL);
int execle  (char *path, char *arg, ..., NULL, char *envp []);
int execlp  (char *file, char *arg, ..., NULL);
int execlpe (char *file, char *arg, ..., NULL, char *envp []);
int exect   (char *path, char *argv [], char *envp []);
int execv   (char *path, char *argv []);
int execve  (char *path, char *argv [], char *envp []);
int execvp  (char *file, char *argv []);
int execvpe (char *file, char *argv [], char *envp []);
```

All these functions do exactly the same thing: they replace the process image with a process image from the absolute executable whose filename is specified in the first argument (path or file). They differ only in the manner in which they supply the parameters:

- The parameter path specifies an absolute pathname. If this file does not exist, the call fails.
- Alternatively, the parameter file specifies a file to be searched via the PATH environment variable, the way the shell does when a filename is specified.
- The parameter argv is a pointer to a NULL-terminated list of parameters.
- Alternatively, you can place the arguments, including the terminating NULL, in the call as a series of args.

- If the parameter envp is specified, it is a pointer to a NULL-terminated list of environment variables. This is typically used when the child process should be given a different environment from the parent process.
- If envp is not specified, the environment variables are taken from the parent's environment (via the global pointer environ).

One further function deserves mention: exect, which is supplied only in newer BSD systems, takes the same parameters as execve but enables program tracing facilities.

The total storage available for the argument list and the environment varies from system to system. System V traditionally has only 5,120 characters. POSIX.1 requires at least 20,480 characters, and this is the standard value for newer BSD systems. Many *Makefiles* take advantage of these large parameter lists, and frequently a package fails to build under System V because the parameter lists are too long. You get the following message:

```
make: execve: /bin/sh: Arg list too long
```

We looked at what we can do to solve these problems in the section called "Arg list too long" in Chapter 5, *Building the Package.*

getrlimit and setrlimit

The Seventh Edition made a number of arbitrary choices about kernel limits. For example, each process was allowed to have 50 files open at any one time. In the course of time, a number of these kernel limits were made configurable, and some systems allowed the process to modify them directly, up to a "hard" limit. SunOS, BSD, and System V.4 supply the system calls getrlimit and setrlimit in order to manipulate this configuration information:

```
#include <sys/time.h>
#include <sys/resource.h>
struct rlimit
  {
  int rlim_cur;                          /* current (soft) limit */
  int rlim_max;                          /* hard limit */
  };

int getrlimit (int resource, struct rlimit *rlp);
int setrlimit (int resource, struct rlimit *rlp);
```

The rlimit structure defines two values for each resource, the current value and the maximum value. getrlimit returns this information, setrlimit sets a new current value. Table 12-1 shows which limits can be set.

Table 12–1: getrlimit and setrlimit Resources

Resource	System	Description
RLIMIT_CORE	All	The maximum size, in bytes, of a core image file.
RLIMIT_CPU	All	The maximum amount of CPU time that a process may consume.
RLIMIT_DATA	All	The maximum size, in bytes, of the process data segment.
RLIMIT_FSIZE	All	The largest size, in bytes, that any file may attain.
RLIMIT_MEMLOCK	4.4BSD	The maximum size, in bytes, which a process may lock into memory using the mlock function.
RLIMIT_NOFILE	All	The maximum number of files that a process may open at one time. This is also one more than the highest file number that the process may use.
RLIMIT_NPROC	4.4BSD	The maximum number of simultaneous processes for the current user id.
RLIMIT_RSS	4.4BSD, SunOS 4	The maximum size, in bytes, that the resident set of a process may attain. This limits the amount of physical memory that a process can occupy.
RLIMIT_STACK	All	The maximum size, in bytes, that the stack segment of a process may attain.
RLIMIT_VMEM	System V.4	The maximum size, in bytes, that the mapped address space of a process may attain.

If your system doesn't have these functions, you can't do much except guess. In some cases, header files contain similar information declared as constants, but it's not a very satisfactory alternative.

Process Groups

Where other operating systems use a single program to perform an operation, UNIX frequently uses a group of cooperating processes. It's useful to be able to define such a group, particularly when the processes access terminals. *Advanced Programming in the UNIX Environment* describes all you will want to know about process groups. Here, we'll look at some minor differences in implementations.

setpgid

setpgid adds a process to a process group:

```
#include <unistd.h>

int setpgid (pid_t pid, pid_t pgrp);
```

`pid` is the process ID of the process that is to be added to the process group, and `pgrp` is the process group to which it should be added. It returns 0 on success and –1 with an error code in `errno` on failure.

Normally you see **setpgid** used to add the calling process to a group, which can be done by setting `pid` to 0. System V versions also allow `pgrp` to be 0. This specifies that the process id should be the same as `pid`, and that this process will become a process group leader.

setpgrp

setpgrp is obsolete. Two different implementations duplicate functionality supplied by other functions:

- In more modern BSD systems, it is the same as **setpgid**:

  ```
  int setpgrp (pid_t pid, pid_t pgrp);
  ```

- In System V, it creates a new process group, with the calling process as group leader, and adds the calling process to the group. It also releases the controlling terminal of the calling process. This is the same as **setsid**:

  ```
  int setpgrp ();
  ```

If you run into trouble with this function, it's best to replace it with **setpgid** or **setsid**, depending on the functionality that was intended.

setsid

setsid creates a new process group, with the calling process as group leader, and adds the calling process to the group. It also releases the calling process from its controlling terminal:

```
#include <unistd.h>

int setsid ();
```

Real and Effective User IDs

Occasionally the UNIX security system causes unintended problems: a trusted program may require access to facilities to which the user should not have unlimited access. For example, the program *ps* requires access to */dev/kmem*, kernel memory, which is usually accessible only to the superuser. Serial communication programs such as *uucp* require access to the serial ports, but in order to avoid conflicts, only trusted users have access to the ports.

UNIX solves this problem by allowing the programs to run always as specific users or groups. If you execute a program that has the `setuid` bit set in the file permissions, it runs as if its owner had *exec*ed it, no matter who really started it. Similarly, the `setgid` bit causes the program to run as if it had been executed in the group to which the file belongs. These user and group ids are called *effective user ID* and *effective group ID*, and they are the only permissions that are relevant when a process accesses a file. Figure 12-1 shows the difference between executing a normal file and a file with `setuid` set.

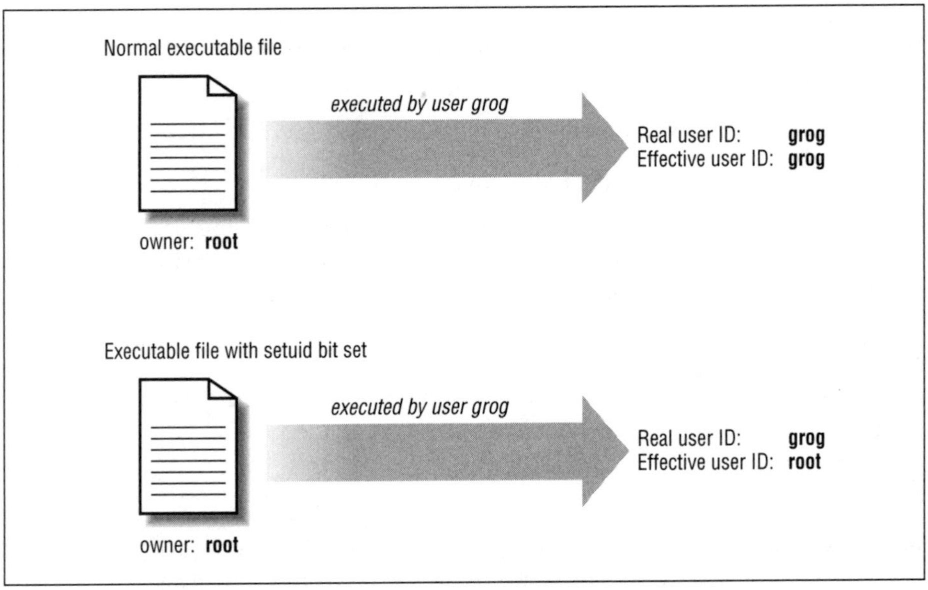

Figure 12-1: What the setuid bit does

Similar considerations apply to group IDs. In the following discussion, we'll consider user IDs, but unless specified otherwise, everything I say about user IDs also applies to group IDs.

A number of subtle problems arise from this scheme. One of the most obvious ones is that programs frequently also need to be able to access your files. There's no guarantee that this will always work. For example, *uucp* needs to be `setuid` to user *uucp* in order to access the communication ports, but it also frequently needs to transfer data to your home directory. If your permissions are set so that *uucp* can't access your home directory, it won't be able to perform the transfer. This is obviously not the intention: somehow, *uucp* needs access both to the serial ports and to your files.

This means that we need to maintain at least two user IDs, the *effective user ID* and the *real user ID*. Modern systems also supply a *saved set user ID*. On System V.4, it's a configuration option (set the configuration constant `_POSIX_SAVED_IDS`). BSD uses the saved set user ID in a different way from System V, as we will see in the next section.

The system manipulates user IDs in the following ways:

- If you execute a program that is not `setuid`, the system sets all IDs to the effective user ID of the process that executes it.
- If you execute a program that has the `setuid` permission set, the system sets the effective user ID to the owner of the program and the real user ID to the effective ID of the process that executes it. If there is a saved set user ID, the system also sets it to the owner of the program.
- At run time, you can change between IDs with the system call `setuid`. A number of alternative calls are also available. We'll look at them in the following sections.

setuid

`setuid` changes the effective user ID. If your current effective user ID is *root*, you can set it to any valid user ID. After that, unfortunately, systems diverge:

- In systems without a saved set user ID, including SunOS 4 and System V.3, `setuid` sets the effective user ID and the real user ID if the current effective user ID is *root*. Otherwise, it sets only the effective user ID. The function call succeeds if the argument to `setuid` is the real user ID or the effective user ID, or if the effective user ID is *root*. Once you have changed from the old effective user ID and *root*, there is no way to change back.
- On System V systems with saved set user ID, `setuid` sets the effective user ID and the real user ID if the current effective user ID is *root*. Otherwise, it sets only the effective user ID. It does not change the saved set user ID. The function call succeeds if the argument to `setuid` is the real user ID, the effective user ID, or the saved set user ID, or if the effective user ID is *root*. This means that you can switch back and forth between the ID of the program owner and the ID of the process that started it.
- On BSD systems with saved set user ID, `setuid` sets the real, effective, and saved set user IDs. The function call succeeds if the argument to `setuid` is the real user ID, or if the effective user ID is *root*. Unlike System V.4, non-*root* users cannot use `setuid` to set the user ID to the saved set user ID. The saved set user ID is of no use to BSD `setuid`. Instead, BSD systems use `seteuid`, which sets only the effective user ID to either the real user ID or the saved set user ID.

setreuid

BSD versions since 4.2BSD have the system call `setreuid`, which takes two parameters:

```
int setreuid (int ruid, int euid);
```

You can use it to swap the effective and real user IDs, so you don't really need a saved set user ID. For nonprivileged users, `ruid` and `euid` can be either the current real user ID or the current effective user ID, or *-1* to indicate no change. This function was needed in BSD up to and including 4.3BSD, since these versions did not support the concept of a saved set user ID. On non-BSD systems only, you can replace this function with `setuid` if your system supports saved set user IDs.

seteuid

As we noted earlier, BSD `setuid` cannot change to the saved set user ID. The BSD solution to this problem, which has been proposed for adoption in a new revision of POSIX.1, is the function `seteuid`. It sets the effective user ID to `euid` if `euid` corresponds either to the real user ID or the saved set user ID. Unlike `setuid`, it sets only the effective user ID.

setruid

In addition to `seteuid`, BSD systems provide the call `setruid`, which sets the real user ID to the effective or real user ID. `setruid` is considered nonportable. Future BSD releases plan to drop it.

Comparison of user ID calls

User IDs are much more complicated than they should be. In fact, you'll want to do only two things, and for non-*root* users they work only with programs that have `setuid` permissions: change from the initial effective user ID to the real user ID, and back again. Changing from effective to real user ID is simple. In all systems, you can use the `setuid` system call though in 4.3BSD and SunOS4, this means that you can't change back. In these systems, it's better to use code such as:

```
int euid = geteuid ();          /* get current effective user ID */
int ruid = getuid ();           /* and real user ID */
setreuid (euid, ruid);          /* and swap them */
```

Changing back again is more complicated:

- On older systems, including XENIX and System V.3, and on System V.4 systems without `_POSIX_SAVED_IDS`, you can't change back. About the only workaround for the older systems is not to change away from the initial effective user ID—you might be able to to spawn a process that does the necessary work under the real user ID.

- On BSD systems up to and including 4.3BSD, and under SunOS 4, you can change back only if you changed with `setreuid`, as in the previous example. In this case, you just need to continue with

  ```
  setreuid (ruid, euid);
  ```

- On System V.4 systems with `_POSIX_SAVED_IDS`, use `setuid (ssuid)`, where `ssuid` is the saved set user ID. You can get the value of `ssuid` by calling `geteuid` before changing the initial effective user ID, since they're the same at program start.
- On BSD systems that support saved set user IDs, use `seteuid (ssuid)`. As with System V.4, you can get the value of `ssuid` by calling `geteuid` before changing the initial effective user ID.

vfork

`vfork` was introduced in 3BSD as a more efficient version of `fork`. In those days, `fork` copied each data area page of the parent process for the child process, which could take a considerable time. Typically, the first thing a child does is to call `exec` to run a new program, which discards the data pages, so this was effectively wasted time. `vfork` modified this behavior so that the pages were shared and not copied.

This is inherently very dangerous. Very frequently the parent waits until the child has done something before continuing. During this time, the child can modify the parent's data, since it is shared. More modern techniques, such as *copy on write*,* have eliminated the need for this function. You *should* be able to replace it with `fork` (the semantics are identical). Unfortunately, some obscene programs rely on the fact that they can manipulate the parent's data before the parent continues. These programs need to be fixed.

wait and Friends

`wait` has been in UNIX as long as anybody can remember:

```
#include <sys/types.h>
#include <sys/wait.h>

pid_t wait (int *status);
```

* With copy on write, the data pages are set to be write-protected. The first write causes an interrupt, effectively a bus error, which the system intercepts. The system makes a copy of the single page and resets write protection for both the original and the copy, allowing the write to proceed.

Unfortunately, various flavors define the value of the status return differently. This is a cosmetic difference, not a real difference. The status information consists of a number of bit fields that depend on the kind of status:

- The low-order 7 bits contain the number of the signal that terminated the process or 0 if the process called **exit**.
- The bit 0x80 is set if a core dump was taken.
- The next 8 bits are the return code if the process called **exit**.

If the process is stopped (if it can be restarted), the low-order 8 bits are set to 127 (0x7f), and the next byte contains the number of the signal that stopped the process.

This information is the same on all versions of UNIX, but there is no agreement on how to represent this information. Older BSD systems defined a union to represent it:

```
union __wait
  {
  int w_status;                        /* status as int */
  struct
    {
    unsigned short w_Termsig:7;        /* termination signal */
    unsigned short w_Coredump:1;       /* core dump indicator */
    unsigned short w_Retcode:8;        /* exit code if w_termsig==0 */
    }
  w_T;
  struct
    {
    unsigned short w_Stopval:8;        /* == W_STOPPED if stopped */
    unsigned short w_Stopsig:8;        /* signal that stopped us */
    }
   w_S;
 };
```

Modern systems define macros:

- WIFEXITED (status) is true if the process terminated via a call to **exit**. If this is true, WEXITSTATUS (status) returns the low order 8 bits of the process' exit value.
- WIFSIGNALED (status) is true if the process was terminated by receiving a signal. If this is true, the following macros apply:
  - WTERMSIG (status) evaluates to the number of the signal that caused the termination of the process.

- `WCOREDUMP (status)` is true if a core dump was created.

- `WIFSTOPPED (status)` is true if the process is stopped and can be restarted. This macro can be true only if the `waitpid` call specified the `UNTRACED` option or if the child process is being traced. If this is true, `WSTOPSIG (status)` returns the number of the signal that caused the process to stop.

Some systems offer both of these options, sometimes incompletely. For example, SunOS 4 defines `w_Coredump` in the `union __wait` but does not define the corresponding `WCOREDUMP` macro.

These varying differences cause problems out of all proportion to the importance of the information contained. In particular, the newer macros do not allow you to change the status, you can only read it. Some programs, for example BSD *make*, modify the status, which makes it difficult to port it to System V or another system that does not understand `union wait`.

waitpid

`waitpid` is a variant of `wait` that waits for a specific process to terminate. It is part of all modern UNIX implementations:

```
#include <sys/wait.h>

pid_t waitpid (pid_t wpid, int *status, int options);
```

`waitpid` waits for process `pid` to terminate. Its behavior is governed by a number of bit-mapped options:

- Set `WNOHANG` to specify to return immediately, even if no status is available. If the status is not available, the functions return the process number 0. Not all systems support this behavior.
- Specify `WUNTRACED` if you want the status of stopped processes as well as processes that have terminated. Some systems do not return complete status information for stopped processes.
- Under System V.4, use `WCONTINUED` to report the status of any process that has continued (in other words, one that is no longer stopped) since the last status report.
- Also under System V.4, you can set the option `WNOWAIT` to specify that the process should not terminate (it remains a zombie). This means that you can call `waitpid` again and get the same information.

The value of `status` is the same as with `wait`. See the previous section for further details.

If you run into problems with `waitpid`, it may be due to a bug. Some versions of System V.3, including most current versions of SCO UNIX, return a process ID if a process is waiting and an error number such as `ECHILD` (10) if nothing is waiting. If your freshly ported program keeps reporting the demise of process 10, this could be the problem. It's almost impossible to work around this bug—about all you can do is to use some other system call.

wait3 and wait4

Newer BSD implementations supply the functions `wait3` and `wait4` as alternatives to `wait`. They correspond to `wait` and `waitpid`, respectively, but return an additional parameter `rusage` with accounting information for the terminated process:

```
pid_t wait3 (int *status, int options, struct rusage *rusage);
pid_t wait4 (pid_t wpid, int *status, int options, struct rusage *rusage);
```

Not all implementations return usage information to `rusage` when the process is stopped (and not terminated). The definition of `struct rusage` is implementation dependent and defined in *sys/resource.h*. See the file *sys/sys/resource.h* in the 4.4BSD Lite distribution for further details.

In This Chapter:
- *Supported Signals*
- *Unreliable and Reliable Signals*
- *Signal Handlers*
- *SIGCLD and SIGCHLD*
- *Interrupted System Calls*
- *Calling Functions from Signal Handlers*
- *Current Signal Implementations*
- *Other Signal-Related Functions*

13

Signals

Signals are another area in UNIX where the initial implementation was inadequate, and multiple implementations have developed in the course of time. If you try to port software that assumes the presence of one implementation and your system doesn't support this implementation, you could be in for a significant amount of rewriting. The situation isn't improved by the number of subtle differences that exist between the various implementations and even between different systems with the same implementation. In this chapter, we'll look at those aspects of signal implementation that relate to porting.

Four different implementations have been developed in the course of UNIX history:

- The Seventh Edition had so-called *unreliable signals* and handled them with the `signal` system call. System V still supplies them with the `signal` system call. As we will see in the section called "Seventh Edition Signal Function", the use of the `signal` function does not automatically imply unreliable signals.
- 4.2BSD introduced the first implementation of *reliable signals*. It uses the functions `signal`, `sigvec`, `sigblock`, `sigsetmask`, and `sigpause`.
- System V introduced an alternative implementation of reliable signals. It uses the functions `sigset`, `sighold`, `sigrelse`, `sigignore`, and `sigpause`.

- Finally, POSIX.1 defined a third implementation of reliable signals. These are based on the BSD signals and use the functions `sigaction`, `sigprocmask`, `sigpending`, and `sigsuspend`.

Most people think of signals as the way the operating system or an outside user stops a program that is misbehaving. More generally, they are a means to cause execution of functions out of sequence and have thus been called *software interrupts*. Hardware interrupts cause the system to interrupt normal processing and perform a specific sequence of instructions. Signals do the same in software: when a process receives a signal, the kernel simulates a call to a predefined routine.* The routine, called a *signal handler*, handles the signal and possibly returns to the "caller."

For every program to supply a signal handler for every conceivable signal would require significant overhead, so the kernel supplies two default methods of handling the signal. The choice of a signal handler or one of the two defaults is called the *disposition* of the signal. Initially, each signal's disposition is set either to ignore the signal or to terminate the process if the signal occurs. In some cases, the system writes a *core* file, a copy of the state of the process, when the process is terminated.

Signals may come from a number of different sources:

- External events. For example, pressing **CTRL-C** or **DEL** on most systems causes the terminal driver to send a SIGINT signal to the foreground process group of the terminal.
- Internal events. For example, `alarm` causes a SIGALRM signal after the specified timeout.
- Hardware interrupts. For example, if a process attempts to access a page that is not part of its address space, it receives a SIGSEGV or SIGBUS signal.
- As the result of another process calling `kill`.

In this chapter, we'll consider which signals are supported by which operating systems and how signals are implemented in different operating systems.

* This is not a real call. When the kernel delivers the signal, it modifies the process stack and registers so that it looks as if the signal handler has just been called. When the process continues executing, it is in the signal handler. Nobody ever really calls the signal handler.

Supported Signals

The Seventh Edition had 15 signals, and current implementations allow up to 31, though not all are used. In the course of time, the meanings have also diverged somewhat. Table 13-1 gives an overview of which signals are present in which implementations.

Table 13-1: Signal Usage

Signal	V7	SVR3	SVR4	BSD	POSIX	Action	Purpose
SIGABRT			•	•	•	core	Abort call[a]
SIGALRM	•	•	•	•	•	kill	Real-time timer expired
SIGBUS	•	•	•	•		core	Bus error
SIGCHLD			•	•	•	ignore	Child status has changed
SIGCLD		•	•			ignore	Child status has changed
SIGCONT		•	•	•	•	ignore	Continue after stop
SIGEMT	•	•	•	•		core	Emulate instruction executed
SIGFPE	•	•	•	•	•	core	Floating-point exception
SIGHUP	•	•	•	•	•	kill	Line hangup
SIGILL	•	•	•	•	•	core	Illegal instruction
SIGINFO			•	•		ignore	Status request from keyboard
SIGINT	•	•	•	•	•	kill	Interrupt program (usually from terminal driver)
SIGIO			•	•		ignore	I/O completion outstanding[b]
SIGIOT	•	•				core	IOT instruction[a]
SIGKILL	•	•	•	•	•	kill	Kill program[c]
SIGPIPE	•	•	•	•	•	kill	Write on a pipe with no reader
SIGPROF			•	•		kill	Profiling timer alarm
SIGPWR		•	•	•		ignore	Power fail/restart
SIGQUIT	•	•	•	•	•	core	Quit program (usually from terminal driver)
SIGSEGV	•	•	•	•	•	core	Segmentation violation
SIGSTOP		•	•	•	•	stop	Stop[c]
SIGSYS	•	•	•	•		core	Invalid system call
SIGTERM	•	•	•	•	•	kill	Software termination signal
SIGTRAP	•	•	•	•		core	Trace trap

Table 13-1: Signal Usage (continued)

Signal	V7	SVR3	SVR4	BSD	POSIX	Action	Purpose
SIGTSTP		•	•	•	•	stop	Stop signal generated from keyboard
SIGTTIN		•	•	•	•	stop	Background read from control terminal
SIGTTOU		•	•	•	•	stop	Background write to control terminal
SIGURG			•	•		ignore	Urgent condition present on socket
SIGUSR1		•	•	•	•	kill	User-defined signal 1
SIGUSR2		•	•	•	•	kill	User-defined signal 2
SIGVTALRM			•			kill	Virtual time alarm
SIGWINCH		•[d]	•	•		ignore	Window size change
SIGXCPU		•	•	•		core	CPU time limit exceeded
SIGXFSZ		•	•	•		core	File size limit exceeded

[a] SIGIOT and SIGABRT usually have the same signal number.
[b] Sometimes called SIGPOLL in System V.
[c] This signal cannot be caught or ignored.
[d] Not available in all versions.

Unreliable and Reliable Signals

The terms *unreliable signals* and *reliable signals* need explaining. The problem relates to what happens when a signal handler is active: if another signal occurs during this time, and it is allowed to be delivered to the process, the signal handler is entered again. Now it's not difficult to write reentrant* signal handlers—in fact, it's a very good idea because it means that you can use one signal handler to handle multiple signals. But if the same signal reoccurs before the signal handler has finished handling the previous instance, the signal could reoccur again and again, and the result can be a stack overflow with repeated signal handler calls.

The original signal implementation, which we call *unreliable signals*, had a simplistic attitude to this problem. It reset the signal dispostion to the default, which meant that if another signal occurred while the previous one was being processed, the system would either ignore the signal (so it would lose the signal) or terminate the process (which is probably not what you want). It was up to the signal

* A *reentrant function* is one that can be called by functions that it has called. In other words, it can be entered again before it has returned. This places a number of restrictions on the function. In particular, it cannot rely on external values and may not use static storage.

handler to reinstate the signal disposition, and this couldn't be done immediately without running the risk of stack overflow.

All newer signal implementations provide so-called *reliable signals.* The signal disposition is not changed on entry to the signal handler, but a new signal is not delivered until the signal handler returns. This concept is called *blocking* the signal: the system notes that the signal is pending, but doesn't deliver it until it is unblocked.

The term *reliable signal* does *not* mean the following:

- The underlying kernel implementation is bug free. Depending on the implementation, there is still a slight chance that the kernel could lose the signal.
- A signal cannot get lost. The method used to queue signals is to set a bit in a bit mask. If multiple signals of the same kind occur while the signal is blocked, only one is delivered.
- You don't need reentrant signal handlers. The system blocks only the signal that is currently being handled. If you have a single handler for multiple signals, it needs to be reentrant. In particular, this means that you should at least be very careful with static variables and preferably use few local variables (since they take up stack space). You should also be careful with the functions you call. We'll take another look at this issue in the section called "Calling Functions from Signal Handlers".

The semantics of each implementation differ in subtle ways, so changing to a different set of signal calls involves more than just changing the function calls and parameters. Here's a brief overview of the differences you might encounter:

- With unreliable signals, after a signal occurs, the signal disposition is reset to default, so the signal handler must reinstate itself before returning. If a second signal occurs before the disposition is reinstated, the process may be terminated (if the default disposition is *terminate*), or the signal may be completely forgotten (if the default disposition is *ignore*).
- The names and purposes of the signals differ significantly from one implementation to the next. See Table 13-1 for an overview.
- In modern implementations, the function call `signal` varies in its meaning. In System V, it uses the old, unreliable Seventh Edition signal semantics, while in BSD it is an interface to the `sigaction` system call, which provides reliable signals. If you're porting BSD `signal` to System V, you should modify the code to use `sigaction` instead.

- The first parameter to a signal handler is always the number of the signal. Both System V.4 and BSD can supply additional parameters to the signal handlers. We'll look at the additional parameters in more detail in the section called "System V.4 Signal Handlers".
- The handling of *interrupted system calls* varies from one system to the next. We'll look into this topic in more detail in the section called "Interrupted System Calls".
- The difference between the signals SIGBUS and SIGSEGV is purely historical: it relates to the PDP-11 hardware interrupt that detected the problem. In modern systems, which signal you get depends on the whim of the implementor. POSIX.1 defines only SIGSEGV, but this doesn't help much if the processor generates SIGBUS anyway. It's best to treat them as equivalent.
- SIGCLD is a System V version of SIGCHLD. A number of hairy problems can arise with SIGCLD; we'll look at them in more detail in the section called "BSD Signal Handlers".
- SIGILL was generated by the abort function in early BSD implementations. Early System V used SIGIOT instead. All modern implementations generate SIGABRT. Frequently you'll find that SIGIOT and SIGABRT are in fact defined to have the same number; if you run into troubles where one or the other is undefined, you could possibly do simply this:

```
#define SIGIOT SIGABRT
```

Then write a handler for SIGABRT.

Signal Handlers

Modern versions of UNIX define signal handlers to be of type

```
void (*signal (int signum, void (*handler))) (int hsignum)
```

This definition is probably one of the most confusing you are likely to come across. To understand it, remember that we are talking about two functions:

- The *signal handler*, called handler in this declaration, takes an int parameter hsignum and returns a void pointer to the old signal handler function, which is of the same type as itself.
- The function signal, which takes two parameters. The first is signum, the number of the signal to be handled, of type int, and the second is a pointer to a signal handler function handler. It also returns a void pointer to a signal handler function.

In fact, in many implementations the signal handler function takes additional parameters, and you may find that your program takes advantage of them. We'll look at these in the following sections.

System V.4 Signal Handlers

The System V.4 signal handler interface offers additional functionality in certain circumstances. If you use the `sigaction` interface, and you set the flag `SA_SIGINFO` in `sa_flags`, the signal handler is invoked as if it were defined

```
void handler (int signum,
              struct siginfo *info,
              struct ucontext *context);
```

`siginfo` is an enormous structure, defined in */usr/include/siginfo.h*, which starts with

```
struct siginfo
  {
  int si_signo;                          /* signal from signal.h */
  int si_code;                           /* code from above */
  int si_errno;                          /* error from errno.h */
... more stuff, including space for further growth
  }
```

`ucontext` is defined in */usr/include/ucontext.h* and contains information about the user context at the time of the signal application. It includes the following fields:

`uc_sigmask`
: Contains the blocked signal mask.

`us_stack`
: Points to the top of stack at the time the signal was delivered.

`uc_mcontext`
: Contains the processor registers and any implementation-specific context data.

For example, assume you had set the signal handler for `SIGFPE` with the call in this example:

```
void bombout_handler (int signum,
                      struct siginfo *info,
                      struct ucontext *context);

sigset_t bombout_mask;
struct sigaction bad_error = {&bombout_handler,  handler for the signal
                              &bombout_mask,     signals to mask
                              SA_SIGINFO};       we want additional info

sigemptyset (&bombout_mask);                     no signals in mask
sigaction (SIGFPE, &bad_error, NULL);
```

On receipt of a SIGFPE,

- signal is set to SIGFPE.
- info->si_signo is also set to SIGFPE.
- On an i386 machine, info->si_code might be, for example, FPE_INTDIV (indicating an integer divide by zero) or FPE_FLTUND (indicating floating-point underflow).
- The value of info->si_errno can't be relied on to have any particular value.
- context->uc_sigmask contains the current signal mask.
- context->uc_stack points to the stack in use at the time the signal was delivered.
- context->uc_mcontext contains the contents of the processor registers at the time of the interrupt. This can be useful for debugging.

BSD Signal Handlers

BSD signal handlers do not use the flag SA_SIGINFO for sa_flags. Signal handlers always receive three parameters:

```
void handler (int signum, int code, struct sigcontext *context);
```

code gives additional information about certain signals—you can find this information in the header file */usr/include/machine/trap.h*. This file also contains information about how hardware interrupts are mapped to signals. context is hardware-dependent context information that can be used to restore process state under some circumstances. For example, for a Sparc architecture it is defined as the following:

```
struct sigcontext
  {
  int    sc_onstack;                          /* sigstack state to restore */
  int    sc_mask;                             /* signal mask to restore */
  /* begin machine dependent portion */
  int    sc_sp;                               /* %sp to restore */
  int    sc_pc;                               /* pc to restore */
  int    sc_npc;                              /* npc to restore */
  int    sc_psr;                              /* psr to restore */
  int    sc_g1;                               /* %g1 to restore */
  int    sc_o0;                               /* %o0 to restore */
  };
```

The program in the following example won't compile under BSD, since BSD doesn't define SA_SIGINFO, and the parameters for bombout_handler are different. We need to modify it a little:

```
void bombout_handler (int signum,
                      int code,
                      struct sigcontext *context);

sigset_t bombout_mask;
struct sigaction bad_error = {&bombout_handler,  handler for the signal
                              &bombout_mask,      signals to mask
                              0};
...the rest stays the same
```

If you enter this signal handler because of a SIGFPE, you might find the following conditions:

- signum will be set to SIGFPE.
- On an i386 machine, code might be, for example, FPE_INTOVF_TRAP (indicating an integer divide by zero) or FPE_FLTUND_TRAP (indicating floating-point underflow).
- The value of sc_onstack would be the previous *sigstack* state.
- context->sc_mask contains the current blocked signal mask, like context->uc_sigmask in the System V.4 example.
- The rest of the context structure shows the same kind of register information that System V.4 stores in context->uc_mcontext.

SIGCLD and SIGCHLD

System V treats the death of a child differently from other implementations. The System V signal SIGCLD differs from the BSD and POSIX.1 signal SIGCHLD and from all other signals by remaining active until you call wait. This can cause infinite recursion in the signal handler if you reinstate the signal via signal or sigset before calling wait. If you use the POSIX.1 sigaction call, you don't have to worry about this problem.

When a child dies, it becomes a *zombie.* As all voodoo fans know, a zombie is one of the Living Dead, neither alive nor dead. In UNIX terminology, when a child process becomes a zombie, the text and data segments are freed, the files are closed, but the process table entry and some other information remain until it is exorcized by the parent process, which is done by calling wait. By default, System V ignores SIGCLD and SIGCHLD, but the system creates zombies, so you can find out about child status by calling *wait.* If, however, you change the default to *explicitly* ignore the signal, the system ignores SIGCHLD and SIGCLD, but it also no longer creates zombie processes. If you set the disposition of SIGCHLD and SIGCLD to *ignore,* but you call wait anyway, it waits until *all* child processes have terminated and then returns –1 (error), with errno set to ECHILD. You can achieve the same effect with sigaction by specifying the SA_NOCLDWAIT flag in sa_flags. There is no way to achieve this behavior in other versions of UNIX. If you find your ported program is collecting zombies (which you can see with the *ps* program), it might be that the program uses this feature to avoid having to call wait. If you experience this problem, you can solve it by adding a signal handler for SIGCLD that just calls wait and returns.

The signal number for SIGCLD is the same as for SIGCHLD. The semantics depend on how you enable it: if you enable it with signal, you get SIGCLD semantics (and unreliable signals), and if you enable it with sigaction you get SIGCHLD and reliable signals. Don't count on this behavior, however. Some versions of System V have special coding to ensure that a separate SIGCLD signal is delivered for each child that dies.

Interrupted System Calls

Traditional UNIX kernels differentiate between *fast* and *slow* system calls. Fast calls are handled directly by the kernel, while slow calls require the cooperation of other processes or device drivers. While the call is being executed, the calling process is suspended.

If a signal for a process occurs while the process is suspended, the behavior depends both on whether the call is fast or slow and on the signal implementation. On traditional systems, if the priority is numerically less than (of a higher priority than) the constant PZERO, the signal is slow and remains pending until the priority rises above PZERO. Otherwise, it is fast, and the system call is interrupted. Typically, this means that disk and network operations are not interrupted, since they run at a priority below PZERO, whereas terminal and serial line operations can be interrupted. Some newer systems treat the relationship between priority and delivering signals more flexibly.

In the Seventh Edition, if a system call was interrupted, it returned an error, and errno was sent to EINTR. It was up to the process to decide whether to repeat the call. This added a significant coding overhead to just about every program; the result was that programs usually did not provide for interrupted system calls, and died when one occurred.

Later signal implementations improved on this state of affairs:

- In 4.2BSD, signals automatically restarted the system calls ioctl, read, readv, wait, waitpid, write, and writev.

- In 4.3BSD, the 4.2BSD signal implementation was modified so that the user could elect not to restart specific system calls after interruption. The default remained to restart the system call.
- In POSIX.1, when you call `sigaction` you can specify that system calls interrupted by specific signals should be restarted. You specify this with the `SA_RESTART` flag in the field `sa_flags`. If this flag is not set, the calls are not restarted.
- SunOS 4 does not have `SA_RESTART`, but it has `SA_INTERRUPT`, which is effectively the reverse of `SA_RESTART`: system calls are restarted unless `SA_INTERRUPT` is set.

On modern systems, the action taken depends on the system calls you have used and the system you are using:

- With System V, you have the choice of no restart (unreliable `signal` or System V `sigset` and friends), or POSIX.1 selective restart based on the signal (`SA_RESTART` with `sigaction`).
- With BSD, you have the choice of no restart (reliable `signal` based on `sigaction`), default restart based on system calls (`sigvec` and friends) or again the POSIX.1 selective restart based on the signal (`SA_RESTART` with `sigaction`).

Calling Functions from Signal Handlers

By definition, signals interrupt the normal flow of program execution. This can cause problems if the signal handler calls a function that has already been invoked and that has saved some local state. The function needs to be written specially to avoid such problems—it should block either all signals during execution, or, preferably, it should be written reentrantly. Either solution is difficult, and typically system libraries do not support this kind of reentrancy. On the other hand, there's not much you can do without calling some library routine. POSIX.1 defines "safe" routines that you can call from a signal handler. They are:

_exit	access	alarm	cfgetispeed	cfgetospeed
cfsetispeed	cfsetospeed	chdir	chmod	chown
close	creat	dup	dup2	execle
execve	fcntl	fork	fstat	getegid
geteuid	getgid	getgroups	getpgrp	getpid
getppid	getuid	kill	link	lseek
mkdir	mkfifo	open	pathconf	pause
pipe	read	rename	rmdir	setgid
setpgid	setsid	setuid	sigaction	sigaddset
sigdelset	sigemptyset	sigfillset	sigismember	sigpending

sigprocmask	sigsuspend	sleep	stat	sysconf
tcdrain	tcflow	tcflush	tcgetattr	tcgetpgrp
tcsendbreak	tcsetattr	tcsetpgrp	time	times
umask	uname	unlink	utime	wait
waitpid	write			

In addition, System V.4 allows `abort`, `exit`, `longjmp`, and `signal`.

Current Signal Implementations

In this section, we'll look at the differences between individual signal implementations. We'll concentrate on what you need to do to convert from one to another. If you *do* need to convert signal code, you should use the POSIX.1 signal implementation whenever practical.

Seventh Edition Signal Function

The Seventh Edition provided only one signal function, `signal`, which is the granddaddy of them all. All systems supply `signal`, though on some systems, such as newer BSD systems, it is a library function that calls `sigaction`. This also means that you can't rely on specific semantics if you use `signal`—avoid it if at all possible. Older UNIX systems (specifically those that did not expect function prototypes to be used) implicitly defined the return type of `signal` to be an `int`. This does not change the meaning of the return value, but it can confuse more pedantic compilers. About the only system still on the market that returns an `int` from `signal` is XENIX.

BSD Signal Functions

The BSD signal functions were the first attempt at reliable signals, and they form the basis of the POSIX.1 implementation. All modern systems offer the POSIX.1 implementation as well, and on many BSD systems the functions described in this section are just an interface to the POSIX.1 functions.

Signal sets

A central difference between the Seventh Edition and System V implementations, on the one side, and the BSD and POSIX.1 implementations, on the other side, is the way signals can be specified. The Seventh Edition functions treat individual signals, which are specified by their numbers. The BSD routines introduced the concept of the *signal set*, a bitmap of type `sigset_t`, that specifies any number of signals, as illustrated in Figure 13-1.

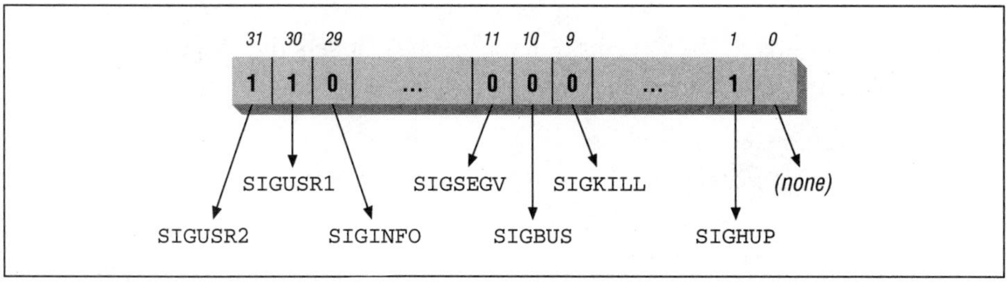

Figure 13-1: BSD and POSIX.1 signal sets

For each signal, if the corresponding bit in the bitmap is set, the signal is said to be included in the set. In this example, the signals specified are SIGUSR2, SIGUSR1, and SIGHUP. This method enables any number of signals to be specified as the parameter of one call.

The kernel maintains two special signal sets for each process: the *signal mask* and the *pending signal set*. The signal mask specifies which signals should not currently be delivered to the process—these signals are said to be *blocked*. This does not mean that they are ignored. If a signal occurs while it is blocked, the kernel notes that it has occurred and sets its bit in the pending signal set. When a subesequent call to **sigsetmask** resets the bit for this signal in the signal mask, the kernel delivers the signal to the process and clears the bit in the pending signal set.

sigsetmask

sigsetmask sets the process signal mask:

```
#include <sys/signal.h>
int sigsetmask (int mask);
```

sigsetmask can be defined in terms of the POSIX.1 function **sigprocmask** using the SIG_SETMASK flag—see Table 13-3 for more details.

sigblock

sigblock modifies the process signal mask. Unlike **sigsetmask**, it performs a logical OR of the specified mask with the current signal mask, so it can only block signals and not enable them.

```
#include <sys/signal.h>
int sigblock (int mask);
```

sigblock can be defined in terms of the POSIX.1 function **sigprocmask** using the SIG_BLOCK flag—see Table 13-3 for more details.

sigvec

`sigvec` corresponds to the Seventh Edition `signal`: it sets the disposition of a signal. In addition, it can block other signals during the processing of a signal.

```
#include <signal.h>
... in signal.h is the definition
struct sigvec
  {
  void      (*sv_handler) ();
  sigset_t sv_mask;
  int       sv_flags;
  };

sigvec (int signum, struct sigvec *vec, struct sigvec *ovec);
```

`signum` is the signal whose disposition is to be changed. `vec` specifies the new disposition of the signal, and the function returns the old disposition to `ovec`.

If `vec->sv_mask` is nonzero, it specifies the signals to block while the signal handler is running. This mask is logically ORed with the current signal mask, so it works like an implicit `sigblock` on entering the signal handler. On exit from the signal handler, the kernel reinstates the previous signal mask.

`flags` can consist of:

- `SV_ONSTAC K`, which specifies the signal to be taken on an alternate signal stack, if one has been defined.
- `SV_INTERRUPT`, which specifies that system calls should not be restarted after the signal handler has completed.

`sigvec` is almost identical to the POSIX.1 function `sigaction` (described in the section called "sigaction")—except the names of the `sigvec` structure and its members are different. Note, however, that the flag `SV_INTERRUPT` has the opposite meaning from the POSIX.1 flag `SA_RESTART`, which frequently has the same numeric value.

sigpause

`sigpause` combines the functionality of `sigmask` and `pause`: it first sets the signal mask and then calls *pause* to wait for a signal to occur.

```
#include <sys/signal.h>
int sigpause (sigset_t sigmask);
```

Typical use of BSD signal functions

Most signal coding consists of initialization. Typical programs set the disposition of the signals in which they are interested during program initialization and don't change them much after that. For example, with BSD signals you might see code like that in the following example:

```
struct sigvec hupvec = {&hup_handler, 0, 0}; /* disposition of SIGHUP */
struct sigvec iovec = {&io_handler, 1 << SIGHUP, 0}; /* disposition of SIGIO */
sigvec (SIGHUP, &hupvec, NULL);              /* instate handlers for SIGHUP, */
sigvec (SIGIO, &iovec, NULL);                /* SIGIO, */
sigvec (SIGURG, &iovec, NULL);               /* and SIGURG */
```

Occasionally a process uses `sigpause`, usually to wait for I/O. In Example 13.3 it blocks the signals `SIGINT` and `SIGQUIT`:

```
sigpause ((1 << SIGINT) | (1 << SIGQUIT));   /* wait for a signal */
```

System V Signal Functions

The following signal functions were implemented in System V and are effectively obsolete: the POSIX.1 functions have replaced them even in System V.3. The syntax of the function calls is more like the Seventh Edition than POSIX.1. In particular, they do not support the concept of a signal set. If you do find it necessary to replace System V signals with POSIX.1 signals, there is considerable scope for simplification by merging multiple System V calls (one per signal) into a single POSIX.1 call.

sigset

`sigset` is the System V reliable equivalent of `signal`:

```
#include <signal.h>
void (*sigset (int sig, void (*disp) (int))) (int);
```

Unlike `signal`, with `sigset` the signal is not disabled when the signal handler is executing—instead it is blocked until the signal handler terminates.

sighold

`sighold` blocks the delivery of signal `sig` by setting the corresponding bit in the process signal mask. Semantically this corresponds to the POSIX.1 function `sigprocmask` with the `SIG_BLOCK` flag, but it can block only one signal per call.

```
#include <signal.h>
int sighold (int sig);
```

sigrelse

sigrelse allows the delivery of signal sig by resetting the corresponding bit in the process signal mask. Semantically this corresponds to the POSIX.1 function sigprocmask with the SIG_UNBLOCK flag, but it can release only one signal per call.

```
#include <signal.h>
int sigrelse (int sig);
```

sigignore

sigignore sets the disposition of signal sig to SIG_IGN—the kernel ignores the signal.

```
#include <signal.h>
int sigignore (int sig);
```

sigpause

```
#include <signal.h>
int sigpause (int sig);
```

sigpause enables the delivery of signal sig and then waits for delivery of any signal.

CAUTION

This is *not* the same as the BSD function sigpause described in the section called "BSD Signal Functions". BSD sigpause takes a signal mask as an argument; System V sigpause takes a single signal number. In addition, BSD sigpause only resets the mask temporarily—until the function return—whereas System V sigpause leaves it in this condition.

Example of System V signal functions

In the example in the the section called "Typical use of BSD signal functions", we looked at what typical BSD code might look like. The System V equivalent of this program might perform the initialization shown in the following example. System V doesn't supply the functionality associated with SIGIO and SIGURG—it uses SIGPOLL instead. See the section called "fcntl" and the section called "SIGPOLL" in Chapter 14, *File Systems*, for more details.

```
sigset (SIGHUP, &hup_handler);              /* instate handlers for SIGHUP */
sigset (SIGPOLL, &io_handler);              /* and SIGPOLL */
```

System V sigpause has a different syntax, so we need to set the signal mask explicitly with calls to sighold and also to release them explicitly with sigrelse.

```
sighold (SIGINT);                    /* block SIGINT */
sighold (SIGQUIT);                   /* and SIGQUIT */
sigpause (0);                        /* wait for something to happen */
sigrelse (SIGINT);                   /* unblock SIGINT */
sigrelse (SIGQUIT);                  /* and SIGQUIT */
```

POSIX.1 Signal Functions

All modern UNIX implementations claim to support POSIX.1 signals. These are the functions to use if you need to rewrite signal code. They are similar enough to the BSD functions to be confusing. In particular, the BSD functions pass signal masks as `longs`, whereas the POSIX.1 functions pass pointers to the signal mask—this enables the number of signals to exceed the number of bits in a `long`.

sigaction

`sigaction` is the POSIX.1 equivalent of `signal`. It specifies the disposition of a signal. In addition, it can specify a mask of signals to be blocked during the processing of a signal and a number of flags whose meaning varies significantly from system to system.

```
#include <signal.h>
struct sigaction
  {
  void     (*sa_handler) ();         /* handler */
  sigset_t sa_mask;                  /* signals to block during processing */
  int      sa_flags;
  };

void sigaction (int sig,
                const struct sigaction *act,
                struct sigaction *oact);
```

`signum` is the signal whose disposition is to be changed. `act` specifies the new disposition of the signal, and the function returns the old disposition to `oact`.

If `act->sa_mask` is nonzero, it specifies which signals to block while the signal handler is running. This is logically ORed with the current signal mask, so it works like an implicit `sigblock` on entering the signal handler.

Table 13-2 provides an overview of the flags.

Table 13-2: sigaction Flags

Parameter	Supported by	Meaning
SA_ONSTACK	BSD, System V	Take the signal on the alternate signal stack, if one has been defined. POSIX.1 does not define the concept of an alternate signal stack—see the section called "sigstack and sigaltstack" for more details. Linux plans similar functionality with the SA_STACK flag, but at the time of writing it has not been implemented.
SA_RESETHAND	System V	Reset the disposition of this signal to SIG_DFL when the handler is entered (simulating Seventh Edition semantics). This is the same as the Linux SA_ONESHOT flag.
SA_ONESHOT	Linux	Reset the disposition of this signal to SIG_DFL when the handler is entered (simulating Seventh Edition semantics). This is the same as the System V SA_RESETHAND flag.
SA_RESTART	BSD, System V	Restart system calls after the signal handler has completed (see the section called "Interrupted System Calls").
SA_SIGINFO	System V	Provide additional parameters to signal handler (see the section called "System V.4 Signal Handlers").
SA_NODEFER	System V	Don't block this signal while its signal handler is active. This means that the signal handler can be called from a function that it calls and thus needs to be reentrant.
SA_NOCLDWAIT	System V	Don't create zombie children on SIGCLD (see the section called "BSD Signal Handlers").
SA_NOCLDSTOP	Linux, System V	Don't generate SIGCHLD when a child stops, only when it terminates.
SA_NOMASK	Linux	Disable the signal mask (allow all signals) during the execution of the signal handler.
SA_INTERRUPT	Linux	Disable automatic restart of signals. This corresponds to the SunOS 4 flag SV_INTERRUPT in the `sigvec` call (see the section called "sigvec"). Currently not implemented.

sigprocmask

`sigprocmask` manipulates the process signal mask. It includes functional modes that correspond to both of the BSD functions `sigblock` and `sigsetmask`:

```
#include <signal.h>
int sigprocmask (int how, const sigset_t *set, sigset_t *oset)
```

The parameter `how` determines how the mask is to be manipulated. It can have the values provided in Table 13-3.

Table 13-3: sigprocmask Functional Modes

Parameter	Meaning
SIG_BLOCK	Create a new signal mask by logically ORing the current mask with the specified set.
SIG_UNBLOCK	Reset the bits in the current signal mask specified in set.
SIG_SETMASK	Replace the current signal mask by set.

sigpending

```
#include <signal.h>
int sigpending (sigset_t *set);
```

`sigpending` returns the pending signal mask to `set`. These are the signals pending delivery but currently blocked, which will be delivered as soon as the signal mask allows. The return value is an error indication and *not* the signal mask. This function does not have an equivalent in any other signal implementation.

sigsuspend

```
#include <sys/signal.h>
int sigsuspend (const sigset_t *sigmask);
```

`sigsuspend` temporarily sets the process signal mask to `sigmask` and then waits for a signal. When the signal is received, the previous signal mask is restored on exit from `sigsuspend`. It always returns –1 (error), with `errno` set to `EINTR` (interrupted system call).

Example of POSIX.1 signal functions

In the example in the section called "Typical use of BSD signal functions", we looked at a simple example of signal setup, and in the two examples in the section called "Example of System V signal functions" and we changed it for System V. Changing it from BSD to POSIX.1 is mainly a matter of changing the names. We change the calls to `sigvec` to `sigaction`, and their parameters are now also of type `struct sigaction` instead of `struct sigvec`.

Unfortunately, there is a problem with this example: POSIX.1 does not define any of the I/O signals to which this example refers. This is not as bad as it sounds, since there are no pure POSIX.1 systems, and all systems offer either SIGIO/SIGURG or SIGPOLL. In the following example, we'll stick with the BSD signals SIGIO and SIGURG:

```
struct sigaction hupvec = {&hup_handler, 0, 0}; /* disposition of SIGHUP */
struct sigaction iovec = {&io_handler, 1 << SIGHUP, 0};/* disposition of SIGIO */
sigaction (SIGHUP, &hupvec, NULL);              /* instate handlers for SIGHUP, */
sigaction (SIGIO, &iovec, NULL);                /* SIGIO, */
sigaction (SIGURG, &iovec, NULL);               /* and SIGURG */
sigset_t blockmask;                             /* create a mask */
sigemptyset (&blockmask);                       /* clear signal mask */
sigaddset (&blockmask, SIGINT);                 /* add SIGINT to the mask */
sigaddset (&blockmask, SIGQUIT);                /* add SIGQUIT to the mask */
```

The following example shows the corresponding call to sigsuspend:

```
sigsuspend (&blockmask);                        /* let the action begin */
```

We'll look at `sigemptyset` and `sigaddset` in the section called "Other Signal-Related Functions". It's unfortunate that this part of the initialization looks so complicated. It's just part of the explicit programming style that POSIX.1 desires. On most systems, you could get the same effect without the calls to `sigemptyset` and `sigaddset` by just defining

```
int blockmask = (1 << SIGINT) | (1 << SIGQUIT);
sigpause ((sigset_t *) &blockmask);             /* let the action begin */
```

The only problem with this approach (and it's a showstopper) is that it's not portable: on a different system, `sigset_t` might not map to `int`.

Signals Under Linux

Linux signals are an implementation of POSIX.1 signals, and we discussed some of the details in the previous section. In addition, it's good to know that:

- For compatibility, SIGIOT is defined as SIGABRT. POSIX.1 does not define SIGIOT.
- As we saw, POSIX.1 does not supply the signals SIOPOLL, SIGIO, and SIGURG. Linux does, but it maps all three signals to the same numerical value.
- If you really want to, you can simulate unreliable signals under Linux with `sigaction` and the SA_ONESHOT flag.

Other Signal-Related Functions

A significant advantage of the BSD and POSIX.1 signal functions over the Seventh Edition and System V versions is that they have signal set parameters. The down side of signal sets is that you need to calculate the values of the bits. The following functions are intended to make manipulating these structures easier. They are usually implemented as macros:

`sigemptyset (sigset_t *set)`
    Sets `set` to the "empty" signal set—in other words, it excludes all signals.

`sigfillset (sigset_t *set)`
    Sets all valid signals in `set`.

`sigaddset (sigset_t *set, int signum)`
    Adds signal `signum` to `set`.

`sigdelset (sigset_t *set, int signum)`
    Removes signal `signum` from `set`.

`sigismember (sigset_t *set, int signum)`
    Returns 1 if `signum` is set in `set` and 0 otherwise.

sigstack and sigaltstack

As we have already discussed, a signal is like a forced function call. On modern processors with stack-oriented hardware, the call uses stack space. In some cases, a signal that arrives at the wrong time could cause a stack overflow. To avoid this problem, both System V and BSD (but not POSIX.1) allow you to define a specific *signal stack*. On receipt of a signal, the stack is switched to the alternate stack, and on return the original stack is reinstated. This can also occasionally be of interest in debugging. If a program gets a signal because of a reference beyond the top of the stack, it's not much help if the signal destroys the evidence.

BSD supplies the **sigstack** system call:

```
#include <sys/signal.h>
struct sigstack
  {
  caddr_t ss_sp;                  /* Stack address */
  int     ss_onstack;             /* Flag, set if currently
                                   * executing on this stack */
  };
int sigstack (const struct sigstack *ss, struct sigstack *oss);
```

- ss may be NULL. If it is not, the process signal stack is set to ss->ss_sp.
- ss->ss_onstack tells sigstack whether the process is currently executing on the stack.
- oss may also be NULL. If it is not, information about the current signal stack is returned to it.

System V supplies the function sigaltstack:

```
#include <signal.h>
typedef struct
  {
  char *ss_sp;                                    /* Stack address */
  int   ss_size;                                  /* Stack size */
  int   ss_flags;                                 /* Flags, see below */
  }
stack_t;
int sigaltstack (const stack_t *ss, stack_t *oss);
```

- ss may be NULL. If it is not, the process signal stack is set to ss->ss_sp, and its size is set to ss->ss_size.
- oss may also be NULL. If it is not, information about the current signal stack is returned to it.
- The structure element ss_flags may contain the following flags:
  - SS_DISABLE specifies that the alternate stack is to be disabled. ss_sp and ss_size are ignored. This flag is also returned in oss when the alternate stack is disabled.
  - SS_ONSTACK (returned) indicates that the process is currently executing on the alternate stack. If this is the case, a modification of the stack is not possible.

setjmp and longjmp

When you return from a function, C language syntax does not give you a choice of where to return to: you return to the instruction after the call. Occasionally, deep in a series of nested function calls, you will discover you need to return several levels down the stack—effectively, you want to perform multiple returns. Standard "structured programming" techniques do not handle this requirement well, and you can't just perform a goto to the location because that would leave the stack in a mess. The library functions setjmp and longjmp provide this *nonlocal return.*

What does this have to do with signals? Nothing, really, except that the receipt of a signal is one of the most common reasons to want to perform a nonlocal return: a signal can interrupt processing anywhere where the process signal mask allows it. In many cases, the result of the signal processing is not related to the processing that was interrupted, and it may be necessary to abort the processing and perform a nonlocal return. For example, if you are redisplaying data in an X window and the size of the window changes, you will get a SIGWINCH signal. Since this requires a complete recalculation of what needs to be displayed, there is no point in continuing the current redisplay operation.

Nonlocal returns are implemented with the functions setjmp, longjmp, and friends. setjmp saves the process context, and longjmp restores it—in other words, it returns to the point in the program where setjmp was called. Unlike a regular function return, a longjmp return may involve discarding a significant part of the stack. There are a number of related functions:

```
#include <setjmp.h>

int setjmp (jmp_buf env);
void longjmp (jmp_buf env, int val);
int _setjmp (jmp_buf env);
void _longjmp (jmp_buf env, int val);
void longjmperror (void);
int sigsetjmp (sigjmp_buf env, int savemask);
void siglongjmp (sigjmp_buf env, int val);
```

The definitions of jmp_buf and sigjmp_buf are less than illuminating: they are just defined as an array of ints long enough to contain the information that the system saves. In fact, they contain the contents of the registers that define the process context—stack pointer, frame pointer, program counter, and usually a number of other registers.

From the user point of view, setjmp is unusual in that it can return more often than you call it. Initially, you call setjmp, and it returns the value 0. If it returns again, it's because the program called longjmp, and this time it returns the value parameter passed to longjmp, which normally should not be 0. The caller can then use this value to determine whether this is a direct return from setjmp, or whether it returned via longjmp:

```
int return_code = setjmp (env);
if (return_code)
  {                       /* non-0 return code: return from longjmp */
  printf ("longjmp returned %d\n", return_code);
  }
```

These functions are confusing enough in their own right, but they also have less obvious features:

- It doesn't make any sense for longjmp to return 0, and System V.4 longjmp never returns 0, even if you tell it to—it returns 1 instead. BSD longjmp returns whatever you tell it to.
- The setjmp functions save information about the state of the function that called them. Once this function returns, this information is no longer valid. For example, the following code does not work:

```
jmp_buf env;                                    /* save area for setjmp */

int mysetjmp ()
  {
  int a = 0;
  if (a = setjmp (env))
    printf ("Bombed out\n");
  return a;
  }

foo ()
  {
  ...
  mysetjmp ();                                  /* catch bad errors */
  ...
  }
```

  The return instruction from mysetjmp to foo frees its local environment. The memory that it occupies, and that the call to setjump saved, is overwritten by the next function call, so a longjmp cannot restore it.
- BSD attempts to determine whether the parameter env to the longjmp functions is invalid (such as in the previous example). If it detects such an error, it calls longjmperror, which is intended to inform that the longjmp has failed. If longjmperror returns, the process is aborted.

  If longjmp does not recognize the error, or if the system is not BSD, the resulting process state is indeterminate. To quote the System V.4 man page: "If longjmp is called even though env was never primed by a call to setjmp, or when the last such call was in a function that has since returned, absolute chaos is guaranteed." In fact, the system will probably generate a SIGSEGV or a SIGBUS, but the core dump will probably show nothing recognizable.
- When longjmp returns to the calling function, automatic variables reflect the last modifications made to them in the function. For example:

```
int foo ()
  {
  int a = 3;
  if (setjmp (env))
```

```
      {
      printf ("a: %d\n", a);
      return a;
      }
    a = 2;
    longjmp (env, 4);
    }
```

At the point where `longjmp` is called, the variable `a` has the value 2, so this function prints `a: 2`.

- When `longjmp` returns to the calling function, register variables normally have the values they had at the time of the call to `setjmp`, since they have been saved in the jump buffer. Since optimizers may reassign automatic variables to registers, this can have confusing results. If you compile the previous example with *gcc* and optimize it, it prints `a: 3`. This is clearly an unsuitable situation: the solution is to declare `a` to be `volatile` (see the section called "ANSI C" in Chapter 20, *Compilers*, for more information). If we do this, `a` will always have the value 2 after the `longjmp`.
- BSD `setjmp` includes the signal mask in the state information it saves, but System V.4 `setjmp` does not save the signal mask. If you want to simulate System V.4 semantics under BSD, you need to use `_setjmp` and `_longjmp`, which do not save the signal mask. In either system, you can use `sigsetjmp`, which saves the signal mask only if `save` is nonzero. Except for the type of its first parameter, the corresponding `siglongjmp` is used in exactly the same manner as `longjmp`.
- The functions must be paired correctly: if you `_setjmp`, you must `_longjmp`, and if you `setjmp` you must `longjmp`.

kill

`kill` is one of the most badly named system calls in the UNIX system. Its function is to send a signal:

```
#include <signal.h>
int kill (pid_t pid, int sig);
```

Normally, `pid` is the process ID of the process that should receive the signal `sig`. There are a couple of additional tricks, however:

- If `pid` is 0, the kernel sends `sig` to all processes whose process group ID is the same as the group ID of the calling process.

- If pid is –1, most implementations broadcast the signal to all user processes if the signal is sent by *root*. Otherwise, the signal is sent to all processes with the same effective user ID. BSD does not broadcast the signal to the calling process, System V does. POSIX.1 does not define this case.
- If pid is < –1, System V and BSD broadcast the signal to all processes whose process group ID is abs (pid) (abs is the absolute value function). Again, non-*root* processes are limited to sending signals to processes with the same effective user ID. BSD can also perform this function with the call killpg.

Another frequent use of kill is to check whether a process exists: kill (pid, 0) does not actually send a signal, but it returns success if the process exists and returns an error indication otherwise.

killpg

killpg broadcasts a signal to all processes whose process group ID is abs (pid). It is supplied with BSD systems:

```
#include <sys/signal.h>

int killpg (pid_t pgrp, int sig);
```

This function sends the signal to the process group of the specified process, assuming that you have the same effective user ID as the recipient process, or you are superuser. You can use pid 0 to indicate your own process group. If you don't have this function, you can possibly replace it with kill (-pgid)—see the previous section on *kill*.

raise

raise is an ANSI C function that enables a process to send a signal to itself. It is defined as

```
int raise (int signum);
```

Older systems don't have raise. You can fake it in terms of kill and getpid:

```
kill (getpid (), signum);
```

sys_siglist and psignal

At the name implies, sys_siglist is a list and not a function. More exactly, it is an array of signal names, indexed by signal number, and is typically supplied with BSD-derived systems. For example,

```
printf ("Signal %d (%s)\n", SIGSEGV, sys_siglist [SIGSEGV]);
```

returns

```
Signal 11 (Segmentation fault)
```

Some systems supply the function `psignal` instead of `sys_siglist`. It prints the text corresponding to a signal.

In This Chapter:
- *File System Structures*
- *Function Calls*
- *Nonblocking I/O*
- *File Locking*
- *Memory-Mapped Files*

14

File Systems

UNIX owes much of its success to the simplicity and flexibility of the facilities it offers for file handling, generally called the *file system*. This term can have two different meanings:

- It can be a part of a hard disk or floppy that can be accessed as a collection of files. It includes regular files and directories. A floppy is usually a single file system, whereas a hard disk can be partitioned into several file systems and possibly also nonfile system parts, such as swap space and bad track areas.
- It can be the software in the kernel that accesses the file systems above.

UNIX has a single file hierarchy, unlike MS-DOS, which uses a separate letter for each file system (`A:` and `B:` for floppies, `C:` to `Z:` for local and network accessible disks). MS-DOS determines the drive letter for the file systems at boot time, whereas UNIX determines only the location of the root file system / at boot time. You add the other file systems to the directory tree by mounting them:

```
$ mount /dev/usr /usr
```

This command mounts the file system on the disk partition */dev/usr* onto the directory */usr*, so if the root directory of */dev/usr* contains a file called *foo*, after mounting you can access it as */usr/foo*.

In addition to filenames, the file system marks files by numbers called inodes. When several file systems are mounted, each has a separate set of inodes. You never think about inodes during normal operation, but we'll have reason to talk about them in this chapter.

Anything useful is bound to attract people who want to make it more useful, so it should come as no surprise that a large number of "improvements" have been made to the file system in the course of time. In the rest of this chapter, we'll look at the following aspects in more detail:

- File systems introduced since the Seventh Edition
- Differences in function calls, in the section called "Function Calls"
- Non-blocking I/O
- File locking
- Memory-mapped files

File System Structures

The original Seventh Edition file system is—at least in spirit—the basis for all current file system implementations. UNIX file systems differ in one important point from almost all non-UNIX file systems. At the lowest level, the file system refers to files by numbers, so-called *inodes*. Inodes are indices in the *inode table*, a part of the file system reserved for describing files. At a higher level, the directory system enables a file to be referred to by a name. This relationship between a name and an inode is called a *link*, and it enables a single file to have multiple names. One consequence of this scheme is that it is usually impossible to determine the filename of an open file.

The Seventh Edition file system is no longer in use in modern systems, though the System V file system is quite similar. Since the Seventh Edition, a number of new file systems have addressed weaknesses of the old file system:

- New file types were introduced, such as *symbolic links*, *FIFO*s, and *sockets*.
- The performance was improved.
- The reliability was increased significantly.
- The length of the filenames was increased.

We'll look briefly at some of the differences in the next few sections.

The Berkeley Fast File System

The first alternative file system to appear was the Berkeley *Fast File System*, (*FFS*), now called the *Unix File System* (*ufs*).* It is described in detail in *A Fast File System for UNIX* by Kirk McKusick, et. al., and *The Design and the Implementation of the*

* Don't confuse the Berkeley FFS with SCO's afs, which is sometimes referred to as a Fast File System. In fact, afs is very similar to s5fs, though later versions have symbolic links and longer filenames.

4.3BSD UNIX Operating System by Sam Leffler, et. al. Its main purpose was to increase speed and storage efficiency. Compared to the Seventh Edition file system, the following differences are relevant to porting software:

- The maximum filename size was increased from 14 to 255 characters.
- The size of the inode number was increased from 16 to 32 bits, thus allowing an effectively unlimited number of files.
- *Symbolic links* were introduced.

A symbolic link differs from a regular link in that it points to another file name, and not an inode number.

Symbolic links

A symbolic link is a file whose complete contents are the name of another file. To access via a symbolic link, the file system first needs to find the directory entry to which it is pointing, then resolve the link to the inode. By contrast, a traditional link (sometimes called *hard link*) links a filename to an inode. Several names can point to the same inode, but it only takes one step to find the file. This seemingly minor difference has a number of consequences:

- A definite relationship exists between the original file and the symbolic link. In a regular link, each of the filenames have the same relationship to the inode; in a symbolic link, the symbolic link name *refers* to the main filename. This difference is particularly obvious if you remove the original file: with a regular link, the other name still works perfectly. With a symbolic link, you lose the file.
- There's nothing to stop a symbolic link from pointing to another symbolic link—in fact, it's quite common and is moderately useful. It also opens the possibility of looping: if the second symbolic link points back to the first, the system gives up after a few iterations with the error code `ELOOP`.
- Symbolic links have two file permissions. In practice, the permission of the link itself is of little consequence—normally it is set to allow reading, writing, and execution for all users (on an *ls -l* listing you see `lrwxrwxrwx`). The permission that counts is still the permission of the original file.
- Symbolic links allow links to different file systems, even (via NFS) to a file system on a different machine. This is particularly useful when using read-only media, such as CD-ROMs. See Chapter 3, *Care and Feeding of Source Trees*, for some examples.

- Symbolic links open up a whole new area of possible errors. It's possible for a symbolic link to point to a file that doesn't exist, so you can't access the file, even if you have a name and the correct permissions.

Other File Systems

Other file systems have emerged since ufs, including:

- The *System V File System, s5fs*, a minor evolution of the Seventh Edition file system with some performance and stability modifications and without multiplexed files. Even in System V, ufs has replaced it. For all practical purposes, you can consider s5fs to be obsolete.
- The *Veritas File System, vxfs*, and the *Veritas Journaling File system, vjfs*. From the point of view of porting, they are effectively compatible with ufs.
- The *Network File System, NFS*,* a method of sharing file systems across networks. It allows a system to mount file systems connected to a different machine. NFS runs on just about any system, including System V.3 and DOS, but unfortunately not XENIX. It can offer a partial escape from the "14 character file limit, no symlinks" syndrome. It is reasonably transparent but unfortunately does not support device files.
- *Remote File Sharing, rfs*. This is AT&T's answer to NFS. Although it has a number of advantages over NFS, it is not widely used.

Along with new file systems, new file types have evolved. We have already looked at symbolic links, which we can think of as a new file type. Others include *FIFOs* (First In First Out) and *sockets*, means of interprocess communications that we looked at in Chapter 12, *Kernel Dependencies*.

In practice, you run into problems only when you port software developed under ufs, vjfs, or vxfs to a s5fs system. If you can, you should change your file system. If you can't do that, here are some of the things that could give you headaches:

- *Filename length*. There's very little you can do about this: if the filenames are longer than your kernel can understand, you have to change them. Some subtle problems arise because some 14-character file systems accept longer names and just silently truncate them; others, notably SCO, signal an error. It should be fairly evident what your file system does when you try a filename that is too long. If your system has the `pathconf` system call, you can also interrogate this programmatically (see the section called "pathconf and fpathconf").

* People just don't seem to be able to agree whether to write file system names in uppercase (as befits an abbreviation) or in lowercase (the way most *mount* commands want to see them). It appears that NFS is written in uppercase more frequently than the other names.

- *Lack of symbolic links* is another big problem. You may need far-reaching source changes to get around this problem, which could bite you early on in the port: you may have an archive containing symbolic links, or the configuration routines might try to create them.

Another, more subtle difference is that BSD and System V do not agree on the question of group ownership. In particular, when you create a file, the group ownership may be that of the directory, or it may be that of the process that creates the file. BSD always gives the file the group of the directory; in System V.4, it is the group of the process, *unless* the "set group ID" bit is set in the directory permissions, in which case the file belongs to the same group as the directory.

Function Calls

The Seventh Edition left a surprising amount of functionality up to the system library. For example, the kernel supplied no method to create a directory or rename a file. The methods that were used to make up for these deficiencies were not always reliable, and in the course of the time, these functions have been implemented as system calls. Current systems offer the following functions, some of them system calls:

chsize

`chsize` changes the end of file of an open file.

```
int chsize (int fd, long size);
```

It originated in XENIX and has been inherited by System V.3.2 and System V.4. It corresponds both in function and in parameters to the System V version of `ftruncate`: if the new end-of-file pointer is larger than the current end-of-file pointer, `chsize` extends the file to the new size.

dup2

All systems offer the system call `dup`, which creates a copy of a file descriptor:

```
int dup (int oldd);
```

`oldd` is an open file descriptor; `dup` returns another file descriptor pointing to the same file. The problem with `dup` is that you don't have any control over the number you get back: it's the numerically smallest file descriptor currently not in use. In many cases, you want a specific number. This is what `dup2` does:

```
int dup2 (int oldd, int newd);
```

With `newd` you specify the number of the new descriptor. If it's currently allocated, `dup2` closes it first. You can fake this with `dup`, but it's painful. The `F_DUPFD` subfunction of fcntl does the same thing as dup2, so you can use it if it is available (see the section called "fcntl"). dup2 is available on nearly every UNIX system, *including* the Seventh Edition. Somehow some earlier versions of System V don't have it, however—recall that System V derived from the Sixth Edition, not the Seventh Edition. See Chapter 1, *Introduction.*

fchdir and Friends

Various systems offer functions with names like fchdir, fchmod, fchown, and fchroot. These are effectively the same as the corresponding functions chdir, chmod, chown, and chroot, except they take the number of an open file instead of its name. For example:

```
#include <sys/stat.h>

int chmod (const char *path, mode_t mode);
int fchmod (int fd, mode_t mode);
```

You can replace them with a corresponding call to ch* if you know the name of the file associated with the file descriptor; otherwise, you could be in trouble.

fcntl

All modern versions of UNIX supply a function called fcntl, which is rather like an ioctl for disk files:

```
#include <sys/fcntl.h>

int fcntl (int fd, int cmd, union anything arg);
```

Table 14-1 shows common command values.

Table 14-1: fcntl Commands

Command	System	Meaning
F_DUPFD	All	Duplicate a file descriptor, like *dup*. Return the lowest numbered descriptor that is higher than the int value arg.
F_GETFD	All	Get the close-on-exec flag associated with fd.
F_SETFD	All	Set the close-on-exec flag associated with fd.
F_FREESP	SVR4, Solaris 2.X	Free storage space associated with a section of the file fd. See the section called "fcntl Locking" for more details.
F_GETFL	All	Get descriptor status flags (see below).
F_SETFL	All	Set descriptor status flags to arg.

Table 14-1: fcntl Commands (continued)

Command	System	Meaning
F_GETOWN	BSD	Get the process ID or the complement of the process group currently receiving SIGIO and SIGURG signals.
F_GETOWN	SVR4	Get the user ID of the owner of the file. This function is not documented for Solaris 2.x.
F_SETOWN	BSD	Set the process or process group to receive SIGIO and SIGURG signals. If arg is negative, it is the complement of the process group. If it is positive, it is a process ID.
F_SETOWN	SVR4	Set the user ID of the owner of the file. This function is not documented for Solaris 2.x.
F_GETLK	All	Get file record lock information. See the section called "File Locking" for more details.
F_SETLK	All	Set or clear a file record lock.
F_SETLKW	All	Set or clear a file record lock, waiting if necessary until it becomes available.
F_CHKFL	SVR3	Check legality of file flag changes.
F_RSETLK	SVR4	Used by *lockd* to handle NFS locks.
F_RSETLKW	SVR4	Used by *lockd* to handle NFS locks.
F_RGETLK	SVR4	Used by *lockd* to handle NFS locks.

As you can see from Table 14-1, arg is not always supplied, and when it is, its meaning and type vary depending on the call.

A couple of these functions deserve closer examination:

- F_SETFD and F_GETFD manipulate the *close-on-exec* flag, which is normally defined in *sys/fcntl.h* as 1. Many programs use the explicit constant 1, which is theoretically nonportable, but which works with current systems. By default, exec inherits open files to the new program. If the close on exec flag is set, exec automatically closes the file.
- F_GETOWN and F_SETOWN have very different meanings for BSD and System V.4. In BSD, they get and set the process ID that receives SIGIO and SIGURG signals; in System V.4, they get and set the file owner, which can also be done with stat or fstat. There is no direct equivalent to the BSD F_SETOWN and F_GETOWN in System V, since the underlying implementation of nonblocking I/O is different. Instead, you call ioctl with the I_SETSIG request—see the section called "SIGPOLL" for more details.

- The request F_CHKFL is defined in the System V.3 header files, but it is not documented.
- F_GETFL and F_SETFL get and set the file status flags that were initally set by open. Table 14-2 shows the flags.

Table 14-2: fcntl File Status Flags

Flag	System	Meaning
O_NONBLOCK	All	Do not block if the operation cannot be performed immediately. Instead, the read or write call returns –1 with errno set to EWOULDBLOCK.
O_APPEND	All	Append each write to the end of file.
O_ASYNC	BSD	Send a SIGIO signal to the process group when I/O is possible.
O_SYNC	System V	write waits for writes to complete before returning.
O_RDONLY	System V	Open for reading only.
O_RDWR	System V	Open for reading and writing.
O_WRONLY	System V	Open for writing only.

getdents and getdirentries

getdents (System V.4) and getdirentries (BSD) are marginally compatible system calls that read a directory entry in a file system–independent format. Both systems provide a header file */usr/include/sys/dirent.h*, which defines a struct dirent, but unfortunately the structures are different. In System V, the structure and the call are:

```
struct  dirent
  {
  ino_t d_ino;
  off_t d_off;
  unsigned short d_reclen;
  char d_name[1];
  };

int getdents(int fd, struct dirent *buf, size_t nbyte);
```

getdirentries is the corresponding BSD system call:

```
struct dirent
  {
  unsigned long d_fileno;      /* "file number" (inode number) of entry */
  unsigned short d_reclen;     /* length of this record */
  unsigned short d_namlen;     /* length of string in d_name */
  char d_name[MAXNAMLEN + 1]; /* name must be no longer than this */
```

```
};

int getdirentries(int fd, char *buf, int nbytes, long *basep);
```

Because of these compatibility problems, you don't normally use these system calls directly—you use the library call **readdir** instead. See the description of **readdir** in the section called "readdir and Friends" for more information.

getdtablesize

Sometimes it's important to know how many files a process is allowed to open. This depends heavily on the kernel implementation: some systems have a fixed maximum number of files that can be opened and may allow you to specify the number a process can open as a configuration parameter when you build a kernel. Others allow an effectively unlimited number of files, but the kernel allocates space for files in groups of about 20. Evidently, the way you find out about these limits depends greatly on the system you are running:

- On systems with a fixed maximum, the constant `NOFILE`, usually defined in */usr/include/sys/param.h*, specifies the number of files you can open.
- On systems with a configurable maximum, you will probably also find the constant `NOFILE`, only you can't rely on it to be correct.
- On some systems that allocate resources for files in groups, the size of these groups may be defined in */usr/include/sys/filedesc.h* as the value of the constant `NDFILE`.
- BSD systems offer the function `getdtablesize` (no parameters) that returns the maximum number of files you can open.
- Modern systems offer the `getrlimit` system call, which allows you to query a number of kernel limits. See the section called "getrlimit and setrlimit" in Chapter 12 for details of `getrlimit`.

ioctl

`ioctl` is a catch-all function that performs functions that weren't thought of ahead of time. Every system has its own warts on `ioctl`, and the most common problem with `ioctl` is a call with a request that the kernel doesn't understand. We can't go into detail about every `ioctl` function, but we do examine terminal driver `ioctl` calls in some depth in the section called "ioctl" in Chapter 15, *Terminal Drivers*.

lstat

`lstat` is a version of `stat`. It is identical to `stat` unless the pathname specifies a symbolic link. In this case, `lstat` returns information about the link itself, whereas `stat` returns information about the file to which the link points. BSD and System V.4 support `lstat`, and it should be available on any system that supports symbolic links.

ltrunc

`ltrunc` truncates an open file in the same way that `ftruncate` does, but the parameters are more reminiscent of `lseek`:

```
int ltrunc (int fd, off_t offset, int whence);
```

`fd` is the file descriptor. `offset` and `whence` specify the new end-of-file value:

- If `whence` is `SEEK_SET`, `ltrunc` sets the file size to `offset`.
- If `whence` is `SEEK_CUR`, `ltrunc` sets the file size to `offset` bytes beyond the current seek position.
- If `whence` is `SEEK_END`, `ltrunc` increases the file size by `offset`.

No modern mainstream system supports `ltrunc`. You can replace a call `ltrunc (fd, offset, SEEK_SET)` with `ftruncate (fd, offset)`. If you have calls with `SEEK_CUR` and `SEEK_END`, you need to first establish the corresponding offset with a call to `lseek`:

```
ftruncate (fd, lseek (fd, offset, SEEK_CUR)); or SEEK_END
```

mkdir and rmdir

Older versions of UNIX did not supply a separate system call to create a directory; they used `mknod` instead. Unfortunately, this meant that only the superuser could create directories. Newer versions supply `mkdir` and `rmdir`. The syntax is:

```
#include <sys/stat.h>
int mkdir (const char *path, mode_t mode)

#include <unistd.h>
int rmdir (const char *path)
```

If your system does not have the `mkdir` system call, you can simulate it by invoking the `mkdir` utility with the library function `system`.

open

Since the Seventh Edition, open has acquired a few new flags. All modern versions of UNIX support most of them, but the following differ between versions:

- O_NDELAY is available only in earlier versions of System V. It applies to devices and FIFOs (see the section called "FIFOs" in Chapter 12 for more information on FIFOs) and specifies that both the call to open and subsequent I/O calls should return immediately without waiting for the operation to complete. A call to read returns 0 if no data is available, which is unfortunately also the value returned at end of file. If you don't have O_NDELAY, or if this ambiguity bugs you, use O_NONBLOCK.
- O_NONBLOCK specifies that both the call to open and subsequent I/O calls should return immediately without waiting for completion. Unlike O_NDELAY, a subsequent call to read returns –1 (error) if no data is available, and errno is set to EAGAIN.
- System V.4 and 4.4BSD have a flag, called O_SYNC in System V.4 and O_FSYNC in 4.4BSD, which specifies that each call to write write should write any buffered data to disk and update the inode. Control does not return to the program until these operations complete. If your system does not support this feature, you can probably just remove it, though you lose a little bit of security. To *really* do the Right Thing, you can include a call to fsync after every I/O.

pathconf and fpathconf

pathconf and fpathconf are POSIX.1 functions that get configuration information for a file or directory:

```
#include <unistd.h>
long fpathconf (int fd, int name);
long pathconf (const char *path, int name);
```

Despite what it is called, the name parameter specifies the *action* to perform. Possible actions are listed in Table 14-3.

Table 14-3: pathconf Actions

Name	Function
_PC_LINK_MAX	Return the maximum number of links that can be made to an inode.
_PC_MAX_CANON	For terminals, return the maximum length of a formatted input line.
_PC_MAX_INPUT	For terminals, return the maximum length of an input line.

Table 14-3: pathconf Actions (continued)

Name	Function
_PC_NAME_MAX	For directories, return the maximum length of a filename.
_PC_PATH_MAX	Return the maximum length of a relative pathname starting with this directory.
_PC_PIPE_BUF	For FIFOs, return the size of the pipe buffer.
_PC_CHOWN_RESTRICTED	Return TRUE if the `chown` system call may not be used on this file. If `fd` or `path` refer to a directory, this information applies to all files in the directory.
_PC_NO_TRUNC	Return TRUE if an attempt to create a file with a name longer than the maximum in this directory would fail with ENAMETOOLONG.
_PC_VDISABLE	For terminals, return TRUE if special character processing can be disabled.

read

The function `read` is substantially unchanged since the Seventh Edition, but note the comments about `O_NDELAY` and `O_NONBLOCK` in the section called "open".

rename

Older versions of UNIX don't have a system call to rename a file: instead, they make a link and then delete the old file. This can cause problems if the process is stopped in the middle of the operation, and so the atomic `rename` function was introduced. If your system doesn't have it, you can still rename a file the old-fashioned way.

revoke

`revoke` is used in later BSD versions to close all file descriptors associated with a special file, even those opened by a different process. It is *not* available with System V.4. Typically, this call is used to disconnect serial lines.

After a process has called `revoke`, a call to `read` on the device from any process returns an end-of-file indication, a call to `close` succeeds, and all other calls fail. Only the file owner and the superuser may use this call.

readdir and Friends

In the Seventh Edition, reading a directory was simple: directory entries were 16 bytes long and consisted of a 2-byte *inode number* and a 14-byte file name. This was defined in a `struct direct`:

```
struct direct
  {
  ino_t d_ino;
  char  d_name[DIRSIZ];
  };
```

With the introduction of ufs, which supports names of up to 256 characters, it was no longer practical to reserve a fixed-length field for the filename, and it became more difficult to access directories. A family of directory access routines was introduced with 4.2BSD:

```
#include <sys/types.h>
#include <dirent.h>
DIR *opendir (const char *filename);
struct dirent *readdir (DIR *dirp);
long telldir (const DIR *dirp);
void seekdir (DIR *dirp, long loc);
void rewinddir (DIR *dirp);
int closedir (DIR *dirp);
int dirfd (DIR *dirp);
```

Along with the `DIR` type, there is a `struct dirent` that corresponds to the Seventh Edition `struct direct`. Unfortunately, System V defines `struct dirent` and `DIR` differently from the original BSD implementation. In BSD, it is as follows:

```
struct dirent                   /* directory entry */
  {
  unsigned long d_fileno;       /* file number of entry */
  unsigned short d_reclen;      /* length of this record */
  unsigned short d_namlen;      /* length of string in d_name */
  char d_name [255 + 1];        /* maximum name length */
  };

/* structure describing an open directory. */
typedef struct _dirdesc
  {
  int   dd_fd;                  /* directory file descriptor */
  long  dd_loc;                 /* offset in current buffer */
  long  dd_size;                /* amount of data from getdirentries */
  char  *dd_buf;                /* data buffer */
  int   dd_len;                 /* size of data buffer */
  long  dd_seek;                /* magic cookie from getdirentries */
  } DIR;
```

System V defines it like this:

```
struct dirent
  {
  ino_t d_ino;                  /* inode number of entry */
  off_t d_off;                  /* offset of directory entry */
  unsigned short d_reclen;      /* length of this record */
  char d_name [1];              /* name of file */
  };
```

```
typedef struct
  {
  int dd_fd;                    /* file descriptor */
  int dd_loc;                   /* offset in block */
  int dd_size;                  /* amount of valid data */
  char *dd_buf;                 /* directory block */
  } DIR;                        /* stream data from opendir() */
```

There are a number of ugly incompatibilities here:

- The field `d_fileno` in the BSD `dirent` struct is not a file descriptor, but an inode number. The System V name `d_ino` makes this fact clearer, but it introduces a name incompatiblity.
- A number of the BSD fields are missing in the System V structures. You can calculate `dirent.d_namlen` by subtracting the length of the other fields from `dirent.d_reclen`. For example, based on the System V `dirent` structure above:

```
d_namlen = dirent.d_reclen
           - sizeof (ino_t)          /* length of the d_ino field */
           - sizeof (d_off)          /* length of the d_off field */
           - sizeof (unsigned short); /* length of the d_reclen field */
```

System V.4 has two versions of these routines: a System V version and a BSD version. Many reports have claimed that the BSD version is broken, though it's possible that the programmers were using the wrong header files. If you *do* run into trouble, you should make sure the header files match the flavor of `dirent` and `DIR` that you have.

readv and writev

`readv` and `writev` perform a so-called *scatter read* and *gather write*. These functions are intended to write to a file a number of pieces of data spread in memory or to read from a file to a number of places.

```
#include <unistd.h>
#include <sys/types.h>
#include <sys/uio.h>
in sys/uio.h is the definition:
struct iovec
  {
  caddr_t iov_base;
  int     iov_len;
  };

int readv(int d, struct iovec *iov, int iovcnt);
int writev (int d, struct iovec *iov, int iovcnt);
```

Each iovec element specifies an address and the number of bytes to transfer to or from it. The total number of bytes transferred would be the sum of the iov_len fields of all iovcnt elements. **readv** and **writev** are available only for BSD and System V.4 systems. If you don't have them, it's relatively easy to fake them in terms of read or write. The reasons why these calls exist at all are:

- Some devices, such as tape drives, write a physical record for each call to write. This can result in a significant drop in performance and tape capacity.
- For tape drives, the only alternative is to copy the data into one block before writing. This, too, impacts performance, though not nearly as much as writing smaller blocks.
- Even for devices that don't write a physical block per write, it's faster to do it in the kernel with just a single function call. You don't have as many context switches.

statfs and statvfs

statfs or statvfs return information about a file system in a format referred to as a *generic superblock*. All current UNIX versions supply one or the other of these functions, but the information they return varies greatly. XENIX, System V.3, BSD, and BSD-derived SunOS operating systems supply statfs. System V.4 supplies statvfs.

BSD systems define statfs like this:

```
typedef quad fsid_t;

#define MNAMELEN 32                    /* length of buffer for returned name */

struct statfs
  {
  short   f_type;                      /* type of filesystem (see below) */
  short   f_flags;                     /* copy of mount flags */
  long    f_fsize;                     /* fundamental file system block size */
  long    f_bsize;                     /* optimal transfer block size */
  long    f_blocks;                    /* total data blocks in file system */
  long    f_bfree;                     /* free blocks in fs */
  long    f_bavail;                    /* free blocks avail to non-superuser */
  long    f_files;                     /* total file nodes in file system */
  long    f_ffree;                     /* free file nodes in fs */
  fsid_t  f_fsid;                      /* file system id */
  long    f_spare[6];                  /* spare for later */
  char    f_mntonname[MNAMELEN];       /* mount point */
  char    f_mntfromname[MNAMELEN];     /* mounted filesystem */
  };
```

SunOS 4.1.3 defines statfs as:

```
#include <sys/vfs.h>

typedef struct
  {
  long    val[2];
  } fsid_t;
struct statfs
  {
  long    f_type;                /* type of info, zero for now */
  long    f_bsize;               /* fundamental file system block size */
  long    f_blocks;              /* total blocks in file system */
  long    f_bfree;               /* free blocks */
  long    f_bavail;              /* free blocks available to non-super-user */
  long    f_files;               /* total file nodes in file system */
  long    f_ffree;               /* free file nodes in fs */
  fsid_t  f_fsid;                /* file system id */
  long    f_spare[7];            /* spare for later */
  };
```

System V.3 and XENIX define:

```
struct  statfs
  {
  short f_fstyp;      /* File system type */
  long  f_bsize;      /* Block size */
  long  f_frsize;     /* Fragment size (if supported) */
  long  f_blocks;     /* Total number of blocks on file system */
  long  f_bfree;      /* Total number of free blocks */
  long  f_files;      /* Total number of file nodes (inodes) */
  long  f_ffree;      /* Total number of free file nodes */
  char  f_fname[6];   /* Volume name */
  char  f_fpack[6]    /* Pack name */
  };

int statfs (const char *path, struct statfs *buf);
int fstatfs (int fd, struct statfs *buf);
```

System V.4 and Solaris 2.X use statvfs, which is defined as:

```
#include <sys/types.h>
#include <sys/statvfs.h>

struct statvfs
  {
  u_long  f_bsize;                  /* preferred file system block size */
  u_long  f_frsize;                 /* fundamental filesystem block size */
  u_long  f_blocks;                 /* total # of blocks on file system */
  u_long  f_bfree;                  /* total # of free blocks */
  u_long  f_bavail;                 /* # of free blocks available */
  u_long  f_files;                  /* total # of file nodes (inodes) */
  u_long  f_ffree;                  /* total # of free file nodes */
  u_long  f_favail;                 /* # of inodes available */
```

```
    u_long  f_fsid;                /* file system id (dev for now) */
    char    f_basetype [FSTYPSZ];  /* target fs type name */
    u_long  f_flag;                /* bit mask of flags */
    u_long  f_namemax;             /* maximum file name length */
    char    f_fstr [32];           /* file system specific string */
    u_long  f_filler [16];         /* reserved for future expansion */
    };

#define ST_RDONLY  0x01            /* read-only file system */
#define ST_NOSUID  0x02            /* does not support setuid/setgid */
#define ST_NOTRUNC 0x04            /* does not truncate long file names */

int statvfs (const char *path, struct statvfs *buf);
int fstatvfs (int fd, struct statvfs *buf);
```

There's not much to say about these functions. If you have problems, hopefully this information can help you figure out what the author intended.

symlink

`symlink` creates a symbolic link in file systems that support symbolic links:

```
#include <unistd.h>

int symlink (const char *real_name, const char *symbolic_name);
```

A symbolic link `symbolic_name` is created to the name `real_name`.

sysfs

`sysfs` is a System V function that returns information about the kinds of file systems configured in the system. This function has the rather strange property of not being compatible with ANSI C—the parameters it accepts depend on the function supplied:

```
#include <sys/fstyp.h>
#include <sys/fsid.h>

int sysfs ((int) GETFSIND, const char *fsname);
```

This call translates `fsname`, a `NUL`-terminated file system–type identifier, into a file system–type index.

```
int sysfs ((int) GETFSTYP, int fs_index, char *buf);
```

This call translates `fs_index`, a file system–type index, into a `NUL`-terminated file system–type identifier in the buffer pointed to by `buf`.

```
int sysfs((int) GETNFSTYP);
```

This call returns the total number of file system types configured in the system.

truncate and ftruncate

These functions set the EOF pointer of a file. truncate finds the file via its filename, and ftruncate requires the file number of an open file.

```
#include <unistd.h>
int truncate (const char *path, off_t length);
int ftruncate (int fd, off_t length);
```

These functions are available with BSD and System V.4. There is a subtle difference between the way the BSD and System V.4 versions work: if the file is smaller than the requested length, System V.4 extends the file to the specified length, while BSD leaves it as it is. Both versions discard any data beyond the end if the current EOF is longer.

If your system doesn't have these functions, you may be able to perform the same function with chsize (see the the section called "chsize") or the fcntl function F_FREESP (see the the section called "fcntl").

ustat

ustat returns information about a mounted file system and is supported by System V and SunOS 4, but not by BSD. The call is:

```
struct ustat
  {
  daddr_t f_tfree;              /* Total blocks available */
  ino_t f_tinode;               /* Number of free inodes */
  char f_fname [6];             /* File system name */
  char f_fpack [6];             /* File system pack name */

int ustat (dev_t dev, struct ustat *buf);
```

On BSD systems, you can get this information with the statfs system call, which requires a pathname instead of a device number.

utime and utimes

utime is available in all versions of UNIX.

```
#include <sys/types.h>
#include <utime.h>

int utime (const char *path, const struct utimbuf *times);
```

utime sets the modification timestamp of the file defined by path to the time specified in times. In the Seventh Edition, times was required to be a valid pointer, and only the file owner or *root* could use the call. All newer versions of UNIX allow `times` to be a `NULL` pointer, in which case the modification timestamp is set to the current time. Any process that has write access to the file can use `utime` in this manner. BSD implements this function in the C library in terms of the function `utimes`:

```
#include <sys/time.h>
sys/time.h defines:
struct timeval
  {
  long tv_sec;                  /* seconds */
  long tv_usec;                 /* and microseconds */
};
int utimes (const char *file, const struct timeval *times);

#include <sys/types.h>
#include <utime.h>
utime.h defines:
struct utimbuf
  {
  time_t actime;                /* access time */
  time_t modtime;               /* modification time */
  };

int utime (char *path, struct utimbuf *times);
```

The difference between `utime` and `utimes` is simply in the format of the access time: `utime` supplies the time in `time_t` format, which is accurate to a second, whereas `utimes` uses the `timeval` struct which is (theoretically) accurate to one microsecond. BSD systems supply the `utime` function as a library call (which, not surprisingly, calls `utimes`). On XENIX and early System V systems you can fake `utimes` using `utime`.

Nonblocking I/O

In early versions of UNIX, all device I/O was *blocking*: if you made a call to `read` and no data was available, or if you made a call to `write` and the device wasn't ready to accept the data, the process would sleep until the situation changed. This is still the default behavior.

Blocking I/O can be restrictive in many situations, and many schemes have been devised to allow a process to continue execution before the I/O operation completes. On current systems, you select nonblocking I/O either by supplying the flag `O_NONBLOCK` to `open` or by calling the `fcntl` function `F_SETFL` with the `O_NONBLOCK` flag (see the section called "fcntl").

One problem with nonblocking I/O is that you don't automatically know when a request is complete. In addition, if you have multiple requests outstanding, you may not really care which finishes first, you just want to know when one finishes.

Two approaches have been used to inform a process when a request completes. One is to call a function that returns information about current request status and that may optionally block until something completes. Traditionally, BSD uses `select` to perform this function, whereas System V uses `poll`.

The other solution is to send a signal (`SIGPOLL` in System V, `SIGIO` or `SIGURG` in BSD) when the request finishes. In both systems, sending a signal has the disadvantage of not supplying any information about the request that completed, so if you have more than one request outstanding, you still need to call `select` or `poll` to handle the situation.

select

`select` is called with the following parameters:

```
#define FD_SETSIZE 512    my maximum FD count, see below
#include <unistd.h>
#include <sys/types.h>
#include <sys/time.h>
```

These header files define the structs:

```
typedef struct fd_set
  {
  fd_mask fds_bits [howmany (FD_SETSIZE, NFDBITS)];
  } fd_set;

struct timeval
  {
  long  tv_sec;               /* seconds */
  long  tv_usec;              /* and microseconds */
  };

int select (int nfds, fd_set *readfds, fd_set *writefds, fd_set *exceptfds,
            struct timeval *timeout);
```

The parameters `readfds`, `writefds`, and `exceptfds` are bitmaps, one bit per possible file descriptor. Recall that file descriptors are small non-negative integers. `select` uses the file descriptor as an index in the bitmap.

This gives us a problem when porting: we don't know how many files our implementation supports. In modern systems, there is usually no fixed limit. The solution chosen is a kludge: "choose a sufficiently high number." The expression howmany (FD_SETSIZE, NFDBITS) evaluates to the number of words of NFDBITS required to store FD_SETSIZE bits:

```
#define howmany(bits, wordsize)  ((bits + wordsize - 1) / wordsize)
```

In 4.4BSD FD_SETSIZE defaults to 256 (in *sys/types.h*). Nowadays, a server with many requestors could quite easily exceed that value. Because of this, you can set it yourself: just define FD_SETSIZE before including */usr/include/sys/types.h*, as indicated in the syntax overview above.

Setting variables of type fd_mask is tricky, so a number of macros are supplied:

```
FD_SET (fd, &fdset)          /* set bit fd in fdset*/
FD_CLR (fd, &fdset)          /* clear bit fd in fdset */
FD_ISSET (fd, &fdset)        /* return value of bit fd in fdset */
FD_ZERO (&fdset)             /* clear all bits in fdset */
```

select examines the files specified in readfds for read completion, the files specified in writefds for write completion, and the files specified in exceptfds for exceptional conditions. You can set any of these pointers to NULL if you're not interested in this kind of event. The action that select takes depends on the value of timeout:

- If timeout is a NULL pointer, select blocks until a completion occurs on one of the specified files.
- If both timeout->tv_sec and timeout->tv_usec are set to 0, select checks for completions and returns immediately.
- Otherwise, select waits for completion up to the specified timeout.

select returns –1 on error conditions, and the number of ready descriptors (possibly 0) otherwise. It replaces the contents of readfds, writefds, and exceptfds with bitmaps indicating which files had a corresponding completion.

So far, we haven't even mentioned nfds. Strictly speaking, it's not needed: you use it to indicate the *number* of file descriptors that are worth examining. By default, open and dup allocate the lowest possible file descriptors, so select can save a lot of work if you tell it the highest file number that is worth examining in the bitmaps. Since file descriptors start at 0, the *number* of file descriptors is 1 higher than the highest file descriptor number.

This baroque function has a couple of other gotchas waiting for you:

- The state of readfds, writefds, and exceptfds is undefined if select returns 0 or –1. System V clears the descriptors, whereas BSD leaves them unchanged. Some System V programs check the descriptors even if 0 is returned, which can cause problems if you port such a program to BSD.

- The return value is interpreted differently in BSD and System V. In BSD, each completion event is counted, so you can have up to three completions for a single file. In System V, the number of files with completions is returned.
- On completion without timeout, Linux decrements the value of `timeout` by the time elapsed since the call. If `timeout` was initially set to 30 seconds, and I/O completes after 5 seconds, the value of `timeout` on return from `select` will be 25 seconds. This can be of use if you have a number of outstanding requests, all of which must complete in a certain time. You can call `select` again for the remaining file descriptors without first calculating how much time remains. In Linux, this feature can be disabled by setting the `STICKY_TIMEOUTS` flag in the COFF/ELF personality used by the process. Other versions of UNIX do not currently suppport this feature, although both System V and BSD suggest that it will be implemented. For example, the man pages for 4.4BSD state:

  > **Select**() should probably return the time remaining from the original timeout, if any, by modifying the time value in place. This may be implemented in future versions of the system. Thus, it is unwise to assume that the timeout value will be unmodified by the *select*() call.

If you find a system without `select` that does support `poll`, you can probably replace `select` with `poll`—it's just a SMOP.*

Typical use of select

Programs that use `select` generally start a number of I/O transfers and then go to some central place to wait for something to happen. The code could look like:

```
if (select (maxfnum,                  /* number of files to check */
            &readfds,                 /* mask of read completions */
            &writefds,                /* mask of write completions */
            &exceptfds,               /* mask of exception completions */
            NULL) > 0)                /* no timeout */
  {                                   /* we have completions, */
  int fd;
  for (fd = 0; fd < maxfnum; fd++)
    {
    if (FD_ISSET (fd, readfds))       /* this file has a read completion */
      read_completion (fd);           /* process it */
    if (FD_ISSET (fd, writefds))      /* this file has a write completion */
      write_completion (fd);          /* process it */
    if (FD_ISSET (fd, exceptfds))     /* this file has a exception completion */
      exception_completion (fd);      /* process it */
    }
```

* To quote the New Hacker's Dictionary: "SMOP: /S-M-O-P/ [Simple (or Small) Matter of Programming] n. 2. Often used ironically ... when a suggestion for a program is made which seems easy to the suggester, but is obviously (to the victim) a lot of work."

`FD_ISSET` is a macro that checks if bit `fd` is set in the bit mask. The `*_completion` functions do whatever is needed on completion of I/O for this file descriptor. See *Advanced Programming in the UNIX Environment* for further information.

poll

`poll` takes a different approach from `select`:

```
#include <stropts.h>
#include <poll.h>

... in poll.h is the definition
struct pollfd
  {
  int fd;                   /* file descriptor */
  short events;             /* requested events */
  short revents;            /* returned events */
  };

int poll (struct pollfd *fds, unsigned long nfds, int timeout);
```

For each file of interest, you set up a `pollfd` element with the file number and the events of interest. `events` and `revents` are again bitmaps. `events` can be made up of the values listed in Table 14-4. These values distinguish between normal data and priority data, a distinction that exists in TCP/IP network connections.

Table 14–4: poll Event Codes

Event	Meaning
POLLIN	Data other than high priority data is available for reading.
POLLRDNORM	Normal data[a] (priority band = 0) is available for reading.
POLLRDBAND	Data from a nonzero priority band is available for reading.
POLLPRI	High priority data is available for reading.
POLLOUT	Normal data may be written without blocking.
POLLWRNORM	The same as POLLOUT: normal data may be written without blocking.
POLLWRBAND	Priority data (priority band > 0) may be written without blocking.

[a] STREAMS recognizes 256 different *data priority bands*. Normal data is sent with priority band 0, but urgent data with a higher priority can "leapfrog" normal data. See *UNIX Network Programming*, by W. Richard Stevens, for further information.

When it succeeds, `poll` sets the corresponding bits in `revents` to indicate which events occurred. In addition, it may set the event bits listed in Table 14-5.

Table 14-5: poll Result Codes

Event	Meaning
POLLERR	An error has occurred on the device or stream.
POLLHUP	A hangup has occurred.
POLLNVAL	The specified fd is not open.

Timeout processing is nearly the same as for `select`, but the parameter `timeout` is specified in milliseconds. Since it is an `int`, not a pointer, you can't supply a `NULL` pointer; instead, you set the value to `INFTIM` (defined in *stropts.h*) if you want the call to block. To summarize:

- If `timeout` is set to `INFTIM`, `poll` blocks until a completion occurs on one of the specified files.
- If `timeout` is set to 0, a check is made for completions, and `poll` returns immediately.
- If `timeout` is nonzero, `poll` waits for completion up to the specified timeout.

Typical use of poll

Like `select`, programs that use `poll` generally start a number of I/O transfers and then go to some central place to wait for something to happen. In this case, the code could look like:

```
if (poll (pollfds, maxfnum, NULL) > 0) /* wait for something to complete */
  {
  int fd;
  for (fd = 0; fd < maxfnum; fd++)
    {
    if (pollfds [fd].revents)           /* something completed */
   ... check the result bits which interest you and
   perform the appropriate actions
    }
  }
```

The code for starting the request and enabling `SIGIO` and `SIGURG` for the line assumes that the file has been opened and the number stored in an array of file numbers.

rdchk

`rdchk` is a XENIX function that checks if data is available for reading on a specific file descriptor:

```
int rdchk (int fd);
```

It returns 1 if data is available, 0 if no data is currently available, and –1 on error (and errno is set). If you don't have it, you can implement it in terms of `select` or `poll`.

SIGPOLL

System V systems can arrange to have the signal SIGPOLL delivered when a request completes. It is not completely general: the file in question must be a STREAMS device, since only STREAMS drivers generate the SIGPOLL signal.

The `ioctl` call I_SETSIG enables SIGPOLL. The third parameter specifies a bit mask of events to wait for. Table 14-6 lists the I_SETSIG event mask bits. As discussed in the section called "poll", these bits accommodate TCP/IP network connections, which allow high-priority data.

Table 14-6: I_SETSIG Event Mask Bits

Mask Bit	Event
S_INPUT	A normal priority message is on the read queue.
S_HIPRI	A high priority message is on the read queue.
S_OUTPUT	The write queue is no longer full.
S_WRNORM	The same as S_OUTPUT: the write queue is no longer full.
S_MSG	A signal message is at the front of the read queue.
S_ERROR	An error message has arrived at the stream head.
S_HANGUP	A hangup message has arrived at the stream head.
S_RDNORM	A normal message is on the read queue.
S_RDBAND	An out-of-band message is on the read queue.
S_WRBAND	We can write out-of-band data.
S_BANDURG	In conjunction with S_RDBAND, generate SIGURG instead of SIGPOLL.

In addition to the call to `ioctl`, the process needs to set up a signal handler for SIGPOLL—the default disposition is to terminate the process, which is probably not what you want.

SIGIO

BSD systems have a similar mechanism to SIGPOLL, called SIGIO. Like SIGPOLL, it also has its restrictions: it can be applied only to terminal or network devices. In addition, when out-of-band data* arrives, a second signal, `SIGURG`, is generated. `SIGIO` and `SIGURG` are enabled by the `O_ASYNC` flag to `open` and a couple of calls to `fcntl` (see Table 14-2 for more details):

- First, specify the process or process group that should receive the signals, using the `fcntl` command `F_SETOWN` in order to enable reception of `SIGURG`.
- If you want to use `SIGIO`, set the `O_ASYNC` file status flag with the `fcntl` command `F_SETFL`.
- As with System V's `SIGPOLL`, you need to define a signal handler for `SIGIO` and `SIGURG`.

File Locking

The Seventh Edition did not originally allow programs to coordinate concurrent access to a file. If two users both had a file open for modification at the same time, it was almost impossible to prevent disaster. This is an obvious disadvantage, and all modern versions of UNIX supply some form of file locking.

Before we look at the functions that are available, it's a good idea to consider the various kinds of lock. There seem to be two of everything. First, the *granularity* is of interest:

File locking
: This applies to the whole file.

Range locking
: This applies only to a range of byte offsets. It is sometimes misleadingly called *record locking*.

With file locking, no other process can access the file when a lock is applied. With range locking, multiple locks can coexist as long as their ranges don't overlap. Secondly, there are two types of lock:

Advisory locks
: These do not actually prevent access to the file. They work only if every participating process ensures that it locks the file before accessing it. If the file is already locked, the process blocks until it gains the lock.

* Sockets use the term *out-of-band* to refer to data that comes in at a higher priority, such as TCP urgent mode. Like STREAMS priority data, this data is presented ahead of normal data.

Mandatory locks
These prevent (block) read and write access to the file but do not stop it from being removed or renamed. Many editors do just this, so even mandatory locking has its limitations.

Finally, there are also two ways in which locks cooperate with each other:

Exclusive locks
These allow no other locks that overlap the range. This is the only way to perform file locking, and it implies that only a single process can access the file at a time. These locks are also called *write locks*.

Shared locks
These allow other shared locks to coexist with them. Their main purpose is to prevent an exclusive lock from being applied. In combination with mandatory range locking, a write is not permitted to a range covered by a shared lock. These locks are also called *read locks*.

There are five different kinds of file or record locking in common use:

- *Lock files*, also called *dot locking*, is a primitive workaround used by communication programs such as *uucp* and *getty*. It is independent of the system platform, but since it is frequently used we'll look at it briefly. It implements advisory file locking.
- After the initial release of the Seventh Edition, a file locking package using the system call `locking` was introduced. The package, which implements mandatory range locking, is still in use today on XENIX systems.
- BSD systems have the system call `flock`, which implements advisory file locking.
- System V, POSIX.1, and more recent versions of BSD support range locking via the `fcntl` system call. BSD and POSIX.1 systems provide only advisory locking. System V supplies a choice of advisory or mandatory locking, depending on the file permissions. If you need to rewrite locking code, `fcntl` is the method you should use.
- System V also supplies range locking via the `lockf` library call. Again, it supplies a choice of advisory or mandatory locking, depending on the file permissions.

The decision between advisory and mandatory locking in System V depends on the file permissions and not on the call to `fcntl` or `lockf`. The `setgid` bit is used for this purpose. Normally, in executables, the `setgid` bit specifies that the executable should assume the effective group ID of its owner group when `exec`ed.

On files that do not have group execute permission, it specifies mandatory locking if it is set, and advisory locking if it is not set. For example:

- A file with permissions 0764 (rwxrw-r--) is locked with advisory locking because its permissions include neither group execute nor setgid.
- A file with permissions 0774 (rwxrwxr--) is locked with advisory locking because its permissions don't include setgid.
- A file with permissions 02774 (rwxrwsr--) is locked with advisory locking because its permissions include both group execute and setgid.
- A file with permissions 02764 is locked with mandatory locking because it has the setgid bit set, but group execute is not set. If you list the permissions of this file with *ls -l*, you get rwxrwlr-- on a System V system, but many versions of *ls*, including BSD and GNU versions, lists rwxrwSr--.

Lock Files

Lock files are the traditional method that *uucp* uses for locking serial lines. Serial lines are typically used either for dialing out, for example with *uucp*, or dialing in, which is handled by a program of the *getty* family. Some kind of synchronization is needed to ensure that both of these programs don't try to access the line at the same time. The other forms of locking we describe apply only to disk files, so we can't use them. Instead, *uucp* and *getty* create *lock files*. A typical lock file has a name like */var/spool/uucp/LCK..ttyb*, and for some reason these double periods in the name have led to the term *dot locking*.

The locking algorithm is straightforward: if a process wants to access a serial line */dev/ttyb*, it looks for a file */var/spool/uucp/LCK..ttyb*. If it finds the file, it checks the contents, which specify the process ID of the owner, and checks if the owner still exists. If it does, the file is locked, and the process can't access the serial line. If the file doesn't exist or if the owner no longer exists, the process creates the file if necessary and puts its own process ID in the file.

Although the algorithm is straightforward, the naming conventions are anything but standardized. When porting software from other platforms, it is absolutely essential that all programs using dot locking should agree on the lock file name and its format.

Let's look at the lock file names for the device */dev/ttyb*, which is major device number 29, minor device number 1. The *ls -l* listing looks like:

```
$ ls -l /dev/ttyb
crw-rw-rw-   1 root     sys       29,   1 Feb 25  1995 /dev/ttyb
```

Table 14-7 describes common conventions.

Table 14-7: uucp Lock File Names and Formats

System	Name	PID Format
4.3BSD	*/usr/spool/uucp/LCK..ttyb*	Binary, 4 bytes
4.4BSD	*/var/spool/uucp/LCK..ttyb*	Binary, 4 bytes
System V.3	*/usr/spool/uucp/LCK..ttyb*	ASCII, 10 bytes
System V.4	*/var/spool/uucp/LK.032.029.001*	ASCII, 10 bytes

A couple of points to note are:

- The digits in the lock file's name for System V.4 are the major device number of the disk on which */dev* is located (32), the major device number of the serial device (29), and the minor device number of the serial device (1).
- Some systems, such as SCO, have multiple names for terminal lines depending on the characteristics that they should exhibit. For example, */dev/tty1a* refers to a line when running without modem control signals, and */dev/tty1A* refers to the same line when running with modem control signals. Clearly only one of these lines can be used at the same time. By convention, the lock file name for both devices is */usr/spool/uucp/LCK..tty1a*.
- The locations of the lock files vary considerably. Apart from those in the table, other possibilities are */etc/locks/LCK..ttyb*, */usr/spool/locks/LCK..ttyb*, and */usr/spool/uucp/LCK/LCK..ttyb*.
- Still other methods exist. See the file *policy.h* in the Taylor *uucp* distribution for further discussion.

Lock files are unreliable. It is quite possible for two processes to go through this algorithm at the same time, both find that the lock file doesn't exist, both create it, and both put their process ID in it. The result is not what you want. Lock files should be used only when no alternative is available.

locking System Call

`locking` comes from the original implementation introduced during the Seventh Edition. It is still available in XENIX. It implements mandatory range locking.

```
int locking (int fd, int mode, long size);
```

`locking` locks a block of data of length `size` bytes, starting at the current position in the file. `mode` can have one of the values listed in Table 14-8.

Table 14-8: locking Operation Codes

Parameter	Meaning
LK_LOCK	Obtain an exclusive lock for the specified block. If any part is not available, sleep until it becomes available.
LK_NBLCK	Obtain an exclusive lock for the specified block. If any part is not available, the request fails, and errno is set to EACCES.
LK_NBRLCK	Obtains a shared lock for the specified block. If any part is not available, the request fails, and errno is set to EACCES.
LK_RLCK	Obtain a shared lock for the specified block. If any part is not available, sleep until it becomes available.
LK_UNLCK	Unlock a previously locked block of data.

flock

`flock` is the weakest of all the lock functions. It provides only advisory file locking.

```
#include <sys/file.h>
(defined in sys/file.h)
#define   LOCK_SH   1          /* shared lock */
#define   LOCK_EX   2          /* exclusive lock */
#define   LOCK_NB   4          /* don't block when locking */
#define   LOCK_UN   8          /* unlock */

int flock (int fd, int operation);
```

`flock` applies or removes a lock on `fd`. By default, if a lock cannot be granted, the process blocks until the lock is available. If you set the flag LOCK_NB, `flock` returns immediately with errno set to EWOULDBLOCK if the lock cannot be granted.

fcntl Locking

In the section called "fcntl", we discussed `fcntl`, a function that can perform various functions on open files. A number of these functions perform advisory record locking, and System V also offers the option of mandatory locking. All locking functions operate on a `struct flock`:

```
struct flock
  {
  short l_type;          /* lock type: read/write, etc. */
  short l_whence;        /* type of l_start */
  off_t l_start;         /* starting offset */
  off_t l_len;           /* len = 0 means until end of file */
  long  l_sysid;         /* Only SVR4 */
  pid_t l_pid;           /* lock owner */
};
```

In this structure,

- `l_type` specifies the type of the lock, listed in Table 14-9.
- The offset is specified in the same way as a file offset is specified to `lseek`: `flock->l_whence` may be set to `SEEK_SET` (offset is from the beginning of the file), `SEEK_CUR` (offset is relative to the current position), or `SEEK_EOF` (offset is relative to the current end of file position).

Table 14-9: flock.l_type Values

Value	Function
F_RDLCK	Acquire a *read* or *shared* lock.
F_WRLCK	Acquire a *write* or *exclusive* lock.
F_UNLCK	Clear the lock.

All `fcntl` lock operations use this struct, which is passed to `fcntl` as the `arg` parameter. For example, to perform the operation `F_FRDLK`, you would write:

```
struct flock flock;
error = fcntl (myfile, F_FRDLK, &flock);
```

The following `fcntl` operations relate to locking:

- `F_GETLK` gets information on any current lock on the file. When calling, you set the fields `flock->l_type`, `flock->l_whence`, `flock->l_start`, and `flock->l_len` to the value of a lock that you want to set. If a lock that would cause a lock request to block already exists, `flock` is overwritten with information about the lock. The field `flock->l_whence` is set to `SEEK_SET`, and `flock->l_start` is set to the offset in the file. `flock->l_pid` is set to the pid of the process that owns the lock. If the lock can be granted, `flock->l_type` is set to `F_UNLK`, and the rest of the structure is left unchanged,
- `F_SETLK` tries to set a lock (`flock->l_type` set to `F_RDLCK` or `F_WRLCK`) or to release a lock (`flock->l_type` set to `F_UNLCK`). If a lock cannot be obtained, `fcntl` returns with `errno` set to `EACCES` (System V) or `EAGAIN` (BSD and POSIX).
- `F_SETLKW` works like `F_SETLK`, except that if the lock cannot be obtained, the process blocks until it can be obtained.
- System V.4 has an additional function, `F_FREESP`, which uses the `struct flock`, but in fact has nothing to do with file locking: it frees the space defined by `flock->l_whence`, `flock->l_start`, and `flock->l_len`. The data in this part of the file is physically removed, a read access returns `EOF`, and a write access writes new data. The only reason this operation uses the `struct flock` (and

the reason we discuss it here) is because `struct flock` has suitable members to describe the area that needs to be freed. Many file systems allow data to be freed only if the end of the region corresponds with the end of file, in which case the call can be replaced with `ftruncate`.

lockf

`lockf` is a library function supplied only with System V. Like `fcntl`, it implements advisory or mandatory range locking based on the file permissions. In some systems, it is implemented in terms of `fcntl`. It supports only exclusive locks:

```
#include <unistd.h>

int lockf (int fd, int function, long size);
```

The functions are similar to those supplied by `fcntl`. `l_type` specifies the type of the lock, as shown in Table 14-10.

Table 14-10: lock Functions

Value	Function
F_ULOCK	Unlock the range.
F_LOCK	Acquire exclusive lock.
F_TLOCK	Lock if possible, otherwise return status.
F_TEST	Check range for other locks.

`lockf` does not specify a start offset for the range to be locked. The start offset is always the current position in the file. You need to use `lseek` to get there if you are not there already. The following code fragments are roughly equivalent:

```
flock->ltype = F_WRLK;      /* lockf only supports write locks */
flock->whence = SEEK_SET;
flock->l_start = filepos;   /* this was set elsewhere */
flock->l_len = reclen;      /* the length to set */
error = fcntl (myfile, F_GETLK, &flock);
```

...and

```
lseek (myfile, SEEK_SET, filepos); /* Seek the correct place in the file */
error = lockf (myfile, F_LOCK, reclen);
```

Which Locking Scheme?

As we've seen, file locking is a can of worms. Many portable software packages offer you a choice of locking mechanisms, and your system may supply a number of them. Which do you take? Here are some rules of thumb:

- `fcntl` locking is the best choice, as long as your system and the package agree on what it means. On System V.3 and V.4, `fcntl` locking offers the choice of mandatory or advisory locking, whereas on other systems it offers only advisory locking. If your package expects to be able to set mandatory locking, and you're running, say, 4.4BSD, the package may not work correctly. If this happens, you may have to choose `flock` locking instead.
- If your system doesn't have `fcntl` locking, you probably have either `flock` or `lockf` locking instead. If the package supports it, use it. Pure BSD systems don't support `lockf`, but some versions simulate it. Since `lockf` can also be used to require mandatory locking, it's better to use `flock` on BSD systems and `lockf` on System V systems.
- You probably won't come across any packages that support `locking`. If you do, and your system supports it, it's not a bad choice.
- If all else fails, use lock files. This is a very poor option, though—it's probably a better idea to consider a more modern kernel.

Memory-Mapped Files

Some systems offer a feature called *memory-mapped files*: the data of a file is mapped to a particular area of memory, so you can access it directly rather than by calling `read` and `write`. This increases performance, since the virtual memory system is more efficient than the file system. The following function calls are used to implement memory mapping:

- `open` and `create` are the file system calls you need to open the file.
- `mmap` maps the file into memory.
- `msync` ensures that updates to the file map are flushed back to the file.
- `munmap` frees the mapped file data.

In the following sections, we'll look at these functions more closely.

mmap

`mmap` maps a portion of a file to memory.

```
#include <sys/types.h>
#include <sys/mman.h>

caddr_t mmap (caddr_t addr, int len, int prot, int flags, int fd, off_t offset);
```

- `addr` specifies the address at which the file should be mapped. Unless you have good reasons to do otherwise, you should specify it as `NULL` and let `mmap` choose a suitable address itself. If `mmap` can't place the memory where it is requested, the subsequent behavior depends on the flag `MAP_FIXED`—see the discussion of flags later in this section.

- `len` specifies the length to map.
- `prot` specifies the accessibility of the resultant memory region and may be any combination of `PROT_EXEC` (pages may be executed), `PROT_READ` (pages may be read), or `PROT_WRITE` (pages may be written). In addition, System V.4 allows the specification `PROT_NONE` (pages may not be accessed at all).
- `flags` is a bitmap that specifies properties of the mapped region. It consists of a combination of the following bit-mapped flags:
  - `MAP_ANON` specifies that the memory is not associated with any specific file. In many ways, this is much the same as a call to `malloc`: you get an area of memory with nothing in it. This flag is available only in BSD.
  - `MAP_FILE` specifies that the region is mapped from a regular file or character-special device. This flag, supplied only in BSD, is really a dummy and is used to indicate the opposite of `MAP_ANON`: if you don't have it, ignore it.
  - `MAP_FIXED` specifies that `mmap` may use only the specified `addr` as the address of the region. The 4.4BSD man page discourages the use of this option.
  - `MAP_INHERIT` permits regions to be inherited across `exec` system calls. Supported only in 4.4BSD.
  - `MAP_PRIVATE` specifies that modifications to the region are private. If the region is modified, a copy of the modified pages is created, and the modifications are copied to them. This flag is used in debuggers and to perform page-aligned memory allocations: `malloc` doesn't allow you to specify the address you want. In some systems, such as System V.4, `MAP_PRIVATE` is defined as 0, so this is the default behavior. In others, such as SunOS 4, you must specify either `MAP_PRIVATE` or `MAP_SHARED`. Otherwise, the call fails with an `EINVAL` error code.
  - `MAP_SHARED` specifies that modifications to the region are shared. The virtual memory manager writes any modifications back to the file.
- On success, `mmap` returns the address of the area that has been mapped. On failure, it returns –1 and sets `errno`.

msync

Writes to the memory-mapped region are treated like any other virtual memory access: the page is marked dirty, and that's all that happens immediately. At some later time the memory manager writes the contents of memory to disk. If this file is shared with some other process, you may need to explicitly flush it to disk, depending on the underlying cooperation between the file system and the virtual memory manager.

System V.4 maps the pages at a low level, and the processes share the same physical page, so this problem does not arise. BSD and older versions of System V keep separate copies of memory mapped pages for each process that accesses them. This makes sharing them difficult. On these systems, the `msync` system call is used to flush memory areas to disk. This solution is not perfect: the possibility still exists that a concurrent read of the area may get a garbled copy of the data. To quote the 4.4BSD man pages:

> Any required synchronization of memory caches also takes place at this time. Filesystem operations on a file that is mapped for shared modifications are unpredictable except after an msync.

Still, it's better than nothing. The call is straightforward:

```
void msync (caddr_t addr, int len);
```

`addr` must be specified and must point to a memory-mapped page; `len` may be 0, in which case all modified pages are flushed. If `len` is not 0, only modified pages in the area defined by `addr` and `len` are flushed.

munmap

`munmap` unmaps a memory-mapped file region:

```
void munmap (caddr_t addr, int len);
```

It unmaps the memory region specified by `addr` and `len`. This is not necessary before terminating a program—the region is unmapped like any other on termination—and it carries the danger that modifications may be lost, since it doesn't flush the region before deallocating. About the only use is to free the area for some other operation.

In This Chapter:

- *Typical Terminal Code*
- *Terminology*
- *Terminal Data Structures*
- *Terminal Driver Modes*
- *ioctl*
- *termios Functions*

15

Terminal Drivers

Terminal I/O is a real can of worms. Even in the Seventh Edition, it wasn't exactly simple. To quote the terminal driver man page, "The terminal handler has clearly entered the race for ever-greater complexity and generality. It's still not complex and general enough for TENEX fans." Since then, things have gone steadily downhill.

The most important terminal driver versions are:

- The "old" terminal driver, derived from the Seventh Edition terminal driver. This driver is still in use in XENIX and older BSD versions.
- The System III/System V terminal driver, also called *termio*.
- The POSIX.1 *termios* routines, derived from *termio*.

Most modern systems support more than one kind of serial line driver. This is known as the *line discipline*. Apart from terminal drivers, the most important line disciplines for asynchronous lines are *SLIP* (*Serial Line Internet Protocol*) and *PPP* (*Point to Point Protocol*). These are very implementation dependent, and we won't discuss them further. The line discipline is set with the `TIOCSETD` `ioctl`, described in the section called "TIOCSETD".

It's beyond the scope of this book to explain all the intricacies and kludges that have been added to terminal handlers over the decades. *Advanced Programming in the UNIX Environment* provides an overview of current practice, and you shouldn't really want to know about older versions unless you have trouble with them. In the following discussion, we'll concentrate on the four areas that cause the most headaches when porting programs:

- The externally visible data structures used for passing information to and from the driver.
- The different operational modes (raw, cooked, cbreak, canonical, and non-canonical).
- The `ioctl` request interface to the terminal driver, one of the favorite problem areas in porting terminal-related software.
- The POSIX.1 *termios* request interface.

The documentation of every driver describes at least two different modes of treating terminal input. The Seventh Edition and BSD drivers define three:

- In *raw* mode, the `read` system call passes input characters to the caller exactly as they are entered. No processing takes place in the driver. This mode is useful for programs that want to interpret characters themselves, such as full-screen editors.
- *cooked* mode interprets a number of special characters, including the newline character \n. A `read` call terminates on a newline character. Cooked mode is the mode used by programs that don't want to be bothered by the intricacies of terminal programming.
- *cbreak* mode performs partial interpretation of the special characters, this time not including the newline character. *cbreak* mode is easier to use than raw mode and is adequate for many purposes. It's a matter of taste whether you prefer this to raw mode.

By contrast, *termio* and *termios* specify two different processing modes for terminal input:

- *canonical** mode performs significant processing on input before passing it to the calling function. Up to 21 input special characters may be used to tell the driver to do things as varied as start and stop output, to clear the input buffer, to send signals to the process, and to terminate a line in a number of different ways.
- *Non-canonical* input mode, in which the driver does not interpret input characters specially (this corresponds roughly to BSD *cbreak* mode).

In fact, subdividing the terminal operation into modes is an oversimplification: a large number of flags modify the operational modes. Later in the chapter we'll look at how to set these modes with *termios.*

---

* The word *canon* refers to (religious) law. The intent is that this should be the correct or standard way to handle input characters. See the *New Hacker's Dictionary* for a lengthy discussion of the term.

Typical Terminal Code

Our discussion so far has been rather abstract. Let's look at a simple example: a program wants to read a single character from the terminal. To do this, it needs to set raw or non-canonical mode, read the character, and then reinstate the previous mode. For the old terminal driver, the code looks like this:

```
struct sgttyb initial_status;                 /* initial termios flags */
struct sgttyb raw_status;                     /* and the same with icanon reset */

ioctl (stdin, TIOCGETA, &initial_status);     /* get attributes */
raw_status = initial_status;                  /* make a copy */
raw_status.sg_flags |= RAW;                   /* and set raw mode */
ioctl (stdin, TIOCSETN, &raw_status);         /* set the new terminal flags */
puts ("? ");
if ((reply = getchar ()) != '\n')             /* get a reply */
  puts ("\n");                                /* and finish the line */
ioctl (stdin, TIOCSETN, &initial_status);     /* set the old terminal flags */
```

With the System V *termio* driver, the code would look like the following:

```
struct termio initial_status;                 /* initial termio flags */
struct termio noicanon_status;                /* and the same with icanon reset */

ioctl (stdin, TCGETA, &initial_status);       /* get attributes */
noicanon_status = initial_status;             /* make a copy */
noicanon_status.c_lflag &= ~ICANON;           /* and turn icanon off */
ioctl (stdin, TCSETA, &noicanon_status);      /* set non-canonical mode */
puts ("? ");
if ((reply = getchar ()) != '\n')             /* get a reply */
  puts ("\n");                                /* and finish the line */
ioctl (stdin, TCSETA, &initial_status))       /* reset old terminal mode */
```

Don't rely on code like this to be *termio* code: *termios* code can look almost identical. Correct *termios* code uses the *termios* functions that we will discuss later in this chapter and looks like the following code:

```
struct termios initial_status;                /* initial termios flags */
struct termios noicanon_status;               /* and the same with icanon reset */

tcgetattr (stdin, &initial_status)1           /* get current attributes */
noicanon_status = initial_status;             /* make a copy */
noicanon_status.c_lflag &= ~ICANON;           /* and turn icanon off */

tcsetattr (stdin, TCSANOW, &noicanon_status);/* set non-canonical mode */
puts ("? ");
if ((reply = getchar ()) != '\n')             /* get a reply */
  puts ("\n");                                /* and finish the line */
tcsetattr (stdin, TCSANOW, &initial_status); /* reset old terminal mode */
```

Terminology

Before we start, it's a good idea to be clear about a few terms that are frequently confused:

- All terminal drivers buffer I/O in two *queues*, an input queue and an output queue. The input queue contains characters that the user has entered and the process has not yet read. The output queue contains characters that the process has written but that have not yet been output to the terminal. These queues are maintained inside the terminal driver. Don't confuse them with buffers maintained in the process data space by the *stdio* routines.
- The term *flush* can mean to discard the contents of a queue or to wait until the contents have all been output to the terminal. Most of the time *flush* means to discard the contents, and that's how we'll use it in this chapter.
- The term *drain* means to wait until the contents of the output queue have been written to the terminal, which is also one of the meanings of *flush*.
- *Special characters*, frequently called *control characters*, are input characters that cause the terminal driver to do something out of the ordinary. For example, **CTRL-D** usually causes the terminal driver to return an end-of-file indication. The term *special characters* is the better term, since you can set them to characters that are not ASCII control characters. For example, even today, the default erase character in System V is the pound sign (#): it's a special character but not an ASCII control character.
- The *baud rate* is the number of units of information a modem can transmit per second. Modems are analog devices that can represent multiple bits in a single unit of information—modern modems encode up to 6 bits per unit. For example, a modern V.32bis modem transfers 14,400 bits per second but runs at only 2400 baud. Baud rates are of interest only to modem designers.
- As the name indicates, the *bit rate* of a serial line indicates how many bits it can transfer per second. Bit rates are often erroneously called *baud rates*, even in official documentation. The number of bytes transferred per second depends on the configuration: normally, an asynchronous serial line transmits one start bit and one stop bit in addition to the data, so it transmits 10 bits per byte.
- *break* is an obsolete method to signal an unusual condition over an asynchronous line. Normally, a continuous voltage or current is present on a line except when data is being transferred. Break effectively breaks (disconnects) the line for a period between .25 and .5 seconds. The serial hardware detects the break and reports it separately. One of the problems with break is that it is intimately related to the serial line hardware.

- *DCE* and *DTE* mean *data communication equipment* and *data terminal equipment*, respectively. In a modem connection, the modem is the DCE, and both terminal and computer are DTEs. In a direct connect, the terminal is the DTE, and the computer is the DCE. Different cabling is required for these two situations.
- *RS-232*, also known as *EIA-232*, is a standard for terminal wiring. In Europe, it is sometimes referred to as *CCITT V.24*, though V.24 does not in fact correspond exactly to RS-232. It defines a number of signals, listed in Table 15-1.

  For more details about RS-232, see *RS-232 Made Easy*, second edition, by Martin Seyer.

Table 15-1: RS-232 Signals

RS-232 Name	Pin	Purpose
PG	1	Protective ground. Used for electrical grounding only.
TxD	2	Transmitted data.
RxD	3	Received data.
RTS	4	Request to send. Indicates that the device has data to output.
CTS	5	Clear to send. Indicates that the device can receive input. Can be used with RTS to implement flow control.
DSR	6	Data set ready. Indicates that the modem (*data set* in older parlance) is powered on.
SG	7	Signal ground. Return for the other signals.
DCD	8	Carrier detect. Indicates that the modem has connection with another modem.
DTR	20	Data terminal ready. Indicates that the terminal or computer is ready to talk to the modem.
RI	22	Ring indicator. Raised by a modem to indicate that an incoming call is ringing.

Terminal Data Structures

In this section, we'll take a detailed look at the data structures you're likely to encounter when porting software from a different platform. I have included typical literal values for the macros. *Don't ever use these values!* They're not guaranteed to be correct for every implementation, and they're included only to help you if you find that the program includes literals rather than macro names. When writing code, always use the names.

Old Terminal Driver Definitions

In the Seventh Edition, most `ioctl` calls that took a parameter referred to a `struct sgttyb`, which was defined in */usr/include/sgtty.h*:

```
struct sgttyb
  {
  char sg_ispeed;                     /* input bit rate code */
  char sg_ospeed;                      /* output bit rate code */
  char sg_erase;                       /* erase character */
  char sg_kill;                        /* kill character */
  int  sg_flags;                       /* Terminal flags (see Table 15-3) */
  char sg_nldly;                       /* delay after \n character */
  char sg_crdly;                       /* delay after \r character */
  char sg_htdly;                       /* delay after tab character */
  char sg_vtdly;                       /* delay after vt character */
  char sg_width;                       /* terminal line width */
  char sg_length;                      /* terminal page length */
  };
```

The bit rates in `sg_ispeed` and `sg_ospeed` are encoded and allow only a certain number of speeds, which are provided in Table 15-2.

Table 15-2: Seventh Edition Bit Rate Codes

Parameter	Value	Meaning
B0	0	Hang up phone
B50	1	50 bits/second
B75	2	75 bits/second
B110	3	110 bits/second
B134	4	134.5 bits/second
B150	5	150 bits/second
B200	6	200 bits/second
B300	7	300 bits/second
B600	8	600 bits/second
B1200	9	1200 bits/second
B1800	10	1800 bits/second
B2400	11	2400 bits/second
B4800	12	4800 bits/second
B9600	13	9600 bits/second
EXTA	14	External A
EXTB	15	External B

The field `sg_flags` contains a bitmap specifying the actions listed in Table 15-3.

Table 15-3: Seventh Edition tty Flags

Parameter	Value (octal)	Value (hex)	Meaning
XTABS	02000	0x400	Replace output tabs by spaces
INDCTL	01000	0x200	Echo control characters as ^a, ^b, etc.
SCOPE	0400	0x100	Enable neat erasing functions on display terminals ("scopes")
EVENP	0200	0x80	Even parity allowed on input (most terminals)
ODDP	0100	0x40	Odd parity allowed on input
RAW	040	0x20	Raw mode: wake up on all characters, 8-bit interface
CRMOD	020	0x10	Map CR into LF; echo LF or CR as CR-LF
ECHO	010	0x8	Echo (full duplex)
LCASE	04	0x4	Map uppercase to lowercase on input
CBREAK	02	0x2	Return each character as soon as typed
TANDEM	01	0x1	Automatic flow control

A second structure defines additional special characters that the driver interprets in cooked mode. They are stored in a `struct tchars`, which is also defined in */usr/include/sgtty.h*:

```
struct tchars
  {
  char t_intrc;                    /* interrupt (default DEL) */
  char t_quitc;                    /* quit (default ^\) */
  char t_startc;                   /* start output (default ^Q)*/
  char t_stopc;                    /* stop output (default ^S) */
  char t_eofc;                     /* end-of-file (default ^D) */
  char t_brkc;                     /* input delimiter (like nl, default -1) */
  };
```

Each of these characters can be disabled by setting it to –1 (octal 0377), as is done with the default `t_brkc`. This means that no key can invoke its effect.

termio and termios Structures

The System V terminal driver defines a `struct termio` to represent the data that the Seventh Edition driver stored in `sgttyb` and `tchars`. In POSIX.1 *termios*, it is called `struct termios`. They are very similar: compared to the Seventh Edition, they appear to have been shorter by moving the special characters, which in `sgttyb` were stored as individual elements, into the array `c_cc`:

```
struct termio
  {
  unsigned short c_iflag;                 /* input modes */
  unsigned short c_oflag;                 /* output modes */
  unsigned short c_cflag;                 /* control modes */
  unsigned short c_lflag;                 /* local modes */
  char c_line;                            /* line discipline */
  unsigned char c_cc [NCC];               /* special chars */
  long c_ispeed;                          /* input speed, some termios */
  long c_ospeed;                          /* output speed, some termios */
  };
```

The variable `c_line` specifies the line discipline. It is defined in *termio* and not in the POSIX.1 *termios* standard, but some System V versions of *termios* have it anyway. `NCC` is the number of special characters. We'll look at them after we look at the flags.

Not all versions of System V define the members `c_ispeed` and `c_ospeed`. Instead, they encode the line speed in `c_cflag`. The correct way to access them is via the *termios* utility functions `cfgetispeed`, `cfsetispeed`, `cfgetospeed`, `cfsetospeed`, and `cfsetspeed`, which we will discuss in the section called "termios Functions". To make matters worse, some older System V *termios* implementations supplied `c_ispeed` and `c_ospeed`, but the implementation didn't use them. In addition, many systems cannot handle different input and output speeds, so setting one speed automatically sets the other as well.

`c_iflag`, `c_oflag`, `c_cflag`, and `c_lflag` (a total of 128 possible bits) take the place of the Seventh Edition `sg_flags`.

c_iflag

`c_iflag` specifies how the driver treats terminal input, which is described in Table 15-4.

Table 15-4: termios c_iflag Bits

Parameter	Value (System V)	Value (BSD)	Meaning
IGNBRK	0x1	0x1	Ignore break condition.
BRKINT	0x2	0x2	Generate a SIGINT signal on break.
IGNPAR	0x4	0x4	Ignore characters with parity errors.
PARMRK	0x8	0x8	If a parity or framing error occurs on input, accept it, and insert into the input stream the three-character sequence 0xff, 0, and the character received.
INPCK	0x10	0x10	Enable input parity check.
ISTRIP	0x20	0x20	Strip bit 7 from character.

Table 15-4: termios c_iflag Bits (continued)

Parameter	Value (System V)	Value (BSD)	Meaning
INLCR	0x40	0x40	Map NL to CR on input.
IGNCR	0x80	0x80	Ignore CR.
ICRNL	0x100	0x100	Map CR to NL on input.
IUCLC[a]	0x200		Map uppercase to lowercase on input.
IXON	0x400	0x200	Enable output flow control with XON/XOFF (**CTRL-S/CTRL-Q**).
IXANY	0x800	0x800	Allow any character to restart output after being stopped by **CTRL-S**.
IXOFF	0x1000	0x400	Enable input flow control with XON/XOFF.
CTSFLOW[a]	0x2000		Enable CTS protocol for a modem line.
RTSFLOW[a]	0x4000		Enable RTS signaling for a modem line.
IMAXBEL[b]	0x2000	0x2000	Ring the terminal bell when the input queue is full.

[a] Not in POSIX.1 or BSD.
[b] Not in POSIX.1 and some versions of System V.

A couple of these flags are not portable:

- IUCLC maps lowercase to uppercase: if you enter a lowercase character, it is converted to an uppercase character and echos that way. Many people consider this a bug, not a feature. There's no good way to implement this on a non-System V system. If you *really* want to have this behavior, you'll have to turn off echo and provide an echo from the program.
- CTSFLOW and RTSFLOW specify flow control via the RS-232 signals CTS and RTS. These are control flags, of course, not input flags, but some versions of System V put them here for backward compatibility with XENIX. Some other versions of System V don't define them at all, and BSD systems and yet other System V systems supply them in `c_cflags`, where they belong.

`c_oflag` specifies the behavior on output, which is described in Table 15-5.

Table 15-5: termios c_oflag Bits

Parameter	Value (System V)	Value (BSD)	Meaning
OPOST	0x1	0x1	Postprocess output
OLCUC[a]	0x2		Map lowercase to uppercase on output
ONLCR	0x4	0x2	Map NL to CR-NL on output
OCRNL	0x8	0x8	Map CR to NL on output

Table 15-5: termios c_oflag Bits (continued)

Parameter	Value (System V)	Value (BSD)	Meaning
ONOCR	0x10	0x10	Suppress CR output at column 0
ONLRET	0x20	0x20	NL performs CR function
OFILL	0x40	0x40	Use fill characters for delay
OFDEL	0x80	0x80	Fill is DEL if set, otherwise NUL.[b]
NLDLY[a]	0x100		Mask bit for newline delays:
NL0	0x0		No delay after NL
NL1	0x100		One character delay after NL
CRDLY[a]	0x600		Mask bits for carriage-return delays:
CR0	0x0		No delay after CR
CR1	0x200		One character delay after CR
CR2	0x400		Two characters delay after CR
CR3	0x600		Three characters delay after CR
TABDLY[a]	0x18000		Mask bits for horizontal-tab delays:
TAB0	0x0		No delay after HT
TAB1	0x800		One character delay after HT
TAB2	0x1000		Two characters delay after HT
TAB3	0x1800		Expand tabs to spaces
BSDLY[a]	0x2000		Mask bit for backspace delays:
BS0	0x0		No delay after BS
BS1	0x2000		One character delay after BS
VTDLY[a]	0x4000		Mask bit for vertical-tab delays:
VT0	0x0		No delay after VT
VT1	0x4000		One character delay after VT
FFDLY[a]	0x8000		Mask bit for form-feed delays:
FF0	0x0		No delay after FF
FF1	0x8000		One character delay after FF

[a] Not in POSIX.1 or BSD.
[b] The ASCII character represented by binary 0 (the C character constant \0). Not to be confused with the null pointer, which in C is usually called NULL.

A number of these flags are not portable:

- System V supplies a large number of flags designed to compensate for mechanical delays in old hard copy terminal equipment. It's doubtful that any of these flags are needed nowadays. If you do have an unbuffered hard copy terminal connected to your BSD machine and it loses characters at the beginning of a line or a page, you should check whether CTS/RTS flow control might help. Or you could buy a more modern terminal.

- `OLCUC` is obsolete, of course, but if that old hardcopy terminal also doesn't support lowercase, and it doesn't upshift lowercase characters automatically, you'll have to do it programatically.

`c_cflag` specifies hardware control aspects of the terminal interface, as shown in Table 15-6.

Table 15-6: termios c_cflag Bits

Parameter	Value (System V)	Value (BSD)	Meaning
`CBAUD`[a]	0xf		Bit rate
`B0`	0		Hang up
`B50`	0x1		50 bps
`B75`	0x2		75 bps
`B110`	0x3		110 bps
`B134`	0x4		134 bps
`B150`	0x5		150 bps
`B200`	0x6		200 bps
`B300`	0x7		300 bps
`B600`	0x8		600 bps
`B1200`	0x9		1200 bps
`B1800`	0xa		1800 bps
`B2400`	0xb		2400 bps
`B4800`	0xc		4800 bps
`B9600`	0xd		9600 bps
`B19200`	0xe		19200 bps
`EXTA`	0xe		External A
`B38400`	0xf		38400 bps
`EXTB`	0xf		External B
`CSIZE`	0x30	0x300	Mask bits for character size:
`CS5`	0x0	0x0	5 bits
`CS6`	0x10	0x100	6 bits
`CS7`	0x20	0x200	7 bits
`CS8`	0x30	0x300	8 bits

Table 15-6: termios c_cflag Bits (continued)

Parameter	Value (System V)	Value (BSD)	Meaning
CSTOPB	0x40	0x400	Send two stop bits (if not set, send 1 stop bit).
CREAD	0x80	0x800	Enable receiver
PARENB	0x100	0x1000	Enable parity
PARODD	0x200	0x2000	Set odd parity if set, otherwise even
HUPCL	0x400	0x4000	Hang up on last close
CLOCAL	0x800	0x8000	Disable modem control lines
RCV1EN[b]	0x1000		See below
XMT1EN[b]	0x2000		See below
LOBLK[b]	0x4000		Block layer output
CTSFLOW[a]	0x10000		CTS flow control of output
CCTS_OFLOW[c]		0x10000	CTS flow control of output
CRTSCTS[c]		0x10000	CTS flow control of output (alternative symbol)
RTSFLOW[a]		0x20000	RTS flow control of input
CRTS_IFLOW[c]		0x20000	RTS flow control of input
MDMBUF[c]	0x100000		Flow control output via carrier

[a] Speeds are encoded differently in BSD—see below.
[b] Not in POSIX.1 or BSD.
[c] Not in POSIX.1 or System V.

Again, some of these flags are available only on specific platforms:

- RCV1EN and XMT1EN are defined in some System V header files, but they are not documented.
- BSD systems supply CRTS_IFLOW and CCTS_OFLOW for RS-232 flow control. Some System V systems supply RTSFLOW and CTSFLOW to mean the same, but other System V systems don't support it, and other systems again put these flags in c_iflag.

c_lflag specifies the behavior specific to the line discipline. This flag varies so much between System V and BSD that I've listed them in separate tables. Table 15-7 describes the standard System V line discipline, and Table 15-8 describes the standard BSD line discipline.

Table 15-7: System V termios c_lflag Bits

Parameter	Value	Meaning
ISIG	0x1	Allow the characters INTR, QUIT, SUSP, and DSUSP to generate signals.
ICANON	0x2	Enable canonical input (erase and kill processing).
XCASE	0x4	In conjunction with ICANON, map uppercase/lowercase to an uppercase only terminal. Lowercase letters are displayed in uppercase, and uppercase letters are displayed with a preceding backslash (\).
ECHO	0x8	Enable echo.
ECHOE	0x10	Erase character removes character from screen.
ECHOK	0x20	Echo NL after line kill character.
ECHONL	0x40	Echo NL even if echo is off.
NOFLSH	0x80	Disable flush after interrupt or quit.

Table 15-8: BSD termios c_lflag Bits

Parameter	Value	Meaning
ECHOKE[a]	0x1	Line kill erases line from screen.
ECHOE	0x2	Erase character removes character from screen.
ECHOK	0x4	Echo NL after line kill character.
ECHO	0x8	Enable echo.
ECHONL	0x10	Echo NL even if echo is off.
ECHOPRT[a]	0x20	Visual erase mode for hard copy.
ECHOCTL[a]	0x40	Echo control chars as ^(Char).
ISIG	0x80	Enable signals INTR, QUIT, SUSP, and DSUSP.
ICANON	0x100	Enable canonical input (erase and kill processing).
ALTWERASE[a]	0x200	Use alternate WERASE algorithm. Instead of erasing back to the first blank space, erase back to the first nonalphanumeric character.
IEXTEN	0x400	Enable DISCARD and LNEXT.
EXTPROC[a]	0x800	This flag carries the comment "External processing". Apart from that, it appears to be undocumented.
TOSTOP	0x400000	If a background process attempts output, send a SIGTTOU to it. By default this stops the process.
FLUSHO[a]	0x800000	Status return only: output being flushed.
NOKERNINFO[a]	0x2000000	Prevent the STATUS character from displaying information on the foreground process group.

Table 15-8: BSD termios c_lflag Bits (continued)

Parameter	Value	Meaning
PENDIN[a]	0x20000000	Pending input is currently being redisplayed.
NOFLSH	0x80000000	Don't flush input and output queues after receiving SIGINT or SIGQUIT.

[a] Not in POSIX.1.

Converting the `c_lflag` bits is even more of a problem:

- `XCASE` is part of the System V uppercase syndrome that we saw with `c_iflag` and `c_oflag`.
- BSD offers a number of echo flags that are not available in System V. In practice, this is a cosmetic difference in the way input works. Consider a BSD program with a line like:

  ```
  term.c_lflag = ECHOKE | ECHOE | ECHOK | ECHOCTL;
  ```

  This fails to compile under System V because `ECHOKE` and `ECHOCTL` are undefined. You can probably ignore these flags. The way to fix it would be to write something like:

  ```
  term.c_lflag = ECHOE | ECHOK
  #ifdef ECHOKE
                 | ECHOKE
  #endif
  #ifdef ECHOCTL
                 | ECHOCTL
  #endif
                ;
  ```

  Note the lonesome semicolon on the last line.
- The flags `FLUSHO` and `PENDIN` are status flags that cannot be set. There's no way to get this information in System V.
- `NOKERNINFO` refers to the `STATUS` character, which we will see in Table 15-9. This is not supported in System V.

Special characters

The number of special characters has increased from 6 in the Seventh Edition (`struct tchars`) to 8 in *termio* and a total of 20 in *termios* (though 4 of the *termios* special characters are "reserved"—in other words, not defined). Despite this high number, there is no provision for redefining `CR` and `NL`.

Table 15-9: termio and termios Special Characters

Name	Index in c_cc (Sys. V)	Default (Sys. V)	Index in c_cc (BSD)	Default (BSD)	Function
CR	None	\r	None	\r	Go to beginning of line. In canonical and cooked modes, complete a read request.
NL	None	\n	None	\n	End line. In canonical and cooked modes, complete a read request.
VINTR	0	DEL	8	CTRL-C	Generate an SIGINT signal.
VQUIT	1	CTRL-|	9	CTRL-|	Generate a SIGQUIT signal.
VERASE	2	#[a]	3	DEL	Erase last character.
VKILL	3	@[a]	5	CTRL-U	Erase current input line.
VEOF	4	CTRL-D	0	CTRL-D	Return end-of-file indication.
VEOL	5	NUL	1	ÿ	Alternate end-of-line character.
VEOL2[b]	6	NUL	2	ÿ	Alternate end-of-line character.
VSWTCH[b c]	7	NUL			*shl* layers: switch shell.
VSTART	8	CTRL-Q	12	CTRL-Q	Resume output after stop.
VSTOP	9	CTRL-S	13	CTRL-S	Stop output.
VSUSP	10	CTRL-Z	10	CTRL-Z	Generate a SIGTSTP signal when typed.
VDSUSP[b]	11	CTRL-Y	11	CTRL-Y	Generate a SIGTSTP signal when the character is read.
VREPRINT[b]	12	CTRL-R	6	CTRL-R	Redisplay all characters in the input queue (in other words, characters that have been input but not yet read by any process). The term "print" recalls the days of hard copy terminals.
VDISCARD[b]	13	CTRL-O	15	CTRL-O	Discard all terminal output until another DISCARD character arrives, more input is typed, or the program clears the condition.
VWERASE[b]	14	CTRL-W	4	CTRL-W	Erase the preceding word.
VLNEXT[b]	15	CTRL-V	14	CTRL-V	Interpret next character literally.

Table 15-9: termio and termios Special Characters (continued)

Name	Index in c_cc (Sys. V)	Default (Sys. V)	Index in c_cc (BSD)	Default (BSD)	Function
VSTATUS[b d]			18	ÿ	Send a SIGINFO signal to the foreground process group. If NOKERNINFO is not set, the kernel also prints a status message on the terminal.

[a] These archaic, teletype-related values are still the default for System V. The file */usr/include/sys/termio.h* contains alternative definitions (VERASE set to CTRL-H and VKILL set to CTRL-X), but these need to be specifically enabled by defining the preprocessor variable _NEW_TTY_CTRL.
[b] Not in POSIX.1.
[c] *shl* layers are a System V method of multiplexing several shells on one terminal. They are not supported on BSD systems.
[d] Not supported on System V.

You frequently see the names listed in Table 15-9 without the leading V. For example, the *stty* program refers to VQUIT as QUIT.

Terminal Driver Modes

Depending on the driver, it looks as if you have a choice of two or three operational modes on input:

- With the *termio* and *termios* drivers, you have the choice of canonical and non-canonical mode.
- With the old terminal driver, you have the choice of raw, cooked, and cbreak modes.

This distinction is not as clear cut as it appears: in fact, you can set up both drivers to do most things you want.

Canonical Mode

To quote Richard Stevens' *Advanced Programming in the UNIX Environment*: "Canonical mode is simple." It takes only about 30 pages for a brief description. Here's an even simpler description: everything in the rest of this chapter applies to canonical mode unless otherwise stated.

Non-Canonical Mode

Non-canonical mode ignores all special characters except INTR, QUIT, SUSP, STRT, STOP, DISCARD, and LNEXT. If you don't want these to be interpreted, you can disable them by setting the corresponding entry in tchars to _POSIX_VDISABLE.

The terminal mode has a strong influence on how a read from a terminal completes. In canonical mode, a read request completes when the number of characters requested has been input, or when the user enters one of the characters CR, NL, VEOL, or (where supported) VEOL2. In non-canonical mode, no special character causes a normal read completion. The way a read request completes depends on two variables, MIN and TIME. MIN represents a minimum number of characters to be read, and TIME represents a time in units of 0.1 second. There are four possible cases:

- Both MIN and TIME are nonzero. In this case, a read completes when either MIN characters have been entered or TIME/10 seconds have passed since a character was entered. The timer starts when a character is entered, so at least one character must be entered for the read to complete.
- MIN is nonzero, TIME is zero. In this case, the read cannot complete until MIN characters have been entered.
- MIN is zero, and TIME is nonzero. The read will complete after entering one character or after *TIME/10* seconds. In the latter case, 0 characters are returned. This is not the same as setting MIN to 1 and leaving TIME as it is: in this case, the read would not complete until at least one character is entered.
- Both MIN and TIME are set to 0. In this case, read returns immediately with any characters that may be waiting.

If MIN is nonzero, it overrides the read count specified to read, even if read requests less than MIN characters: the remaining characters are kept in the input queue for the next read request. This can have the unpleasant and confusing effect that at first nothing happens when you type something in and then suddenly multiple reads complete.

Non-canonical mode does not interpret all the special characters, but it needs space to store MIN and *TIME*. In 4.4BSD, two of the reserved characters are used for this purpose. Most other implementations, including XENIX, System V, and some older BSDs do it differently, and this can cause problems:

- The value of *VEOF* is used for *VMIN*. This value is normally **CTRL-D**, which is decimal 4: if you switch from canonical to non-canonical mode and do not change MIN, you may find that a read of a single character does not complete until you enter a total of four characters.

- The value of *VEOL* is used for *TIME*. This is normally 0.

Raw Mode

Raw mode does almost no interpretation of the input stream. In particular, no special characters are recognized, and there is no timeout. The non-canonical mode variables MIN and *TIME* do not exist. The result is the same as setting MIN to 1 and TIME to 0 in non-canonical mode.

Cooked Mode

The cooked mode of the old terminal driver is essentially the same as canonical mode, within the limitations of the driver data structures—*termios* offers some features that are not available with the old terminal driver, such as alternate end-of-line characters.

cbreak Mode

To quote the Seventh Edition manual, "CBREAK is a sort of half-cooked (rare?) mode."

In terms of *termios*, it is quite close to non-canonical mode: the only difference is that cbreak mode turns off echo. Non-canonical mode does not specify whether echo is on or off.

Emulating Old Terminal Driver Modes

Table 15-10 illustrates how you can define old driver terminal modes with *termios*. You'll see that a large number of entries are not defined: raw and cbreak modes do not specify how these parameters are set. You can set them to whatever you feel appropriate.

Table 15-10: Defining Terminal Modes with termios

Flag	Raw Mode	cbreak Mode
BRKINT	off	on
INPCK	off	on
ISTRIP	off	not defined
ICRNL	off	not defined
IXON	off	not defined

Table 15-10: Defining Terminal Modes with termios (continued)

Flag	Raw Mode	cbreak Mode
OPOST	off	not defined
CSIZE	CS8	not defined
PARENB	off	not defined
ECHO	off	off
ISIG	off	not defined
ICANON	off	off
IEXTEN	off	not defined
VMIN	1	1
VTIME	0	0

gtty and stty

You may still occasionally run into the system calls `stty` and `gtty`, which are left-overs from the Seventh Edition. You can replace `stty` with the `ioctl` function TIOCSETP, and you can replace `gtty` with the `ioctl` request TIOCGETP. You can read more on both these requests in the section called "TIOCGETP and TIOCSETP".

The Linux Terminal Driver

Linux has the great advantage of being a recent development, so it doesn't have a number of the warts of older terminal drivers. It goes to some trouble to be compatible, however:

- In addition to POSIX.1 *termios*, the kernel also directly supports System V *termio*.
- The library *libbsd.a* includes `ioctl` calls for the old terminal driver, which Linux users call the BSD driver.
- The only line discipline you can expect to work under Linux is the standard tty line discipline N_TTY.

ioctl

`ioctl` is the file system catch-all: if there isn't any other function to do the job, then somebody will bend `ioctl` to do it. Nowhere is this more evident than in terminal I/O handling. As a result of this catch-all nature, it's not easy to represent `ioctl` parameters in C.

We'll look at the semantics first. The `ioctl` function call takes three parameters:

- A file number.
- A *request*, which we'll look at in more detail in the next section.
- When present, the meaning is defined by the request. It could be an integer, another request code, or a pointer to some structure defined by the request.

ioctl Request Codes

The key to understanding `ioctl` is the request code. Request codes are usually subdivided into a number of fields. For example, 4.4BSD defines four fields, shown in Figure 15-1.

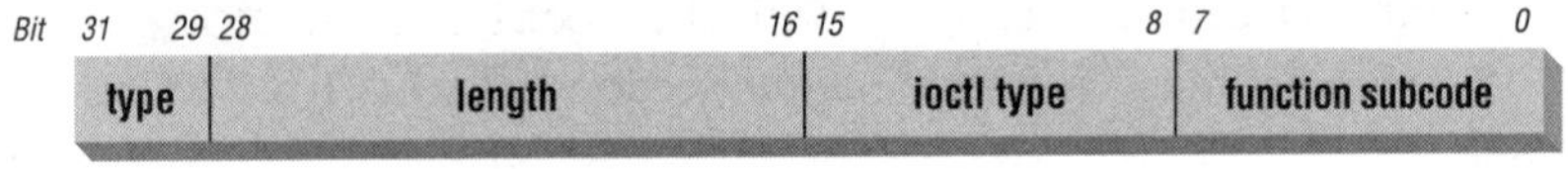

Figure 15-1: 4.4BSD ioctl request

type
The first three bits specify the type of parameter. IOC_VOID (0x20 in the first byte) specifies that the request takes no parameters, IOC_OUT (0x40 in the first byte) specifies that the parameters are to be copied out of the kernel (in other words, that the parameters are to be returned to the user), and IOC_IN (0x80 in the first byte) specifies that the parameters are to be copied in to the kernel (they are to be passed to `ioctl`).

length
The next 13 bits specify the length of the parameter in bytes.

ioctl type
The next byte specifies the type of request. This is frequently a mnemonic letter. In 4.4BSD, this field is set to the lowercase letter *t* for terminal ioctls.

function subcode

The final byte is a number used to identify the request uniquely.

This encoding depends heavily on the operating system. Other systems (especially, of course, 16-bit systems) encode differently, but the general principle remains the same.

Both the request code and the third parameter, where present, do not map easily to C language data structures. As a result, the definition of the function varies significantly. For example, XENIX and BSD declare it as:

```
#include <sys/ioctl.h>
int ioctl (int fd, unsigned long request, char *argp)
```

System V.4 has:

```
#include <unistd.h>
int ioctl (int fs, int request,                /* arg */ ...);
```

Strictly speaking, since the request code is not a number, both `int` and `unsigned long` are incorrect, but they both do the job.

When debugging a program, it's not always easy to determine which request has been passed to `ioctl`. If you have the source code, you will see something like

```
ioctl (stdin, TIOCGETA, &termstat);
```

Unfortunately, a number of `ioctl` calls are embedded in libraries to which you probably don't have source, but you can figure out what's going on by setting a breakpoint on `ioctl`. In this example, when you hit the breakpoint, you will see something like:

```
(gdb) bt
#0  ioctl (file=0, request=1076655123, parameter=0xefbfd58c "") at ioctl.c:6
#1  0x10af in main () at foo.c:12
```

The value of `request` looks completely random. In hexadecimal it starts to make a little more sense:

```
(gdb) p/x request
$1 = 0x402c7413
```

If we compare this with the request code layout in the previous example, we can recognize a fair amount of information:

type

The first byte starts with `0x40`, `IOC_OUT`: the parameter exists and defines a return value.

length

The next 13 bits are 0x2c, the length to be returned (this is the length of struct termios).

ioctl type

The next byte is 0x74, the ASCII character *t*, indicating that this is a terminal ioctl request.

function subcode

The last byte is 0x13 (decimal 19).

The meaning of the 32 bits is easy enough to understand when it's deciphered like this, but doing it yourself is a lot different. The first problem is that there is no agreed place where the ioctl requests are defined. The best place to start is in the header file *sys/ioctl.h*, which in the case of 4.4BSD leads you to the file *sys/ioccom.h* (*sys/sys/ioccom.h* in the 4.4BSD distribution). Here you find code like:

```
#define IOCPARM_MASK     0x1fff          /* parameter length, at most 13 bits */
#define IOCPARM_LEN(x)   (((x) >> 16) & IOCPARM_MASK)
#define IOCBASECMD(x)    ((x) & ~(IOCPARM_MASK << 16))
#define IOCGROUP(x)      (((x) >> 8) & 0xff)
#define IOC_VOID         0x20000000      /* no parameters */
#define IOC_OUT          0x40000000      /* copy out parameters */
#define IOC_IN           0x80000000      /* copy in parameters */
```

These define the basic parts of the request. Next come the individual types of request:

```
#define _IOC(inout,group,num,len) \  pass a structure of length len as parameter
  (inout | ((len & IOCPARM_MASK) << 16) | ((group) << 8) | (num))
#define _IO(g,n)      _IOC(IOC_VOID, (g), (n), 0)     No parameter
#define _IOR(g,n,t) _IOC(IOC_OUT,  (g), (n), sizeof(t)) Return parameter from kernel
#define _IOW(g,n,t)  _IOC(IOC_IN,    (g), (n), sizeof(t)) Pass parameter to kernel
/* this should be _IORW, but stdio got there first */
#define _IOWR(g,n,t) _IOC(IOC_INOUT, (g), (n), sizeof(t)) Pass and return parameter
```

With these building blocks, we can now understand the real definitions:

```
#define TIOCSBRK  _IO('t', 123)              /* set break bit */
#define TIOCCBRK  _IO('t', 122)              /* clear break bit */
#define TIOCSDTR  _IO('t', 121)              /* set data terminal ready */
#define TIOCCDTR  _IO('t', 120)              /* clear data terminal ready */
#define TIOCGPGRP _IOR('t', 119, int)        /* get pgrp of tty */
#define TIOCSPGRP _IOW('t', 118, int)        /* set pgrp of tty */
```

These define four requests without parameters (_IO), a request that returns an int parameter from the kernel (_IOR), and a request that passes an int parameter to the kernel (_IOW).

Terminal ioctls

For a number of reasons, it's difficult to categorize terminal driver `ioctl` calls:

- As the terminal driver has changed over the course of time, some implementors have chosen to keep the old `ioctl` codes and give them new parameters. For example, the Seventh Edition call TIOCGETA returned the terminal parameters to a `struct sgttyb`. The same call in System V returns the values to a `struct termio`, and in 4.4BSD it returns the values to a `struct termios`.
- The documentation for many `ioctl` calls is extremely hazy: although System V supports the old terminal driver discipline, the documentation is very scant. Just because an `ioctl` function is not documented in the man pages doesn't mean that it isn't supported: it's better to check in the header files (usually something like *sys/termio.h* or *sys/termios.h*).
- Many `ioctl` calls seem to duplicate functionality. There are minor differences, but even they are treacherous. For example, in the Seventh Edition the TIOCSETA function drains the output queue and discards the content of the input queue before setting the terminal state. The same function in 4.4BSD sets the state immediately. To get the Seventh Edition behavior, you need to use TIOCSETAF. The behavior in System V is not documented, which means that you may be at the mercy of the implementor of the device driver: on one system, it may behave like the Seventh Edition, on another like 4.4BSD.

In the following sections, we'll attempt to categorize the most frequently used `ioctl` functions in the kind of framework that POSIX.1 uses for *termios*. Table 15-11 provides an index to the mess.

Table 15-11: ioctl Parameters

Name	Function	Parameter 3
TCFLSH	Flush I/O	int *
TCGETA	Get terminal state	struct termio *
TCGETS	Get terminal state	struct termios *
TCSBRK	Drain output, send break	int *
TCSETA	Set terminal state	struct termio *
TCSETAF	Drain I/O and set state	struct termio *
TCSETAW	Drain output and set state	struct termio *
TCSETS	Set terminal state	struct termios *
TCSETSF	Drain I/O and set state	struct termios *
TCSETSW	Drain output and set state	struct termios *
TCXONC	Set flow control	int *
TIOCCBRK	Clear break	None

Table 15-11: ioctl Parameters (continued)

Name	Function	Parameter 3
TIOCCDTR	Clear DTR	None
TIOCCONS	Set console	int *
TIOCDRAIN	Drain output queue	None
TIOCFLUSH	Flush I/O	int *
TIOCGETA	Get current state	struct termio *
TIOCGETC	Get special chars	struct tchars *
TIOCGETD	Set line discipline	int *ldisc
TIOCGETP	Get current state	struct sgttyb *
TIOCGPGRP	Get process group ID	pid_t *
TIOCGSID	Get session ID	pid_t *
TIOCGSOFTCAR	Get DCD indication	int *
TIOCGWINSZ	Get window size	struct winsize *
TIOCHPCL	Hang up on clear	None
TIOCMBIC	Clear modem state bits	int *
TIOCMBIS	Set modem state bits	int *
TIOCMGET	Get modem state	int *
TIOCMSET	Set modem state	int *
TIOCNXCL	Clear exclusive use	None
TIOCNOTTY	Drop controlling terminal	None
TIOCOUTQ	Get output queue length	int *
TIOCSBRK	Send break	None
TIOCSCTTY	Set controlling tty	None
TIOCSDTR	Set DTR	None
TIOCSETA	Set terminal state	struct sgttyb *
TIOCSETAF	Drain I/O and set state	struct termios *
TIOCSETAW	Drain output and set state	struct termios *
TIOCSETC	Set special chars	struct tchars *
TIOCSETD	Set line discipline	int *ldisc
TIOCSETN	Set state immediately	struct sgttyb *
TIOCSETP	Get current state	struct sgttyb *
TIOCSPGRP	Set process group ID	pid_t *
TIOCSSOFTCAR	Set DCD indication	int *
TIOCSTART	Start output	None
TIOCSTI	Simulate input	char *

Table 15-11: ioctl Parameters (continued)

Name	Function	Parameter 3
TIOCSTOP	Stop output	None
TIOCSWINSZ	Set window size	struct winsize *

Terminal Attributes

One of the most fundamental groups of `ioctl` requests get and set the terminal state. This area is the biggest mess of all. Each terminal driver has its own group of requests, the request names are similar enough to be confusing, different systems use the same request names to mean different things, and even in *termios*, there is no agreement between BSD and System V about the names of the requests.

Table 15-12 gives an overview.

Table 15-12: Comparison of sgttyb, termio, and termios ioctls

Function	sgtty Request	termio Request	termios Request (BSD)	termios Request (System V)
Get current state	TIOCGETA	TCGETA	TIOCGETA	TCGETS
Get special chars	TIOCGETC	TCGETA	TIOCGETA	TCGETS
Set terminal state immediately	TIOCSETN	TCSETA	TIOCSETA	TCSETS
Drain output and set state		TCSETAW	TIOCSETAW	TCSETSW
Drain I/O and set state	TIOCSETA	TCSETAF	TIOCSETAF	TCSETSF
Set special chars	TIOCSETC	TCSETAF	TIOCSETAF	TCSETSF

TIOCGETA

The call `ioctl (fd, TIOCGETA, term)` places the current terminal parameters in the structure `term`. The usage differs depending on the system:

System	Structure for "term"
Seventh Edition	sgttyb
System V	termio
4.4BSD	termios

The Seventh Edition request `TIOCSETN` only sets the terminal state described in the first six bytes of `struct sgettyb`.

TIOCSETA

The call `ioctl (fd, TIOCSETA, term)` sets the current terminal state from `term`. The usage differs depending on the system:

System	Structure for "term"	Description
Seventh Edition	`sgttyb`	Drain the output queue and flush the input queue before setting the parameters.
System V.3	`termio`	The drain and flush behavior is not documented.
4.4BSD	`termios`	Perform the action immediately with no drain or flush. This is used to implement the `tcsetattr` function with the TCSANOW option.

TIOCGETP and TIOCSETP

`TIOCGETP` and `TIOCSETP` are obsolete versions of `TIOCGETA` and `TIOCSETA` respectively. They affect only the first six bytes of the `sgttyb` structure (`sg_ispeed` to `sg_flags`). These requests correspond in function to the obsolete Seventh Edition system calls `stty` and `gtty`.

TIOCSETAW

The call `ioctl (fd, TIOCSETAW, void *term)` waits for any output to complete, then sets the terminal state associated with the device. 4.4BSD uses this call to implement the `tcsetattr` function with the `TCSADRAIN` option. In XENIX, the parameter `term` is of type `struct termio`; in other systems, it is of type `struct termios`.

TIOCSETAF

The call `ioctl (fd, TIOCSETAF, void *term)` waits for any output to complete, flushes any pending input, and then sets the terminal state. 4.4BSD uses this call to implement the `tcsetattr` function with the `TCSAFLUSH` option. In XENIX, the parameter `term` is of type `struct termio`; in other systems, it is of type `struct termios`.

TIOCSETN

The call `ioctl (fd, TIOCSETN, struct sgttyb *term)` sets the parameters but does not delay or flush input. This call is supported by System V.3 and the Seventh Edition. In the Seventh Edition, this function works only on the first six bytes of the `sgttyb` structure.

TIOCHPCL

The call `ioctl (fd, TIOCHPCL, NULL)` specifies that the terminal line is to be disconnected (hung up) when the file is closed for the last time.

TIOCGETC

The call `ioctl (fd, TIOCGETC, struct tchars *chars)` returns the terminal special characters to `chars`.

TIOCSETC

The call `ioctl (fd, TIOCSETC, struct tchars *chars)` sets the terminal special characters from `chars`.

TCGETS

The call `ioctl (fd, TCGETS, struct termios *term)` returns the current terminal parameters to `term`. This function is supported by System V.4.

TCSETS

The call `ioctl (fd, TCSETS, struct termios *term)` immediately sets the current terminal parameters from `term`. This function is supported by System V.4 and corresponds to the 4.4BSD call `TIOCSETA`.

TCSETSW

The call `ioctl (fd, TCSETSW, struct termios *term)` sets the current terminal parameters from `term` after all output characters have been output. This function is supported by System V.4 and corresponds to the 4.4BSD call `TIOCSETAW`.

TCSETSF

The call `ioctl (fd, TCSETSF, struct termios *term)` flushes the input queue and sets the current terminal parameters from `term` after all output characters have been output. This function is supported by System V.4 and corresponds to the 4.4BSD call `TIOCSETAF`.

TCGETA

The call `ioctl (fd, TCGETA, struct termio *term)` stores current terminal parameters in `term`. Not all *termios* parameters can be stored in a `struct termio`; you may find it advantageous to use `TCGETS` instead (see the previous section on `TCGETS`).

TCSETA

The call `ioctl (fd, TCSETA, struct termio *term)` sets the current terminal status from `term`. Parameters that cannot be stored in `struct termio` are not affected. This corresponds to `TCSETA`, except that it uses a `struct termio *` instead of a `struct termios *`.

TCSETAW

The call `ioctl (fd, TCSETAW, struct termio *term)` sets the current terminal parameters from `term` after draining the output queue. This corresponds to `TCSETW`, except that it uses a `struct termio *` instead of a `struct termios *`.

TCSETAF

The call `ioctl (fd, TCSETAF, struct termio *term)` flushes the input queue and sets the current terminal parameters from `term` after all output characters have been output. This corresponds to `TCSETF`, except that it uses a `struct termio *` instead of a `struct termios *`.

TIOCGWINSZ

The call `ioctl (fd, TIOCGWINSZ, struct winsize *ws)` puts the window size information associated with the terminal in `ws`. The window size structure contains the number of rows and columns (and pixels if appropiate) of the devices attached to the terminal. It is set by user software and is the means by which most full screen–oriented programs determine the screen size. The `winsize` structure is defined as:

```
struct winsize
  {
  unsigned short  ws_row;          /* rows, in characters */
  unsigned short  ws_col;          /* columns, in characters */
  unsigned short  ws_xpixel;       /* horizontal size, pixels */
  unsigned short  ws_ypixel;       /* vertical size, pixels */
  };
```

Many implementations ignore the members `ws_xpixel` and `ws_ypixel` and set them to 0.

TIOCSWINSZ

The call `ioctl (fd, TIOCSWINSZ, struct winsize *ws)` sets the window size associated with the terminal to the value at `ws`. If the new size is different from the old size, a `SIGWINCH` (window changed) signal is sent to the process group of the terminal. See `TIOCGWINSZ` for more details.

TIOCSETD

The call `ioctl (fd, TIOCSETD, int *ldisc)` changes the line discipline to `ldisc`. Not all systems support multiple line disciplines, and both the available line disciplines and their names depend on the system. Here are some typical ones:

`OTTYDISC`
: In System V, the "old" (Seventh Edition) tty discipline

`NETLDISC`
: The Berknet line discipline

`NTTYDISC`
: In System V, the "new" (termio) tty discipline

`TABLDISC`
: The Hitachi tablet discipline

`NTABLDISC`
: The GTCO tablet discipline

`MOUSELDISC`
: The mouse discipline

`KBDLDISC`
: The keyboard line discipline

`TTYDISC`
: The *termios* interactive line discipline

`TABLDISC`
: The tablet line discipline

`SLIPDISC`
: The Serial IP (SLIP) line discipline

TIOCGETD

The call `ioctl (fd, TIOCGETD, int *ldisc)` returns the current line discipline at `ldisc`. See the discussion in the previous section on `TIOCSETD`.

Hardware Control

TIOCSBRK

The call `ioctl (fd, TIOCSBRK, NULL)` sets the terminal hardware into break condition. This function is supported by 4.4BSD.

TIOCCBRK

The call `ioctl (fd, TIOCCBRK, NULL)` clears a terminal hardware BREAK condition. This function is supported by 4.4BSD.

TIOCSDTR

The call `ioctl (fd, TIOCSDTR, NULL)` asserts Data Terminal Ready (DTR). This function is supported by 4.4BSD. See the section called "Terminology" for details of the DTR signal.

TIOCCDTR

The call `ioctl (fd, TIOCCDTR, NULL)` resets DTR. This function is supported by 4.4BSD. See the section called "Terminology" for details of the DTR signal.

TIOCMSET

The call `ioctl (fd, TIOCMSET, int *state)` sets modem state. It is supported by 4.4BSD, SunOS, and System V.4, but not all terminals support this call. `*state` is a bitmap representing the parameters listed in Table 15-13.

Table 15-13: TIOCMSET and TIOCMGET State Bits

Parameter	Meaning
TIOCM_LE	Line Enable
TIOCM_DTR	Data Terminal Ready
TIOCM_RTS	Request To Send
TIOCM_ST	Secondary Transmit
TIOCM_SR	Secondary Receive
TIOCM_CTS	Clear To Send
TIOCM_CAR	Carrier Detect
TIOCM_CD	Carrier Detect (synonym)
TIOCM_RNG	Ring Indication
TIOCM_RI	Ring Indication (synonym)
TIOCM_DSR	Data Set Ready

TIOCMGET

The call `ioctl (fd, TIOCMGET, int *state)` returns the current state of the terminal modem lines. See the description of `TIOCMSET` for the use of the bitmapped variable `state`.

TIOCMBIS

The call `ioctl (fd, TIOCMBIS, int *state)` sets the modem state in the same manner as `TIOMSET`, but instead of setting the `state` bits unconditionally, each bit is logically ORed with the current state.

TIOCMBIC

The call `ioctl (fd, TIOCMBIC, int *state)` clears the modem state: each bit set in the bitmap `state` is reset in the modem state. The other state bits are not affected.

TCSBRK

The call `ioctl (fd, TCSBRK, int nobreak)` drains the output queue and then sends a break if `nobreak` is not set. This function is supported in System V and SunOS. In contrast to the 4.4BSD function `TIOCSBRK`, `TCSBRK` resets the break condition automatically.

TCXONC

The call `ioctl (fd, TCXONC, int type)` specifies flow control. It is supported in System V and SunOS. Table 15-14 shows the possible values of `type`.

Table 15-14: TCXONC and tcflow Type Bits

Parameter	Value	Meaning
`TCOOFF`	0	Suspend output
`TCOON`	1	Restart suspended output
`TCIOFF`	2	Suspend input
`TCION`	3	Restart suspended input

Not all drivers support input flow control via `TCXONC`.

Queue Control

TIOCOUTQ

The call `ioctl (fd, TIOCOUTQ, int *num)` sets the current number of characters in the output queue to `*num`. This function is supported by BSD and SunOS.

TIOCSTI

The call `ioctl (fd, TIOCSTI, char *cp)` simulates typed input. It inserts the character at `*cp` into the input queue. This function is supported by BSD and SunOS.

TIOCSTOP

The call `ioctl (fd, TIOCSTOP, NULL)` stops output on the terminal. It's like typing **CTRL-S** at the keyboard. This function is supported by 4.4BSD.

TIOCSTART

The call `ioctl (fd, TIOCSTART, NULL)` restarts output on the terminal, like typing **CTRL-Q** at the keyboard. This function is supported by 4.4BSD.

TIOCDRAIN

The call `ioctl (fd, TIOCDRAIN, NULL)` suspends process execution until all output is drained. This function is supported by 4.4BSD.

TIOCFLUSH

The call `ioctl (fd, TIOCFLUSH, int *what)` flushes the input and output queues. This function is supported by 4.4BSD, System V.3, and the Seventh Edition. The System V.3 and Seventh Edition implementations ignore the parameter `what` and flush both queues. 4.4BSD flushes the queues if the corresponding bits `FREAD` and `FWRITE` are set in `*what`. If no bits are set, it clears both queues.

TCFLSH

The call `ioctl (fd, TCFLSH, int type)` flushes the input or output queues, depending on the flags defined in Table 15-15.

Table 15-15: TCFLSH Type Bits

Parameter	Value	Meaning
`TCIFLUSH`	0	Flush the input queue
`TCOFLUSH`	1	Flush the output queue
`TCIOFLUSH`	2	Flush both queues

This function is supported by System V. It does the same thing as `TIOCFLUSH`, but the semantics are different.

Session Control

TIOCGPGRP

The call `ioctl (fd, TIOCGPGRP, pid_t *tpgrp)` sets `*tpgrp` to the ID of the current process group with which the terminal is associated. 4.4BSD uses this call to implement the function `tcgetpgrp`.

TIOCSPGRP

The call `ioctl (fd, TIOCSPGRP, pid_t *tpgrp)` associates the terminal with the process group `tpgrp`. 4.4BSD uses this call to implement the function `tcsetpgrp`.

TIOCSCTTY

`TIOCSCTTY` makes the terminal the controlling terminal for the process. This function is supported by BSD and SunOS systems. On BSD systems, the call is `ioctl (fd, TIOCSCTTY, NULL)` and on SunOS systems, it is `ioctl (fd, TIOCSCTTY, int type)`. Normally the controlling terminal is set only if no other process already owns it. In those implementations that support `type` the superuser can set `type` to 1 in order to force the takeover of the terminal, even if another process owns it. In 4.4BSD, you would first use the *revoke* system call (see the section called "revoke" in Chapter 14, *File Systems*) to force a close of all file descriptors associated with the file.

System V and older versions of BSD have no equivalent of this function. In these systems, when a process group leader without a controlling terminal opens a terminal, it automatically becomes the controlling terminal. There are methods to override this behavior: in System V, you set the flag `O_NOCTTY` when you open the terminal. In old BSD versions, you subsequently release the control of the terminal with the `TIOCNOTTY` request, which we'll look at in the next section.

TIOCNOTTY

Traditionally, the first time a process without a controlling terminal opened a terminal, it acquired that terminal as its controlling terminal. We saw in the previous section on `TIOCSCTTY` that this is no longer the default behavior in BSD and that you can override it in System V. Older BSD versions, including SunOS, did not offer either of these choices. Instead, you had to accept that you acquired a controlling terminal and then release the controlling terminal again with ioctl `TIOCNOTTY`. If you find this code in a package and your system doesn't support it, you can eliminate it. If your system is based on System V, you should check the call to `open` for the terminal and ensure that the flag `O_NOCTTY` is set.

A second use for `TIOCNOTTY` was after a `fork`, when the child might want to relinquish the controlling terminal. This can also be done with `setsid` (see the section called "setsid" in Chapter 12, *Kernel Dependencies*).

TIOCGSID

The call `ioctl (fd, TIOCGSID, pid_t *pid)` stores the terminal's session ID at `pid`. This function is supported by System V.4.

Miscellaneous Functions

TIOCEXCL

The call `ioctl (fd, TIOCEXCL, NULL)` sets exclusive use on the terminal. No further opens are permitted except by *root*.

TIOCNXCL

The call `ioctl (fd, TIOCNXCL, NULL)` clears exclusive use of the terminal (see `TIOCEXCL`). Further opens are permitted.

TIOCCONS

The call `ioctl (fd, TIOCCONS, int *on)` sets the console file. If `on` points to a nonzero integer, kernel console output is redirected to the terminal specified in the call. If `on` points to zero, kernel console output is redirected to the standard console. This is usually used on workstations to redirect kernel messages to a particular window.

TIOCGSOFTCAR

The call `ioctl (fd, TIOCGSOFTCAR, int *set)` sets `*set` to 1 if the terminal data carrier detect (DCD) signal or the software carrier flag is asserted and to 0 otherwise. This function is supported only in SunOS 4.x, and is no longer present in Solaris 2. See the section called "Terminology" for a description of the DSR line.

TIOCSSOFTCAR

The call `ioctl (fd, TIOCSSOFTCAR, int *set)` is a method to fake a modem carrier detect signal. It resets software carrier mode if `*set` is zero and sets it otherwise. In software carrier mode, the `TIOCGSOFTCAR` call always returns 1; otherwise it returns the real value of the DCD interface signal. This function is supported only in SunOS 4.x, and is no longer present in Solaris 2.

termios Functions

It should come as no surprise that people have long wanted a less bewildering interface to terminals than the `ioctl` calls that we looked at in the previous section. In POSIX.1, a number of new functions were introduced with the intent of bringing some sort of order into the chaos. A total of eight new functions were introduced, split into three groups. In addition, another six auxiliary functions were added:

- `tcgetattr` and `tcsetattr` get and set terminal attributes using `struct termios`.
- `tcgetpgrp` and `tcsetpgrp` get and set the program group ID.
- `tcdrain`, `tcflow`, `tcflush`, and `tcsendbreak` manipulate the terminal hardware.
- `cfgetispeed`, `cfsetispeed`, `cfgetospeed`, `cfsetospeed`, `cfsetspeed`, and `cfmakeraw` are auxiliary functions to manipulate *termios* entries.

These functions do not add new functionality but attempt to provide a more uniform interface. In some systems, they are system calls, whereas in others, they are library functions that build on the `ioctl` interface. If you are porting a package that uses *termios* and your system doesn't supply it, you have the choice of rewriting the code to use `ioctl` calls, or you can use the 4.4BSD library calls supplied in the 4.4BSD Lite distribution (*usr/src/lib/libc/gen/termios.c*). In the following sections, we'll look briefly at each function.

Direct termios Functions

tcgetattr

`tcgetattr` corresponds to `TIOCGETA` described in the section called "TIOCGETA". It returns the current *termios* state to `term`.

```
#include <termios.h>
int tcgetattr (int fd, struct termios *term)
```

tcsetattr

`tcgetattr` sets the current *termios* state from `term`.

```
#include <termios.h>
int tcsetattr (int fd, int action, struct termios *t)
```

`action` can have one of the values listed in Table 15-16.

Table 15-16: tcsetattr Action Flags

Parameter	Meaning
TCSANOW	Change terminal parameters immediately. Corresponds to the `ioctl` request TIOCSETA.
TCSADRAIN	First drain output, then change the parameters. Used when changing parameters that affect output. Corresponds to the `ioctl` call TIOCSETAW.
TCSAFLUSH	Discard any pending input drain output, then change the parameters. Corresponds to the `ioctl` call TIOCSETAF.

See the section called "TIOCSETA" for details of the corresponding `ioctl` interfaces.

In addition, some implementations define the parameter `TCSASOFT`: if this is specified in addition to one of the flags listed in Table 15-16, the values of the fields `c_cflag`, `c_ispeed`, and `c_ospeed` are ignored. This is typically used when the device in question is not a serial line terminal.

tcgetpgrp

`tcgetpgrp` returns the ID of the current process group with which the terminal is associated. It corresponds to the `ioctl` call `TIOCGPGRP` described in the section called "TIOCGPGRP".

```
#include <sys/types.h>
#include <unistd.h>
pid_t tcgetpgrp (int fd);
```

tcsetpgrp

`tcsetpgrp` associates the terminal with the process group `tpgrp`. It corresponds to the `ioctl` call `TIOCSPGRP` described in the section called "TIOCSPGRP".

```
#include <sys/types.h>
#include <unistd.h>
int tcsetpgrp (int fd, pid_t pgrp_id);
```

tcdrain

`tcdrain` suspends the process until all output is drained. It corresponds to the `ioctl` call `TIOCDRAIN` described in the section called "TIOCDRAIN".

```
#include <termios.h>
int tcdrain (int fd);
```

tcflow

`tcflow` specifies flow control. It corresponds to the `ioctl` call `TCXONC`. See the description of `TCXONC` in the section called "TCXONC" for the meaning of the parameter `action`.

```
#include <termios.h>
int tcflow (int fd, int action);
```

tcflush

`tcflush` flushes input or output queues for `fd`.

```
#include <termios.h>
int tcflush (int fd, int action);
```

`action` may take the values shown in Table 15-17.

Table 15-17: tcflush Action Bits

Parameter	Meaning
TCIFLUSH	Flush data received but not read.
TCOFLUSH	Flush data written but not transmitted.
TCIOFLUSH	Flush both data received but not read and data written but not transmitted.

This function corresponds to the `ioctl` request `TCFLSH` described in the section called "TCFLSH".

tcsendbreak

`tcsendbreak` sends a break indication on the line. This is equivalent to the `ioctl` request `TCSBRK` described in the section called "TCSBRK".

```
#include <termios.h>
int tcsendbreak (int fd, int len);
```

termios Auxiliary Functions

In addition to the *termios* functions in the previous section, a number of library functions manipulate `termios struct` entries. With one exception, they handle line speeds. They don't have any direct effect on the line—you need a `tcsetattr` for that—but they provide a link between the viewpoint of the application and the underlying implementation.

There is still no agreement on how to represent line speeds. BSD systems use the bit rate as an integer and store it in the fields `c_ispeed` and `c_ospeed`. They leave it to the driver to explain it to the hardware, so you can effectively specify any speed the hardware is capable of handling. By contrast, System V still uses the small numeric indices that were used in the Seventh Edition* (see the section called "Old Terminal Driver Definitions"), which allow the field to be stored in 4 bits. They are located in the field `c_cflag`. This is *not* a good idea because these speeds are the only ones System V knows about. If you have a V.32bis or V.42bis modem that claims to be able to transfer data at up to 57,600 bps, you won't be

* These constants were originally the values that were written to the interface hardware to set the speed.

able to take full advantage of its capabilities with System V. In addition, only one speed constant sets both the input and output speeds. The functions for setting input and output speed are effectively the same.

In addition to these problems, SCO UNIX System V.3 further complicates the issue by providing the fields `s_ospeed` and `s_ispeed` in the `struct termios`. The functions `cfsetispeed` and `cfsetospeed` set these fields in addition to the four bits in `c_cflag`, but the functions `cfgetispeed` and `cfgetospeed` retrieve the values from `c_cflags`, so it's not clear what use the fields `c_ispeed` and `c_ospeed` are intended to be.

Setting the bit rates is thus not quite as simple as it might appear. The preprocessor variables `B9600` and friends might not equate to the kind of constant that the *termios* implementation needs, and no place is designated in the *termios* structure to store the bit rates.

This problem is solved by the following functions, which are normally macros:

`speed_t cfgetispeed (struct termios *t)`
: Returns `t`'s input speed in `speed_t` format. It is undefined if the speed is not representable as `speed_t`.

`int cfsetispeed (struct termios *t, speed_t speed)`
: Sets `t`'s input speed to the internal representation of `speed`.

`speed_t cfgetospeed (struct termios *t)`
: Returns `t`'s output speed in `speed_t` format. The result is undefined if the speed is not representable as `speed_t`.

`int cfsetospeed (struct termios *t, speed_t speed)`
: Sets `t`'s output speed to the internal representation of `speed`.

`void cfsetspeed (struct termios *t, speed_t speed)`
: Sets both input and output speed to the internal representation of `speed`.

`void cfmakeraw (struct termios *t)`
: Sets the whole structure `t` to default values.

In This Chapter:
- *Problems with UNIX Time Functions*
- *Getting the Current Time*
- *Setting the Current Time*
- *Converting Time Values*
- *Suspending Process Execution*

16

Timekeeping

UNIX timekeeping is an untidy area, made more confusing by national and international laws and customs. Broadly, there are two kinds of timekeeping functions: one group is concerned with getting and setting system times, and the other group is concerned with converting time representations between a bewildering number of formats.

Before we start, we'll define some terms:

Time zone
: A definition of the time at a particular location relative to the time at other locations. Most time zones are bound to political borders and vary from one another in steps of one hour, although a number of time zones are offset from adjacent time zones by 30 minutes. Time zones tend to have three-letter abbreviations (TLAs) such as *PST* (*Pacific standard time*), *EDT* (*Eastern daylight time*), *BST* (*British summer time*), *AET* (*Australian eastern time*), and *MEZ* (*Mitteleuropäische Zeit*). As these examples show, you should not rely on the letter combination *ST* to represent *Standard Time.*

UTC
: The international base time zone and has the distinction of being one of those abbreviations that nobody can expand. It means *universal coordinated time,* despite the order of the letters. It obviously doesn't stand for the French *temps universel coordonné.* It corresponds very closely, but not exactly, to Greenwich mean time (GMT), the local time in England in the winter, and is the basis of all UNIX timestamps. The result is that for most of us, UTC is *not* the current local time, though it might be close enough to be confusing or far enough off to be annoying.

Epoch
From the standpoint of UNIX, you can consider the *Epoch* to be the beginning of recorded history: it's 00:00:00 UTC, 1 January 1970. All system internal dates are relative to the Epoch.

Daylight saving time
A method of making the days appear longer in summer by setting the clocks forward, usually by one hour. Thus, in summer, the sun appears to set one hour later than would otherwise be the case.

Problems with UNIX Time Functions

Even after clarifying these definitions, timekeeping remains a pain. We'll look at the main problems in the following sections:

Difficulty of Using

The time functions are not easy to use: to get them to do anything useful requires a lot of work. You'd think that UNIX would supply a primitive call upon which you could easily build, but unfortunately no such call is available. The ones that are available do not operate in an intuitively obvious way. For example, no standard function is available for returning the current time in a useful format.

Differing Implementations

No single system call is supported across all platforms. Functions are implemented as system calls in some systems and as library functions in others. As a result, it doesn't make sense to maintain our distinction between system calls and library functions when it comes to timekeeping. In our discussion of the individual functions, we'll note which systems implement them as system calls and which as library calls.

Differing Time Formats

There are at least four different time formats:

- The `time_t` format represents the number of seconds since the Epoch. This format is not subject to time zones or daylight saving time, but it is accurate only to one second, which is not accurate enough for many applications.
- The `struct timeval` format is something like an extended `time_t` with a resolution of 1 microsecond:

```
#include <sys/time.h>

struct timeval
```

```
{
long    tv_sec;                         /* seconds since Jan. 1, 1970 */
long    tv_usec;                        /* and microseconds */
};
```

It is used for a number of newer functions, such as `gettimeofday` and `setitimer`.

- Many library routines represent the calendar time as a struct `tm`. It is usually defined in */usr/include/time.h*:

```
struct tm
  {
  int   tm_sec;                     /* seconds after the minute [0-60] */
  int   tm_min;                     /* minutes after the hour [0-59] */
  int   tm_hour;                    /* hours since midnight [0-23] */
  int   tm_mday;                    /* day of the month [1-31] */
  int   tm_mon;                     /* months since January [0-11] */
  int   tm_year;                    /* years since 1900 */
  int   tm_wday;                    /* days since Sunday [0-6] */
  int   tm_yday;                    /* days since January 1 [0-365] */
  int   tm_isdst;                   /* Daylight Savings Time flag */
  long  tm_gmtoff;                  /* offset from UTC in seconds */
  char  *tm_zone;                   /* timezone abbreviation */
  };
```

Unlike `time_t`, a `struct tm` does not uniquely define the time: it may be a UTC time or it may be local time, depending on the time zone information for the system.

- Dates as a text string are frequently represented in a strange manner, for example `Sat Sep 17 14:28:03 1994\n`. This format includes a `\n` character, which is seldom needed—often you have to chop it off.

Daylight Saving Time

The support for daylight saving time was rudimentary in the Seventh Edition, and the solutions that have arisen since then are not completely compatible. In particular, System V handles daylight saving time via environment variables, so one user's view of time could be different from the next. Recent versions of BSD handle daylight saving time via a database that keeps track of local regulations.

National Time Formats

Printable representations of dates and times are very much a matter of local customs. For example, the date *9/4/94* (in the U.S.) would be written as *4/9/94* in Great Britain and *04.09.94* in Germany. The time written as *4:23 p.m.* in the U.S. would be written *16.23* in France. The situation gets even worse if you want to use the names of the days and months. As a result, many timekeeping functions refer to the *locale* ANSI C. The locale describes country-specific information. Since it does not vary from one system to the next, we won't look at it in more detail—see the *POSIX Programmer's Guide*, by Donald Lewine, for more information.

Global Timekeeping Variables

A number of global variables define various aspects of timekeeping:

`timezone`
: Used in System V and XENIX to specify the number of minutes that the standard time zone is west of Greenwich. It is set from the environment variable `TZ`, which has a rather bizarre syntax. For example, in Germany daylight saving time starts on the last Sunday of March and ends on the last Sunday of September (not in October, as in some other countries, including the U.S.). To tell the system about this, you would use the following `TZ` string:

```
MEZ-1MSZ-2;M3.5,M9.5
```

This states that the standard time zone is called *MEZ* and that it is one hour ahead of UTC, that the summer time zone is called *MSZ* and that it is two hours ahead of UTC. Summer time begins on the (implied Sunday of the) fifth week in March and ends in the fifth week of September.

The punctuation varies. This example comes from System V.3, which requires a semicolon in the indicated position. Other systems allow a comma there, which works until you try to move the information to System V.3.

`altzone`
: Used in SVR4 and XENIX to specify the number of minutes that the daylight saving time zone is west of Greenwich.

`daylight`
: Used in SVR4 and XENIX to indicate that daylight saving time is currently in effect.

`tzname`
: Used in BSD, SVR4, and XENIX as a pointer to two strings; it specifies the name of the standard time zone and the daylight saving time zone, respectively.

In the sections that follow we'll look at how to get the current time, how to set the current time, how to convert time values, and how to suspend process execution for a period of time.

Getting the Current Time

The system supplies the current time via the system calls `time` or `gettimeofday`—only one of these is a system call, but the system determines which one it is.

time

```
#include <sys/types.h>
#include <time.h>

time_t time (time_t *tloc);
```

`time` returns the current time in `time_t` form, both as a return value and at `tloc` if this is not `NULL`. `time` is implemented as a system call in System V and as a library function (which calls `gettimeofday`) in BSD. Since it returns a scalar value, a call to `time` can be used as a parameter to functions like `localtime` or `ctime`.

ftime

`ftime` is a variant of `time` that returns time information with a resolution of one millisecond. It originally came from 4.2BSD but is now considered obsolete.

```
#include <sys/types.h>
#include <sys/timeb.h>

typedef long time_t;                      /* (typically) */

struct timeb
  {
  time_t   time;                          /* the same time returned by time */
  unsigned short millitm;                 /* Milliseconds */
  short    timezone;                      /* System default time zone */
  short    dstflag;                       /* set during daylight savings time */
  };

struct timeb *ftime (struct timeb *tp);
```

The time zone returned is the system default, possibly not what you want. System V.4 deprecates* the use of this variable as a result. Depending on which

* The term *deprecate* comes from *deprecatus*, a religious term meaning "to seek to avert by prayer." Nowadays, used to indicate functionality that the implementors or maintainers wish would go away. This term seems to have come from Berkeley. To quote the *New Hackers Dictionary*:

> **deprecated**: adj. Said of a program or feature that is considered obsolescent and in the process of being phased out, usually in favor of a specified replacement. Deprecated features can, unfortunately, linger on for many years. This term appears with distressing frequency in standards documents when the committees writing

parameters are actually used, a number of alternatives to `ftime` exist. In many cases, `time` supplies all you need. However, `time` is accurate only to one second.

On some systems, you may be able to define `ftime` in terms of `gettimeofday`, which returns the time of the day with a 1- microsecond resolution—see the next section. On other systems, unfortunately, the system clock does not have a finer resolution than one second, and you are stuck with `time`.

gettimeofday

```
#include <sys/time.h>

struct timeval
  {
  long    tv_sec;                      /* seconds since Jan. 1, 1970 */
  long    tv_usec;                     /* and microseconds */
  };

int gettimeofday (struct timeval *tp,
                  struct timezone *tzp); /* (BSD) */
int gettimeofday (struct timeval *tp);  /* (System V.4) */
```

`gettimeofday` returns the current system time, with a resolution of 1 microsecond, to `tp`. The name is misleading, since the `struct timeval` representation does not relate to the time of day. Many implementations ignore `tzp`, but others, such as SunOS 4, return time zone information there.

In BSD, `gettimeofday` is a system call. In some versions of System V.4, it is emulated as a library function defined in terms of `time`, which limits its resolution to 1 second. Other versions of System V appear to have implemented it as a system call, though this is not documented.

Setting the Current Time

Setting the system time is similar to getting it, except that for security reasons only the superuser (*root*) is allowed to perform the function. It is normally executed by the *date* program.

adjtime

```
#include <sys/time.h>

int adjtime (struct timeval *delta, struct timeval *olddelta);
```

---

the documents realize that large amounts of extant (and presumably happily working) code depend on the feature(s) that have passed out of favor. See also {dusty deck}.

`adjtime` makes small adjustments to the system time and is intended to help synchronize time in a network. The adjustment is made gradually—the system slows down or speeds up the passage of time by a fraction of a percent until it has made the correction, in order not to confuse programs like *cron*, which are watching the time. As a result, if you call `adjtime` again, the previous adjustment still might not be complete; in this case, the remaining adjustment is returned in `olddelta`. `adjtime` was introduced in 4.3BSD and is also supported by System V. It is implemented as a system call in all systems.

settimeofday

```
#include <sys/time.h>

int gettimeofday (struct timeval *tp, struct timezone *tzp);
int settimeofday (struct timeval *tp, struct timezone *tzp);
```

`settimeofday` is a BSD system call that is emulated as a library function in System V.4. It sets the current system time to the value of `tp`. The value of `tzp` is no longer used. In System V, this call is implemented in terms of the `stime` system call, which sets the time only to the nearest second. If you really need to set the time more accurately in System V.4, you can use `adjtime`.

stime

```
#include <unistd.h>

int stime (const time_t *tp);
```

`stime` sets the system time and date. This is the original Seventh Edition function that is still available in System V. It is *not* supported in BSD. Use `settimeofday` on BSD systems.

Converting Time Values

As advertised, a large number of time conversion functions are available, and they are made all the more complicated because many are supported only on specific platforms. All are library functions. Many return pointers to static data areas that are overwritten by the next call. Solaris attempts to solve this problem with versions of the functions with the characters `_r` (for *reentrant*) appended to their names. These functions use a user-supplied buffer to store the data they return.

strftime

```
#include <sys/types.h>
#include <time.h>
#include <string.h>

size_t strftime (char *s, size_t maxsize, char *format, struct tm *tm);
```

strftime converts the time at tm into a formatted string at s. format specifies the format of the resultant string, which can be no longer than maxsize characters. format is similar to the format strings used by printf but contains strings related to dates. strftime has a rather strange return value: if the complete date string, including the terminating NULL character, fits into the space provided, it returns the length of the string—otherwise it returns 0, which implies that the date string has been truncated.

strftime is available on all platforms and is implemented as a library function. System V.4 considers ascftime and cftime to be obsolete. The man pages state that strftime should be used instead.

strptime

```
#include <time.h>

char *strptime (char *buf, char *fmt, struct tm *tm);
```

strptime is a library function supplied with SunOS 4. It converts the date and time string buf into a struct tm value at tm. This call bears the same relationship to scanf that strftime bears to printf.

ascftime

```
#include <sys/types.h>
#include <time.h>

int ascftime (char *buf, char *fmt, tm *tm);
```

ascftime converts the time at tm into a formatted string at buf. format specifies the format of the resultant string. This is effectively the same function as strftime, except that no provision is made to supply the maximum length of buf. ascftime is available on all platforms and is implemented as a library function.

asctime and asctime_r

```
#include <sys/types.h>
#include <time.h>

char *asctime (const struct tm *tm);
char *asctime_r (const struct tm *tm, char *buf, int buflen);
```

asctime converts a time in struct tm format into the same kind of string that is returned by ctime. asctime is available on all platforms and is always a library function.

asctime_r is a version of asctime that returns the string to the user-provided buffer res, which must be at least buflen characters long. It returns the address of res. It is supplied as a library function on Solaris systems.

cftime

```
#include <sys/types.h>
#include <time.h>

int cftime (char *buf, char *fmt, time_t *clock);
```

cftime converts the time at clock into a formatted string at buf. format specifies the format of the resultant string. This is effectively the same function as strftime, except that no provision is made to supply the maximum length of buf, and the time is supplied in time_t format. cftime is available on all platforms and is implemented as a library function.

ctime and ctime_r

```
#include <sys/types.h>
#include <time.h>
extern char *tzname[2];

char *ctime (const time_t *clock);
char *ctime_r (const time_t *clock, char *buf, int buflen);
```

ctime converts the time clock into a string in the form Sat Sep 17 14:28:03 1994\n, which has the advantage of consistency: it is not a normal representation anywhere in the world and immediately brands any printed output with the word *UNIX*. It uses the environment variable TZ to determine the current time zone. You can rely on the string to be exactly 26 characters long, including the final \0 and to contain that irritating \n at the end. ctime is available on all platforms and is always a library function.

ctime_r is a version of ctime that returns its result in the buffer pointed to by buf. The length is limited to buflen bytes. ctime_r is available on Solaris platforms as a library function.

dysize

```
#include <time.h>

int dysize (int year);
```

dysize returns the number of days in year. It is supplied as a library function in SunOS 4.

gmtime and gmtime_r

```
#include <time.h>

struct tm *gmtime (const time_t *clock);
struct tm *gmtime_r (const time_t *clock, struct tm *res);
```

gmtime converts a time in time_t format into struct tm format, like localtime. As the name suggests, however, it does not account for local time zones—it returns a UTC time (this was formerly called Greenwich mean time, thus the name of the function). gmtime is available on all platforms and is always a library function.

gmtime_r is a version of gmtime that returns the string to the user-provided buffer res. It returns the address of res. It is supplied as a library function on Solaris systems.

localtime and localtime_r

```
#include <time.h>

struct tm *localtime (const time_t *clock);
struct tm *localtime_r (const time_t *clock, struct tm *res);
```

localtime converts a time in time_t format into struct tm format. Like ctime, it uses the time zone information in tzname to convert to local time. localtime is available on all platforms and is always a library function.

localtime_r is a version of localtime that returns the string to the user-provided buffer res. It returns the address of res. It is supplied as a library function on Solaris systems.

mktime

```
#include <sys/types.h>
#include <time.h>
time_t mktime (struct tm *tm);
```

mktime converts a local time in struct tm format into a time in time_t format. It does not use tzname in the conversion—it uses the information at tm->tm_zone instead. The argument passed is both input and output. In addition to converting the time, mktime also sets the members wday (day of week) and yday (day of year) of the struct tm to agree with day, month, and year. tm->tm_isdst determines whether daylight saving time is applicable:

- If it is > 0, `mktime` assumes daylight saving time is in effect.
- If it is 0, it assumes that no daylight saving time is in effect.
- If it is < 0, `mktime` tries to determine whether daylight saving time is in effect and is often wrong.

`mktime` is available on all platforms and is always a library function.

timegm

```
#include <time.h>

time_t timegm (struct tm *tm);
```

`timegm` converts a `struct tm` time, assumed to be UTC, to the corresponding `time_t` value. This is effectively the same as `mktime` with the time zone set to UTC and is the converse of `gmtime`. `timegm` is a library function supplied with SunOS 4.

timelocal

```
#include <time.h>

time_t timelocal (struct tm *tm);
```

`timelocal` converts a `struct tm` time, assumed to be local time, to the corresponding `time_t` value. This is similar to `mktime`, but it uses the local time zone information instead of the information in `tm`. It is also the converse of `localtime`. `timelocal` is a library function supplied with SunOS 4.

difftime

```
#include <sys/types.h>
#include <time.h>

double difftime (time_t time1, time_t time0);
```

`difftime` returns the difference in seconds between two `time_t` values. This is effectively the same as `(int) time1 - (int) time0`. `difftime` is a library function available on all platforms.

timezone

```
#include <time.h>

char *timezone (int zone, int dst);
```

`timezone` returns the name of the time zone that is `zone` minutes west of Greenwich. If `dst` is nonzero, the name of the daylight saving time zone is returned instead. This call is obsolete—it was used at a time when time zone information was stored as the number of minutes a place was located west of Greenwich. Nowadays, since the information is stored with a time zone name, there should be no need for this function.

tzset

```
#include <time.h>

void tzset ();
```

tzset sets the value of the internal variables used by localtime to the values specified in the environment variable TZ. It is called by asctime. In System V, it sets the value of the global variable daylight. tzset is a library function supplied with BSD and System V.4.

tzsetwall

```
#include <time.h>

void tzsetwall ();
```

tzsetwall sets the value of the internal variables used by localtime to the default values for the site. tzsetwall is a library function supplied with BSD and System V.4.

Suspending Process Execution

Occasionally, you may want to suspend process execution for a short period of time. For example, the *tail* program with the *–f* option waits until a file has grown longer, so it needs to relinquish the processor for a second or two between checks on the file status.

Typically, sleep is used to suspend execution. However, some applications need to specify the length of time more accurately than sleep allows, so a couple of alternatives have arisen: nap suspends execution for a number of milliseconds, and usleep suspends it for a number of microseconds.

nap

nap is a XENIX variant of sleep with finer resolution:

```
#include <time.h>

long nap (long millisecs);
```

nap suspends process execution for at least millisecs milliseconds. In practice, the XENIX clock counts in intervals of 20 ms, so this is the maximum accuracy with which you can specify `millisecs`. You can simulate this function with `usleep` (see the section called "usleep" for more details).

setitimer

BSD systems and derivatives maintain three (possibly four) interval timers:

- A *real time* timer, `ITIMER_REAL`, which keeps track of real elapsed time.
- A *virtual* timer, `ITIMER_VIRTUAL`, which keeps track of process execution time—in other words, the amount of CPU time that the process has used.
- A *profiler* timer, `ITIMER_PROF`, which keeps track of both process execution time and time spent in the kernel on behalf of the process. As the name suggests, it is used to implement profiling tools.
- A *real time profiler* timer, `ITIMER_REALPROF`, used for profiling Solaris 2.X multithreaded processes.

These timers are manipulated with the system calls `getitimer` and `setitimer`:

```
#include <sys/time.h>

struct timeval
  {
  long  tv_sec;                         /* seconds */
  long  tv_usec;                        /* and microseconds */
  };

struct itimerval
  {
  struct  timeval it_interval;          /* timer interval */
  struct  timeval it_value;             /* current value */
  };

int getitimer (int which, struct itimerval *value);
int setitimer (int which, struct itimerval *value, struct itimerval *ovalue);
```

`setitimer` sets the value of a specific timer `which` to `value` and optionally returns the previous value in `ovalue` if this is not a `NULL` pointer. `getitimer` just returns the current value of the timer to `value`. The resolution is specified to an accuracy of 1 microsecond, but it is really limited to the accuracy of the system clock, which is more typically in the order of 10 milliseconds. In addition, as with all timing functions, there is no guarantee that the process can run immediately when the timer expires.

In the struct `itimerval`, `it_value` is the current value of the timer, which is decremented depending on the type of timer (real, virtual, or whatever) as previously described. When it_value is decremented to 0, a signal is generated, and it_value is reloaded from it_interval. If the result is 0, no further action occurs; otherwise, the system continues decrementing the counter. In this way, one call to setitimer can cause the system to generate continuous signals at a specified interval.

The signal that is generated depends on the timer. Table 16-1 provides an overview.

Table 16-1: setitimer Signals

Timer	Signal
Real time	SIGALRM
Virtual	SIGVTALRM
Profiler	SIGPROF
Real-time profiler[a]	SIGPROF

[a] Only Solaris 2.x

The only timer you're likely to see is the real time timer. If you don't have it, you can fake it with alarm. In System V.4, setitimer is implemented as a library function that calls an undocumented system call. See *The Magic Garden Explained: The Internals of UNIX System V Release 4* for more details.

setitimer is used to implement the library routine usleep, described in a section later in this chapter.

sleep

```
#include <unistd.h>

unsigned sleep (u_int seconds);
```

The library routine sleep suspends program execution for approximately seconds seconds. It is available on all UNIX platforms.

usleep

usleep is a variant of sleep that suspends program execution for a very short time:

```
#include <unistd.h>
void usleep (u_int microseconds);
```

usleep sleeps for at least microseconds microseconds. It is supplied on BSD and System V.4 systems as a library function that uses the setitimer system call.

select and poll

If your system doesn't supply any timing function with a resolution of less than one second, you might be able to fake it with the functions `select` or `poll`. `select` can wait for nothing if you ask it to, and since the timeout is specified as a `struct timeval` (see the section called "Differing Time Formats" earlier in this chapter), you can specify times down to microsecond accuracy. You can use `poll` in the same way, except that you specify its timeout value in milliseconds.

For example,

```
void usleep (int microseconds)
  {
  struct timeval timeout;
  timeout.tv_usec = microseconds % 1000000;
  timeout.tv_sec = microseconds / 1000000;
  select (0, NULL, NULL, NULL, &timeout);
  }
```

or

```
void usleep (int microseconds)
  {
  poll (0, NULL, microseconds / 1000);
  }
```

In This Chapter:
- *ANSI C, POSIX.1, and Header Files*
- *Names and Locations*
- *Problems with Header Files*

17

Header Files

When the C language was young, header files were required to define structures and occasionally to specify that a function did something out of the ordinary, such as taking a `double` parameter or returning a `float` result. Then ANSI C and POSIX came along and changed all that.

Header files seem a relatively simple idea, but in fact they can be a major source of annoyance in porting. In particular:

- ANSI and POSIX.1 have added a certain structure to the usage of header files, but many old-fashioned headers are still in use.
- ANSI and POSIX.1 have also placed more stringent requirements on data types used in header files. This can cause conflicts with older systems, especially if the author has commited the sin of trying to out-guess the header files.
- C++ has special requirements for header files. If your header files don't fulfill these requirements, the GNU *protoize* program can usually fix them.
- There is still no complete agreement on the names of header files or in which directories they should be placed. In particular, System V.3 and System V.4 frequently disagree as to whether a header file should be in */usr/include* or in */usr/include/sys*.

ANSI C, POSIX.1, and Header Files

ANSI C and POSIX.1 have had a far-reaching effect on the structure of system header files. We'll look at the changes in the C language in more detail in Chapter 20, *Compilers*. The following points are relevant to the use of header files:

- ANSI C prefers to have an ANSI-style prototype for every function call it encounters. If it doesn't find one, it can't check the function call semantics as thoroughly, and it may issue a warning. It's a good idea to enable all such warnings, but this kind of message makes it difficult to recognize the real errors hiding behind the warnings. In C++, the rules are even stricter: not having a prototype is an error, and your source file doesn't compile.
- To do a complete job of error checking, ANSI C requires the prototype in the new, embedded form:

  ```
  int foo (char *zot, int glarp);
  ```

  Not:

  ```
  int foo (zot, glarp);
  char *zot;
  int glarp;
  ```

  Old C compilers don't understand this new kind of prototype.
- Header files usually contain many definitions that are not part of POSIX.1. A mechanism is needed to disable these definitions if you are compiling a program intended to be POSIX.1 compatible.*

The result of these requirements is spaghetti header files: you frequently see code like this excerpt from the header file *stdio.h* in 4.4BSD:

```
/*
 * Functions defined in ANSI C standard.
 */
__BEGIN_DECLS
void     clearerr __P((FILE *));
int      fclose __P((FILE *));

#if !defined(_ANSI_SOURCE) && !defined(_POSIX_SOURCE)
extern int sys_nerr;            /* perror(3) external variables */
extern __const char *__const sys_errlist[];
#endif
void     perror __P((const char *));

__END_DECLS

/*
 * Functions defined in POSIX 1003.1.
 */
#ifndef _ANSI_SOURCE
#define L_cuserid       9       /* size for cuserid(); UT_NAMESIZE + 1 */
```

* Writing your programs to conform to POSIX.1 may be a good idea if you want them to run on as many platforms as possible. On the other hand, it may be a bad idea: POSIX.1 has very rudimentary facilities in some areas. You may find it confines your program more than you want.

```
#define L_ctermid       1024  /* size for ctermid(); PATH_MAX */

__BEGIN_DECLS
char    *ctermid __P((char *));

__END_DECLS
#endif /* not ANSI */

/*
 * Routines that are purely local.
 */
#if !defined (_ANSI_SOURCE) && !defined(_POSIX_SOURCE)
__BEGIN_DECLS
char    *fgetln __P((FILE *, size_t *));

__END_DECLS
```

Well, it *does* look vaguely like C, but this kind of header file scares off most people. A number of conflicts have led to this kind of code:

- The ANSI C library and POSIX.1 carefully define a subset of the total available functionality. If you want to abide strictly to the standards, any extension must be flagged as an error, even if it would work.
- The C++ language has a different syntax from C, but both languages share a common set of header files.

These solutions have caused new problems, which we'll examine in this chapter.

ANSI and POSIX.1 Restrictions

Most current UNIX implementations do not conform completely with POSIX.1 and ANSI C, and every implementation offers a number of features that are not part of either standard. A program that conforms with the standards must not use these features. You can specify that you wish your program to be compliant with the standards by defining the preprocessor variables `_ANSI_SOURCE` or `_POSIX_SOURCE`, which maximizes the portability of the code, by preventing the inclusion of certain definitions. In our example, the array `sys_errlist` (see the section called "strerror and sys_errlist" in Chapter 18, *Function Libraries*) is not part of POSIX.1 or ANSI, so the definition is not included if either preprocessor variable is set. If we refer to `sys_errlist` anyway, the compiler signifies an error, since the array hasn't been declared. Similarly, `L_cuserid` is defined in POSIX.1 but not in ANSI C, so it is defined only when `_POSIX_SOURCE` is defined and `_ANSI_SOURCE` is not defined.

Declarations for C++

C++ has additional requirements for symbol naming: *function overloading* allows different functions to have the same name. Assemblers don't think this is funny at all, and neither do linkers, so the names need to be changed to be unique. In addition, the names need to somehow reflect the class to which they belong, the kind of parameters that the function takes, and the kind of value it returns. This is done by a technique called *function name encoding*, or more commonly, *function name mangling*. The parameter and return value type information is appended to the function name according to a predetermined rule. To illustrate, let's look at a simple function declaration:

```
double Internal::sense (int a, unsigned char *text, Internal &p, ...);
```

- First, two underscores are appended to the name of the function. With the initial underscore we get for the assembler, the function name is now `_sense__`.
- Then the class name, `Internal` is added. The length of the name, which must be specified, is added first: `_sense__8Internal`.
- Next, the parameters are encoded. Simple types like `int` and `char` are abbreviated to a single character (in this case, `i` and `c`). If they have modifiers like `unsigned`, these, too, are encoded and precede the type information. In this case, we get just plain `i` for the `int` parameter, and `PUc` (a pointer to unsigned characters for the second parameter: `_sense__8InternaliPUc`.
- Class or structure references can't be coded ahead of time, so again the length of the name and the name itself is used. In this case, since we have a reference, the letter *R* is placed in front of the name: `_sense__8InternaliPUcR8Internal`.
- Finally, the ellipses are specified with the letter *e*: `_sense__8InternaliPUcR8Internale`.

For more details on function name mangling, see *The Annotated C++ Reference Manual*, by Margaret Ellis and Bjarne Stroustrup.

This difference in naming is a problem when a C++ program really needs to call a function written in C. Since the name in the object file is not mangled, the C++ compiler must not output a reference to a mangled name. Theoretically, the compiler also needs to take into account other differences between C++ calls and C calls. Since you can't just assume that a function written in another language adheres to the same conventions, you have to indicate that a called function is written according to C conventions rather than according to C++ conventions.

This is done with the following elegant construct:

```
extern "C"
  {
  char  *ctermid (char *);
  };
```

In ANSI C, the same declaration would be:

```
  char  *ctermid (char *);
```

In K&R C it would be:

```
  char  *ctermid ();
```

It would be a pain to have a separate set of header files for each version. Instead, the implementors defined preprocessor variables that evaluate to language constructs for certain places:

- `__BEGIN_DECLS` is defined as `extern "C" {` for C++ and nothing otherwise.
- `__END_DECLS` is defined as `};` for C++ and nothing otherwise.
- `__P(foo)` is defined as `foo` for C++ and ANSI C, and nothing otherwise. This is the reason why the arguments to `__P()` are enclosed in double parentheses: the outside level of parentheses gets stripped by the preprocessor.

In this implementation, *sys/cdefs.h* defines these preprocessor variables. What happens if *sys/cdefs.h* isn't included before *stdio.h*? Lots of error messages. So one of the first lines in *stdio.h* is `include <sys/cdefs.h>`. This is not the only place that *sys/cdefs.h* is included. In this particular implementation from 4.4BSD, it is included from *assert.h*, *db.h*, *dirent.h*, *err.h*, *fnmatch.h*, *fstab.h*, *fts.h*, *glob.h*, *grp.h*, *kvm.h*, *locale.h*, *math.h*, *netdb.h*, *nlist.h*, *pwd.h*, *regex.h*, *regexp.h*, *resolv.h*, *runetype.h*, *setjmp.h*, *signal.h*, *stdio.h*, *stdlib.h*, *string.h*, *time.h*, *ttyent.h*, *unistd.h*, *utime.h*, and *vis.h*. This places an additional load on the compiler, which reads in a 100-line definition file multiple times. It also creates the possibility for compiler errors. *sys/cdefs.h* defines a preprocessor variable `_CDEFS_H_` in order to avoid this problem: after the obligatory UCB copyright notice, it starts with the following:

```
#ifndef _CDEFS_H_
#define _CDEFS_H_

#if defined(__cplusplus)
#define __BEGIN_DECLS   extern "C" {
#define __END_DECLS     };
#else
#define __BEGIN_DECLS
#define __END_DECLS
#endif
```

This common technique was introduced by ANSI C: the preprocessor processes the body of the header file only the first time. After that, the preprocessor variable `_CDEFS_H_` is defined, and the body is not processed again.

Note the following about this method:

- There are no hard and fast rules for the naming and definition of these auxiliary variables. The result is that not all header files use this technique. For example, in FreeBSD 1.1, the header file *machine/limits.h* defines a preprocessor variable `_MACHINE_LIMITS_H` and interprets the body of the file only if this preprocessor variable was not set on entry. BSD/OS 1.1, on the other hand, does not. The same header file is present, and the text is almost identical, but nothing stops you from including and interpreting *machine/limits.h* multiple times. The result can be that a package that compiles just fine under FreeBSD may fail to compile under BSD/OS.
- The ANSI standard defines numerous standard preprocessor variables to ensure that header files are interpreted only the first time they are included. The variables all start with a leading `__`, and the second character is either another `_` or an uppercase letter. It's a good idea to avoid using such symbols in your sources.
- We could save including *sys/cdefs.h* multiple times by checking `_CDEFS_H_` before including it. Unfortunately, this would establish an undesirable relationship between the two files. If for some reason it becomes necessary to change the name of the preprocessor variable or perhaps to give it different semantics (like giving it different values at different times, instead of just defining it), you have to modify all the header files that refer to the preprocessor variable.

ANSI Header Files

The ANSI C language definition, also called *Standard C*, was the first to attempt some kind of standardization of header files. As far as it goes, ANSI C works well, but unfortunately it covers only a comparatively small number of header files. In ANSI C:

- The only header files you should need to include are *assert.h*, *ctype.h*, *errno.h*, *float.h*, *limits.h*, *locale.h*, *math.h*, *setjmp.h*, *signal.h*, *stdarg.h*, *stddef.h*, *stdio.h*, *stdlib.h*, *string.h*, and *time.h*.
- You may include headers in any order.

- You may include any header more than once.
- Header files do not depend on other header files.
- Header files do not include other header files.

If you can get by with just the ANSI header files, you won't have much trouble. Unfortunately, real-life programs usually require headers that aren't covered by the ANSI standard.

Type Information

A large number of system and library calls return information that can be represented in a single machine word. The machine word of the PDP-11, on which the Seventh Edition ran, was only 16 bits wide, and in some cases you had to squeeze the value to get it in the word. For example, the Seventh Edition file system represented an inode number in an `int`, so each file system could have only 65536 inodes. When 32-bit machines were introduced, people quickly took the opportunity to extend the length of these fields, and modern file systems such as ufs or vxfs have 32-bit inode numbers.

These changes were an advantage, but they bore a danger with them: nowadays, you can't be sure how long an inode number is. Current systems really do have different-sized fields for inode numbers, and this presents a portability problem. Inodes aren't the only element that has changed: consider the following structure definition, which contains information returned by system calls:

```
struct process_info
  {
  long pid;                    /* process number */
  long start_time;             /* time process was started, from time () */
  long owner;                  /* user ID of owner */
  long log_file;               /* file number of log file */
  long log_file_pos;           /* current position in log file */
  short file_permissions;      /* default umask */
  short log_file_major;        /* major device number for log file */
  short log_file_minor;        /* minor device number */
  short inode;                 /* inode number of log file */
  }
```

On most modern systems, the `long`s take up 32 bits and the `short`s take up 16 bits. Because of alignment constraints, we put the longest data types at the front and the shortest at the end. (See the section called "Data Alignment" in Chapter 11, *Hardware Dependencies*, for more details.) And for older systems, these fields are perfectly adequate. But what happens if we port a program containing this structure to a 64-bit machine running System V.4 and vxfs? We've already seen that the inode numbers are now 32 bits long, and System V.4 major and minor device numbers also take up more space. If you port this package to 4.4BSD, the field `log_file_pos` needs to be 64 bits long.

Clearly, it's an oversimplification to assume that any particular kind of value maps to a `short` or a `long`. The correct way to do this is to define a type that describes the value. In modern C, the previous structure definition becomes:

```
struct process_info
  {
  pid_t   pid;                /* process number */
  time_t  start_time;         /* time process was started, from time () */
  uid_t   owner;              /* user ID of owner */
  long    log_file;           /* file number of log file */
  pos_t   log_file_pos;       /* current position in log file */
  mode_t  file_permissions;   /* default umask */
  short   log_file_major;     /* major device number for log file */
  short   log_file_minor;     /* minor device number */
  inode_t inode;              /* inode number of log file */
  }
```

It's important to remember that these type definitions are all in the mind of the compiler and that they are defined in a header file, which is usually called *sys/types.h*. The system handles them as integers of appropriate length. If you define them in this manner, you give the compiler an opportunity to catch mistakes and generate more reliable code. Check your man pages for the types of the arguments on your system if you run into trouble. In addition, Appendix A contains an overview of the more common types used in UNIX systems.

Names and Locations

If you look at the directory hierarchy */usr/include*, you may be astounded by the sheer number of header files, over 400 of them on a typical UNIX system. Fortunately, many of them are in subdirectories, and you usually won't have to worry about them, except for one subdirectory: */usr/include/sys*.

In early versions of UNIX, this directory contained the header files used for compiling the kernel. Nowadays, this directory is intended to contain header files that relate to the UNIX implementation, though the usage varies considerably. You will frequently find files that directly include files from */usr/include/sys*. In fact, it may come as a surprise that this is not supposed to be necessary. Often you will also see code like the following:

```
#ifdef USG                       /* System V */
#include <sys/err.h>
#else                            /* non-System V system */
#include <err.h>
#endif
```

This simplified example shows what you need to do because System V keeps the header file *err.h* in */usr/include/sys*, whereas other flavors keep it in */usr/include*. In order to include the file correctly, the source code needs to know what kind of system it is running on. If it guesses wrong (for example, if USG is not defined when it should be) or if the author of the package didn't allow for System V, either out of ignorance or because the package has never been compiled on System V, the compilation fails with a message about missing header files.

Frequently, the decisions made by the kind of code in the last example are incorrect. Some header files in System V have changed between System V.3 and System V.4. If, for example, you port a program written for System V.4 to System V.3, you may find code like:

```
#include <wait.h>
```

This fails in most versions of System V.3, because there is no header file */usr/include/wait.h*; the file is called */usr/include/sys/wait.h*. There are a couple of actions you could take:

- You could start the compiler with a supplementary *–I/usr/include/sys*, which causes it to search */usr/include/sys* for files specified without any pathname component. The problem with this approach is that you need to do it for every package that runs into this problem.
- You could consider doing what System V.4 does in many cases: create a file called */usr/include/wait.h* that contains just an obligatory copyright notice and an #include directive enclosed in #ifdefs:

```
/* THIS IS PUBLISHED NON-PROPRIETARY SOURCE CODE OF O'REILLY  */
/* & ASSOCIATES Inc.                                          */
/* The copyright notice above does not evidence any actual or */
/* intended restriction on the use of this code.              */
#ifndef _WAIT_H
#define _WAIT_H
#include <sys/wait.h>
#endif
```

Problems with Header Files

It's fair to say that no system is supplied with completely correct system header files. Your system header files will probably suffer from at least one of the following problems:

- "Incorrect" naming. The header files contain the definitions you need, but they are not in the place you would expect.

- Incomplete definitions. Function prototypes or definitions of structures and constants are missing.
- Incompatible definitions. The definitions don't match your compiler, which is particularly often the case with C++ on systems that don't have a native C++ compiler. The *gcc* utility program *protoize*, which is run when installing *gcc*, is supposed to take care of these differences, and it may be of use even if you choose not to install *gcc*.
- Incorrect `#ifdefs`. For example, the file may define certain functions only if `_POSIX_SOURCE` is defined, even though `_POSIX_SOURCE` is intended to restrict functionality, not to enable it. The System V.4.2 version *math.h* surrounds `M_PI` (the constant pi) with:

  ```
  #if (__STDC__ && !defined(_POSIX_SOURCE)) || defined(_XOPEN_SOURCE)
  ```

  In other words, if you include *math.h* without defining `__STDC__` (ANSI C) or `_XOPEN_SOURCE` (X Open compliant), `M_PI` is not defined.
- The header files may contain syntax errors that the native compiler does not notice but which cause other compilers to refuse them. For example, some versions of XENIX *curses.h* contain the lines:

  ```
  #ifdef M_TERMCAP
  #  include <tcap.h>      /* Use: cc -DM_TERMCAP ...  -lcurses -ltermlib */
  #else
  # ifdef M_TERMINFO
  #  include <tinfo.h>     /* Use: cc -DM_TERMINFO ...  -ltinfo [-lx] */
  # else
     ERROR -- Either "M_TERMCAP" or "M_TERMINFO" must be #define'd.
  # endif
  #endif
  ```

  This does not cause problems for the XENIX C compiler, but *gcc*, for one, complains about the unterminated character constant starting with `define'd`.
- The header files may be "missing." In the course of time, header files have come and gone, and the definitions have been moved to other places. In particular, the definitions that used to be in *strings.h* have been moved to *string.h* (and changed somewhat on the way), and *termio.h* has become *termios.h*. (See the section called "termio and termios Structures" in Chapter 15, *Terminal Drivers*, for more details.)

The solutions to these problems are many and varied. They usually leave you feeling dissatisfied:

- Fix the system header files. This sounds like heresy, but if you have established beyond any reasonable doubt that the header file is to blame, changing it is about all you can do, assuming that you can convince your system administrator that it is necessary. If you do choose to fix the system header file, be sure to consider whether the change will break some other program that relies on its present behavior. In addition, you should report the bugs to your vendor and remember to re-apply the updates when you install a newer version of the operating system.

- Use the system header files, but add the missing definitions in local header files, or, worse, in the individual source files. This "solution" is a particularly obnoxious one, especially when, as so often, the declarations are not dependent on a particular `ifdef`. In almost any system with reasonably complete header files discrepancies will exist between the declarations in the system header files and the declarations in the package. Even if the discrepancies are only cosmetic, they will stop an ANSI compiler from compiling. For example, your system header files may declare `getpid` to return `pid_t`, but the package declares it to return `int`.

  About the only legitimate use of this style of "fixing" is to declare functions that really cause incorrect compilation if you don't declare them. Even then, declare them only inside an `ifdef` for a specific operating system. In the case of `getpid`, you're better off not declaring it. The compiler assumes the correct return values. Nevertheless, you will see mismatched argument types surprisingly often in packages that have already been ported to a number of operating systems, and it's one of the most common causes problems when porting.

- Make your own copies of the header files, and use them instead. This is the worst idea of all. If anything changes in your system's header files, you will never find out about it. It also means you can't give your source tree to somebody else: in most systems, the header files are subject to copyright.

In This Chapter:
- *Standard Library Functionality*
- *Block Memory Access Functions*
- *Regular Expression Routines*
- *termcap and terminfo*

18

Function Libraries

In this chapter, we'll look at functions usually supplied in libraries with the system. If you have the sources, porting a single library function that doesn't require specific kernel functionality is usually relatively trivial. Out of the hundreds of libraries in existence, we'll look only at those libraries that are available on a large number of systems. In the following sections, we'll cover:

- Functions that are found in the standard C library frequently enough that their absence can be a problem.
- Block memory functions, which modern compilers frequently treat as special cases.
- Regular expression libraries—five of them, all incompatible with each other.
- *terminfo* and *termlib*, in the section called "termcap and terminfo". We'll also briefly touch on *curses*.

If the program you're porting requires a function, you can often get the source code and create your own library. See Appendix E for places to get sources.

Standard Library Functionality

The content of the standard C library *libc.a* reminds me of the joke, "The nice thing about standards is that there are so many to choose from." Different systems have very different views on what should and should not be part of the standard library, and a number of systems don't supply some functions at all. In this section, we'll look at frequently used functions and what to do if your system doesn't have them.

alloca

alloca allocates memory in the stack, as opposed to malloc, which allocates memory in the heap:

```
void *alloca (size_t size);
```

alloca has a significant speed advantage over malloc. malloc needs to search and update a free space list. alloca typically just needs to change the value of a register and is thus very fast. It is often included with the package you are compiling, but you may need to set a flag or modify the *Makefile* in order to include it. Versions for VAX, HP 300, i386, and Tahoe processors are located in the 4.4BSD Lite distribution as *lib/libc/<machine>/gen/alloca.s.* On the down side, it is a somewhat system-dependent function, and it's possible that it might break after a new kernel release. You can almost always replace alloca with malloc, though doing so may be impact performance.

bcopy

bcopy is a BSD function that substantially corresponds to memmove:

```
#include <string.h>

void bcopy (const void *src, void *dst, size_t len);
```

Unlike memcpy, it is guaranteed to move correctly when the source and destination fields overlap. If your system has memmove, you can define bcopy as:

```
#define bcopy(s, d, l) memmove (d, s, l)
```

The operands have a different sequence from those of memmove.

bzero

bzero is a BSD function to clear an area of memory to 0. It is a subset of the standard function memset, and you can define it as:

```
#define bzero(d, l) memset (d, '\0', l)
```

fnmatch

fnmatch is a routine that matches patterns according to the shell filename rules:

```
#include <fnmatch.h>

int fnmatch (const char *pattern, const char *string, int flags);
```

fnmatch compares string against pattern. It returns 0 if string matches pattern and FNM_NOMATCH otherwise. The flags in Table 18-1 specify the kind of match to perform.

Table 18-1: fnmatch Flags

Flag	Meaning
FNM_NOESCAPE	Interpret the backslash character (\e) literally.
FNM_PATHNAME	Slash characters in string must be explicitly matched by slashes in pattern.
FNM_PERIOD	Leading periods in strings match periods in patterns. Not all versions of fnmatch implement this flag.

fnmatch is supplied with later BSD versions only. If you need it, it is in the 4.4BSD Lite distribution as *lib/libc/gen/fnmatch.c*.

getcwd and getwd

getcwd and getwd both return the name of the current working directory. This is the function behind the *pwd* command:

```
#include <stdio.h>

char *getcwd (char *buf, size_t size);
char *getwd (char *buf);
```

getwd has the great disadvantage that the function does not know the length of the pathname, and so it can write beyond the end of the buffer. As a result, it has been replaced by getcwd, which specifies a maximum length for the returned string. You can define getwd as:

```
#define getwd(d) getcwd (d, MAXPATHLEN)
```

MAXPATHLEN is a kernel constant defining the maximum pathname length. It is normally defined in */usr/include/sys/param.h*.

gethostname and uname

There is no one function call that returns the name of the system on all UNIX platforms. On BSD systems, *gethostname* returns the current host name:

```
#include <unistd.h>
int gethostname (char *name, int namelen);
```

gethostname returns a NUL-terminated string if the space defined by namelen allows it. This function is supported in System V.4 but not in standard versions of System V.3 and XENIX.

On System V systems, the system call uname returns a number of items of information about the system, including the name. It is also supported as a library function by most BSD systems.

```
#include <sys/utsname.h>                    sys/utsname.h defines
struct utsname
  {
  char sysname [9];                        /* Internal system name */
  char nodename [9];                       /* External system name */
  char release [9];                        /* Operating system release */
  char version [9];                        /* Version of release */
  char machine [9];                        /* Processor architecture */
  };
int uname (struct utsname *name);
```

The systems that *do* support *uname* apply a different meaning to the field *sysname*. For example, consider the output of the following program, which was compiled and run on Interactive UNIX/386 System V.3 Version 2.2 and BSD/386 version 1.1, both running on an Intel 486 platform:

```
#include <sys/utsname.h>
main ()
{
  struct utsname myname;
  uname (&myname);
  printf ("sysname %s nodename %s release %s version %s machine %s\n",
          myname.sysname,
          myname.nodename,
          myname.release,
          myname.version,
          myname.machine);
  }
$ uname                 On the System V.3 machine:
sysname adagio nodename adagio release 3.2 version 2 machine i386
$ uname                 On the BSD/386 machine:
sysname BSD/386 nodename allegro release 1.1 version 0 machine i386
```

System V puts the node name in sysname, whereas BSD uses it for the name of the operating system. This information is by no means complete. In particular, neither version tells you explicitly whether the system is running System V or BSD, and there is no indication of the vendor at all on the System V system.

index

index searches the string s forward for the first occurrence of the *character* c. If it finds one, it returns a pointer to the character. Otherwise it returns NULL. It is essentially the same as the ANSI function strchr, and you can define it as:

```
#define index strchr
```

malloc

`malloc` has always been around, but the semantics have changed over time. In the Seventh Edition and XENIX, a call to `malloc` with length 0 returned a valid pointer, whereas later versions return a `NULL` pointer, indicating an error. As a result, programs that ran on older versions might fail on more recent implementations.

memmove

`memmove` copies an area of memory:

```
#include <string.h>
void *memmove (void *dst, const void *src, size_t len);
```

This is the same function as `memcpy`, except that `memmove` is guaranteed to move overlapping data correctly. Except for the parameter sequence, it is the same as `bcopy` (see the section called "bcopy"). If you don't have either function, you can find `bcopy` in the 4.4BSD library source (*lib/libc/string/bcopy.c*), as well as versions in assembler:

lib/libc/vax/string/memmove.s
lib/libc/hp300/string/bcopy.s
lib/libc/tahoe/string/bcopy.s

A generic version of `memmove` in C can be found in the GNU C library in *sysdeps/generic/memmove.c*. See Appendix E to locate these sources. Note also the comments about memory move functions in the section called "Block Memory Access Functions".

remove

```
#include <stdio.h>
int remove (const char *path);
```

On BSD systems, `remove` is a synonym for the system call `unlink`. This means that it makes sense to use it only for files. On System V.4 systems, it is slightly more complicated: if called for a file, it does the same as `unlink`, for directories it does the same as `rmdir`.

rindex

`rindex` (reverse *index*) searches the string `s` for the last occurrence of *character* `c` and returns a pointer to the character if it is found, and `NULL` otherwise. It is essentially the same function as `strrchr`, and you can define it as:

```
#define rindex strrchr
```

snprintf and vsnprintf

`snprintf` and `vsnprintf` are versions of `sprintf` and `vsprintf` that limit the length of the output string:

```
int sprintf (char *str, const char *format, ...);
int snprintf (char *str, size_t size, const char *format, ...);
int vsprintf (char *str, char *format, va_list ap);
int vsnprintf (char *str, size_t size, const char *format, va_list ap);
```

The argument `size` specifies the maximum length of the output string, including the trailing `\0`. These functions are supplied in 4.4BSD Lite as *usr/src/lib/libc/stdio/snprintf.c* and *usr/src/lib/libc/stdio/vsnprintf.c*. Alternatively, you can remove the second parameter and use `sprintf` or `vsprintf` instead.

strcasecmp and strncasecmp

`strcasecmp` and `strncasecmp` perform an unsigned comparison of two ASCII strings, ignoring case (they consider `a` to be the same thing as `A`):

```
#include <string.h>

int strcasecmp (const char *s1, const char *s2);
int strncasecmp (const char *s1, const char *s2, size_t len);
```

`strncasecmp` differs from `strcasecmp` by comparing at most `len` characters. Both functions stop comparing when a `NUL` character is detected in one of the strings. You can find both functions in the 4.4BSD Lite distribution (*lib/libc/string/strcasecmp.c*).

strdup

`strdup` allocates memory with `malloc` and copies a string to it:

```
#include <string.h>

char *strdup (const char *str);
```

It is included in the 4.4BSD Lite distribution (*lib/libc/string/strdup.c*).

strerror and sys_errlist

`strerror` returns an error message string for a specific error:

```
#include <string.h>

extern char *sys_errlist [];
extern int sys_nerr;
char *strerror (int errnum);
```

errnum is the number of the error; strerror returns a pointer to a text string for the error or NULL if none is found.

Most library implementations also define sys_errlist, an array of description strings for errors, and sys_nerr, the total number of error messages—in other words, the number of messages in sys_errlist. If you don't find this variable anywhere in your man pages, don't give up: it's frequently hidden in an unexpected library. For example, NonStop UX version B22 doesn't define or document sys_errlist anywhere, but it is in *libc.a* all the same.

The implementation of strerror is trivial:

```
char *strerror (int errnum)
  {
  if (errnum < sys_nerr)
    return sys_errlist [errnum];
  else
    {
    static char bogus [80];
    sprintf (bogus, "Unknown error: %d", errnum);
    return bogus;
    }
  }
```

Don't assume that your system doesn't have sys_errlist just because you can't find a definition in the header files. Many systems install it via the back door because packages such as X11 use them. The safest way to find out if your system includes sys_errlist is to search the system libraries. The shell script *findf*, described in the section called "Missing functions" in Chapter 21, *Object Files and Friends*, can do this for you.

stricmp and strnicmp

These are somewhat uncommon alternatives to strcasecmp and strncasecmp, which are described earlier in this chapter.

Block Memory Access Functions

Many programs spend the bulk of their execution time moving areas of memory about or comparing them. The C language supplies a rich set of functions, such as memcpy, memmove, strcpy, strchr, strlen, and friends. Unfortunately, their performance frequently leaves something to be desired. Many C libraries still write the move in C. You can write memcpy as:

```
char *memcpy (char *d, char *s, int len)
  {
  char *dest = d;
  while (len--)
```

```
    *d++ = *s++;
  return dest;
  }
```

On an Intel 386 architecture, *gcc* compiles quite a tight little loop with only 7 instructions,* but it also requires another 15 instructions to set up the function environment and remove it again. In addition, the calling sequence `memcpy (bar, foo, 10)` might compile in 5 instructions. Many machines supply special instructions for block memory operations, but even those that don't can do it faster without a function call. The block memory functions are thus ideal candidates for inline functions that the compiler can optimize. Many compilers now do so, including *gcc* and the System V.4 CCS compilers. In this situation, the compiler can recognize that only a few bytes are to be moved and that they are word-aligned, so it can use native load and store operations. When you enable optimization, *gcc* can compile the `memcpy (bar, foo, 10)` into only 6 simple instructions: the loop has disappeared completely, and we just have 3 load and 3 store instructions. This approach isn't appropriate for moves of 1000 bytes, of course. Here, the compiler uses 4 instructions to set up a block move instruction, for a total of 5 instructions.

These examples are typical of what a smart compiler can do if it has inside information about what the function does. Normally this information is compiled into the compiler, and it doesn't need a header file to know about the function. This can have a number of consequences for you:

- The compiler "knows" the parameter types for the function. If you define the function differently, you get a possibly confusing error message:

  ```
  memcpy.c:3: warning: conflicting types for built-in function `memcpy'
  ```

  If you get this message, you can either ignore it or, better, remove the definition. The compiler knows what to do without it.

- When debugging, you can't just put a breakpoint on `memcpy`. There is no such function, or if it has been included to satisfy references from modules compiled by other compilers, it may not be called when you expect.

- If you have a program written for a compiler that knows about the block memory functions, you may need to add definitions if your compiler doesn't support them.

* See the section called "Stack Frames" in Chapter 21, for a discussion of parameter passing.

Regular Expression Routines

Regular expressions are coded descriptions of text strings. They are used by editors and utilities such as *grep* for searching and matching actual text strings. There's nothing very special about routines that process regular expressions, but no agreement about standards and there is no agreement about how to write a regular expression. The only regular thing about them is the regularity with which programs fail to link due to missing functions. There are at least five different popular packages, and the names are similar enough to cause significant confusion.

In all cases, the intention of the routines is the same:

- A *compilation* function converts a string representation of a regular expression into an internal representation that is faster to interpret.
- A *search* function applies the regular expression to a text string, searching for a match.

In addition, the Eighth Edition *regex* package has support for a replacement function based on the results of a previous search.

Regular expression syntax also comes in two basic flavors:

- The documentation of the older syntax usually states that it is the same syntax that *ed* uses. *ed* is an editor that is now almost completely obsolete,* so it's good to know that the stream editor *sed*, which is still in current use, uses the same syntax.
- The newer syntax is the same that *egrep* uses. It is similar to that of *ed* but includes a number of more advanced expressions.

If you get software that expects one package, but you have to substitute another, you should expect changes in behaviour. Regular expressions that worked with the old package may not work with the new one, or they may match differently. A particularly obvious example is the use of parentheses to group expressions. All forms of regular expressions perform this grouping, but the old syntax requires the parentheses to be escaped: `\(expr\)`, whereas the new syntax does not: `(expr)`.

Apart from the intention of the functions, they also perform their tasks in *very* different ways. They might store compiled program in an area that the caller supplies, they might *malloc* it, or they might hide it where the user can't find it. In some cases, the compiled expression is stored in a `struct` along with other information intended for use by the calling functions. In others, this information is not

* *ed* does have its uses, though. If you have serious system problems (like */usr* crashed), it's nice to have a copy of *ed* on the root file system. It's also useful when your only connection to the machine is via a slow modem line: over a 2400 bps line, redrawing a 24×80 screen with a full-screen editor takes 8 seconds, and simple editing is faster with *ed*.

returned at all, and in still others again it is returned in global arrays, and in still others, it is returned via optional arguments. Translating from one flavor to another takes a lot of time.

Three packages are widely available: Henry Spencer's Eighth Edition package, the 4.4BSD POSIX.2 version, and the GNU POSIX.2 version. See Appendix E for information on the sources of these packages. If you *do* have to port to a different regular expression package, choose a POSIX.2 implementation. Although it is by far the most complicated to understand, it is probably the only one that will be around in a few years.

Regular expressions are used for two purposes: searching and replacing. When replacing text that a regular expression matches, it's nice to be able to refer to parts of the text. By convention, you define these subexpressions with parentheses. For instance, the expression `foo\(.*\)bar\(.*\)baz` defines two such subexpressions. The regular expression matches all strings containing the texts `foo`, `bar`, and `baz` with anything in between them. The first marked subexpression is the text between `foo` and `bar`, and the second one is the text between `bar` and `baz`.

regexpr

The *regexpr* routines have traditionally been supplied with System V and XENIX systems. They were originally part of the *ed* editor and thus implement the *ed* style of regular expressions. Despite the name of the package, there is no function called `regexpr`.

The routines themselves are normally in a library *libgen.a*. In addition, for some reason many versions of System V and XENIX include the complete *source* to the functions in the header file *regexp.h*, whereas the header file *regexpr.h* contains only the declarations. There are three routines:

```
#include <regexpr.h>

extern char *loc1, *loc2, *locs;
extern int nbra, regerrno, reglength;
extern char *braslist [], *braelist [];

char *compile (const char *instring,
               char *expbuf,
               char *endbuf);
int step (const char *string, char *expbuf);
int advance (const char *string, char *expbuf);
```

- `compile` compiles the regular expression `instring`. The exact behavior depends on the value of `expbuf`. If `expbuf` is `NULL`, `compile` *malloc*s space for the compiled version of the expression and returns a pointer to it. If `expbuf` is non-`NULL`, `compile` places the compiled form there if it fits between `expbuf` and `endbuf`, and it returns a pointer to the first *free* byte. If the regular expression does not fit in this space, `compile` aborts. If the compilation succeeds, the length of the compiled expression is stored in the global variable `reglength`.

If the compilation fails, `compile` returns `NULL` and sets the variable `regerrno` to one of the values in Table 18-2.

- `step` compares the string `string` with the compiled expression at `expbuf`. It returns nonzero if it finds a match and 0 if it does not. If there is a match, the pointer `loc1` is set to point to the start of the match, and `loc2` is set to point past the last character of the match.

  If the regular expression contains parenthesized subexpressions, `step` stores the locations of the start and end of each matching substring in the global arrays `braslist` (start) and `braelist` (end). It stores the total number of such subexpressions in `nbra`.

- `advance` has the same function as `step`, but it restricts its matching to the beginning of the string. In other words, a successful match always causes `loc1` to point to the beginning of the string.

Table 18–2: regcomp Error Codes

Error Code	Meaning
11	Range endpoint too large.
16	Bad number.
25	\digit out of range.
36	Illegal or missing delimiter.
41	No remembered search string.
42	\(\) imbalance.
43	Too many \(.
44	More than 2 numbers given in \{ \}.
45	} expected after \.
46	First number exceeds second in \{ \}.
49	[ ] imbalance.
50	Regular expression overflow.

regcmp

regcmp is another regular expression processor used in System V and XENIX. Like *regexpr*, it implements the *ed* style of regular expressions with some extensions. It is also normally part of the library *libgen.a*.

```
#include <libgen.h>

char *regcmp (const char *string1,
              /* char *string2 */ ...
              (char *) 0);
char *regex (const char *re,
             const char *subject,
             /* char *ret0, *ret1, ... *retn */ );
extern char *__loc1;
```

- regcmp can take multiple input arguments, which it concatenates before compilation. This can be useful when the expression is supplied on a number of input lines, for example. It always *mallocs* space for its compiled expression, and returns a pointer to it.
- regex searches the string subject for a match by the compiled regular expression re. On success, it returns a pointer to the next character after the match and sets the global pointer __loc1 to the address of the first character of the match. Optionally, it returns up to 10 matched substrings at ret0 and the parameters that follow. You specify them with the $n regular expression element discussed below.

The regular expression syntax is slightly different from that of *ed* and *sed*:

- The character $ represents the end of the text being searched, not the end of the logical line. Use \n to specify the end of the line.
- You can use the syntax x+ to represent one or more occurrences of x.
- You can use the syntax {m}, where m is an integer, to indicate that the immediately preceding item should match exactly m times.
- You can use the syntax {m,}, where m is an integer, to indicate that the preceding item should immediately match at least m times.
- You can use the syntax {m,n}, where m and n are integers, to indicate that the previous subexpression should match at least m and at most n times.
- (...), not \(...\), is used to mark subexpressions.
- The syntax (exp) groups the characters exp so that operators such as * and + work on the whole expression and not just the preceding character. For example, the regular expression (abc)+ matches abcabcabcabc, and abc+ matches abcccccc.
- The syntax (exp)$*n*, where *n* is an integer, matches the expression exp and returns the address of the matched string to the call parameter ret*n* of the call to regex. It will even try to return the address if you didn't supply parameter ret*n*, so it's good practice to supply all the parameters unless you are in control of the regular expressions.

regex: re_comp and re_exec

regex is the somewhat confusing name given to the functions **re_comp** and **re_exec**, which were introduced in 4.0BSD. Note particularly that there is no function called **regex**, and that the name is spelled without a final *p*. *regex* also implements *ed*-style regular expressions. There are two functions:

```
char *re_comp (char *sp);
int re_exec (char *p1);
```

- **re_comp** compiles the regular expression `sp` and stores the compiled form internally. On successful compilation, it returns a `NULL` pointer, and on error a pointer to an error message.
- **re_exec** searches the string `p1` against the internally stored regular expression. It returns 1 if the string p1 matches the last compiled regular expression, 0 if the string p1 fails to match the last compiled regular expression, and –1 if the compiled regular expression is invalid.

No publicly available versions of *regex* are available, but it's relatively simple to define them in terms of POSIX.2 *regex*.

Eighth Edition regexp

The Eighth Edition regexp package has gained wider popularity due to a widely available implementation by Henry Spencer of the University of Toronto. It consists of the functions *regcomp*, *regexec*, *regsub*, and *regerror*:

```
#include <regexp.h>

regexp * regcomp (const char *exp);
int regexec (const regexp *prog, const char *string);
void regsub (const regexp *prog, const char *source, char *dest);
void regerror (const char *msg);
```

In contrast to earlier packages, Eighth Edition *regexp* implements *egrep*-style regular expressions. Also in contrast to other packages, the compiled form of the regular expression includes two arrays that **regexec** sets for use by the programmer: `char *startp []` is an array of start addresses of up to nine subexpressions (expressions enclosed in parentheses), and `char *endp []` is an array of the corresponding end addresses. The subexpressions are indexed 1 to 9; `startp [0]` refers to the complete expression.

regcomp compiles the regular expression `exp` and stores the compiled version in an area that it *mallocs*. It returns a pointer to the compiled version on success or `NULL` on failure.

regexec matches the string string against the compiled regular expression prog. It returns 1 if a match was found and 0 otherwise. In addition, it stores the start and end addresses of the first nine parenthesized subexpressions in prog->startp and prog->endp.

regsub performs a regular expression substitution, a function not offered by the other packages. You use it after regcomp finds a match and stores subexpression start and end information in startp and endp. It copies the input string source to dest, replacing expressions of the type &n, where n is a single digit from 1 to 9, by the substring defined by startp [n] and endp [n].

regerror determines the action to be taken if an error is detected in regcomp, regexec, or regsub. The default regerror prints the message and terminates the program. If you want, you can replace it with your own routine.

POSIX.2 regex

As if there weren't enough regular expression libraries already, POSIX.2 also has a version of *regex*. It is intended to put an end to the myriad other flavors of regular expressions and thus supplies all the functionality of the other packages. Unfortunately, it re-uses the function names of Eighth Edition *regexp*. This is the only similarity: the POSIX.2 functions take completely different parameters. The header file of the 4.4BSD package starts with:

```
#ifndef _REGEX_H_
#define _REGEX_H_                          /* never again */

#ifdef _REGEXP_H_
BAD NEWS -- POSIX regex.h and V8 regexp.h are incompatible
#endif
```

The Eighth Edition *regexp.h* contains similar code, so if you accidentally try to use both, you get an error message when you try to compile it.

The POSIX.2 *regex* package offers a seemingly infinite variety of flags and options. It consists of the functions *regcomp*, *regexec*, *regerror*, and *regfree*. They match regular expressions according to the POSIX.2 regular expression format, either *ed* format (so-called *basic regular expressions*, the default) or *egrep* format (*extended regular expressions*). The 4.4BSD implementations refer to them as *obsolete regular expressions* and *modern regular expressions*, respectively. You choose the kind of expression via flag bits passed to the compilation function regcomp. Alternatively, you can specify that the string is to be matched exactly, in which case no characters have any special significance.

Here are the functions:

```
#include <sys/types.h>
#include <regex.h>

int regcomp (regex_t *preg, const char *pattern, int cflags);
int regexec (const regex_t *preg,
             const char *string,
             size_t nmatch,
             regmatch_t pmatch [],
             int eflags);
size_t regerror (int errcode,
                 const regex_t *preg,
                 char *errbuf,
                 size_t errbuf_size);
void regfree (regex_t *preg);
```

- `regcomp` compiles the regular expression `pattern` and stores the result at `preg`. It returns 0 on success and an error code on failure. `cflags` modifies the way in which the compilation is performed. These flags are listed in Table 18-3.
- `regexec` matches the string `string` against the compiled regular expression `preg`. If `nmatch` is nonzero and `pmatch` is non-`NULL`, start and end information for up to `nmatch` subexpressions is returned to the array `pmatch`. `regexec` also supports a number of flags in `eflags`, described in Table 18-4.
- `regerror` is analogous to the C library function `perror`: it converts the error code `errcode` for regular expression `preg` into a human-readable error message at `errbuf`, up to a maximum of `errbuf_size` bytes.

Table 18-3: cflags Bits for regcomp

Flag Bit	Function
REG_BASIC	Compile basic ("obsolete") REs. This is the default.
REG_EXTENDED	Compile extended ("modern") REs.
REG_NOSPEC	Compile a literal expression (no special characters). This is not specified by POSIX.2. You may not combine REG_EXTENDED and REG_NOSPEC.
REG_ICASE	Ignore case when matching.
REG_NOSUB	Compile to report only whether the text matched, don't return subexpression information. This makes the search faster.
REG_NEWLINE	Compile for newline-sensitive matching. By default, a newline character in the searched text does not have any special meaning. With this flag, ^ and $ match beginnings and ends of lines, and expressions bracketed with [^...] do not match new lines.
REG_PEND	Specify that the expression ends at `re_endp`, thus allowing NUL characters in expressions. This is not defined in POSIX.2

Table 18-4: eflags Bits for regexec

Flag Bit	Meaning
`REG_NOTBOL`	Do not match the beginning of the expression with `^`.
`REG_NOTEOL`	Do not match the end of the expression with `$`.
`REG_STARTEND`	Specify that the string starts at `string + pmatch[0].rm_so` and ends at `string + pmatch[0].rm_eo`. This can be used with `cflags` value `REG_PEND` to match expressions containing `NUL` characters.

As in the Eighth Edition *regexp*, `regcomp` returns additional information about the expression:

- If you compile the expression with the `REG_PEND` bit set in `cflags`, you can set `re_endp` to point to the real end of the regular expression string supplied to `regcomp`, thus allowing `NULL` characters in the regular expression.
- After compilation, `regcomp` sets `re_nsub` to the number of subexpressions it found. For each subexpression, `regexec` can return start and end address information if you call it with appropriate parameters.

In addition, `regexec` stores information about matched subexpressions in a structure of type `regmatch_t`, unless you specify the flag `REG_NOSUB`. This contains at least the fields `rm_so` and `rm_eo`, which are *offsets* from the start of the string of the first and last character of the match. They are of type `regmatch_t`.

No fewer than three versions of POSIX.2 *regex* are generally available. Henry Spencer's *regex* is included in the 4.4BSD distribution, and the GNU project has the older *regex* and newer *rx*. See Appendix E.

termcap and terminfo

When full-screen editors started to appear in the late seventies, Bill Joy at UCB wrote *ex*, out of which grew *vi*. One of the problems he had experienced was that just about every terminal has a different command set. Even commands as simple as positioning the cursor were different from one terminal to the next. In order to get the editor to work over a range of terminals, he devised *termcap*, the terminal capabilities database, which, with a few access routines, allowed a program to determine the correct control sequences for most common functions.

A few years later, while writing the game *rogue*, Ken Arnold extended the routines and created a new package, *curses*, which offered higher-level functions.

Finally, USG improved on *curses* and introduced *terminfo*, a new implementation of the same kind of functionality as *termcap*. It was designed to address some of the weaknesses of *termcap* and, as a result, is not compatible with it. More programs use *termcap* than *terminfo*: *terminfo* is usually restricted to System V systems, and *termcap* has been around longer and is available on most systems. Some programs use both, but there aren't very many of them.

There are a number of gotchas waiting for you with *termcap*, *termlib*, and *curses*:

- *termcap* isn't perfect, to put it mildly. It relies on a marginally human-readable definition file format, which means that the access routines are slow. When AT&T incorporated *termcap* into System V, they addressed this problem and created *terminfo*, with a so-called *compiled* representation of the terminal data.
- Both *termcap* and *terminfo* are passive services: your program has to explicitly ask for them in order for them to work. Many programs don't use either, and many use only one or the other.
- Though the BSD *curses* package offered a bewildering number of functions, users asked for more. When AT&T incorporated *curses* into System V, they added significant enhancements. *curses* goes a level of complexity beyond *termcap* and *terminfo* and supplies a huge number of functions to perform all kinds of activities on a terminal. It's like a can of worms: avoid opening it if you can; otherwise, refer to *UNIX Curses Explained* by Berny Goodheart. If you have a BSD system and need System V *curses*, you can try the *ncurses* package. (See Appendix E.)
- BSD versions of UNIX have still not incorporated *terminfo* or the additional *curses* routines, although they have been available for some time.

In this section, we'll look at the differences in the implementations and what can be done about them. For more information, read *Programming with curses*, by John Strang, for a description of BSD *curses*; *Termcap and Terminfo*, by John Strang et. al. for a description of *termcap* and *terminfo*; and *UNIX Curses Explained*, by Berny Goodheart, for a description of both versions of *curses*.

termcap

The heart of *termcap* is the terminal description, which may be specified with an environment variable or stored in a file containing definitions for a number of terminals. There is no complete agreement on the location of this file:

- If the *termcap* routines find the environment variable `TERMCAP`, and it doesn't start with a slash (/), they try to interpret it as a *termcap* entry.

- If the *termcap* routines find the environment variable TERMCAP, and it *does* start with a slash, they try to interpret it as the name of the *termcap* file.
- If TERMCAP isn't specified, the location depends on a constant compiled into the *termcap* library. Typical directories are */etc*, */usr/lib*, and */usr/share*. Don't rely on finding only one of these files: it's not uncommon to find multiple copies on a machine, only one of which is of any use to you. If the system documentation doesn't tell you where the *termcap* file is located, you can usually find out with the aid of *strings* and *grep*. For example, BSD/OS gives:

  ```
  $ strings libtermcap.a |grep /termcap
  .termcap /usr/share/misc/termcap
  ```

  SCO UNIX gives:

  ```
  $ strings libtermcap.a |grep /termcap
  /etc/termcap
  /etc/termcap
  ```

The file *termcap* contains entries for all terminals known to the system. On some systems it can be up to 200 KB in length. This may not seem very long, but every program that uses *termcap* must read it until it finds the terminal definition: if the terminal isn't defined, it reads the full length of the file.

Here's a typical entry:

```
vs|xterm|vs100|xterm terminal emulator (X Window System):\
        :AL=\E[%dL:DC=\E[%dP:DL=\E[%dM:DO=\E[%dB:IC=\E[%d@:UP=\E[%dA:\
        :al=\E[L:am:\
        :bs:cd=\E[J:ce=\E[K:cl=\E[H\E[2J:cm=\E[%i%d;%dH:co#80:\
        :cs=\E[%i%d;%dr:ct=\E[3k:\
        :dc=\E[P:dl=\E[M:\
        :im=\E[4h:ei=\E[4l:mi:\
        :ho=\E[H:\
        :is=\E[r\E[m\E[2J\E[H\E[?7h\E[?1;3;4;6l\E[4l:\
        :rs=\E[r\E[m\E[2J\E[H\E[?7h\E[?1;3;4;6l\E[4l\E<:\
        :k1=\EOP:k2=\EOQ:k3=\EOR:k4=\EOS:kb=^H:kd=\EOB:ke=\E[?1l\E>:\
        :kl=\EOD:km:kn#4:kr=\EOC:ks=\E[?1h\E=:ku=\EOA:\
        :li#65:md=\E[1m:me=\E[m:mr=\E[7m:ms:nd=\E[C:pt:\
        :sc=\E7:rc=\E8:sf=\n:so=\E[7m:se=\E[m:sr=\EM:\
        :te=\E[2J\E[?47l\E8:ti=\E7\E[?47h:\
        :up=\E[A:us=\E[4m:ue=\E[m:xn:
v2|xterms|vs100s|xterm terminal emulator, small window (X Window System):\
        :co#80:li#24:tc=xterm:
vb|xterm-bold|xterm with bold instead of underline:\
        :us=\E[1m:tc=xterm:
#
# vi may work better with this termcap, because vi
# doesn't use insert mode much
vi|xterm-ic|xterm-vi|xterm with insert character instead of insert mode:\
        :im=:ei=:mi@:ic=\E[@:tc=xterm:
```

The lines starting with the pound sign (#) are comments. The other lines are terminal capability definitions: each entry is logically on a single line, and the lines are continued with the standard convention of terminating them with a backslash (\). As in many other old UNIX files, fields are separated by colons (`:`).

The first field of each description is the *label*, the name of the terminal to which the definition applies. The terminal may have multiple names, separated by vertical bars (|). In our example, the first entry has the names `vs`, `xterm`, and `vs100`. The last part of the name field is a description of the kind of terminal. In the second entry, the names are `vi`, `xterm-ic`, and `xterm-vi`.

Both 4.4BSD *termcap* and System V *terminfo* recommend the following conventions for naming terminals:

- Start with the name of the physical hardware, for example, *hp2621*.
- Avoid hyphens in the name.
- Describe operational modes or configuration preferences for the terminal with an indicator, separated by a hyphen. Use the following suffixes, listed in Table 18-5, where possible:

Table 18–5: Conventions for Terminal Names

Suffix	Meaning	Example
-w	Wide mode (more than 80 columns)	vt100-w
-am	With automatic margins (usually default)	vt100-am
-nam	Without automatic margins	vt100-nam
-n	Number of lines on screen	aaa-60
-na	No arrow keys (leave them in local)	concept100-na
-np	Number of pages of memory	concept100-4p
-rv	Reverse video	concept100-rv

The fields that follow describe individual capabilities in the form *capability=definition*. The capabilities are abbreviated to two characters, and case is significant. See the O'Reilly Nutshell *Programming with curses* for a list of the currently defined abbreviations and their meanings. Depending on the capability, the definition may be a truth value (true or false), a number, or a string. For example,

- The first entry for `vs` (`AL=\E[%dL`) states that the capability `AL` (insert *n* new blank lines) can be invoked with the string `\E[%dL`. `\E` represents an ESC character. The characters `[` and `L` are passed to the terminal literally. The program uses `sprintf` to replace the `%d` with the number of lines to insert.

- The next entry, am, has no parameter. This is a Boolean or truth value, which, in this case, means that the terminal supports automatic margins. The presence of the capability means that it is true, the absence means that it is false.
- The entry co#80 specifies a numeric parameter and states that the capability co (number of columns) is 80.

There is almost nothing in the syntax of the definition file that requires that a particular capability have a particular type, or even which capabilities exist. This is simply a matter of agreement between the program and the capabilities database. If your program wants the capability co and wants it to be numeric, it calls tgetnum. For example, the following code checks first the information supplied by ioctl TIOCGWINSZ (see the section called "TIOCGWINSZ" in Chapter 15, *Terminal Drivers*), then the *termcap* entry, and if both of them are not defined, it defaults to a configurable constant:

```
if (! (maxcols = winsize.ws_col)
    && (! (maxcols = tgetnum ("co"))) )
     maxcols = MAXCOLS;
```

The only exception to this rule is the capability tc, which refers to another capability. In the sample *termcap* entry shown previously, the entry for vi and friends consists of only five entries, but the last one is a tc entry that refers to the vs entry above it.

This lack of hard and fast rules means that *termcap* is extensible: if you have a terminal that can change the number of colors that can be displayed at one time, and for some reason you want to use this feature, you might define a *termcap* variable XC specifying the string to output to the terminal to perform this function. The danger is that somebody else might write a program that uses the variable XC for some other purpose.

termcap functions: termlib

Along with *termcap* come library functions, normally in a library called *libtermcap.a*, though a number of systems include them in *libc.a*. They help you query the database and perform user-visible functions such as writing to the terminal. There aren't many functions, but they are nonetheless confusing enough:

```
char PC;                                    /* padding character */
char *BC;                                   /* backspace string */
char *UP;                                   /* Cursor up string */
short ospeed;                               /* terminal output speed */

tgetent (char *bp, char *name);
tgetnum (char *id);
tgetflag (char *id);
char *tgetstr (char *id, char **sbp);
```

```
char *tgoto (char *cm, int destcol, int destline);
tputs (register char *cp, int affcnt, int (*outc) ());
```

Before you start, you need two areas of memory: a 1 KB temporary buffer for the *termcap* entry, which we call `buf`, and a buffer for the string capabilities that you need, which we call `sbuf`. The initialization function `tgetent` fills `sbuf` with the *termcap* entry, and the function `tgetstr` transfers strings from `buf` to `sbuf`. After initialization is complete, `buf` can be deallocated.

In addition, you need a `char` pointer `sbp`, which must be initialized to point to `sbuf`. `tgetstr` uses it to note the next free location in `sbuf`.

If you don't specify a specific *termcap* string as the value of the `TERMCAP` environment variable, you need to know the name of your terminal in order to access it in the *termcap* file. By convention, this is the value of the `TERM` environment variable, and you can retrieve it with the library function `getenv`.

- `tgetent` searches the *termcap* file for a definition for the terminal called `name` and places the entry into the buffer, which must be 1024 bytes long, at `buf`. All subsequent calls use this buffer. Unfortunately, they do not explicitly reference the buffer: `tgetent` saves its address in a static pointer internal to the *termcap* routines. `tgetent` returns 1 on success, 0 if the terminal name was not found, or -1 if the termcap database could not be found.

- `tgetnum` looks for a numeric capability `id` and returns its value if found. If the value is not found, it returns –1.

- `tgetflag` looks for a Boolean capability `id` and returns 1 if it is present and 0 otherwise.

- `tgetstr` looks for a string capability `id`. If it is found, the function copies it into the buffer pointed to by the pointer at `*sbp`. `tgetstr` then updates `sbp` to point past the string. It returns the address of the string in `sbuf` if found, or `NULL` if not. This method ensures that the strings are null-terminated (which is not the case in `buf`) and that they are stored efficiently (though a 1 KB buffer is no longer the overhead it used to be).

- `tgoto` generates a positioning string to move the cursor to column `destcol` and line `destline` using the `cm` (cursor position) capability. This capability contains format specifications that `tgoto` replaces with the representation of the actual row and column numbers. It returns a pointer to the positioning string, which again is stored in a static buffer in the package. It also attempts to avoid using the characters `\n`, **CTRL-D**, or **CTRL-@**. The resulting string may contain binary information that corresponds to tab characters. Depending on how it is set up, the terminal driver may replace these tab characters with blanks, which is obviously not a good idea. To ensure that this does not happen, turn off `TAB3` on a *termio* or *termios* system (see Chapter 15, Table 15-5) or reset `XTABS` in `sgttyp.sg_flags` with the old terminal driver (see Table 15-3).

This is all that `tgoto` does. It does not actually output anything to the terminal.

- `tputs` writes the string at `cp` to the screen. This seems unnecessary, since `write` and `fwrite` already do the same thing. The problem is that the output string `cp` may contain padding information for serial terminals, and only `tputs` interprets this information correctly. `affcnt` is the number of lines on the screen affected by this output, and `outc` is the address of a function that outputs the characters correctly. Often enough, this is something like `putchar`.

Problems with termcap

Sooner or later you'll run into problems with *termcap*. Here are some favorite ones:

Missing description

It could still happen that the *termcap* database doesn't include a description for your terminal. This isn't the problem it used to be, since most modern terminals come close to the ANSI standard. If in doubt, try `ansi` or `vt100`. This is, of course, not a good substitute for complete documentation for your terminal.

Incomplete description

It's much more likely that you *will* find a terminal description for your terminal but that it's incomplete, which, surprisingly, is often the case. This happens surprisingly often. For example, the *xterm* definition supplied in X11R5 has 56 capabilities, and the definition supplied with X11R6 has 85. `xterm` hasn't changed significantly between X11R5 and X11R6: the capabilities were just missing from the entry in X11R5. Frequently, you'll find that a feature you're looking for, in particular the code generated by a particular function key, is missing from your *termcap* entry. If nothing else helps, you can find out what codes the key generates with od:

```
$ od -c                              display stdin in character format
^[[11~^[[12~^[[13~^[[14~ RETURN
0000000  033   [   1   1   ~ 033   [   1   2   ~ 033   [   1   3   ~ 0000020
033   [   1   4   ~  \n
0000025
```

In this example, I pressed the keys **F1**, **F2**, **F3**, and **F4** on an *xterm*, and this is what echos on the first line. *od* doesn't display anything until its `read` completes, so I pressed **RETURN** to show the text.

The first `0000000` in the *od* display is just a counter for characters. The real data comes next. It shows that the sequences generated are:

- `033` (**ESC**, which is represented as `\E` in *termcap* entries).
- `[1` and the number of the function key and a tilde (`~`).

These sequences can then be translated into the *termcap* capabilities:

```
k1=\E[11~:k2=\E[12~:k3=\E[13~:k4=\E[14~:
```

Incorrect description

If we look at the previous example more carefully, we'll notice something strange: these capabilities aren't the same as the ones in the example for *xterm* in the section called "termcap". What's wrong with this picture? A good question. Both under X11R5 and X11R6, *xterm* on an Intel architecture gives you the codes shown above. The codes for **F5** to **F10** are as shown in the *termcap* entry, but the entries for **F1** to **F4** are just plain wrong. I don't know of any way to generate them with *xterm*, which is typical of *termcap* entries: if you run into trouble, first make sure that your descriptions are correct.

Obsolete information

Another interesting thing about the *xterm* example is that it tells you the size of the terminal: `co#80` says that this terminal has 80 columns, and `li#65` says that it has 65 lines. This information can be an approximation at best, since X11 allows you to resize the window. Most modern systems supply the `SIGWINCH` signal, which is delivered to the controlling process when a window is resized (see the section called "TIOCSWINSZ" in Chapter 15). This information is just plain misleading, but there's a lot of it in just about any *termcap* file. The 4.4BSD man page flags a number of capabilities that are considered obsolete, including such things as the character used to backspace or the number of function keys.

terminfo

terminfo is the System V replacement for *termcap*. At first sight it looks very similar, but there are significant differences:

- Instead of reading the *termcap* file, the *terminfo* routines require a "compiled" version.

- Instead of storing all entries in a single file, *terminfo* stores each entry in a different file and puts them in a directory whose name is the initial letter of the terminal name. For example, the *terminfo* description for *xterm* might be stored in */usr/lib/terminfo/x/xterm.*
- The substitution syntax has been significantly expanded: in *termcap*, only `tgoto` could handle parameter substitution (see the section called "termcap functions: termlib"); in *terminfo*, the substitution syntax is more general and offers many more features.
- The program *tic* (terminfo compiler) compiles *terminfo* descriptions.
- The programs *infocmp*, which is supplied with System V, and *untic*, which is part of *ncurses*, dump compiled *terminfo* entries in source form.

As an example of a *terminfo* definition, let's look at the definition for an *xterm*. This should contain the same information as the *termcap* entry in the section called "termcap":

```
xterm|xterm-24|xterms|vs100|xterm terminal emulator (X Window System),
        is2=\E7\E[r\E[m\E[?7h\E[?1;3;4;6l\E[4l\E8\E>,
        rs2=\E7\E[r\E[m\E[?7h\E[?1;3;4;6l\E[4l\E8\E>,
        am, bel=^G,
        cols#80, lines#24,
        clear=\E[H\E[2J, cup=\E[%i%p1%d;%p2%dH,
        csr=\E[%i%p1%d;%p2%dr,
        cud=\E[%p1%dB, cud1=\n, cuu=\E[%p1%dA, cuu1=\E[A,
        cub=\E[%p1%dD, cub1=\b,        cuf=\E[%p1%dC, cuf1=\E[C,
        el=\E[K, ed=\E[J,
        home=\E[H, ht=^I, ind=^J, cr=^M,
        km,
        smir=\E[4h, rmir=\E[4l, mir,
        smso=\E[7m, rmso=\E[m, smul=\E[4m, rmul=\E[m,
        bold=\E[1m, rev=\E[7m, blink@, sgr0=\E[m, msgr,
        enacs=\E)0, smacs=^N, rmacs=^O,
        smkx=\E[?1h\E=, rmkx=\E[?1l\E>,
        kf1=\EOP, kf2=\EOQ, kf3=\EOR, kf4=\EOS,
        kf5=\E[15~, kf6=\E[17~, kf7=\E[18~, kf8=\E[19~, kf9=\E[20~,
        kf10=\E[21~,
        kf11=\E[23~, kf12=\E[24~, kf13=\E[25~, kf14=\E[26~, kf15=\E[28~,
        kf16=\E[29~, kf17=\E[31~, kf18=\E[32~, kf19=\E[33~, kf20=\E[34~,
        kfnd=\E[1~, kich1=\E[2~, kdch1=\E[3~,
        kslt=\E[4~, kpp=\E[5~, knp=\E[6~,
        kbs=\b,        kcuu1=\EOA, kcud1=\EOB, kcuf1=\EOC, kcub1=\EOD,
        meml=\El, memu=\Em,
        smcup=\E7\E[?47h, rmcup=\E[2J\E[?47l\E8,
        sc=\E7, rc=\E8,
        il=\E[%p1%dL, dl=\E[%p1%dM, il1=\E[L, dl1=\E[M,
        ri=\EM,
        dch=\E[%p1%dP, dch1=\E[P,
        tbc=\E[3g,
        xenl,
```

```
xterm-65|xterm with tall window 65x80 (X Window System),
        lines#65,
        use=xterm,
xterm-bold|xterm with bold instead of underline (X Window System),
        smul=\E[1m, use=xterm,
#
# vi may work better with this entry, because vi
# doesn't use insert mode much
xterm-ic|xterm-vi|xterm with insert character instead of insert mode,
        smir@, rmir@, mir@, ich1=\E[@, ich=\E[%p1%d@, use=xterm,
```

The entries look very similar, but there are a few minor differences:

- The names for the capabilities may be up to five characters long. As a result, the names are different from the *termcap* names.
- Capabilities are separated by commas instead of colons.
- Definitions may be spread over several lines: there is no need to terminate each line of a definition with a backslash.
- The last character in each entry must be a comma. If you remove it, you will thoroughly confuse *tic*.

terminfo functions

terminfo has a number of functions that correspond closely to *termlib*. They are also the low-level routines for *curses*:

```
#include <curses.h>
#include <term.h>
TERMINAL *cur_term;

int setupterm (char *term, int fd, int *error);
int setterm (char *term);
int set_curterm (TERMINAL *nterm);
int del_curterm (TERMINAL *oterm);
int restartterm (char *term, int fildes, int *errret);
char *tparm (char *str, long int p1 ... long int p9);
int tputs (char *str, int affcnt, int  (*putc) (char));
int putp (char *str);
int vidputs (chtype attrs, int  (*putc) (char));
int vidattr (chtype attrs);
int mvcur (int oldrow, int oldcol, int newrow, int newcol);
int tigetflag (char *capname);
int tigetnum (char *capname);
int tigetstr (char *capname);
```

terminfo can use an environment variable TERMINFO, which has a similar function to TERMCAP: it contains the name of a directory to search for *terminfo* entries. Since *terminfo* is compiled, there is no provision for stating the capabilities directly in TERMINFO.

- `setupterm` corresponds to the *termcap* function `tgetent`: it reads in the *terminfo* data and sets up all necessary capabilities. The parameter `term` is the name of the terminal but may be `NULL`, in which case `setupterm` calls `getenv` to get the name of the terminal from the environment variable `TERM`. `fd` is the file descriptor of the output terminal (normally 1 for `stdout`), and `error` is an error status return address.
- `setterm` is a simplified version of `setupterm`: it is equivalent to `setupterm (term, 1, NULL)`.
- `setupterm` allocates space for the terminal information and stores the address in the global pointer `cur_term`. You can use `set_curterm` to set it to point to a different terminal entry in order to handle multiple terminals.
- `del_curterm` deallocates the space allocated by `setupterm` for the terminal `oterm`.
- `restartterm` performs a subset of `setupterm`: it assumes that the `cur_term` is valid but that terminal type and transmission speed may change.
- `tparm` substitutes the real values of up to nine parameters (`p1` to `p9`) into the string `str`. This can be used, for example, to create a cursor-positioning string like `tgoto`, but it is much more flexible.
- `tputs` is effectively the same function as *termcap* `puts` described in the section called "termcap functions: termlib".
- `putp` is effectively `tputs (str, stdout, putchar)`.
- `vidputs` sets the terminal attributes for a video terminal.
- `vidattr` is effectively `vidputs (attr, putchar)`.
- `mvcur` provides optimized cursor motion depending on the terminal capabilities and the relationship between the current cursor position *(oldrow, oldcol)* and the new position *(newrow, newcol)*.
- `tigetflag`, `tigetnum`, and `tigetstr` correspond to the *termcap* functions `tgetnum`, `tgetflag`, and `tgetstr` described in the section called "termcap functions: termlib".

printcap

termcap was developed in the days when "terminal" did not always mean a display terminal, and the capabilities thus include a number of functions relating to hard copy terminals. Nevertheless, they are not sufficient to describe the properties of modern printers, and BSD systems have developed a parallel system called *printcap*, which is a kind of *termcap* for printers. It is used primarily by the spooling system.

printcap differs from *termcap* in a number of ways:

- The *printcap* capabilities are stored in a file called */etc/printcap*, even in systems where *termcap* is stored in some other directory.
- The syntax of the *printcap* file is identical to the syntax of *termcap*, but the capabilities differ in name and meaning from *termcap* capabilities.
- There is no environment variable corresponding to `TERMCAP`.
- There are no user-accessible routines. The functions used by the spool system actually have the same names as the corresponding *termcap* functions, but they are private to the spooling system. In a BSD source tree, they are located in the file *usr.sbin/lpr/common_source/printcap.c*.

A better way to look at *printcap* is to consider it part of the spooling system, but occasionally you'll need to modify */etc/printcap* for a new printer.

In This Chapter:
- *Terminology*
- *Additional make Features*
- *BSD make*

19

make

Nowadays, only the most trivial UNIX package comes without a *Makefile*, and you can assume that the central part of building just about any package is:

```
$ make
```

We won't go into the details of how *make* works. You can find this information in the Nutshell Handbook *Managing Projects with make*, by Andrew Oram and Steve Talbott. In this chapter, we'll look at the aspects of *make* that differ between implementations. We'll also take a deeper look at BSD *make*, because it is significantly different from other flavors and because very little documentation is available for it.

Terminology

In the course of the evolution of *make* the terminology has changed. Both the old and the new terminology are in current use, which can be confusing at times. In the following list, we'll look at the terms we use in this book and relate them to others that you might encounter:

- A *rule* looks like the following:

  ```
  target: dependencies
     command
     command
  ```

- A *target* is the name by which you invoke a rule. *make* implicitly assumes that you want to create a file of this name.

- The *dependencies* are the files or targets upon which the target *depends*: if any of the dependencies do not exist, if they are newer than the current target file, or if the corresponding target needs to be rebuild, the target is rebuilt (in other words, its commands are executed). Some versions of *make* use the terms *prerequisite* or *source* to represent what we call dependencies.
- The *commands* are single-line shell scripts that get executed in sequence if the target needs to be rebuilt.
- *variables* are environment variables that *make* imports, explicitly named variables, or *implicit variables* such as `$@` and `$<`. Variables used to be called *macros*. They aren't really macros, since they don't take parameters, so the term *variable* is preferable. BSD *make* uses the term *local variable* for implicit variables. As we will see, they don't correspond exactly. SunOS uses the term *dynamic macros* for implicit variables.

Additional make Features

A number of versions of *make* offer additional features beyond those of the version of *make* described in *Managing Projects with make.* In the following sections, we'll look at:

- Internal variables
- Variables with special meanings
- Targets with special meanings
- Including other source files from the *Makefile*
- Conditional execution
- Variations on assignments to variables
- Functions
- Multiple targets

All versions of *make* supply internal variables, but the list differs between individual implementations. We'll defer discussing internal variables until the section called "Variables", later in this chapter.

Variables with Special Meanings

A number of regular variables have taken on special meanings in some versions of *make*. Here's an overview:

- VPATH is a list of directory names to search for files named in dependencies. It is explicitly supported in GNU *make*, where it applies to all file searches, and is also supported, but not documented, in some versions of System V.4. GNU *make* also supports a directive `vpath`.

- `MAKE` is the name with which *make* was invoked. It can be used to invoke subordinate *makes* and has the special property that it will be invoked even if you have specified the *-n* option to *make*. The *-n* indicates that you just want to see the commands that would be executed, and you don't want to execute them.
- In all modern versions of *make*, `MAKEFLAGS` is a list of the flags passed to *make*. *make* takes the value of the environment variable `MAKEFLAGS`, if it exists, and adds the command-line arguments to it. It is automatically passed to subordinate *makes*.
- `SHELL` is the name of a shell to be used to execute commands. Since many versions of *make* execute simple commands directly, you may find that `SHELL` doesn't have any effect unless you include a shell metacharacter like `;`.

The exact semantics of these variables frequently vary from one platform to another—in case of doubt, read your system documentation.

Special Targets

All versions of *make* define a number of targets that have special meanings. Some versions define additional targets:

- `.BEGIN` is a target to be executed before any other target. It is supported by BSD *make*.
- `.INIT` is a target to be executed before any other target. It is supported by SunOS and Solaris *make*.
- `.END` is a target to be executed after all other targets have been executed. It is supported by BSD *make*.
- `.DONE` is a target to be executed after all other targets have been executed. It is supported by SunOS and Solaris *make*.
- `.FAILED` is a target to be executed after all other targets have been executed. It is supported by SunOS and Solaris *make*.
- `.INTERRUPT` is a target to be executed if *make* is interrupted. It is supported by BSD *make*.
- `.MAIN` is the default target to be executed if no target was specified on the command line. If this target is missing, *make* executes the first target in the *Makefile*. It is supported by BSD *make*.

- `.MAKEFLAGS` is an alternate method to supply flags to subordinate *makes*. It is supported by BSD *make*.
- `.PATH` is an alternate method to specify a search path for files not found in the current directory. It is supported by BSD *make*.
- `.MUTEX` is used in System V.4 to synchronize parallel *makes*.
- GNU *make* uses the target `.PHONY` to indicate targets, such as `clean` and `install`, that do not create files. If by chance you have a file *install* in your directory, *make* determines that `make install` does not need to be executed, since *install* is up to date. If you use GNU *make*, you can avoid this problem with:

  ```
  .PHONY: all install clean
  ```

  If you don't have GNU *make*, you can usually solve the problem with

  ```
  all install clean:      .FORCE
          install commands

  .FORCE:
  ```

  In this example, `.FORCE` looks like a special target, as it is meant to. In fact, the name is not important: you simply need a name that doesn't correspond to a real file.

In addition to special targets, BSD *make* also has *special sources* (in other words, special dependencies). We'll look at them in the section called "Special Sources".

include Directive

Many modern *makes* allow you to include other files when processing the *Makefile*. Unfortunately, the syntax is varies greatly:

- In GNU *make*, the syntax is simply `include` *`filename`*.
- In BSD *make*, the syntax is `.include` <*`filename`*> or `.include` *`"filename"`*. The syntax resembles that of the C preprocessor. The first form searches only the system directories, the second form searches the current directory before searching the system directories.
- In SunOS, Solaris, and System V.4 *make*, the syntax is `include` *`filename`*, and the text `include` must be at the beginning of the line.
- SunOS and Solaris *make* automatically include a file *make.rules* in the current directory if it exists. Otherwise, they include the file */usr/share/lib/make/make.rules*.

Conditional Execution

A number of versions of *make* support conditional execution of commands. GNU *make* has commands reminiscent of the C preprocessor:

```
.c.o:
ifeq (${CC},gcc)
        ${CC} -traditional -O3 -g $*.c -c -o $<
else
        ${CC} -O $*.c -c -o $<
endif
```

BSD *make* has a different syntax, which also vaguely resembles the C preprocessor. Apart from standard `.if`, `.else`, and `.endif`, BSD *make* also provides an `.ifdef` directive and additional operators analogous to `#if defined`:

- `.if make (`*variable*`)` checks whether *variable* is a main target of *make* (in other words, if it was mentioned on the command line that invoked *make*).
- `.if empty (`*variable*`)` tests whether *variable* represents the empty string.
- `.if exists (`*variable*`)` tests whether the file *variable* exists.
- `.if target (`*variable*`)` tests whether *variable* represents a defined target.

SunOS and Solaris have so-called *conditional macros*:

```
foo bar baz:=   CC = mycc
```

This tells *make* that the variable (macro) `CC` should be set to `mycc` only when executing the targets `foo`, `bar`, and `baz`.

Other Forms of Variable Assignment

Simply expanded variables

make normally expands variables until no variable references remain in the result. Take the following *Makefile*, for example:

```
CFLAGS = $(INCLUDE) $(OPT)
OPT    = -g -O3
INCLUDE= -I/usr/monkey -I/usr/dbmalloc

all:
        @echo CFLAGS: ${CFLAGS}
```

If you run *make*, you get:

```
$ make
CFLAGS: -I/usr/monkey -I/usr/dbmalloc -g -O3
```

On the other hand, you can't change the definition to:

```
CFLAGS = $(CFLAGS) -I/usr/monkey
```

If you do this, you get:

```
$ make
makefile:7: *** Recursive variable `CFLAGS' references itself (eventually).
Stop.
```

make would loop trying to expand `$(CFLAGS)`. GNU *make* solves this with *simply expanded* variables, which go through one round of expansion only. You specify them with the assignment operator `:=` instead of the usual `=`. For example:

```
CFLAGS = -g -O3
CFLAGS := $(CFLAGS) -I/usr/monkey
```

In this case, `CFLAGS` expands to `-g -O3 -I/usr/monkey`.

define directive

You frequently see multiline shell script fragments in *make* rules. They're ugly and error-prone, because in conventional *make*, you need to put this command sequence on a single line with lots of backslashes and semicolons. GNU *make* offers an alternative with the *define* directive. For example, to check for the existence of a directory and create it if it doesn't exist, you might normally write:

```
${INSTDIR}:
        if [ ! -d $@ ]; then \
          mkdir -p $@; \
        fi
```

With GNU *make*, you can define this as a command:

```
define makedir
if [ ! -d $@ ]; then
  mkdir -p $@
fi
endef
${INSTDIR}:
        ${makedir}
```

Override variable definitions

Conventional versions of *make* have three ways to define a *make* variable. In order of precedence, they are:

1. Define it on the command line used to invoke *make*:

```
$ make CFLAGS="-g -O3"
```

2. Define it in the *Makefile*.
3. Define it in an environment variable. This can be confusing because most shells allow you to write the environment variable on the same line as the invocation of *make*:

   ```
   $ CFLAGS="-g -O3" make
   ```

   This looks almost identical to the first form, but the precedence is lower.

The command-line option has the highest priority. This is usually a good idea, but there are times when you want the declaration in the *Makefile* to take precedence: you want to override the definition on the command line. GNU *make* allows you to specify it with the *override* directive. For example, you might want to insist that the optimization level be limited to *–O2* when you're generating debugging symbols. In GNU *make*, you can write:

```
override CFLAGS=-O2
```

Functions

In addition to supplying variables, GNU *make* supplies built-in *functions*. You call them with the syntax `${function arg,arg,arg}`. These functions are intended for text manipulation and have names like `subst`, `findstring`, `sort`, and such. Unfortunately there is no provision for defining your own functions.

Multiple Targets

All forms of *make* support the concept of *multiple targets*. They come in two flavors:

- *Single-colon targets*, in which the target name is followed by a single colon. Each target of the same name may specify dependencies—this is how *Makefile* dependencies are specified—but only one rule may have commands. If any of the dependencies require the target to be rebuilt, these commands are executed. If you supply commands to more than one rule, the behavior varies: some versions of *make* prints a warning or an error message, and generally they execute only the last rule with commands. Under these circumstances, however, BSD *make* executes the first rule with commands.
- *Double-colon targets* have two colons after the target name. Each of these is independent of the others: each may contain commands, and each gets executed only if the dependencies for that rule require it. Unfortunately, if multiple rules need to be executed, the sequence of execution of the rules is not defined. Most versions of *make* execute them in the sequence in which they appear in the *Makefile*, but it has been reported that some versions of BSD *make* execute in reverse order, which breaks some *Imakefiles*.

BSD make

With the Net/2 release, the Computer Sciences Research Group in Berkeley released a completely new *make* with many novel features. Most BSD-flavored software that has come out in the last few years uses it. Unfortunately, it contains a number of incompatibilities with other *makes*. It is part of the 4.4BSD Lite distribution—see Appendix E for further details. The package includes hard copy documentation, which refers to it as *PMake*, a name that does not occur anywhere else. You may also see the name *bsdmake*.

We've already described some of the trivial differences between BSD *make* and other flavors. In the following sections we'll look at some more significant differences. In the section called "BSD Makefile Configuration System", we'll investigate the BSD *make* features that are designed to make configuration easier.

Additional Rule Delimiter

An additional delimiter is allowed between target and dependency in rules. Apart from the single and double colon, which have the same meaning as they do with other *makes*, there is the exclamation point (`!`) delimiter. This is the same as the single colon delimiter in that the dependencies are the sum of all dependencies for the target and that only the first rule set gets executed. However, the commands are always executed, even if all the dependencies are older than the target.

Assignment Operators

BSD *make* supplies five different types of variable assignment:

- `=` functions as in other versions of *make*: the assignment `CFLAGS = -g` unconditionally sets `CFLAGS` to *–g*.
- `+=` adds to a definition. If `CFLAGS` is set as shown in the previous example, writing `CFLAGS += -O3` results in a new value *–g -O3*.
- `?=` assigns a value only if the variable is currently undefined. This assignment can be used to set default values.
- `:=` assigns and expands immediately. This is the same as the GNU *make* `:=` assignment.
- `!=` expands the value and passes it to a shell for execution. The result from the shell is assigned to the variable after changing newline characters to spaces.

Variables

BSD *make* has clarified the definitions of variables somewhat. Although nothing is really new in this area, the terminology is arranged in a more understandable manner. It defines four different kinds of variables, the first three of which correspond to the kinds of variable assignment in other *makes*. In order of priority, they are:

- Environment variables
- *Global* variables (called *variables* in other flavors of *make*)
- Command-line variables
- *Local variables*, which correspond roughly to implicit variables in other *makes*

BSD *make* allows the use of the implicit variable symbols (`$@` and friends) but doesn't recommend it. Since they don't match other versions of *make* very well anyway, it makes sense not to use them. Local variables are really variables that *make* predefines. Table 19-1 compares them to traditional *make* variables:

Table 19–1: make Local Variables

Traditional	BSD	Meaning
	`.ALLSRC, $>`	The list of all dependencies ("sources") for this target.
		(GNU *make*) The list of all dependencies of the current target. Only the member name is returned for dependencies that represent an archive member. Otherwise, this is the same as BSD `.ALLSRC`.
`$@`	`.ARCHIVE`	The name of the current target. If the target is an archive file member, the name of the archive file.
`$$@`	`.TARGET, $@`	The complete name of the current target, even if it represents an archive file.[a]
`$<`		The name of the current dependency that has been modified more recently than the target. Traditionally, it can be used only in suffix rules and in the `.DEFAULT` entry, but most modern versions of *make* (except BSD *make*) allow it to be used in normal rules as well.
	`.IMPSRC, $<`	The *implied source*—in other words, the name of the source file (dependency) implied in an implicit rule.
`$%`	`.MEMBER`	The name of an archive member. For example, if the target name is *libfoo.a(bar.o)*, `$@` evaluates to *libfoo.a* and `$%` evaluates to *bar.o*. This variable is supported by GNU, SunOS, and System V.4 *make*.
`$?`	`.OODATE, $?`	The dependencies for this target that were newer than the target.[b]

Table 19-1: make Local Variables (continued)

Traditional	BSD	Meaning
`$*`		The raw name of the current dependency, without suffix, but possibly including directory components. This variable can be used only in suffix rules.
`${*F}`	`.PREFIX, $*`	The raw filename of the current dependency. It does not contain any directory component.
`${*D}`		The directory name of the current dependency. For example, if `$@` evaluates to `foo/bar.o`, `${@D}` evaluates to `foo`. Supported by GNU, SunOS, and System V.4 *make*.
	`.CURDIR`	The name of the directory in which the top-level *make* was started.

[a] `$@` can be used only to the right of the colon in a dependency line. Supported by SunOS and System V.4 *make*.
[b] Confusingly, BSD *make* refers to these dependencies as *out of date*, thus the name of the variable.

Variable Substitution

In BSD *make*, variable substitution has reached a new level of complexity. All versions of *make* support the syntax `${SRC:.c=.o}`, which replaces a list of names of the form `foo.c bar.c baz.c` with M`foo.o bar.o baz.o`.. BSD *make* generalizes this syntax into `${variable[:modifier[:...]]}`. In the following discussion, BSD *make* uses the term *word* where we would usually use the term *parameter*. In particular, a filename is a word. *modifier* is an uppercase letter:

- `E` replaces each word in the variable with its suffix.
- According to the documentation, `H` strips the "last component" from each "word" in the variable. A better definition is: it returns the directory name of each filename. If the original filename didn't have a directory name, the result is set to `.` (current directory).
- `M`*`pattern`* selects those words from the variable that match *pattern*. *pattern* is a *globbing pattern* like that used by shells to specify wildcard filenames.
- `N`*`pattern`* selects those words from the variable that *don't* match *pattern*.
- `R` replaces each word in the variable with everything but its suffix.
- `S/`*`old`*`/`*`new`*`/` replaces the first occurrence of the text *`old`* with *`new`*. The form `S/`*`old`*`/`*`new`*`/g` replaces all occurrences.
- `T` replaces each word in the variable with its "last component," in other words with the filename part.

This is heavy going, and it's already more than the documentation tells you. The following example shows a number of the features:

```
SRCS = foo.c bar.c baz.cc zot.pas glarp.f src/mumble.c util/grunt.f
LANGS = ${SRCS:E}
DIRS = ${SRCS:H}
OBJS = ${SRCS:T}
CSRCS = ${SRCS:M*.c}
PASSRCS = ${SRCS:M*.pas}
FSRCS = ${SRCS:M*.f}
PROGS = ${SRCS:R}
PROFS  = ${CSRCS:S/./_p./g:.c=.o}

all:
        @echo Languages: ${LANGS}
        @echo Objects: ${OBJS}
        @echo Directories: ${DIRS}
        @echo C sources: ${CSRCS}
        @echo Pascal sources: ${PASSRCS}
        @echo Fortran sources: ${FSRCS}
        @echo Programs: ${PROGS}
        @echo Profiled objects: ${PROFS}
```

If you run it, you get:

```
$ make
Languages: c c cc pas f c f
Objects: foo.c bar.c baz.cc zot.pas glarp.f mumble.c grunt.f
Directories: . . . . . src util
C sources: foo.c bar.c src/mumble.c
Pascal sources: zot.pas
Fortran sources: glarp.f util/grunt.f
Programs: foo bar baz zot glarp src/mumble util/grunt
Profiled objects: foo_p.o bar_p.o src/mumble_p.o
```

Special Sources

In addition to special targets, BSD *make* includes *special sources* (recall that *source* is the word that it uses for dependencies). Here are the more important special sources:

- `.IGNORE`, `.SILENT`, and `.PRECIOUS` have the same meaning as the corresponding special targets in other versions of *make*.
- `.MAKE` causes the associated dependencies to be executed even when the options *-n* (just list commands, don't perform them) or *-t* (just update timestamps, don't perform *make*) are specified. This enables *make* to perform subsidiary *makes* even when these options are specified. If this seems a strange thing to want to do, considering that the result of the main *make* could

depend on subsidiary *makes* to such an extent that it would not even make sense to run *make -n* if the subsidiary *makes* did not run correctly—for example, if the subsidiary *make* were a *make depend*.

- `.OPTIONAL` tells *make* that the specified dependencies are not crucial to the success of the build, and that *make* should assume success if it can't figure out how to build the target.

Specifying Dependencies

We have seen that the bulk of a well-written *Makefile* can consist of dependencies. BSD *make* offers the alternative of storing these files in a separate file called *.depend*. This avoids the problem of different flavors of *makedepend* missing the start of the dependencies and adding them again.

BSD Makefile Configuration System

One of the intentions of BSD *make* is to facilitate configuration. The *Makefiles* for *gcc* illustrate the difference that BSD *make* makes. In its entirety, the top-level *Makefile* is:

```
SUBDIR= cc cpp lib cc1 libgcc cc1plus cc1obj #libobjc
.include <bsd.subdir.mk>
```

The complete *Makefile* in the subdirectory *cc1* (the main pass of the compiler) reads:

```
#       @(#)Makefile    6.2 (Berkeley) 2/2/91

PROG=    gcc1
BINDIR=  /usr/libexec
SRCS=    c-parse.c c-lang.c  c-lex.c c-pragma.c  \
         c-decl.c c-typeck.c c-convert.c c-aux-info.c \
         c-iterate.c

CFLAGS+= -I. -I$(.CURDIR) -I$(.CURDIR)/../lib
YFLAGS=
NOMAN=   noman

.if exists(${.CURDIR}/../lib/obj)
LDADD=  -L${.CURDIR}/../lib/obj -lgcc2
DPADD=  ${.CURDIR}/../lib/obj/libgcc2.a
.else
LDADD=  -L${.CURDIR}/../lib/ -lgcc2
DPADD=  ${.CURDIR}/../lib/libgcc2.a
.endif
```

```
LDADD+= -lgnumalloc
DPADD+= ${LIBGNUMALLOC}

.include <bsd.prog.mk>
```

The standard release *Makefile* for *gcc* is about 2500 lines. Clearly, a lot of work has been devoted to getting the BSD *Makefiles* so small. The clue is the last line of each *Makefile*:

```
.include <bsd.subdir.mk>
```

Or:

```
.include <bsd.prog.mk>
```

These files are supplied with the system and define the hardware and software used on the system. They are usually located in */usr/share/mk*, and you can modify them to suit your local preferences.

This configuration mechanism has little connection with the new BSD *make*. It could equally well have been done, for example, with GNU *make* or System V *make*. Unfortunately, the significant incompatibilities between BSD *make* and the others mean that you can't just take the configuration files and use them with other flavors of *make*.

The BSD system places some constraints on the *Makefile* structure. To get the best out of it, you may need to completely restructure your source tree. To quote the *bsd.README*:

> It's fairly difficult to make the BSD .mk files work when you're building multiple programs in a single directory. It's a lot easier [to] split up the programs than to deal with the problem. Most of the agony comes from making the "obj" directory stuff work right, not because we switch to a new version of *make*. So, don't get mad at us, figure out a better way to handle multiple architectures so we can quit using the symbolic link stuff.

On the other hand, it's remarkably easy to use the BSD *make* configuration once you get used to it. It's a pity that the *make* itself is so incompatible with other *makes*: although the system works well, it's usually not worth restructuring your trees and rewriting your *Makefiles* to take advantage of it.

Note a couple of other points about the configuration method:

- *make depend* is supported via an auxiliary file *.depend*, which *make* reads after reading the *Makefile*.

- The configuration files are included at the *end* of the *Makefile*, which is due to the way that BSD *make* works. Unlike other *makes*, if multiple targets with a single colon exist, only the first is executed, but if multiple declarations of the same variable exist, only the last takes effect.

The configuration files consist of one file, *sys.mk*, which *make* automatically reads before doing anything else, and a number of other files, one of which is usually included as the last line in a *Makefile*. These are usually:

- *bsd.prog.mk* for a *Makefile* to make an executable binary.
- *bsd.lib.mk* for a *Makefile* to make a library.
- *bsd.subdir.mk* to make binaries or libraries in subdirectories of the current directory.

In addition, another file, *bsd.doc.mk*, is supplied to make hard copy documentation. In keeping with the Cinderella nature of documentation, no other file refers to it. If you want to use it, you include it *in addition* to one of the other three. This file is required only for hard copy documentation, not for man pages, which *are* installed by the other targets.

sys.mk

sys.mk contains global definitions for all *makes*. *make* reads it in before looking for any *Makefiles*. The documentation states that it is not intended to be modified, but since it contains default names for all tools, as well as default rules for *makes*, there is every reason to believe that you *will* want to change this file. There's no provision to override these definitions anywhere else. How you handle this dilemma is your choice. I personally prefer to change *sys.mk* (and put up with having to update it when a new release comes), but you could create another file *bsd.own.mk*, like FreeBSD does, and put your personal choices in there. The last line of the FreeBSD *sys.mk* is:

```
.include <bsd.own.mk>
```

With this method you can override the definitions in *sys.mk* with the definitions in *bsd.own.mk*. It's up to you to decide whether this solution is better.

bsd.prog.mk

bsd.prog.mk contains definitions for building programs. Table 19-2 lists the targets that it defines.

Table 19-2: bsd.prog.mk Targets

Target	Purpose
`all`	Build the single program `${PROG}`, which is defined in the *Makefile*.
`clean`	Remove `${PROG}`; any object files; and the files *a.out*, *Errs*, *errs*, *mklog*, and *core*.
`cleandir`	Remove all of the files removed by the target `clean` and also the files *.depend*, *tags*, *obj*, and any manual pages.
`depend`	*make* the dependencies for the source files, and store them in the file *.depend*.
`install`	Install the program and its manual pages. If the *Makefile* does not itself define the target `install`, the targets `beforeinstall` and `afterinstall` may also be used to cause actions immediately before and after the `install` target is executed.
`lint`	Run *lint* on the source files.
`tags`	Create a *tags* file for the source files.

In addition, *bsd.prog.mk* supplies default definitions for the variables listed in Table 19-3. The operator `?=` is used to ensure that they are not redefined if they are already defined in the *Makefile*. (See the section called "Assignment Operators" for more details about the `?=` operator.)

Table 19-3: Variables Defined in bsd.prog.mk

Variable	Purpose
`BINGRP`	Group ownership for binaries. Defaults to *bin*.
`BINOWN`	Owner for binaries. Defaults to *bin*.
`BINMODE`	Permissions for binaries. Defaults to 555 (read and execute permission for everybody).
`CLEANFILES`	Additional files that the `clean` and `cleandir` targets should remove. *bsd.prog.mk* does not define this variable, but it adds the file *strings* to the list if the variable `SHAREDSTRINGS` is defined.
`DPADD`	Additional library dependencies for the target `${PROG}`. For example, if you write `DPADD=${LIBCOMPAT} ${LIBUTIL}` in your *Makefile*, the target depends on the compatibility and utility libraries.
`DPSRCS`	Dependent sources—a list of source files that must exist before compiling the program source files. Usually for building a configuration file that is required by all sources. Not all systems define this variable.
`LIBC`	The C library. Defaults to */lib/libc.a*.
`LIBCOMPAT`	The 4.3BSD compatibility library. Defaults to */usr/lib/libcompat.a*.
`LIBCURSES`	The *curses* library. Defaults to */usr/lib/libcurses.a*.

Table 19-3: Variables Defined in bsd.prog.mk (continued)

Variable	Purpose
LIBCRYPT	The *crypt* library. Defaults to */usr/lib/libcrypt.a.*
LIBDBM	The *dbm* library. Defaults to */usr/lib/libdbm.a.*
LIBDES	The *des* library. Defaults to */usr/lib/libdes.a.*
LIBL	The *lex* library. Defaults to */usr/lib/libl.a.*
LIBKDB	Defaults to */usr/lib/libkdb.a.*
LIBKRB	Defaults to */usr/lib/libkrb.a.*
LIBM	The math library. Defaults to */usr/lib/libm.a.*
LIBMP	Defaults to */usr/lib/libmp.a.*
LIBPC	Defaults to */usr/lib/libpc.a.*
LIBPLOT	Defaults to */usr/lib/libplot.a.*
LIBTELNET	Defaults to */usr/lib/libtelnet.a.*
LIBTERM	Defaults to */usr/lib/libterm.a.*
LIBUTIL	Defaults to */usr/lib/libutil.a.*
SRCS	List of source files to build the program. Defaults to `${PROG}.c`.
STRIP	If defined, this should be the flag passed to the install program to cause the binary to be stripped. It defaults to *-s.*

The variables in Table 19-4 are not defined in *bsd.prog.mk* but are used if they have been defined elsewhere.

Table 19-4: Variables used by bsd.prog.mk

Variable	Purpose
COPTS	Additional flags to supply to the compiler when compiling C object files.
HIDEGAME	If defined, the binary is installed in */usr/games/hide*, and a symbolic link is created to */usr/games/dm.*
LDADD	Additional loader objects. Usually used for libraries.
LDFLAGS	Additional loader flags.
LINKS	A list of pairs of filenames to be linked together. For example, `LINKS=${DESTDIR}/bin/test${DESTDIR}/bin/[` links */bin/test* to */bin/[.*
NOMAN	If set, *make* does not try to install man pages. This variable is defined only in *bsd.prog.mk* and not in *bsd.lib.mk* or *bsd.man.mk.*
PROG	The name of the program to build. If not supplied, nothing is built.
SRCS	List of source files to build the program. If SRC is not defined, it's assumed to be `${PROG}.c`.

Table 19-4: Variables used by bsd.prog.mk (continued)

Variable	Purpose
SHAREDSTRINGS	If defined, the *Makefile* defines a new `.c.o` rule that uses *xstr* to create shared strings.
SUBDIR	A list of subdirectories that should be built as well as the targets in the main directory. Each target in the main *Makefile* executes the same target in the subdirectories. Note that the name in this file is SUBDIR, though it has the same function as the variable SUBDIRS in *bsd.subdir.mk*.

If the file *../Makefile.inc* exists, it is included before the other definitions. This is one possibility for specifying site preferences, but of course it makes assumptions about the source tree structure, so it's not completely general.

The file *bsd.man.mk* is included unless the variable NOMAN is defined. We'll take another look at *bsd.man.mk* in the section called "bsd.man.mk".

bsd.lib.mk

bsd.lib.mk contains definitions for making library files. It supplies the same targets as *bsd.prog.mk* but defines or uses a much more limited number of variables.

Table 19-5: Variables Defined or Used in bsd.lib.mk

Variable	Purpose
LDADD	Additional loader objects.
LIB	The name of the library to build. The name is in the same form that you find in the *-l* option to the C compiler—if you want to build *libfoo.a*, you set `LIB` to `foo`.
LIBDIR	Target installation directory for libraries. Defaults to */usr/lib*.
LIBGRP	Library group owner. Defaults to *bin*.
LIBOWN	Library owner. Defaults to *bin*.
LIBMODE	Library mode. Defaults to 444 (read access for everybody).
LINTLIBDIR	Target directory for lint libraries. Defaults to */usr/libdata/lint*.
NOPROFILE	If set, only standard libraries are built. Otherwise (the default), both standard libraries (*libfoo.a*) and profiling libraries (*libfoo_p.a*) are built.[a]
SRCS	List of source files to build the library. Unlike in *bsd.prog.mk*, there is no default value.

[a] A *profiling library* is a library that contains additional code to aid profilers, programs that analyze the CPU usage of the program. We don't cover profiling in this book.

Given the choice of compiling *foo.s* or *foo.c*, *bsd.lib.mk* chooses *foo.s*. Like *bsd.prog.mk*, it includes *bsd.man.mk*. Unlike *bsd.prog.mk*, it does this even if NOMAN is defined.

bsd.subdir.mk

bsd.subdir.mk contains definitions for making files in subdirectories. Since only a single program target can be made per directory, BSD-style directory trees tend to have more branches than others, and each program is placed in its own subdirectory. For example, if I have three programs *foo*, *bar*, and *baz*, I might normally write a *Makefile* with the following rule:

```
all:    foo bar baz

foo:    foo.c foobar.h conf.h

bar:    bar.c foobar.h zot.h conf.h

baz:    baz.c baz.h zot.h conf.h
```

As we have seen, this is not easy to do with the BSD configuration scheme. Instead, you might place all the files necessary to build *foo* in the subdirectory *foo*, and so on. You could then write:

```
SUBDIRS = foo bar baz
.include <bsd.subdir.mk>
```

foo/Makefile could then contain:

```
PROG  = foo
DPADD = foo.c foobar.h conf.h
.include <bsd.prog.mk>
```

The *Makefiles* for *bar* and *baz* are similar now.

bsd.subdir.mk is structured in the same way as *bsd.prog.mk*. Use *bsd.prog.mk* for making files in the same directory and *bsd.subdir.mk* for making files in subdirectories. If you want to do both, use *bsd.prog.mk* and define SUBDIR instead of SUBDIRS.

bsd.man.mk

bsd.man.mk contains definitions for installing man pages. It is included from *bsd.prog.mk* and *bsd.lib.mk*, so the target and variables are available from both of these files as well. It defines the target maninstall, which installs the man pages and their links, and uses or defines the variables described in Table 19-6.

Table 19-6: Variables Defined or Used by bsd.man.mk

Variable	Meaning
MANDIR	The base path of the installed man pages. Defaults to */usr/share/man/cat*. The section number is appended directly to MANDIR, so that a man page *foo.3* would be installed in */usr/share/man/cat3/foo.3*.
MANGRP	The group that owns the man pages. Defaults to *bin*.
MANOWN	The owner of the man pages. Defaults to *bin*.
MANMODE	The permissions of the installed man pages. Defaults to 444 (read permission for anybody).
MANSUBDIR	The subdirectory into which to install machine-specific man pages. For example, i386 specific pages might be installed under */usr/share/man/cat4/i386*. In this case, MANSUBDIR would be set to /i386.
MANn	(n has the values 1 to 8). Manual page names, which should end in .[1-8]. If no MANn variable is defined, MAN1=${PROG}.1 is assumed.
MLINKS	A list of pairs of names for manual page links. The first filename in a pair must exist, and it is linked to the second name in the pair.

bsd.own.mk

Not all variants of the BSD configuration system use *bsd.own.mk*. Where it is supplied, it contains default permissions and may be used to override definitions in *sys.mk*, which *include*s it.

bsd.doc.mk

bsd.doc.mk contains definitions for formatting hard copy documentation files. It varies significantly between versions and omits even the obvious, such as formatting the document. It does, however, define the variables in Table 19-7, which can be of use in your own *Makefile*.

Table 19-7: Variables Defined in bsd.doc.mk

Variable	Meaning
PRINTER	Not a printer name at all, but an indicator of the kind of output format to be used. This is the argument to the *troff* option *-T*. Defaults to ps (PostScript output).
BIB	The name of the *bib* processor. Defaults to bib.
COMPAT	Compatibility mode option for *groff* when formatting documents with Berkeley me macros. Defaults to *-C*.
EQN	How to invoke the *eqn* processor. Defaults to eqn -T${PRINTER}.
GREMLIN	The name of the *gremlin* processor. Defaults to grn.

Table 19-7: Variables Defined in bsd.doc.mk (continued)

Variable	Meaning
`GRIND`	The name of the *vgrind* processor. Defaults to `vgrind -f`.
`INDXBIB`	Name of the *indxbib* processor. Defaults to `indxbib`.
`PAGES`	Specification of the page range to output. Defaults to `1-`.
`PIC`	Name of the *pic* processor. Defaults to `pic`.
`REFER`	Name of the *refer* processor. Defaults to `refer`.

In This Chapter:

20

Compilers

The central tool in building software is the compiler. In UNIX, the compiler is really a collection of programs that compile sources written in the C language. In this chapter, we'll consider the following topics:

- The way the C language has evolved since its introduction, and some of the problems that this evolution has caused.
- C++, an evolution of C.
- The way the compiler is organized.
- How to use the individual parts of the compiler separately—in particular, the assembler and the linker.

We'll defer how the assembler and the linker work until the next chapter—to understand them, we first need to look at object files in more detail.

There are, of course, lots of other languages besides C, but on a UNIX platform C is the most important. Even if you use another language, some of the information in this chapter will be of use to you because many other languages output C source code.

The C Language

The C language has evolved a lot since its appearance in the early '70s. It started life as a Real Man's language: cryptic, small, tolerant of obscenities almost to the point of encouraging them. Now it has passed through countless committees, put on weight, and become somewhat sedate, pedantic, and much less tolerant. Along with these changes, it has developed a lot of idiosyncracies that plague the life of the portable software writer. First, let's take a look at the flavors that are commonly available.

Kernighan and Ritchie

Kernighan and Ritchie or *K&R* is the name given to the dialect of C described in the first edition of *The C Programming Language*, by Brian Kernighan and Dennis Ritchie. This book was the first to describe the C language and has become something of a bible. In 1988, a second edition appeared, which describes an early version of ANSI C, *not* K&R C.

The K&R dialect is now completely obsolete, though many older versions of UNIX C resemble it. Compared to ANSI C (also called *Standard C*), it lacks a number of features and has a few incompatibilities. In particular, strings were always allocated separately for each instance, and so could be modified if desired. For example, you could encounter code like this:

```
complain (msg)
char *msg;
{
  char *message = "Nothing to complain about\n";
  if (msg)                      /* parameter supplied? */
    strcpy (message, msg);      /* yes, save in message */
  puts (message);               /* say what we have to say */
  }
```

When the parameter `msg` is non-`NULL`, it is copied into the string `message`. If you call this function with a `NULL` message, it displays the last message again. For example:

```
complain (NULL);            prints Nothing to complain about
complain ("Bad style");     prints Bad style
complain (NULL);            prints Bad style
```

This may fail with modern C compilers. The ANSI Standard says that string constants are not writable, but real-world compilers differ in the way they handle this situation.

UNIX C

A period of over ten years elapsed between the publication of K&R and the final adoption of the ANSI C Standard. During this time, the language didn't stand still, but there was no effective standards document beyond K&R. The resultant evolution in the UNIX environment is based on the portable C compiler first described in the paper "Portability of C Programs and the UNIX System," published by S.C. Johnson and Dennis Ritchie in 1978, and is frequently referred to as "UNIX C." UNIX C is not a standard or even a series of standards—it's better to consider it a set of marginally compatible extensions to K&R C. You can find more information in *The Evolution of C—Past and Future*, by L. Rosler, but you can't rely on the degree to which your particular compiler (or the one for which your software package was written) agrees with that description. From a present-day standpoint, it's enough to know that these extensions exist, and otherwise treat the compilers like K&R. In case of doubt, the documentation that comes with the compiler is about the only even remotely reliable help.

The following is a brief summary of what had changed by the time *The Evolution of C—Past and Future* appeared:

- Optional function prototyping similar to that of ANSI C was introduced. One difference exists: if a function accepts a variable number of parameters, UNIX C uses the form:

  ```
  int printf (char *format, );
  ```

  whereas ANSI C uses the form:

  ```
  int printf (char *format, ...);
  ```

- The `enum` type specifies a way to define classes of constants. For example, traditionally I could write:

  ```
  #define RED 0
  #define GREEN 1
  #define BLUE 2

  int colour;
  int x;
  colour = BLUE;
  x = RED;
  ```

  With `enums`, I can write:

  ```
  enum colours {red, green, blue};
  enum texture {rough, smooth, slimy};

  enum colours colour;
  enum texture x;
  colour = blue;
  x = red;
  ```

  This syntax is intended to make error checking easier. As you can see in the second example, something seems to be wrong with the assignment to `x`, which was not evident in the K&R example. The compiler can see it, too, and should complain, although many modern compilers compile the second program without any comment. In addition, the symbols are visible to the compiler, which means that the debugger can use them as well. Preprocessor macros never make it to the code generation pass of the compiler, so the debugger doesn't know about them. The keyword `const` was added to specify that a variable may not be changed in the course of program execution.

- The preprocessor directive `#elif` was added.
- The preprocessor pseudofunction `defined (`*`identifier`*`)` was added.
- The data type `void` was added.

ANSI C

In 1989, the C programming language was finally standardized by the American National Standards Institute (ANSI) as standard X3.159-1989. In the following year, it was adopted by the International Standards organization (ISO) as standard ISO/IEC 9899:1990. There are minor textual differences in the two standards, but the language defined is the same. The existence of two standards causes a certain amount of confusion: some people call it ANSI C, some call it Standard C, and I suppose you could call it ISO C, though I haven't heard that name. I call it ANSI C because the name is more specific: the word "Standard" doesn't indicate which standard you're referring to.

The following discussion is intended to show the differences between ANSI C and older versions. It's not intended to teach you ANSI C—see *Practical C Programming*, by Steve Oualline, and the *POSIX Programmer's Guide*, by Donald A. Lewine for that information.

ANSI C introduced a large number of changes, many of them designed to help the compiler detect program errors. You can find a reasonably complete list in Appendix C of K&R. Here are the most important changes that affect the porting of software:

- A number of changes have been made in the preprocessor. We'll look at these in the section called "Differences in the ANSI C Preprocessor".
- The keywords `void`, `signed`, and `const` were adopted from the portable C compiler.
- The keyword `volatile` was added to tell an optimizer not to assume that the value of the variable will stay the same from one reference to another. Variables normally stay unchanged unless you execute an explicit assignment

statement or call a function, and most optimizers rely on this behavior. This assumption may not hold true if a signal interrupts the normal course of execution, or if you are sharing the memory with another process. If the value of a variable might change without your influence, you should declare the variable `volatile` so that the optimizer can handle it correctly. We saw an example of this kind of problem in the section called "setjmp and longjmp" in Chapter 1, *Signals*.

- You can state the type of numeric constants explicitly: for example, you can write a long constant 0 as `0L`, and a double 0 would be `0D`.
- Implicit string literal concatenation is allowed—the following two lines are completely equivalent:

```
"first string"  "second string"
"first stringsecond string"
```

  K&R C allows only the second form.

- `void` pointers are allowed. Previous versions of C allowed the type `void`, but not pointers to objects of that type. You use a `void` pointer to indicate that the object you are pointing to is of indeterminate type. Before you can use the data, you need to cast it to a specific data type.
- In strict ANSI C, you must declare or define functions before you call them. You use a function *declaration* to tell the compiler that the function exists, what parameters it takes, and what value (if any) it returns. A function *definition* is the code for the function and includes the declaration. Strict ANSI C function definitions and declarations include *function protyping*, which specifies the nature of each parameter, though most implementations allow old-style definitions. Consider the following function definition in K&R C:

```
foobar (a, b, c, d)
char *c;
struct baz *a;
{
body
}
```

  This definition does not specify the return type of the function; it may or may not return `int`. The types of two of the parameters are specified, the others default to `int`. The parameter type specifiers are not in the order of the declaration. In ANSI C, this would become:

```
void foobar (struct baz *a, int b, char *c, int d)
{
body
}
```

This definition states all types explicitly, so we can see that foobar does not, in fact, return any value.

- The same syntax can also be used to declare the function, though you can also abbreviate it to:

```
void foobar (struct baz *, int, char, int);
```

This helps catch one of the most insidious program bugs. Consider the following code, which is perfectly legal K&R:

```
extern foobar ();        /* define foobar without parameters */
int a, b;                /* two integers */
struct baz *c;           /* and a struct baz */

foobar (a, b, c);        /* call foobar (int, int, struct baz *) */
```

In this example, I have supplied the parameters to foobar in the wrong sequence: the struct baz pointer is the first parameter, not the third. In all likelihood, foobar will try to modify the struct baz and will use the value of a—possibly a small integer—to do this. If I call foobar without parameters, the compiler won't notice, but by the time I get my almost inevitable segmentation violation, foobar will probably have overwritten the stack and removed all evidence of how the problem occurred.

Differences in the ANSI C Preprocessor

At first sight, the C preprocessor doesn't seem to have changed between K&R C and ANSI C. This is intentional: for the casual user, everything is the same. When you scratch the surface, however, you discover a number of differences. The following list reflects the logical sequence in which the preprocessor processes its input:

- A method called *trigraphs* represents characters not found in the native character set of some European countries. The character sequences in Table 20-1 are considered identical.

Table 20-1: ANSI C Trigraphs

Character	Trigraph
#	??=
[	??(
\	??/
]	??)
^	??'
{	??>

Table 20-1: ANSI C Trigraphs (continued)

Character	Trigraph
|	??!
}	??>
~	??-

To illustrate, let's look at a possibly barely recognizable program:

```
??=include <unistd.h>
main ()
  ??<
  printf ("Hello, world??/n");
  ??>
```

Not surprisingly, most programmers hate trigraphs. To quote the *gcc* manual: "You don't want to know about this brain-damage." Many C compilers, including the GNU C compiler, give you the opportunity to turn off support for trigraphs, since they can bite you when you're not expecting them.

- Any line may end with a backslash, indicating that it should be *spliced.* In other words, the preprocessor removes the backslash character and the following newline character and joins the line to the following line. K&R C performed line splicing only during the definition of preprocessor macros, which can be dangerous. Trailing blanks can nullify the meaning of the backslash character, and it's easy to oversee one when deleting lines that follow it.
- Unlike UNIX C, formal macro parameters in strings are not replaced by the actual parameters. In order to be able to create a string that includes an actual parameter, the operator # was introduced. A formal parameter preceded by a # is replaced by the actual parameter surrounded by string quotes.

```
#define foo(x)  open (#x)
foo (/usr/lib/libc.a);
```

Thus, you can replace the previous code with the following:

```
open ("/usr/lib/libc.a");
```

In many traditional versions of C, you could have got the same effect from:

```
#define foo(x)  open ("x")
foo (/usr/lib/libc.a);
```

- In K&R C, problems frequently arose when concatenating two parameters. Since both parameter names are valid identifiers, you can't just write one after the other, because that would create a new valid identifer, and nothing would be substituted. For example, consider the X11 macro `Concat`, which joins two names together to create a complete pathname from a directory and a filename:

```
Concat(dir, file);
```

I obviously can't just write the following:

```
#define Concat(dir, file) dirfile
```

That will always just give me the text `dirfile`, which isn't much use. The solution that the X Consortium used for K&R C was:

```
#define Concat(dir,file)dir/**/file
```

This relies on the fact that most C compilers derived from the portable C compiler simply remove comments and replace them with nothing. This works most of the time, but the standard has no basis for it, and some compilers replace the sequence `/**/` with a blank, which breaks the mechanism. ANSI C introduced the operator `##` to address this problem. `##` removes itself and any white space (blanks or tab characters) to either side. For ANSI C, *Imake.tmpl* defines `Concat` as:

```
#define Concat(dir,file)dir##file
```

- The `#include` directive now allows the use of preprocessor directives as an argument. *imake* uses this to `#include` the *<vendor>.cf* file.
- Conditional compilation now includes the `#elif` directive, which significantly simplifies nested conditional compilation. In addition, a number of logical operators are available: `||` and `&&` have the same meaning as in C, and the operator `defined` checks whether its operand is defined. This allows code like:

  ```
  #if defined BSD || defined SVR4 || defined ULTRIX
  foo
  #elif defined SVR3
  bar
  #endif
  ```

  If you want, you can surround the operand of `defined` with parentheses, but you don't need to.
- The use of the preprocessor directive `#line`, which had existed in previous versions of C, was formalized. `#line` supports preprocessors that output C code. `#line` tells the compiler to reset the internal line number and filename used for error reporting purposes to the specified values. In the following example, the file *bar.c* contains just:

```
#line 264 "foo.c"
slipup!
```

the compiler would report the error like this:

```
$ gcc -O bar.c -o bar
foo.c:264: parse error before `!'
gnumake: *** [bar] Error 1
```

Although the error was really detected on line 2 of *bar.c*, the compiler reports the error as if it had occurred on line 264 of *foo.c*.

- The line *slipup!* suggests that it is present to draw attention to an error. This is a fairly common technique, though it's obviously just a kludge, especially as the error message requires you to look at the source to figure out what the problem is. ANSI C introduced another directive to do the Right Thing. Instead of `slipup!`, I can enter:

  ```
  #error Have not finished writing this thing yet
  ```

  This produces (from *gcc*):

  ```
  $ make bar
  gcc -O bar.c -o bar
  foo.c:270: #error Have not finished writing this thing yet
  gnumake: *** [bar] Error 1
  ```

  I couldn't write `Haven't`, because that causes *gcc* to look for a matching apostrophe (`'`). Since there isn't one, it would die with a less obvious message, whether or not an error really occurred.

- To quote the Standard:

  > A preprocessor line of the form **# pragma** *token-sequence*$_{opt}$ causes the processor to perform an implementation-dependent action. An unrecognized pragma is ignored.

  This is not a Good Thing. Implementation-dependent actions are the enemy of portable software, and about the only redeeming fact is that the compiler ignores an unrecognized pragma. Since almost nobody uses this feature, you can hope that your compiler will, indeed, ignore any pragmas it finds.

Assertions

Assertions provide an alternative form of preprocessor conditional expression. They are specified in the form:

```
#assert question (answer)
```

In the terminology of the documentation, this *asserts* (states) that the answer to *question* is *answer.* You can test it with the construct:

```
#if #question(answer)
...
#endif
```

The code between `#if` and `#endif` is compiled if the answer to `question` is `answer`. An alternative way to use this facility is in combination with the compiler directive *–Aquestion(answer).* This method is intended for internal use by the compiler: typically, it tells the compiler the software and platform on which it is running. For example, compiling *bar.c* on UnixWare 1.0 with *gcc* and the *–v* option reveals:

```
/usr/local/lib/gcc-lib/i386-univel-sysv4.2/2.4.5/cpp \
-lang-c -v -undef -D__GNUC__=2 -Di386 -Dunix -D__svr4__ \
-D__i386__ -D__unix__ -D__svr4__ -D__i386 -D__unix \
-D__svr4__ -Asystem(unix) -Acpu(i386)  -Amachine(i386) \
bar.c /usr/tmp/cca000N1.i
```

The *–A* options passed by *gcc* to the preprocessor specify that this is a `unix` system and that the cpu and machine are both `i386`. It would be helpful if this information stated that the operating system was `svr4`, but unfortunately this is not the default for System V.4. *gcc* has also retrofitted it to System V.3, where the assertion is *–Asystem(svr3),* which makes more sense, and to BSD systems, in which the assertion is *–Asystem(bsd).*

C++

C++ is an object-oriented evolution of C that started in the early '80s, long before the ANSI C standard evolved. It is almost completely upwardly compatible with ANSI C, to a large extent because ANSI C borrowed heavily from C++, so we don't run much danger by considering it the next evolutionary step beyond ANSI C.

The last thing I want to do here is explain the differences between ANSI C and C++: *The Annotated C++ Reference Manual,* by Margaret A. Ellis and Bjarne Stroustrup, spends nearly 450 very carefully written pages defining the language and drawing attention to its peculiarities. From our point of view, there is not too much to say about C++.

One of the more popular C++ translators is AT&T's *cfront,* which, as the name suggests, is a front-end preprocessor that generates C program code as its output. Although this does not make the generated code any worse, it does make debugging much more difficult.

Since C++ is almost completely upwards compatible from ANSI C, a C++ compiler can usually compile ANSI C. This assumes well-formed ANSI C programs: most ANSI C compilers accept a number of anachronisms either with or without warnings—for example, K&R-style function definitions. The same anachronisms are no longer part of the C++ language and cause the compilation to fail.

C++ is so much bigger than C that it is not practicable to even think about converting a C++ program to C. Unless there are some really pressing reasons, it's a whole lot easier to obtain the current version of the GNU C compiler, which can compile both C and C++ (and Objective C, if you're interested).

C and C++ have different function linking conventions. Since every C++ program calls C library functions, there is potential for errors if you use the wrong calling convention. We looked at this aspect in the section called "Declarations for C++" in Chapter 17, *Header Files*.

Other C Dialects

Before the advent of ANSI C, the language was ported to a number of non-UNIX architectures. Some of these added incompatible extensions. Many added incompatible library calls. One area is of particular interest: the Microsoft C compiler, which was originally written for MS-DOS. It was subsequently adapted to run under XENIX and SCO UNIX System V. Since our emphasis is on UNIX and UNIX-like systems, we'll talk about the XENIX compiler, though the considerations also apply to SCO UNIX and MS-DOS.

The most obvious difference between the XENIX C compiler and most UNIX compilers is in the options, which are described in Appendix B, but a couple of architectural limitations have caused incompatibilities in the language. We'll look at them in the following section.

Intel 8086 Memory Models

The original MS-DOS compiler ran on the Intel 8086 architecture. This architecture has 1 MB of real memory, but the addresses are only 16 bits long. In order to address memory, each machine instruction implicitly adds the contents of one of four *segment registers* to the address, so at any one time the machine can address a total of 256 KB of memory. In order to address more memory, the C implementation defines a 32-bit pointer type, the so-called *far address*, in software. Accessing memory via a far pointer requires reloading a segment register before the access and is thus significantly slower than access via a 16-bit *near address*. This has a number of consequences:

- Near addresses are simply offsets within a segment: if the program expects the address to point to a different segment, it accesses the wrong data.
- Far pointers are 32 bits wide, containing the contents of the segment register in one half and the offset within the segment in the other half. The segment register contains bits 4 through 19 of a 20-bit address, and the offset contains bits 0 through 15. To create an absolute address from a far pointer, the hardware performs effectively:

```
struct fp
  {
  short segment_reg;          /* 16 bits, bits 4 through 19 of address */
  short offset;               /* 16 bits, bits 0 through 15 of address */
  }
long abs_address = (fp.segment_reg << 4) + fp.offset;
```

As a result, many possible far pointer contents could resolve to the same address. This complicates pointer comparison significantly. Some implementations solved this problem by declaring *huge* pointers, which are normalized 20-bit addresses in 32-bit words.

MS-DOS C uses a number of different executable formats, along with three pointer types. Each of them has default pointer sizes associated with them. You choose your model by supplying the appropriate option to the compiler, and you can override the default pointer sizes with the explicit use of the keywords `near`, `far`, or (where available) `huge`:

- The *tiny model* occupies a single segment and thus can always use near addresses. Apart from the obvious compactness of the code, this model has the advantage that it can be converted to a *.COM* file.
- The *small model* occupies a single data segment and a single code segment. Here, too, you can always use near pointers, but you need to be sure you're pointing into the correct segment.
- The *medium model* (sometimes called *middle model*) has multiple code segments and a single data segment. As a result, code pointers are far and data pointers are near.
- The *compact model* is the inverse of the medium model. Here, code is restricted to one segment, and data can have multiple segments. Static data is restricted to a single segment. As a result, code pointers are near, and data pointers are far.

- The *large model* can have multiple code and multiple data segments. Static data is restricted to a single segment. All pointers are far.
- The *huge model* is like the large model except that it can have multiple static data segments. The name is unfortunate, since it suggests some connection with huge pointers. In fact, the huge model uses far pointers.

What does this mean to you? If you're porting from MS-DOS to UNIX, you may run into these keywords `near`, `far`, and `huge`. This isn't a big deal: you just need to remove them, or better still, define them as an empty string. You may also find a lot of pointer-checking code, which will probably get quite confused in a UNIX environment. If you do find this kind of code, the best thing to do is to `ifdef` it out (`#ifndef unix`).

Converting from UNIX to MS-DOS can be a lot more complicated. You'll be better off using a 32-bit compiler, which doesn't need this kind of kludge. Otherwise, you may have to spend a considerable amount of time figuring out the memory architecture most suitable for your package.

Other Differences in MS-DOS

MS-DOS compilers grew up in a very different environment from UNIX. As a result, a number of detail differences exist. None of them are very serious, but it's good to be forewarned:

- MS-DOS compilers do not adhere to the traditional UNIX organization of preprocessor, compiler, assembler, and loader.
- They don't use the assembler directly, though they can usually output assembler code for use outside the compilation environment.
- The assembler code output by MS-DOS compilers is in the standard Intel mnemonics, which are not compatible with UNIX assemblers.
- Many MS-DOS compilers combine the preprocessor and the main compiler pass, which makes for faster compilation and less disk I/O.
- Many rely on the Microsoft linker, which was not originally written for C and has significant limitations.
- Many MS-DOS compilers still run in real mode, which limits them to 640K code and data. This is a severe limitation, and it is not uncommon to have to modify programs in order to prevent the compiler from dying of amnesia. This leads to a different approach with header files, in particular: in UNIX, it's common to declare everything just in case, whereas in MS-DOS it may be a better idea to not declare anything unless absolutely necessary.

Compiler Organization

The traditional UNIX compiler is derived from the portable C compiler and divides the compilation into four steps, traditionally called *phases* or *passes*, controlled by the compiler control program *cc*. Most more modern compilers also adhere to this structure:

1. The preprocessor, called *cpp*, reads in the the source files, handles the preprocessor directives (those starting with #), and performs macro substitution.
2. The compiler itself, usually called *cc1*, reads in the preprocessor output and compiles to assembler source code. In SunOS, this pass is called *ccom*.
3. The assembler *as* reads in this output and assembles it, producing an object file.
4. The loader takes the object file or files and links them together to form an executable. To do so, it also loads a low-level initialization file, normally called *crt0.o*, and searches a number of libraries.

cc usually performs these passes invisibly. The intermediate outputs are stored in temporary files or pipes from one pass to the next. It is possible, however, to call the passes directly or to tell *cc* which pass to execute—we'll look at how to do that in the next section. By convention, a number of suffixes are used to describe the intermediate files. For example, the GNU C compiler recognizes the suffixes in Table 20-2 for a program *foo*.

Table 20–2: C Compiler Intermediate Files

File	Contents	Created by Compiler?
foo.c	Unpreprocessed C source code	no
foo.cc	Unpreprocessed C++ source code	no
foo.cxx	Unpreprocessed C++ source code	no
foo.C	Unpreprocessed C++ source code	no
foo.i	Preprocessed C source code	yes
foo.ii	Preprocessed C++ source code	yes
foo.m	Objective C source code	no
foo.h	C header file	no
foo.s	Assembler source code	yes
foo.S	Assembler code requiring preprocessing	no
foo.o	Object file	yes

Here's what you need to do to go through the compilation of *foo.c* to the executable *foo*, one pass at a time:

`$ gcc -E foo.c -o foo.i`	*preprocess*
`$ gcc -S foo.i`	*compile*
`$ gcc -c foo.s`	*assemble*
`$ gcc foo.o -o foo`	*link*

The form of the commands varies slightly: if you don't tell the preprocessor where to put the output file, *gcc* writes it to *stdout*. Other preprocessors may put a special suffix on the base filename, or if you specify the *-o* option, the compiler might put it in the file you specify. If you don't tell the linker where to put the output file, it writes to *a.out*.

Compiling an object file from an assembler file is the same as compiling from a source file or a preprocessed file. *gcc* decides what to do based on the suffix of the input file.

You can also run any combination of contiguous passes like this:

`$ gcc -S foo.c`	*preprocess and compile*
`$ gcc -c foo.c`	*preprocess, compile and assemble*
`$ gcc -o foo foo.c`	*preprocess, compile, assemble, link*
`$ gcc -c foo.i`	*compile and assemble*
`$ gcc -o foo foo.i`	*compile, assemble, link*
`$ gcc -o foo foo.s`	*assemble and link*

The location of the C compiler is, unfortunately, anything but standardized. The control program *cc* is normally in */usr/bin*, or occasionally in */bin*, but the other components might be stored in any of the following: */usr/lib*, */usr/ccs/lib* (System V.4), */usr/lib/cmplrs/cc* (MIPS), or */usr/local/lib/gcc-lib* (*gcc* on most systems).

Other Compiler Organizations

Some modern compilers have additional passes. Some optimizers fit between the compiler and the assembler: they take the output of the compiler and output optimized code to the assembler. An extreme example is the MIPS compiler, which has a total of eight passes: the preprocessor *cpp*, the front end *cc1*, the *ucode** linker *uld*, the procedure merge pass *umerge*, the global optimizer *uopt*, the code generator *ugen*, the assembler *as1*, and the linker *ld*. Despite this apparent complexity, you can consider this compiler as if it had only the traditional four passes: the five passes from the front end up to the code generator perform the same function as the traditional *cc1*.

* *ucode* is a kind of intermediate code used by the compiler. It is visible to the user, and you have the option of building and using *ucode* libraries.

The C Preprocessor

You can use the preprocessor *cpp* for other purposes than preprocessing C source code. It is a reasonably good macro processor, and it has the advantage that its functionality is available on every system with a C compiler; in some cases, however, it is available only via the C compiler. It is one of the mainstays of *imake*, and occasionally packages use it for other purposes as well.

There are two ways to invoke *cpp*: you can invoke it with *cc* and the *–E* option, or you can start it directly. If at all possible, you should start it via *cc* rather than running it directly. On some systems you can't rely on *cc* to pass the correct options to *cpp*. You also can't rely on all versions of *cpp* to use the same options—you can't even rely on them to be documented. You can find a list comparing the more common preprocessor options in the section called "cpp Options" in Appendix B.

Choosing a Compiler

Most systems still supply a C compiler, and under most circumstances, you would use the one supplied. In some cases, bugs in the native system compiler, compatibility problems, or just the fact that you don't have the normal compiler may lead to your using a different compiler. This situation is becoming more common as software manufacturers unbundle their compilers.

Using a different compiler is not necessarily a Bad Thing and can frequently be an improvement. In particular, *gcc*, the GNU C compiler from the Free Software Foundation, is very popular. It's the standard C compiler for a number of systems, including OSF/1, 4.4BSD, and Linux. It can do just about everything except run in minimal memory, and it has the advantage of being a well-used compiler. Chances are that somebody has compiled your package with *gcc* before, so you are less likely to run into trouble with *gcc* than with the native compiler of a little-known system. In addition, *gcc* is capable of highly optimized code, in many cases significantly better than the code created by the native compiler.

Compilers are becoming more standardized, and so are the bugs you are liable to run into. If you have the choice between compiling for K&R or ANSI, choose ANSI: the K&R options may use "features" that were not universally implemented, whereas the ANSI versions tend to pay more attention to the standard. If you do run into a bug, chances are someone has seen it before and has taken steps to work around it. In addition, compiling for ANSI usually means that the prototypes are declared in ANSI fashion, which increases the chance of subtle type conflicts being caught.

Neither you nor the *Makefile* may expect the following:

- *gcc* compiles both K&R (*–traditional*) and ANSI dialects. However, even some software supplied by the Free Software Foundation breaks when compiled with *gcc* unless the *–traditional* option is used.
- Many compilers do not compile correctly when both optimization and debugging information are specified (*–O* and *–g* options), though most of them recognize the fact and turn off one of the options. Even if the compiler ostensibly supports both options, bugs may prevent it from working well. For example, *gcc* version 2.3.3 generated invalid assembler output for System V.4 C++ programs when both options were specified. Even when compilers do create debugging information from an optimizing compilation, the results can be confusing due to the action of the optimizer:
  - The optimizer may remove variables. As a result, you may not be able to set or display their values.
  - The optimizer may rearrange program flow. This means that single-stepping might not do what you expect, and you may not be able to set breakpoints on certain lines because the code there has been eliminated.
  - Some optimizers remove stack frames,* which makes for faster code, particularly for small functions. *gcc* does this with the *–O3* option.

  Stack frame removal in particular makes debugging almost impossible. These aren't bugs, they're features. If they cause problems for you, recompile without optimization.
- Some compilers limit the length of identifiers, which can cause the compiler to treat two different identifiers as the same. If you run into this problem, change the compiler. Modern compilers don't have such limits, and a compiler that does is liable to have more tricks in store for you.
- With a System V compiler, you might find:

  ```
  $ cc -c frotzel.c -o frotzel.o
  cc: Error: -o would overwrite frotzel.o
  ```

  System V compilers use the option *–o* only to specify the name of the final executable, which must not coincide with the name of the object file. In many *Makefiles* from the BSD world, on the other hand, this is the standard default rule for compiling from *.c* to *.o*.

---

* See the section called "Stack Frames" in Chapter 21, *Object Files and Friends*, for further information on stack frames.

- All C compilers expect at least some of their options in a particular sequence. The documentation is frequently hazy about which operands are sequence-sensitive, or what interactions exist between specific operands.

The last problem deserves more discussion. A well-documented example is that the linker searches library specifications (the *–l* option) in the sequence in which they are specified on the compiler invocation line. We'll investigate that in more detail in the section called "Missing functions" in Chapter 21. Here's an example of another operand sequence problem:

```
$ cc foo.c -I../myheaders
```

If *foo.c* refers to a file *bar.h* in the directory *../myheaders*, some compilers won't find the header because they don't interpret the *–I* directive until after they try to compile *foo.c*. The man page for System V.4 *cc* does state that the compiler searches directories specified with *–I* in the order in which they occur, but it does not warn you that the sequence of *–I* options and filenames is important.

In This Chapter:
- *Object Formats*
- *The Assembler*
- *The Linker*
- *Dumping to Object Files*
- *Process Initialization and Stack Frames*
- *Object Archive Formats*

21

Object Files and Friends

Object files store compiled programs. Usually, you manipulate them only as part of the build process, in which you can treat them as a black box. You don't need to know what they look like inside.

Sometimes, however, some aspects of the true nature of object files become apparent—for example:

- Your program bombs out with a segmentation violation while trying to write to a location that the debugger tells you is valid. So why did it bomb out? It might be that the location was in the text segment, a part of the address space that is read-only.
- You find that the debugger refuses to look at a program because it doesn't have any symbols—whatever *that* may mean.
- You recompile programs and run out of disk space. For some reason, the object files are suddenly 10 times the size that they used to be.

The information in this chapter is some of the most technical in the entire book, which is why I've left it to the end. We look at a number of topics that are related only by their dependence on object files. So far, the inter-platform differences we've seen have been the result of a choice made by the software people who implemented the system. In this chapter, we come a whole lot closer to the hardware. You can almost feel the clocks tick and the pipelines fill. You definitely see instructions execute. You'll find it an interesting look under covers that are usually locked shut.

A number of programs manipulate the object files either because that's their purpose—for example, assemblers or linkers—or because they want to play tricks to install more comfortably. For example, Emacs and TEX both write themselves out as object files during the build process. If anything goes wrong with these programs, you need to open the black box and look inside. In this chapter, we'll examine the tools that manipulate object files and some of the background information that you need to know to solve problems.

Not many programs manipulate object files. The kernel uses absolute object files when creating a process—this is the most frequent use of an object file. In addition, the *assembler* creates them from assembly sources. In most UNIX systems, the assembler is the only program that creates object files from scratch. The *linker* or *link editor* joins object files together to form a larger object file, and debuggers access specific debugging information in the object file. These are the only programs that have intimate understanding of the object file format.

A number of smaller programs do relatively trivial tasks with object files:

ar
: This archiver is usually used for archiving binary files, but it does not know very much about their contents.

nm
: This name list display program displays the symbol table or *name list* of an object file or an archive of object files. We'll look at the symbol table in more detail in the section called "String Table and Name List".

size
: Displays size information from an object file.

strings
: Displays printable strings in an object file.

strip
: Removes unnecessary information from an object file.

In the rest of this chapter, we'll look at the following topics:

- The kernel process model that the object file supports.
- The assembler, including some of the syntax, the symbol table, relocation, and debugging symbols.
- The linker, including the way it searches libraries, and some of the problems that can occur during linking.
- The internal structure of function libraries, and how this affects what they can and cannot do.

- How Emacs and TeX dump themselves as object files.
- How `exec` starts programs.

Object Formats

The purpose of object files is to make it as easy as possible to start a process, so it makes sense to look at the process image in memory first. Modern UNIX systems run on stack-based systems with virtual memory. We touched on the concept of virtual memory in Chapter 11, *Hardware Dependencies*. Since UNIX is a multiprogramming system, it is possible for more than one process to run from a single object file. These facts have a significant influence on the way the system manages processes. For each process, the system allocates at least three segments in which program code and data is stored:

- A *text segment*, which contains the executable code of the program and read-only data. Modern systems create code where the program may not write to its text segment—it is so-called *pure text*. This has two significant advantages for the memory manager. First, all processes in the system that are run from this program can share the same text segment, which significantly reduces the memory requirements when, say, 20 copies of a shell are running. In addition, since the text is not modified, the memory management routines never need to swap it out to disk. The copy on disk is always the same as the copy in memory. This also means that the copy on disk can be the copy in the object file: it does not take up any space in the swap partition.

  Older systems also provided for *impure text* segments that could be modified by the program. This use is obsolete, but is still supported by modern systems.
- A *data segment*, which consists of two parts:
  - Global data that has been initialized in the program. This data can be modified, of course, so it takes up space in the swap partition, but the first time the page is referenced, the memory manager must load it from the object file.
  - *bss** *data*, noninitialized global data. Since the data is not initialized, it does not need to be loaded from a file. The first time the page is referenced, the memory manager just creates an empty data page. After that, the data gets paged to the swap partition in the same way as initialized data.

---

* The name comes from the assembler directive *bss* (Block Starting with Symbol), which was used in older assemblers to allocate uninitialized memory and allocate the address of the first word to the label of the directive. A directive *bes* (Block Ending with Symbol) allocated the address of the last word to the label.

- A *stack segment*. Like bss data, the stack segment is not initialized and, therefore, is not stored in the object file. Unlike any of the other segments, it does not contain any fixed addresses. At the beginning of program execution, it is almost empty, and all data stored in it is relative to the top of the stack or another stack marker. We'll look at stack organization in more detail in the section called "Stack Frames".
- In addition, many systems have *library segments*. From the point of view of memory management, these segments are just additional text and data segments, but they are loaded at run time from another object file, the *library file*.

Older systems without virtual memory stored the data segment below the stack segment with a gap in between, the so-called *break*. The stack grew down into the break as the result of *push* or *call* instructions, and the data segment grew up into the break as the result of system calls `brk` and `sbrk` (*set break*). This additional space in the data segment is typically used for memory allocated by the library call `malloc`. With a virtual memory system, the call to `sbrk` is no longer necessary, but some versions of UNIX still require it, and all support it. Table 21-1 summarizes this information:

Table 21-1: Kinds of Segments

Property	Text Segment	Initialized Data	bss Data	Stack Segment
In object file	yes	yes	no	no
Access	read/execute	read/write	read/write	read/write
Paged out	no	yes	yes	yes
Fixed size	yes	yes	maybe	no

Object files contain the information needed to set up these segments. Before we continue, we should be aware of a change in terminology:

- The object file for a process is called a *program*.
- The images of process segments in an object file are called *sections*.

Three main object file formats are in current use:

- The *a.out* format is the oldest and has remained essentially unchanged since the Seventh Edition. It supplies support for a text section and a data section, as well as relocation information for both sections. It is used by XENIX and BSD systems.

- The *COFF* (Common Object File Format) was introduced in System V and offers an essentially unlimited number of segments, including library segments. It is now obsolete on UNIX but happens to be in use in Microsoft Windows NT.
- The *ELF* (Executable and Linking Format) was introduced for System V.4. From our point of view, it offers essentially the same features as COFF. ELF shows promise as the executable format of the future because it greatly simplifies the use of shared libraries. Currently the Linux project is moving from *a.out* to ELF.

With the exception of library segments, there's not much to choose between the individual object formats, but the internal structures and the routines that handle them are very different. Let's take an *a.out* header from a BSD system as an example. The header file *sys/exec.h* defines:

```
struct exec
  {
  long  a_magic;                /* magic number */
  unsigned long a_text;         /* text segment size */
  unsigned long a_data;         /* initialized data size */
  unsigned long a_bss;          /* uninitialized data size */
  unsigned long a_syms;         /* symbol table size */
  unsigned long a_entry;        /* entry point */
  unsigned long a_trsize;       /* text relocation size */
  unsigned long a_drsize;       /* data relocation size */
  };

/* a_magic */
#define OMAGIC              0407  /* old impure format */
#define NMAGIC              0410  /* read-only text */
#define ZMAGIC              0413  /* demand load format */
#define QMAGIC              0314  /* compact demand load format */
```

This header includes:

- A *magic number*. This specifies the exact kind of file (for example, whether it is relocatable or absolute). The program *file* can interpret this magic number and report the kind of object file.
- The length of the *text section*, an image of the text segment. The text section immediately follows the header.
- The length of the *data section*, which contains the data to be loaded into the initialized global data part of the data segment at run time. The data section immedately follows the text section.

- The length of the bss data. As we have seen, bss data does not need to be stored in the object file. Since the bss data is not initialized, no space is needed for it in the object file.
- The length of the symbol table. The symbol table itself is stored after the data section.
- The *entry point*, the address in the text segment at which execution is to start.
- The lengths of the text and data relocation tables, which are stored after the symbol table.

If you look at the list of contents carefully, you'll notice that there are no start addresses for the segments, and there isn't even any mention of the stack segment. The start address of the text and data segments is implicit in the format, and it's frequently difficult information to figure out. On 32-bit machines, the text segment typically starts at a low address, for example `0` or `0x1000`.* The data segment may start immediately after the text segment (on the following page), or it might start at a predetermined location such as `0x40000000`. The stack segment is usually placed high in the address space. Some systems place it at `0x7fffffff`, others at `0xefffffff`. The best way to find out these addresses is to look through the address space of a typical process with a symbolic debugger.

The magic number is worth closer examination. I said that it occupies the first two bytes of the header, but in our example it is a `long`, four bytes. In fact, the magic number is used in two different contexts:

- The first two bytes in the file are reserved for the magic number in all systems. The information in these bytes should be sufficient to distinguish the architecture.
- The following two bytes may contain additional information for specific systems, but it is often set to 0.

The Assembler

Assembly is the second oldest form of programming.† It is characterized by being specific about the exact instructions that the machine executes, which makes an

* Why `0x1000`? It's a wonderful debugging aid for catching `NULL` pointers. If the first page of memory is not mapped, you'll get a segmentation violation or a bus error if you try to access data at that address.

† The oldest form of programming, of course, used no computational aids whatsoever: in some form or another, the programmer wrote down direct machine code and then entered it into memory with a loader or via front-panel switches. Assembly added the symbolic character to this operation.

assembler program much more voluminous than a higher-level language. Nevertheless, there is nothing difficult about it, it's just tedious.

Assembler programming involves two aspects that don't have much in common:

- The instruction set of the machine in question. The best source of information for this aspect is the hardware description of the machine. Even if you get an assembler manual for the machine, it is not as authoritative as the hardware description.
- The syntax of the assembler. This is where the problems start: first, little documentation is available. Second, assembler syntax diverges greatly, and the documentation you get may not match your assembler.

The i386 is a particularly sorry example of incompatible assembler syntax. The UNIX assemblers available for the i386 (at least three of them, not even compatible with each other) use modified forms of the old UNIX *as* syntax, whereas all books about the assembler and the hardware of the i386 use a syntax related to the Microsoft assembler *MASM*. They don't even agree on such basics as the names of the instructions and the sequence of the operands.

Although nowadays it is used almost only for assembling compiler output, *as* frequently offers features specifically intended for human programmers. In particular, most assemblers support some kind of preprocessing: they may use the macro preprocessor *m4* or the C preprocessor when processing assembler source. See the description of the flags in the section called "as Options" in Appendix C for more information.

Assembler Syntax

Assembler syntax is a relatively involved topic, but there are some general rules that apply to just about every assembler. In this section, we'll see how to fight our way through an assembler listing.

- Assemblers are *line-oriented*: each instruction to the assembler is placed on a separate line.
- An instruction line consists of four parts:
  - If the optional *label* is present, the assembler assigns a value to it. For most instructions, the value is the current value of the *location counter*, the relative address of the instruction in the current section. In UNIX, if the label is present it is followed by a colon. Other assemblers frequently require that only labels start at the beginning of the line and recognize them by this fact.

The assembler usually translates the source file in a single pass. This means that when it encounters the name of a label that is farther down in the source file, it cannot know its value or even if it exists. Some assemblers require that the name of the label be followed with the letter `b` (*backwards*) for labels that should have already been seen in the text, and `f` (*forwards*) for labels that are farther down. In order to avoid ambiguity, these assemblers also require that the labels be all digits. Many other assemblers also support this syntax, so `1b` is not a good name for a label.

- The next field is the *instruction*. In this context, *assembler instructions* are commands to the assembler and may be either *directives*, which tell the assembler to do something not directly related to emitting code, or *machine instructions*, which emit code. In UNIX, directives frequently start with a period.
- The third field contains the `operands` for the instruction. Depending on the instruction, they may not be required.
- The fourth field is a comment field. It is usually delimited by a pound sign (`#`).

- The operands of instructions that take a source operand and a destination operand are usually specified in the sequence *src, dest.*
- Register names are usually preceded with a percent sign (`%`).
- Literal values are usually preceded with a dollar sign (`$`).

For example, consider the instruction:

```
fred: movl    $4,%eax # example
```

This instruction emits a `movl` instruction, which moves the literal* value 4 to the register `eax`. The symbol `fred` is set to the address of the instruction.

We can't go into all the details of the assembly language for all machines, but the descriptions in Appendix C will hopefully give you enough insight to be able to read existing assembler source. You'll need more information before you can write it. One of the few reasonably detailed *as* manuals is *Using as*, by Dean Elsner and Jay Fenlason, which is included as part of the GNU *binutils* distribution.

* `movl` means "move long", not "move literal". In this particular assembler, we know that it is a literal value because of the dollar sign, just as we know that `eax` is a register name because it is preceded by a percent sign.

Assembler Symbols

Local symbols define instruction addresses. High-level constructs in C, such as `if`, `while`, and `switch`, require a number of `jump` (`go to`) instructions in assembler, and the compiler must generate labels for the instructions. Local symbols are also used to label literal data constants, such as strings.

Global symbols are defined in the source. The word *global* has different meanings in C and assembler: in C, it is any symbol defined in the data or text segments, whether or not it is visible outside the module. In assembler, a global symbol is one that is visible outside the module.

Note these points:

- C local variables are generated automatically on the stack and do not retain their names after compilation. They do not have a fixed location because their position on the stack depends on what was already on the stack when the function was called. If the function is recursive, they could even be in many different places on the stack at the same time. As a result, there is nothing that the assembler or the linker can do with the symbols, and the compiler discards them.
- There is a possibility of conflict between the local symbols generated by the compiler and global symbols declared in the program. Most compilers avoid this conflict by placing an underscore (_) in front of all symbols defined in the program, and not using the underscore for local symbols. Others solve the problem by placing a period in front of local symbols, which is not legal in a C identifier.

To see how this all works, let's look at different aspects of what the compiler and assembler do with a small program in the next few sections:

```
char global_text [] = "This is global text in the data area";
void inc (int *x, int *y)
{
  if (*x)
    (*x)++;
  else
    (*y)++;
  puts (global_text);        /* this is an external function */
  puts ("That's all, folks");
  }
```

We compile this program on a BSD/OS machine using *gcc* version 2.5.8, with maximum optimization and debugging symbols:

```
$ gcc -O2 -g -S winc.c
```

The *–S* option tells the compiler control program to stop after running the compiler. It stores the assembly output in *winc.s*, which looks like this:

```
        .file   "winc.c"
gcc2_compiled.:
___gnu_compiled_c:
.stabs "/usr/lemis/book/porting/grot/",100,0,0,Ltext0  name of the source directory
.stabs "winc.c",100,0,0,Ltext0  name of the source file
.text                           select text section
Ltext0:                         internal label: start of text
.stabs "int:t1=r1;-2147483648;2147483647;",128,0,0,0
.stabs "char:t2=r2;0;127;",128,0,0,0
... a whole lot of standard debugging output omitted
.stabs "void:t19=19",128,0,0,0
.globl _global_text              specify an externally defined symbol
.data                            select data section
.stabs "global_text:G20=ar1;0;36;2",32,0,1,0   debug info for global symbol
_global_text:                    variable label
        .ascii "This is global text in the data area "  and text
.text                            select text section
LC0:
        .ascii "That's all, folks "
        .align 2                 start on a 16 bit boundary
.globl _inc                      define the function inc to be external
_inc:                            start of function inc
        .stabd 68,0,3            debug information: start of line 3
        pushl %ebp
        movl %esp,%ebp
        movl 8(%ebp),%eax
        movl 12(%ebp),%edx
        .stabd 68,0,4            debug information: start of line 4
LBB2:
        cmpl $0,(%eax)
        je L2
        .stabd 68,0,5            debug information: start of line 5
        incl (%eax)
        jmp L3
        .align 2,0x90
L2:
        .stabd 68,0,7            debug information: start of line 7
        incl (%edx)
L3:
        .stabd 68,0,8            debug information: start of line 8
        pushl $_global_text
        call _puts
        .stabd 68,0,9            debug information: start of line 9
        pushl $LC0
        call _puts
        .stabd 68,0,10           debug information: start of line 10
LBE2:
        leave
        ret
.stabs "inc:F19",36,0,3,_inc     debug information for inc
.stabs "x:p21=*1",160,0,2,8      debug information for x
```

```
.stabs "y:p21",160,0,2,1          debug information for y
.stabs "x:r21",64,0,2,0
.stabs "y:r21",64,0,2,2
.stabn 192,0,0,LBB2
.stabn 224,0,0,LBE2
```

We'll look at various aspects of this output in the next few sections. For now, we should notice:

- As advertised, the names of the global symbols `global_text`, `inc`, and `puts` have been changed to `_global_text`, `_inc`, and `_puts`.
- The compiler has created the local symbols `Ltext0`, `LC0`, `LBB2`, `LBE2`, `L2`, and `L3`. Clearly it likes to start the names of local symbols with the letter `L` and distinguish them with numbers at the end. But what has happened to `L1`, for example? The compiler generated it, but the optimizer optimized it away. If you compile this same program without the optimizer, the labels will all still be there.
- The compiler has assigned the local symbol `LC0` to the string `"That's all, folks"` so that the assembler can refer to it.
- The variables `x` and `y` have disappeared, since they exist only on the stack.

Relocation Information

The previous example shows another dilemma that afflicts the linker: the program is not complete. It refers to the external symbol `_puts`, and in addition, it does not have a `main` function. The only way to use the program is for a function in another object file to call `_inc`. In order to do this, we need to give the linker information about the following:

- The names of the external symbols that the object file references (`_puts` in our example).
- Symbols defined in the object file that can be referenced by other object files (`_global_text` and `_inc` in our example).
- Where external symbols are referenced in the object code.
- Where locations in the text and data segments are referenced in the object code.

Why do we need to know where *internal* locations are referenced? The linker takes the text and data sections from a large number of object files and makes a single text section and a single data section out of them. The locations of the original sections from the individual object files differ from one occasion to the next, but the addresses in the final executable must reflect the correct references. If an instruction refers to an address in the data or text section or to an external symbol, the assembler can't just put the address of the item in the instruction, since the address is allocated by the linker. Instead, it places the *offset* from the beginning of the text or data section or from the external symbol into the instruction or data word and generates a *relocation record* in the output file. These relocation records contain the following information:

- The *address* of the data that needs to be relocated. From the linker's point of view, the data may be an instruction, in which case the linker needs to modify only the address portion of the instruction, or the data may be a pointer—in other words, an indirect address.
- The *length* of the data. For a data pointer, this is the length of the pointer. For an instruction, it is the length of the address field of the instruction. Some systems have strange instruction formats, and this can become quite complicated.
- About the section in which the data will be located. This could be the current text or data section, or it could be a reference to an external symbol.
- For an external symbol, a pointer to information about the symbol.

Object files contain separate relocation tables for each section that can contain address data—at least the text and data sections. Referring again to the example, we see that the compiler has output `.text` and `.data` directives. These are used to tell the assembler in which section it should put the output that follows. It also supplies relocation information for the output file.

String Table and Name List

The relocation information includes a significant number of strings, among other things. The strings are stored in the *string table*, which is simply a list of strings terminated with a NUL (`\0`) character. Other parts of the object file refer to strings by their offset in the string table.

As we saw in the example, the assembler has a directive (`.globl` in this example) that outputs information about externally visible symbols, such as `global_text`. Some assemblers need to be told about external references (such as `_puts` in the example), and others don't, like the GNU assembler *gas* that I used to create the example. For both external definitions and external references, *gas* outputs an entry for the *symbol table entry* to the output file with information about the symbol. This symbol table is one of the better-known parts of an object file and is usually called the *name list*. The structure differs strongly from one flavor of UNIX to the next, but all name lists contain the following information:

- The index of the symbol's name in the *string table.*
- The type of the symbol (undefined, absolute, text, data, bss, common).
- The *value* of the symbol, if it has one (undefined symbols don't, of course).

The library function `nlist` accesses the symbol table and returns a symbol table entry. The call is:

```
#include <nlist.h>

int nlist (const char *filename, struct nlist *nl);
```

This function has confusing semantics: the symbol table structure `struct nlist` does not contain the name of the symbol. Instead, it contains a *pointer* to the name of the symbol. On disk, the symbol is located in the string list, but in your program, you supply the strings in advance. For the System V.4 ELF format, the structure is:

```
struct nlist
  {
  char  *n_name;                /* name of symbol */
  long  n_value;                /* value of symbol */
  short n_scnum;                /* section number */
  unsigned short  n_type;       /* type and derived type */
  char  n_sclass;               /* storage class */
  char  n_numaux;               /* number of auxiliary entries */
  };
```

To use the `nlist` function, you create an array of `struct nlist` entries with `n_name` set to the symbols you are looking for. The last entry contains a `NULL` string to indicate the end of the list. `nlist` searches the symbol table and fills in information for the symbols it finds and sets all fields except `n_name` to 0 if it can't find the string.

The return value differs from one system to another:

- If *filename* doesn't exist or if it isn't an object file, `nlist` returns –1.
- If all symbols were found, `nlist` returns 0.
- If some symbols were not found, BSD `nlist` returns the number of symbols not found. System V `nlist` still returns 0.

Examining Symbol Tables: The nm Program

You can display the complete symbol table of an object file or an archive with the program *nm.* Invoke it simply with:

```
$ nm filename
```

nm output is frequently used by tools such as shell scripts during building. This can be a problem because the format of the printout depends strongly on the object file format. In the following sections, we'll look at the differences between *nm* output for *a.out*, COFF, and ELF files.

nm display of a.out format

With an *a.out* file, *nm* output looks like:

```
$ nm /usr/lib/libc.a

syscall.o:                              this is the object filename
00000028 T _syscall
         U cerror

sigsuspend.o:
00000030 T _sigsuspend
         U cerror
```

The lines with the filename and colon tell you the name of the archive member (in other words, the object file) from which the following symbols come. The other lines contain a value (which may be missing if it is not defined), a type letter, and a symbol name.

That's all there is to *a.out* symbols. As we will see, *a.out* handles debugging information separately. On the other hand, this means that the type letters are reasonably easy to remember. Uppercase represents global symbols, lower case represents local symbols. Table 21-2 gives an overview.

Table 21-2: a.out Symbol Types

Type Letter	Meaning
–	Symbol table entries (see the *–a* option)
A	Absolute symbol (not relocatable)
B	bss segment symbol
C	Common symbol
D	Data segment symbol
f	Filename (always local)
T	Text segment symbol
U	Indefined

nm display of COFF format

By contrast, COFF gives something like this:

```
$ nm /usr/lib/libc.a
Symbols from /lib/libc.a[printf.o]:     this is the object filename

Name                    Value   Class          Type          Size    Line  Section

printf.c               |        | file |                    |       |      |
DGROUP                 |       0|static|                    |       |      |.data
printf                 |       0|extern|                    |       |      |.text
_doprnt                |       0|extern|                    |       |      |
_iob                   |       0|extern|                    |       |      |
```

These columns have the following meaning:

`Name`
: The name of the symbol.

`Value`
: The value of the symbol.

`Class`
: The *storage class* of the symbol. There are a large number of storage classes, and the System V.3 man pages don't describe them. See *Understanding and Using COFF*, by Gintaras R. Gircys, for a complete list. The one that interests us is `extern` (externally defined symbols).

`Type`
: In conjunction with *Class*, *Type* describes the type of symbol more accurately, when it is needed. The symbols we're looking at don't require a more accurate description.

`Size`
: Specifies the size of the entry. This is used in symbolic debug information.

`Line`
: Line number information, which is also used for symbolic debug information.

`Section`
: The section to which the symbol belongs. In our example, the familiar `.text` and `.data` occur, but this could be any of the myriad COFF section names.

nm display of ELF format

The differences between COFF and ELF are less obvious:

```
$ nm /lib/libc.so.1

Symbols from /lib/libc.so.1:
```

```
[Index]   Value      Size     Type  Bind  Other Shndx    Name

[1]       |          0|         0|FILE |LOCL |0     |ABS     |../../libc.so.1
[2]       |        148|         0|SECT |LOCL |0     |1       |
... skipping
[32]      |     208976|        12|OBJT |LOCL |0     |12      |libdirs
[33]      |     208972|         4|OBJT |LOCL |0     |12      |rt_dir_list
[34]      |          0|         0|FILE |LOCL |0     |ABS     |dlfcns.c
[35]      |      57456|       384|FUNC |LOCL |0     |8       |dl_delete
[36]      |      56240|        72|FUNC |LOCL |0     |8       |lmExists
[37]      |      56112|       128|FUNC |LOCL |0     |8       |appendLm
[38]      |      56320|       464|FUNC |LOCL |0     |8       |dl_makelist
[39]      |     214960|         4|OBJT |LOCL |0     |15      |dl_tail
```

These columns have the following meanings:

`Index`
: Simply, the index of the symbol in the symbol list.

`Value`
: The value of the symbol.

`Size`
: The size of the associated object in bytes.

`Type`
: The type of the object. This can be `NOTY` (no type specfied), `OBJT` (a data object), `FUNC` (executable code), `SECT` (a section name), or `FILE` (a filename).

`Bind`
: Specifies the scope of the symbol. `GLOB` specifies that the symbol is global in scope, `WEAK` specifies a global symbol with lower precedence, and `LOCL` specifies a local symbol.

`Other`
: Currently unused and contains 0.

`Shndx`
: May be `ABS`, specifying an absolute symbol (in other words, not relocatable); `COMMON`, specifying a bss block; or `UNDEF`, specifying a reference to an external symbol. A number in this field is an index to the section table of the section to which the symbol relates. Since *nm* doesn't tell you which section this is, the information is not very useful.

Problems with nm output

As we have seen, the output of *nm* depends a lot on the object file format. You frequently see shell scripts that use *nm* to look inside a file and extract information. They go seriously wrong if the object file format is not what they expect. If there isn't an alternative script with which to look at your kind of object file, you have to modify it yourself.

Debugging Information

Symbolic debuggers have a problem. They relate to the object file, but they want to give the impression that they are working with the source file. For example, the program addresses that interest you are source file line numbers, not absolute addresses, and you want to refer to variables by their names, not their addresses. In addition, you expect the debugger to know the types of variables, so that when you ask the debugger to display a variable of type `char *`, it displays a string, and when you ask it to display a `float`, you get the correct numeric value.

The object file structures we have seen so far don't help too much. Information is available for global symbols, both in the text and data sections, but the type information is not detailed enough to tell the debugger whether a data variable is a `char *` or a `float`. The symbol table information contains no information at all about local variables or line numbers. In addition, the symbol table information goes away at link time, so it wouldn't be of much help anyway.

For these reasons, separate data structures for debugging information were introduced. In the *a.out* format, they have nothing to do with the rest of the file. In COFF and ELF, they are more integrated, but debugging information has one thing in common in all object formats: it is at the end of the file so that it can be easily removed when it is no longer wanted—debugging information can become *very* large. It's not uncommon to see debugging information increase the size of an executable by a factor of 5 or 10. In extreme cases, such as in libraries, it can become 50 times as big.

Frequently, you'll see a *make all* that creates an executable with debugging symbols, and a *make install* that installs the same executable but removes the debugging symbols. This process is called *stripping* and can be done by the program *strip* or by *install* with the *–s* option. In order to do this, the debugging information has to be in its own section at the end of the file, which is how all object file formats solve the problem.

Debugging information is supplied in the assembler source in the form of *directives*. In the example in the section called "Assembler Symbols", which is from an assembler designed to create *a.out* relocatables, this job is performed by the `.stabs`, `.stabn`, and `.stabd` directives. These directives are discussed in more detail in Appendix C, the section called "Debug Information". Let's look at the directives in the example.

- At the beginning of the file, a lot of `.stabs` directives define standard data types, so many that we have omitted most of them. The compiler outputs these directives even if the data type isn't used in the program, and they're handy to have in case you want to cast to this data type when debugging.
- Throughout the file, you find individual `.stabd 68` directives. These specify that the line number specified in the last parameter starts at this point in the text.
- At the end of the function `_inc`, information about the function itself and the variables associated with it appear in additional `.stabs` directives.
- Finally, information about the block structure of the function appears in the `.stabn` directive.

This information is very dependent on the object file format. If you need more information, the best source is the accompanying system documentation.

The Linker

You usually encounter the *linker* as the last pass of the C compiler. As the name *ld* implies, the linker was called the *loader* in the Seventh Edition, though all modern systems call it a link editor.* Traditionally, the compiler compiles object files and then runs the linker to create an executable program. This is logical, since a single executable is always composed of multiple object files,† whereas a one-to-one relationship exists between source files and object modules.

The most important function performed by the linker is symbol resolution. To understand this, we need to define a few terms:

- The *symbol list*, sometimes called a *symbol table*, is an internal data structure where the linker stores information about all symbols whose names it has encountered. It contains the same kind of information about the symbols as we saw in `struct nlist` in the section called "String Table and Name List".
- An *undefined symbol* is only partially undefined. We know at least its name, but some part of its value is unknown.

---

* Properly, the loader was the part of the operating system that loaded a program into memory prior to execution. Once, long before the advent of UNIX, the two functions were almost synonymous.

† Even if you supply only a single object file yourself, you need the C startup code in *crt0.o* and library modules from system libraries such as *libc.a*.

Initially, the symbol list is empty, but every file that is included adds to the list. A number of cases can occur:

- The file refers to an undefined symbol. In this case, if the linker has not yet seen this symbol, it enters it into the symbol list and starts a list of references to it. If the symbol is already in the symbol list, the linker adds a reference to the symbol's reference list.
- The file refers to a symbol that has already been defined. In this case, the linker simply performs the required relocation.
- The file defines a symbol. There are three possibilities here:
  - If the symbol has not been encountered before, it is just added to the symbol list.
  - If the symbol is already marked as undefined, the linker updates the symbol information and performs the required relocation for each element in the reference list.
  - If the symbol is known and defined, it is now doubly defined. The linker prints an error message and does not create an output file.

At the same time as it creates the symbol list, the linker copies data and text sections into the areas it has allocated for them. It copies each individual section to the current end of the area. The symbol list entries reflect these addresses.

Function Libraries

Many of the functions you use in linking an executable program are located in *function libraries*, a kind of object file archive built by *ar*. The linker knows about the format of *ar* archives and is able to extract the object files from the archive. The resultant executable contains code from the object files specified on the command line and from the object files found in the libraries. The functions in the libraries are just like any others you may include. They run in user context, not kernel context, and are stored in libraries simply for convenience. We can consider three groups:

- The standard* C library, normally */usr/lib/libc.a*. This library contains at least the functions needed to link simple C programs. It may also contain functions not directly connected with the C language, such as network interface functions—BSD does it this way.

* Note the lowercase use of the word *standard*. Whether or not the library conforms to the ANSI/ISO C Standard, it is a standard part of a software development system.

- Additional libraries supporting system functions not directly concerned with the C programming language. Networking functions may also fall into this category—System V does it this way.
- Libraries supporting third party packages, such as the X11 windowing system.

Library Search

You can specify object files to the linker in two different ways: you specify that an object file is to be *included* in the output or that a library file is to be *searched* by specifying its name on the command line. The *library search* is one of the most powerful functions performed by the linker. Instead of including the complete library in the output file, the linker checks each object file in the library for definitions of currently undefined symbols. Any object file that contains a symbol needed by the program is included in the executable file. This has a number of implications:

- The linker includes only object files that define symbols referenced by the program, so the program is a lot smaller than it would be if you included the complete library.
- We don't want to include anything that isn't required, so each object file usually defines a single function. In some rare cases, it may define a small number of related functions that always get included together.
- Each object file may refer to other external symbols, so including one file in an archive may require including another one.
- If you compile a library with symbols, each single-function object file will contain debugging information for all the external information defined in the header files. This information is usually many times the size of the function text and data.
- Once the library has been searched, the linker forgets it. This has important consequences that we'll examine in the upcoming section, the section called "Missing functions".

For reasons shrouded in history, you don't specify the pathname of the library file—instead you tell the linker the names of directories that may contain the libraries you are looking for and a coded representation of the library name. For example, if you want to include */opt/lib/libregex.a* in your search path, you would include *–L/opt/lib -lregex* in your compiler or linker call:

- *–L/opt/lib* tells the linker to include */opt/lib* in the list of directories to search.

- *–lregex* tells the linker to search for the file *libregex.a* in *each* of the directories to search.

This can be a problem if you have four files */usr/lib/libfoo.a*, */usr/lib/libbar.a*, */opt/lib/libfoo.a*, and */opt/lib/libbar.a*, and you want to search only */opt/lib/libfoo.a* and */usr/lib/libbar.a*. In this case, you can name the libraries explicitly.

To keep the pain of linking executables down to tolerable levels, the compiler control program (usually *cc*) supplies a few library paths and specifications for free—normally the equivalent of `-L/usr/lib -lc`, which at least finds the library */usr/lib/libc.a* and also supplies the path to all other libraries in */usr/lib*. You need only specify *additional* paths and libraries. Occasionally, this behavior is undesirable. Suppose you deliberately want to exclude the standard libraries—for example, when you're building an executable for a different version of the operating system? Some compilers give you an option to forget these libraries. For example, in *gcc* it is *–nostdlib*.

Like most aspects of UNIX, there is no complete agreement on where to store library files, but most systems come close to the following arrangement:

- */usr/lib* contains the basic system libraries as well as startup code like *crt0.o* and friends, which are bound in to supply low-level support for the C language. We'll look at this in the next section.
- Some of these files used to be stored in */lib*. Nowadays */lib* tends either not to be present or, for compatibility's sake, it is a symlink to */usr/lib*.
- System V.4 systems place BSD compatibility libraries in */usr/ucblib*.* Many of these functions duplicate functions in */usr/lib*.
- */usr/X11/lib*, */usr/X/lib*, */usr/lib/X11*, */usr/lib/X11R6*, and others are some of the places that the X11 libraries might be hidden. This directory probably contains all the parts of X11 and related code that are on your system.

Shared Libraries

Some libraries can be very big. The X11R6 version *libX11.a*, containing the standard X11 functions, runs to 630 KB on BSD/OS. The Motif library *libXm.a* is nearly 1.4 MB in size. This can lead to enormous executables, even if the program itself is relatively small—the "500 KB Hello world" syndrome. Since these functions are used in many programs, many copies of a function may be active at any one time in the system. For example, just about every program uses the function `printf`, which with its auxiliary functions can be quite big. To combat this, modern UNIX

* As explained earlier, UCB stands for the University of California at Berkeley, the home of the Berkeley Software Distributions. You'll frequently find BSD-derived software stored in directories whose names start with the letters *ucb*.

flavors support *shared libraries*: the library itself is no smaller, but it is in memory only once.

Two different library schemes are in current use: *static shared libraries** and *dynamic shared libraries*. Static shared libraries contain code that has been linked to run at a specific address, which means that you could have difficulties if your program refers to two libraries with overlapping address ranges or if you use a different version of the library with functions at slightly different addresses. Dynamic libraries get around this problem by linking at run time, which requires a *dynamic linker*. Unless you're building shared libraries, a topic beyond the scope of this book, you don't need to worry about the difference between the two. If you do find yourself in the situation where you need to build shared libraries, your best source of information is your operating system documentation.

A shared library performs two different functions:

- When you link your program, it supplies information about the locations of the functions and data in the library. Some systems, such as SunOS 4, supply a "stub" file with a name like *libc.sa.1.9*. Since it does not contain the code of the functions, it is relatively small—on SunOS 4.1.3, it is 7996 bytes. Other systems, such as System V.4, supply only a single library file with a name like *libc.so*. The linker includes only enough information for the dynamic loader to locate the functions in the library file at run time.
- At run time, the shared library supplies the functions and data. The filename is of the form *libc.so.1.9*.

It's important to ensure that you use the same library to perform these two actions. If a function or a data structure changes between versions of the library, a program written for a different version may work badly or crash. This is a common problem: most programs are distributed in executable form and thus contain preconceived notions about what the library looks like. Since we're linking the program ourselves, we should not encounter this problem. If you do run into problems, you can always fall back to static (unshared) libraries.

Other Linker Input

In addition to the user-specified object files and libraries, the C programming language requires a few auxiliary routines to set up its run-time environment. These are stored in one or more auxiliary object files in a place known to the compiler,

* Don't confuse static shared libraries with the term *static libraries*, which are traditional, nonshared libraries.

usually */usr/lib*. For example, under System V.4, we can see how the compiler control program starts the linker if we use the *–v* option to the compiler:

```
$ gcc -v -u baz -o foo foo.o -L. -lbaz -lbar
/usr/ccs/bin/ld -V -Y P,/usr/ccs/lib:/usr/lib -Qy -o foo -u baz
/usr/ccs/lib/crt1.o /usr/ccs/lib/crti.o /usr/ccs/lib/values-Xa.o
/opt/lib/gcc-lib/i386-unknown-sysv4.2/2.5.8/crtbegin.o
-L. -L/opt/lib/gcc-lib/i386-unknown-sysv4.2/2.5.8 -L/usr/ccs/bin
-L/usr/ccs/lib -L/opt/lib foo.o -lbaz -lbar -lgcc -lc
/opt/lib/gcc-lib/i386-unknown-sysv4.2/2.5.8/crtend.o
/usr/ccs/lib/crtn.o -lgcc
```

The same example in BSD/OS specifies the files */usr/lib/crt0.o*, *foo.o*, *–lbar*, *–lbaz*, *–lgcc*, *–lc*, and *–lgcc*—only fractionally more readable. This example should make it clear why almost nobody starts the linker directly.

Merging Relocatable Files

Occasionally, you want to merge a number of object files into one large file. We've seen one way of doing that: create an object file library with *ar*. You can also use the linker to create an object file. The alternative you choose depends on why you want to make the file. If you are creating a function library, use *ar*. As we have seen, the linker includes individual object files from the archive when you build an executable program later. It also happily includes a relocatable object created by a previous invocation of the linker, but in this case it includes the complete object, even if you don't need all the functions.

You don't often need to create relocatable objects with the linker: the only real advantage over a library is that the resultant object is smaller and links faster. If you want to do it, you specify an option, usually *–r*. For example:

```
$ ld -r foo.o bar.o baz.o -o foobarbaz.o
```

This links the three object files *foo.o*, *bar.o*, and *baz.o* and creates a new object file *foobarbaz.o* that contains all the functions and data in the three input files.

Problems with the Link Editor

Once you have compiled all your objects, you're still not home. Plenty can go wrong with the linkage step. In this section we'll look at some of the more common problems.

Invalid linker flags

You normally invoke the linker via the compiler rather than calling it directly. This is a good idea, as we saw in the previous section. If you have a *Makefile* with an explicit linker call, and you run into trouble with linker flags, and the system documentation doesn't help, consider replacing the linker invocation with a compiler invocation.

Invalid object files

Occasionally, the package you are building may already contain object files. It's unlikely that you can use them, but *make* is far too simplistic to notice the difference, and the result is usually some kind of message from the linker saying that it can't figure out what kind of file it is. If you're in doubt, use the *file* command:

```
$ file *.o
gram.o: 386 executable not stripped
main.o: ELF 32-bit LSB relocatable 80386 Version 1
scan.o: sparc executable not stripped
util.o: 80386 COFF executable not stripped - version 30821
```

Here are four different kinds of object files in the same directory. Occasionally, you will see files like this that are there for a good reason: due to license reasons, because there are no corresponding sources, and because there will be one object for each architecture that the package supports. In this example, however, the filenames are different enough that you can be reasonably sure that these files are junk left behind from previous builds. If the object files remain after a *make clean*, you should remove them manually (and fix the *Makefile*).

Suboptimal link order

We have seen that the linker takes all objects it finds and puts their code and data into the code and data segments in the order in which they appear. From the point of view of logic flow, this works fine, but it can have significant performance implications on modern machines. You might find that 95% of the execution time of a program is taken up by 5% of the code. If this code is contiguous, it probably can fit into the cache of any modern machine. If, on the other hand, it is scattered throughout memory, it requires much more cache, possibly more than the machine can supply. This can result in a dramatic drop in performance.

Most linkers do not help you much in arranging functions. The simplest way is to put one function in a file, like you do in an archive, and specify the functions in sequence in the linker invocation. For example, if you have five functions `foo`, `bar`, `baz`, `zot`, and `glarp`, and you determine that you need three functions next to each other in the sequence `foo`, `glarp`, and `zot`, you can invoke the linker with:

```
$ cc -o foobar foo.o glarp.o zot.o bar.o baz.o
```

Missing functions

The UNIX library mechanism works well and is reasonably standardized from one platform to the next. The main problem you are likely to encounter is that the linker can't find a function that the program references. There can be a number of reasons for this:

- The symbol may not be a function name at all but a reference to an undefined preprocessor variable. For example, in *xfm* version 1.1, the source file *FmInfo.c* contains:

```
if (S_ISDIR(mode))
  type = "Directory";
else if (S_ISCHR(mode))
  type = "Character special file";
else if(S_ISBLK(mode))
  type = "Block special file";
else if(S_ISREG(mode))
  type = "Ordinary file";
else if(S_ISSOCK(mode))
  type = "Socket";
else if(S_ISFIFO(mode))
  type = "Pipe or FIFO special file";
```

  sys/stat.h defines the macros of the form `S_IS`*foo*. They test the file mode bits for specific file types. System V does not define `S_ISSOCK` (the kernel doesn't have sockets), so a pre-ANSI compiler assumes that `S_ISSOCK` is a reference to an external function. The module compiles correctly, but the linker fails with an undefined reference to `S_ISSOCK`. The obvious solution is conditional compilation, since `S_ISSOCK` is a preprocessor macro, and you can test for it directly with `#ifdef`:

```
      type = "Ordinary file";
#ifdef S_ISSOCK
    else if(S_ISSOCK(mode))
      type = "Socket";
#endif
    else if(S_ISFIFO(mode))
```

- The function is in a different library, and you need to specify it to the linker. A good example is networking code in the standard C library. A reference to `socket` links just fine with no additional libraries on a BSD platform, but on some versions of System V.3, you need to specify `-linet`, and on System V.4 and other versions of System V.3, you need to specify `-lsocket`. The *findf* script can help here. It uses *nm* to output symbol information from the files specified in `LIBS` and searches the output for a function definition whose name matches the parameter supplied. The search parameter is a regular expression, so you can search for a number of functions at once. For example, to search for `strcasecmp` and `strncasecmp`, you might enter:

```
$ findf str.*casecmp
/usr/lib/libc.a(strcasecmp.o): _strcasecmp
/usr/lib/libc.a(strcasecmp.o)): _strncasecmp
/usr/lib/libc_p.a(strcasecmp.po):       _strcasecmp
/usr/lib/libc_p.a(strcasecmp.po)):      _strncasecmp
```

Because of the differences in *nm* output format, *findf* looks very different on BSD systems and on System V. You may find that you need to modify the script to work on your system. The following script shows a version for 4.4BSD:

```
LIBS="/usr/lib/lib* /usr/X11R6/lib/lib*"
nm $LIBS 2>/dev/null \
  | awk -v fun=$1 \
  '/^\// {file = $1};
  /^[^\/].*:/{member = $1};
  $3 ~ fun && $2 ~ /T/ {
  sub (":$", "", file); ;
  sub (":$", "):", member);
  print file "(" member "\t" $3}'
```

The corresponding script for a system like System V.4, which uses ELF format, is shown below:

```
LIBS="/usr/lib/lib* /usr/X11R6/lib/lib*"
nm $LIBS 2>/dev/null \
  | sed 's:|: :g' \
  | gawk -v fun=$1 \
  '/^Symbols from/ {file = $3};
  $8 ~ fun && $4 ~ /FUNC/ { print file member "\t" $8 }'
```

Some versions of System V *awk* have difficulty with this script, which is why this version uses GNU *awk*.

- The function is written in a different language, and the internal name differs from what the compiler expected. This commonly occurs when you try to call a C function from C++ and forget to tell the C++ compiler that the called function is written in C. We discussed this in the section called "Declarations for C++" in Chapter 17, *Header Files*.
- The function is part of the package but has not been compiled because a configuration parameter is set incorrectly. For example, *xpm*, a pixmap conversion program, uses `strcasecmp`. Knowing that it is not available on all platforms, the author included the function in the package, but it gets compiled only if the *Makefile* contains the compiler flag `-DNEED_STRCASECMP`.

- The function is supplied in a library within the package, but the *Makefile* is in error and tries to reference the library before building it. The purpose of *Makefiles* is to avoid this kind of problem, but it happens often enough to be annoying. It's also not always immediately obvious that this is the cause. If you suspect that this is the reason for a problem you're experiencing but are not sure, try to build all libraries first and see if that helps.
- The function is really not supplied in your system libraries. In this case, you need to find an alternative. We looked at this problem in detail in Chapter 18, *Function Libraries.*
- The first reference to a symbol comes after the linker has searched the library in which it is located.

Let's look at the last problem in more detail. When the linker finishes searching a library, it continues with the following file specifications. It is possible that another file later in the list will refer to an object file contained in the library that was not included in the executable. In this case, the symbol will not be found. Consider the following three files:

foo.c
```
main ()
  {
  bar ("Hello");
  }
```

bar.c
```
void bar (char *c)
  {
  baz (c);
  }
```

baz.c
```
void baz (char *c)
  {
  puts (c);
  }
```

We compile them to the corresponding object files and then make libraries *libbar.a* and *libbaz.a*, which contain just the single object file *bar.o* and *baz.o*, respectively. Then we try to link:

```
$ gcc -c foo.c
$ gcc -c bar.c
$ gcc -c baz.c
$ ar r libbaz.a baz.o
$ ar r libbar.a bar.o
$ gcc -o foo foo.o -L. -lbaz -lbar
Undefined                         first referenced
 symbol                               in file
baz                                   ./libbar.a(bar.o)
```

```
ld: foo: fatal error: Symbol referencing errors. No output written to foo
$ gcc -o foo foo.o -L. -lbar -lbaz
$
```

In the first link attempt, the linker included *foo.o*, then searched *libbaz.a*, and didn't find anything of interest. Then it went on to *libbar.a* and found it needed the symbol baz, but by that time it was too late. You can solve the problem by putting the reference *–lbar* before *–lbaz*.

This problem is not even as simple as it seems. You sometimes find that libraries contain mutual references, although it's bad practice. If *libbar.a* also contained an object file *zot.o*, and baz referred to it, you would have to link with:

```
$ gcc -o foo foo.o -L. -lbar -lbaz -lbar
```

An alternative seems even more of a kludge: with the *–u* option, the linker enters an undefined symbol in its symbol table. In this example, we could also have written:

```
$ gcc -u baz -o foo foo.o -L. -lbaz -lbar
$
```

Dumping to Object Files

Some programs need to perform significant processing during initialization. For example, Emacs macros are written in Emacs LISP, and they take some time to load. Startup would be faster if they were already in memory when the program is started. The only normal way to have them in memory is to compile them in, and it's very difficult to initialize data at compile time as intricately as a program like Emacs does at run time.

The solution chosen is simple in concept: Emacs does it once at run time. Then it dumps itself to disk in object file format. It copies the text section directly from its own text area, since there is no way it can be changed, and it writes the data section from its current data area, including all of what used to be bss. It doesn't need to copy the stack section because it is recreated on initialization.

This rather daring approach works surprisingly well as long as Emacs knows its own object file format. UNIX doesn't provide any way to find out because there is usually no reason why a program *should* know its own object file format. The result can be problems when porting a package like this to a system with a different object format: the port runs fine until the first executable dumps, but the dumped executable does not have a format that the kernel can recognize.

Other programs that use this technique are *gcl* (GNU common LISP) and TEX.

Process Initialization and Stack Frames

In the section called "exec" in Chapter 12, *Kernel Dependencies*, we examined the myriad flavors of `exec`. They all pass arguments and environment information to the newly loaded program. From a C program viewpoint, the arguments are passed as a parameter to `main`, and the environment is just there for the picking. In this section, we'll look more closely at what goes on between `exec` and `main`. In order to understand their interaction, we need to look more closely at parameter passing.

Stack Frames

Most modern machines have a stack-oriented architecture, even if the support is rather rudimentary in some cases. Everybody knows what a stack is, but here we'll use a more restrictive definition: a *stack* is a linear list of storage elements, each relating to a particular function invocation. These are called *stack frames*. Each stack frame contains:

- The parameters with which the function was invoked.
- The address to which to return when the function is complete.
- Saved register contents.
- Variables local to the function.
- The address of the previous stack frame.

With the exception of the return address, any of these fields may be omitted.* Typical stack implementations supply two hardware registers to address the stack:

- The *stack pointer* points to the last used word of the stack.
- The *frame pointer* points to somewhere in the middle of the stack frame.

The resultant memory image looks like the stack in Figure 21-1.

The individual parts of the stack frames are built at various times. In the following sections, we'll see how the stack gets set up and freed.

* Debuggers recognize stack frames by the frame pointer. If you don't save the frame pointer, it will still be pointing to the previous frame, so the debugger will report that you are in the previous function. This frequently happens in system call linkage functions, which typically do not save a stack linkage, or on the very first instruction of a function, before the linkage has been built. In addition, some optimizers remove the stack frame.

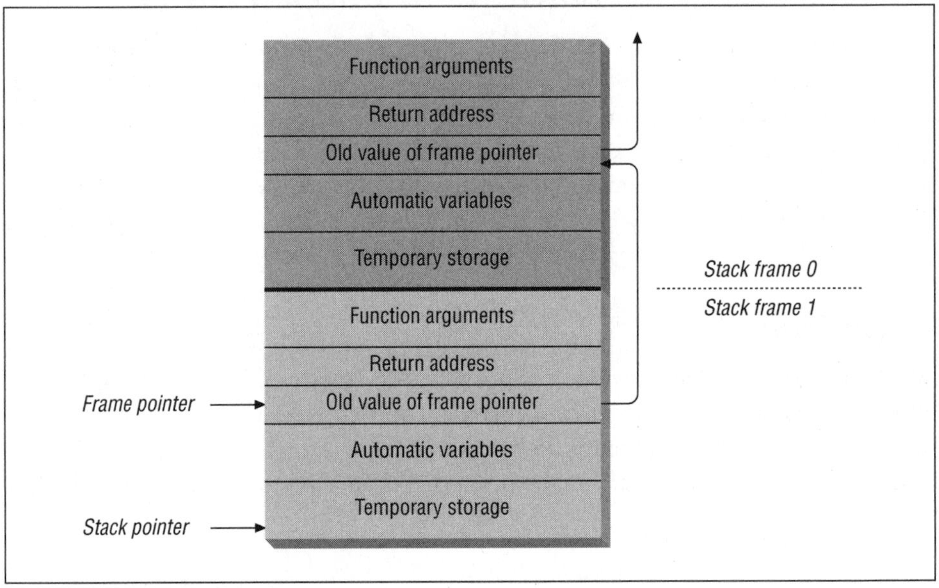

Figure 21-1: Function stack frame

Setting Up the Initial Parameters

exec builds the initial stack. The exact details are implementation dependent, but most come close to the way BSD/OS does it, so we'll look at that.

The stack is always allocated at a fixed point in memory, 0xefbfe000 in the case of BSD/OS, and grows downward, like the stacks on almost every modern architecture. At the very top of the stack is a structure with information for the *ps* program:

```
struct ps_strings
  {
  char    **ps_argv;           /* first of 0 or more argument pointers */
  int     ps_argc;             /* the number of argument pointers */
  char    **ps_envp;           /* first of 0 or more environment pointers */
  int     ps_nenv;             /* the number of environment pointers */
};
```

This structure is supplied for convenience and is not strictly necessary. Many systems, for example FreeBSD, do not define it.

Next, exec places on the stack all environment variable strings, followed by all the program arguments. Some systems severely limit the maximum size of these strings—we looked at the problems that that can cause in the section called "Arg list too long" in Chapter 5, *Building the Package*.

After the variable strings come two sets of NULL-terminated pointers, the first to the environment variables, the second to the program arguments.

Finally, comes the number of arguments to **main**, the well-known parameter **argc**. At this point, the stack looks like the one in Figure 21-2.

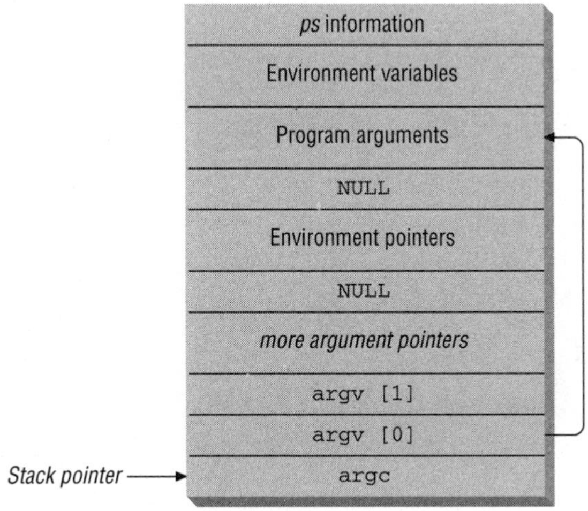

Figure 21-2: Stack frame at start of program

At this point, all the data for **main** is on the stack, but it's not quite in the form that **main** needs. In addition, there's no return address. But where could **main** return to? All this work has been done in the kernel by **exec**: we need to return to a place in the program. These problems are solved by the function **start**, the *real* beginning of the program. It calls **main** and then calls **exit** with the return value from **main**. Before doing so, it may perform some run-time initializations. A minimal **start** function looks like this stripped down version of GNU libc *start.c*, which is the unlikely name of the source file for *crt0.o*:

```
static void start (int argc, char *argp)
{
  char **argv = &argp;    /* set up a pointer to the first argument pointer */
  __environ = &argv [argc + 1]; /* The environment starts just after argv */
  asm ("call L_init");          /* call the .init section */
  __libc_init (argc, argv, __environ); /* Do C and C++ library initializations*/
  exit (main (argc, argv, __environ)); /* Call the user program */
}
```

The asm directive is used for C++ initialization—we'll look at that in the section called "Initializing C++ Programs". But what's this? start calls main with three parameters! The third is the address of the environment variable pointers. This is one of the best-kept secrets in UNIX: main really has three parameters:

```
int main (int argc, char *argv [], char *envp []);
```

It isn't documented anywhere, but it's been there at least since the Seventh Edition. It's unlikely to go away because there isn't really any other good place to store the environment variables.

By the time we have saved the stack linkage in main, the top of the stack looks like the one in Figure 21-3.

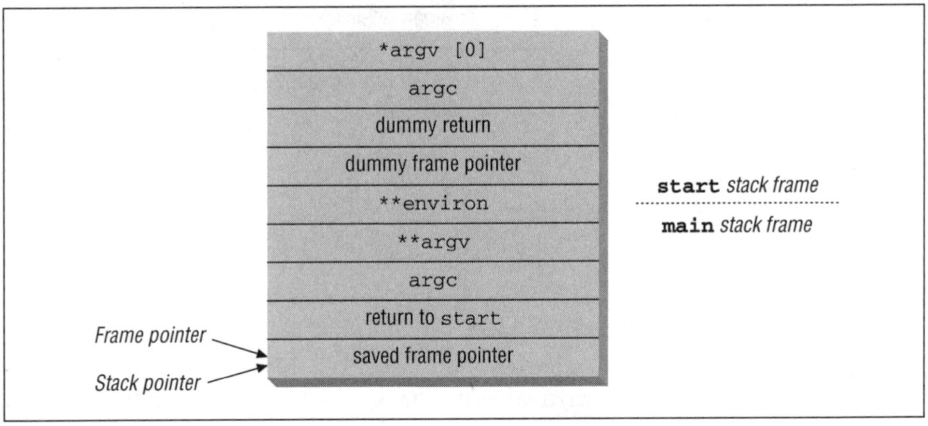

Figure 21-3: Stack frame after entering main

Initializing C++ Programs

What we've seen so far is not enough for C++: before entering main, the program may need to initialize global class instances. Since this is system library code, it can't know what global classes exist. The solution depends on the system:

- System V systems place information about class construction functionbs in a special section, .init. The initialization file *crtn.o* contains a default .init section containing a single return instruction. If a C++ program has global initializers, it creates an .init section to initialize them. If any object module before *ctrn.o* has an .init section, it is included before the .init section in *ctrn.o*. During program initialization, the function start calls the .init section to execute the global constructors—this is the purpose of the asm directive in the section called "Setting Up the Initial Parameters".

- Systems based on *a.out* formats do not have this luxury. Instead, they compile special code into `main` to call the appropriate constructors.

The difference between these two approaches can be important if you are debugging a C++ program that dies in the global constructors.

Stack Growth During Function Calls

Now that we have an initial stack, let's see how it grows and shrinks during a function call. We'll consider the following simple C program compiled on the i386 architecture:

```
foo (int a, int b)
{
  int c = a * b;
  int d = a / b;
  printf ("%d %d\n", c, d);
  }

main (int argc, char *argv [])
{
  int x = 4;
  int y = 5;
  foo (y, x);
  }
```

The assembler code for the calling sequence for `foo` in `main` is:

```
pushl -4(%ebp)          value of x
pushl -8(%ebp)          value of y
call _foo               call the function
addl $8,%esp            and remove parameters
```

Register `ebp` is the *base pointer*, which we call the *frame pointer*. `esp` is the stack pointer.

The `push` instructions decrement the stack pointer and then place the word values of `x` and `y` at the location to which the stack pointer now points.

The `call` instruction pushes the contents of the current instruction pointer (the address of the instruction following the `call` instruction) onto the stack, thus saving the return address, and loads the instruction pointer with the address of the function. We now have the stack shown in Figure 21-4.

The called function `foo` saves the frame pointer (in this architecture, the register is called *ebp*, for *extended base pointer*) and loads it with the current value of the stack pointer register `esp`.

```
_foo:  pushl %ebp              save ebp on stack
       movl %esp,%ebp          and load with current value of esp
```

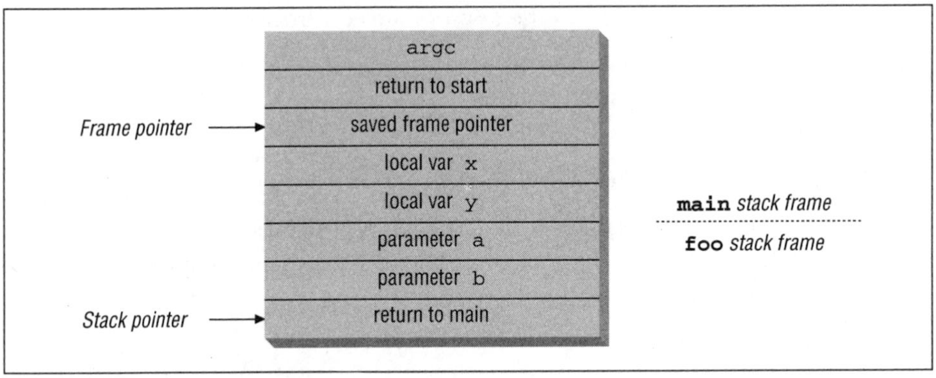

Figure 21-4: Stack frame after call instruction

At this point, the stack linkage is complete, and this is where most debuggers normally set a breakpoint when you request one to be placed at the entry to a function.

Next, `foo` creates local storage for `c` and `d`. They are each 4 bytes long, so it subtracts 8 from the `esp` register to make space for them. Finally, it saves the register `ebx`—the compiler has decided that it will need this register in this function.

```
subl $8,%esp          create two words on stack
pushl %ebx            and save ebx register
```

At this point, our stack is now complete and looks like the one shown in Figure 21-1.

Figure 21-5 shows the effect of entering another function.

The frame pointer isn't absolutely necessary: you can get by without it and refer to the stack pointer instead. The problem is that during the execution of the function, the compiler may save further temporary information on the stack, so it's difficult to keep track of the value of the stack pointer. That's why most architectures use a frame pointer, which *does* stay constant during the execution of the function. Some optimizers, including newer versions of *gcc*, give you the option of compiling without a stack frame. This makes debugging almost impossible.

On return from the function, the sequence is reversed:

```
movl -12(%ebp),%ebx   and restore register ebx
leave                 reload ebp and esp
ret                   and return
```

The first instruction reloads the saved register `ebx`, which could be stored anywhere in the stack. This instruction does not modify the stack.

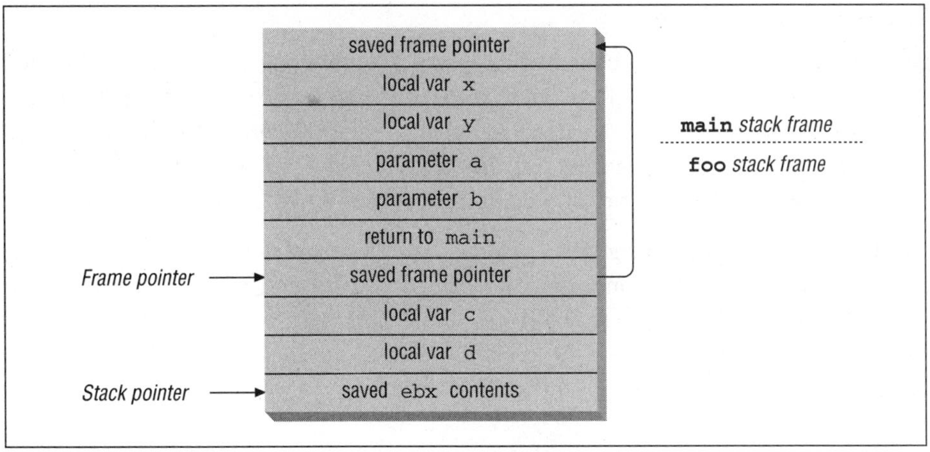

Figure 21-5: Complete stack frame after entering called function

The *leave* instruction loads the stack pointer `esp` from the frame pointer `ebp`, which effectively discards the part stack below the saved `ebp` value. Then it loads `ebp` with the contents of the word to which it points, the saved `ebp`, effectively reversing the stack linkage. The stack now looks like it did on entry.

Next, the `ret` instruction pops the return address into the instruction pointer, causing the next instruction to be fetched from the address following the `call` instruction in the calling function.

The function parameters `x` and `y` are still on the stack, so the next instruction in the calling function removes them by adding to the stack pointer:

```
addl $8,%esp                and remove parameters
```

Object Archive Formats

As we have seen, object files are frequently collected into *libraries*, which from our current point of view are *archives* maintained by *ar*. One of the biggest problems with *ar* archives is that there are so many different forms. You're likely to come across the following ones:

- The so-called *common archive format*. This format starts with the magic string `!<arch>\n`. It is used both in System V.4 and in BSD versions since 4BSD.

- The *PORT5AR* format, which starts with the magic string <ar>. System V.3 defines it but doesn't use it.
- The Seventh Edition archive, which starts with the magic number `0177545`. It is also used by XENIX and System V.2 systems. In System V.3 systems, *file* reports this format as `x.out randomized archive`. 4.4BSD *file* refers to it as `old PDP-11 archive`, while many System V.4 *files* don't recognize it at all. UnixWare is one that does, calling the format a `pdp11/pre System V ar archive`.

As long as you stick to modern systems, the only archive type you're likely to come across is the common archive format. If you do find one of the others, you should remember that you're interested not in the archive but in its contents. If you have another way to get the contents, like the original object or source files, you don't need to worry about the archive.

III

Appendixes

A

Comparative Reference to UNIX Data Types

Table A-1 lists a number of typedefs that are defined in System V.4 and 4.4BSD. The list is not intended to be exhaustive, but it might be of assistance if you run into trouble with a new typedef. Note the following about the table:

- There is a significant deviation even between 4.4BSD and System V.4, although both systems have gone to some trouble to be portable.
- 4.4BSD uses a construct long long to describe 64-bit integers. This is not officially part of the C language but is supported by the GNU C compiler, which is the standard compiler for 4.4BSD. The System V.4 compilers do not support long long, so they have to define quad as a structure containing two longs.

Table A-1: System Type Definitions

Type	System	Definition	Description
addr_t	SVR4	char *	Core address type
amq_mount_tree	4.4BSD	struct amq_mount_tree	
amq_mount_tree_p	4.4BSD	amq_mount_tree *	
ansistat_t	SVR4	struct ansi_state	
audio_info_t	4.4BSD	struct audio_info	
auto_tree	4.4BSD	struct auto_tree	
bitstr_t	4.4BSD	unsigned char	
bool_t	4.4BSD	int	Truth value
boolean_t	4.4BSD	int	
boolean_t	SVR4	enum boolean	
caddr_t	4.4BSD	char *	Core address
cat_t	4.4BSD	unsigned char	

Table A-1: System Type Definitions (continued)

Type	System	Definition	Description
cc_t		unsigned char	
cc_t[a]		char	
charstat_t	SVR4	struct char_stat	
chr_merge_t	SVR4	struct chr_merge	
clock_t	4.4BSD	unsigned long_	
clock_t	SVR4	long	
cnt_t	SVR4	short	Count type
comp_t	4.4BSD	u_short	
comp_t	SVR4	ushort	
create_t	SVR4	enum create	
daddr_t		long	Disk address
dblk_t	SVR4	struct datab	
dev_t		unsigned long	Device number
dirent_t	SVR4	struct dirent	
dmask_t	SVR4	unsigned short	
dpt_dma_t	SVR4	struct ScatterGather	
dpt_sblk_t	SVR4	struct dpt_srb	
emask_t	SVR4	unsigned short	
emcp_t	SVR4	unsigned char *	
emip_t	SVR4	struct emind *	
emop_t	SVR4	struct emout *	
emp_t	SVR4	struct emtab *	
entryno_t	SVR4	int	
ether_addr_t	SVR4	u_char []	
eucioc_t	SVR4	struct eucioc	
faddr_t	SVR4	char *	Far address (XENIX compatibility)
fhandle_t	4.4BSD	struct fhandle	
fhandle_t	SVR4	struct svcfh	
fixpt_t	4.4BSD	unsigned long	Fixed point number
fpos_t	4.4BSD	off_t	
fpos_t	SVR4	long	
frtn_t	SVR4	struct free_rtn	
fsid_t	4.4BSD	struct { long val[2]; }	File system ID type
gdp_t	SVR4	struct gdp	
gdpmisc_t	SVR4	struct gdpmisc	

Table A-1: System Type Definitions (continued)

Type	System	Definition	Description
gid_t	4.4BSD	unsigned long	Group ID
gid_t	SVR4	uid_t	GID type
gid_t[b]		unsigned short	Group ID
greg_t	SVR4	int	
gregset_t	SVR4	greg_t []	
hostid_t	SVR4	long	
id_t	SVR4	long	Process ID, Group ID, etc.
idata_t	SVR4	struct idata	
index_t	SVR4	short	Index into bitmaps
indx_t	4.4BSD	u_int16_t	
ino_t		unsigned long	Inode number
inode_t	SVR4	struct inode	
instr_t	SVR4	char	
int8_t	4.4BSD	char	8-bit signed integer
int16_t	4.4BSD	short	16-bit integer
int32_t	4.4BSD	int	32-bit integer
int64_t	4.4BSD	long long	64-bit integer
ioctl_t	4.4BSD	void *	Third arg of ioctl
jdata_t	SVR4	struct jdata	
k_fltset_t	SVR4	unsigned long	Kernel fault set type
k_sigset_t	SVR4	unsigned long	Kernel signal set type
key_t	4.4BSD	long	IPC key type
key_t	SVR4	int	IPC key type
klm_testargs	SVR4	struct klm_testargs	
klm_testrply	SVR4	struct klm_testrply	
kmabuf_t	SVR4	struct kmabuf	
kmasym_t	SVR4	struct kmasym	
kvm_t	4.4BSD	struct __kvm	
label_t	SVR4	struct {int val [6];}	setjmp/longjmp save area
level_t	SVR4	lid_t	User's view of security level
lid_t	SVR4	unsigned long	Internal representation of security level
lock_data_t	4.4BSD	struct lock	
lock_t	SVR4	short	Lock work for busy wait
major_t	SVR4	unsigned long	Major part of device number
mblk_t	SVR4	struct msgb	

Table A-1: System Type Definitions (continued)

Type	System	Definition	Description
minor_t	SVR4	unsigned long	Minor part of device number
mode_t	4.4BSD	unsigned short	Permissions
mode_t	SVR4	unsigned long	File attribute type
n_time		u_long	ms since 00:00 GMT
nfsv2fh_t	4.4BSD	union nfsv2fh	
nl_catd	SVR4	nl_catd_t *	
nlink_t	4.4BSD	unsigned short	Link count
nlink_t	SVR4	unsigned long	File link type
nmcp_t	SVR4	unsigned char *	
nmp_t	SVR4	struct nmtab *	
nmsp_t	SVR4	struct nmseq *	
o_dev_t	SVR4	short	Old device type
o_gid_t	SVR4	o_uid_t	Old GID type
o_ino_t	SVR4	unsigned short	Old inode type
o_mode_t	SVR4	unsigned short	Old file attribute type
o_nlink_t	SVR4	short	Old file link type
o_pid_t	SVR4	short	Old process ID type
o_uid_t	SVR4	unsigned short	Old UID type
off_t	4.4BSD	quad_t	File offset type
off_t	SVR4	long	File offset type
paddr_t	4.4BSD	long	Physical address type
paddr_t	SVR4	unsigned long	Physical address type
pgno_t	4.4BSD	u_int32_t	
pid_t	4.4BSD	long	Process ID
pid_t	SVR4	long	Process ID type
priv_t	SVR4	unsigned long	
ptr_t	4.4BSD	void *	Pointer type
ptrdiff_t		int	Difference between two pointers
pvec_t	SVR4	unsigned long	Kernel privilege vector
qaddr_t	4.4BSD	quad_t *	
qband_t	SVR4	struct qband	
qshift_t	4.4BSD	u_quad_t	
quad_t	4.4BSD	long long	
queue_t	SVR4	struct queue	
recno_t	4.4BSD	u_int32_t	

Table A-1: System Type Definitions (continued)

Type	System	Definition	Description
regoff_t	4.4BSD	off_t	
rf_token_t	SVR4	struct rf_token	
rlim_t	SVR4	unsigned long	
rm_t	SVR4	enum rm	
rune_t	4.4BSD	int	"rune" type: extended character
rval_t	SVR4	union rval	
s_token	SVR4	u_long	
scrnmap_t	SVR4	unsigned char []	Screen map type
scrnmapp_t	SVR4	unsigned char *	Pointer to screen map type
segsz_t	4.4BSD	long	Segment size
sel_t	SVR4	unsigned short	Selector type
sema_t	SVR4	int	
sig_atomic_t		int	
sig_t	4.4BSD	void (*) (int	Return type of signal function
sigset_t	4.4BSD	unsigned int	
size_t	4.4BSD	int	
size_t	SVR4	unsigned	
speed_t	4.4BSD	long	
speed_t	SVR4	unsigned long	
spl_t	SVR4	int	
srqtab_t	SVR4	unsigned char []	
ssize_t	4.4BSD	int	To return byte count or indicate error
stack_t	SVR4	struct sigaltstack	
stridx_t	SVR4	ushort []	String map index type
strmap_t	SVR4	unchar []	String map table type
sv_t	SVR4	char	
swblk_t	4.4BSD	long	swap offset
symfollow_t	SVR4	enum symfollow	
sysid_t	SVR4	short	System ID
tcflag_t		unsigned long	
tcl_addr_t	SVR4	struct tcl_addr	
tcl_data_t	SVR4	union tcl_data	
tcl_endpt_t	SVR4	struct tcl_endpt	
tco_addr_t	SVR4	struct tco_addr	

Table A-1: System Type Definitions (continued)

Type	System	Definition	Description
tco_endpt_t	SVR4	struct tco_endpt	
tcoo_addr_t	SVR4	struct tcoo_addr	
tcoo_endpt_t	SVR4	struct tcoo_endpt	
time_t		long	Time of day in seconds
tpproto_t	SVR4	struct tpproto	
tpr_t	4.4BSD	struct session *	
ttychar_t	4.4BSD	unsigned char [] []	
u_char		unsigned char	
u_int		unsigned int	
u_int16_t	4.4BSD	unsigned short	16-bit unsigned int
u_int32_t	4.4BSD	unsigned int	32-bit unsigned int
u_int64_t	4.4BSD	unsigned long long	64-bit unsigned int
u_int8_t	4.4BSD	unsigned char	64-bit unsigned int
u_long		unsigned long	Abbreviation
u_quad_t	4.4BSD	unsigned long long	quads
u_short		unsigned short	Abbreviation
uchar_t	SVR4	unsigned char	
uid_t	4.4BSD	unsigned long	User ID
uid_t	SVR4	long	User ID
uid_t[b]		unsigned short	User ID
uinfo_t	SVR4	struct master *	
uint		unsigned int	Abbreviation
uint_t	SVR4	unsigned int	
uio_rw_t	SVR4	enum uio_rw	
uio_seg_t	SVR4	enum uio_seg	
ulong	SVR4	unsigned long	Abbreviation
ulong_t	SVR4	unsigned long	
unchar	SVR4	unsigned char	Abbreviation
use_t	SVR4	unsigned char	use count for swap
ushort		unsigned short	Abbreviation
ushort_t	SVR4	unsigned short	
vcexcl_t	SVR4	enum vcexcl	
vfs_namemap_t	4.4BSD	struct vfs_namemap	
vifbitmap_t	4.4BSD	u_long	
vifi_t	4.4BSD	u_short	Type of a vif index

Table A-1: System Type Definitions (continued)

Type	System	Definition	Description
vpix_page_t	SVR4	struct vpix_page	
wchar_t	4.4BSD	int	Wide character type
wchar_t	SVR4	long	Wide character type
whymountroot_t	SVR4	enum whymountroot	
xdrproc_t		bool_t(*) ()	

[a] Only 4.4BSD telnet
[b] Only 4.4BSD Kerberos

In This Appendix:
- *C Compiler Options*
- *gcc Dialect Options*
- *gcc Debugging Options*
- *gcc Warning Options*
- *cpp Options*

B

C Compiler Options

There is little standardization in the choice of compiler options from one compiler to another, though a couple of options (*–o* and *–c*, for example) are the same across all platforms. Even the *–o* option differs slightly in meaning from one system to another, however. If there is *any* reliable documentation, it's what was supplied with your compiler. This doesn't help you, of course; if you have a *Makefile* from some unfamiliar machine, and you're trying to figure out what the options there mean.

This table should fill that gap: if you find an option, chances are this table can help you guess what it means. If you're looking for a way to tell *your* compiler what to do, read its documentation.

This appendix provides the following comparative references between the GNU, SGI IRIX, SCO UNIX, Solaris, SunOS, System V.3, System V.4, and XENIX versions of the C compiler control program and the C preprocessor.

- Options used by the C compiler control program (*cc* or *gcc*), starting after this section.
- *gcc*-specific options specifying dialect
- *gcc*-specific debugging options
- *gcc*-specific warning options
- Options used by the C preprocessor *cpp*

C Compiler Options

`-a` *gcc*, SunOS

Generate extra code to write profile information for *tcov*.

`-a` *`align`* some MS-DOS compilers

Align in `structs` to *`align`* boundary.

`-A` SVR3

Linker output should be an absolute file (i.e., the opposite of the *–r* option).

`-A` *gcc*, SVR4

–A`question`(*`answer`*) asserts that the answer to *`question`* is *`answer`*. This can used with the preprocessor conditional *`#if #question(answer)`*.

`-A-` *gcc*, SVR4

Disable standard assertions. In addition, SVR4 *cc* undefines all standard macros except those beginning with `__`.

`-acpp` SGI

Use alternative *cpp* based on GNU *cpp*.

`-align` *`block`* SunOS

Force the global bss symbol *`block`* to be aligned to the beginning of a page.

`-ansi` *gcc*, SGI

Enforce strict ANSI compatibility.

`-ansiposix` SGI

Enforce strict ANSI compatibility and define `_POSIX_SOURCE`.

`-B` *gcc*

Specify the path of the directory from which the compiler control program *gcc* should start the individual passes of the compiler.

`-B dynamic` SunOS, SVR4

Dynamic linking: tell the linker to search for library files named *libfoo.so* and then *libfoo.a* when passed the option *–lfoo*.

`-B static` SunOS, SVR4

Static linking: tell the linker to just search for *libfoo.a* when passed the option *–lfoo*.

`-b` *`target`* *gcc*

Cross-compile for machine *`target`*.

`-C` — *gcc*, SGI ANSI C, SCO UNIX, SunOS, SVR4

Tell the preprocessor not to discard comments. Used with the *–E* option.

`-c` — all

Stop compiler after producing the object file, do not link.

`-call_shared` — older MIPS

Produce an executable that uses shareable objects (default). On more modern SGI machines, this is called *–KPIC*.

`-cckr` — SGI

Define K&R-style preprocessor variables.

`-common` — SGI

Cause multiple definitions of global data to be considered to be one definition, and do not produce error messages.

`-compat` — SCO UNIX

Create an executable that is binary compatible across a number of Intel-based systems. Use XENIX libraries to link.

`-cord` — SGI

Rearrange functions in the object file to reduce cache conflicts.

`-CSON` — SCO UNIX

Enable common subexpression optimization. Used in conjunction with the *–O* option.

`-CSOFF` — SCO UNIX

Disable common subexpression optimization. Used in conjunction with the *–O* option.

`-D` — all

Define a preprocessor macro. The form *–Dfoo* defines *foo* but does not give it a value. This can be tested with `#ifdef` and friends. The form *–Dfoo=3* defines *foo* to have the value 3. This can be tested with `#if`.

`-d` — XENIX, SCO UNIX

Report the compiler passes and arguments as they are executed.

`-d` *when* — *gcc*

Make dumps during compilation for debugging the compiler. *when* specifies when the dump should be made. Most options should not be needed by normal users, however the forms *–dD* (leave all macro definitions in the preprocessor output), *–dM* (dump only the macro definitions in effect at the end of preprocessing), and *–dN* (like *–dD* except that only the macro names are output) can be used with the *–E* option in order to debug preprocessor macros.

`-dalign` SunOS on Sun-4 systems

Generate double load/store instructions for better performance.

`-dD` *gcc*

Special case of the *-d* option: leave all macro definitions in the preprocessor output. The resulting output will probably not compile, but it's useful for debugging preprocessor macros.

`-dl` SVR3

Don't generate line number information for the symbolic debugger.

`-dM` *gcc*

Special case of the *-d* option: dump only the macro definitions in effect at the end of preprocessing.

`-dn` SVR4

Don't use dynamic linking. This option cannot be used with the *-G* option.

`-dollar` SGI

Allow the symbol `$` in C identifiers.

`-dos` SCO UNIX, XENIX

Create an executable for MS-DOS systems.

`-dryrun` SunOS

Display the commands that the compiler would execute, but do not execute them

`-ds` SVR3

Don't generate symbol attribute information for the symbolic debugger. Together they are the opposite of the *-g* option.

`-dsl`

Combines *-ds* and *-dl.*

`-dy` SVR4

Use dynamic linking where possible. This is the default.

`-E` all

Write preprocessor output to standard output, then stop. Some compilers interpret the *-o* option and write the output there instead if specified.

`-EP` SCO UNIX, XENIX

Use this instead of the *-E* option to generate preprocessor output without `#line` directives. The output is written to standard output. In addition, SCO UNIX copies the output to a file with the suffix *.i.*

`-F` *num* SCO UNIX, XENIX

Set the size of the program stack to *num* (hexadecimal) bytes.

`-f` *gcc*

A family of options specifying details of the C dialect to be compiled. See the section called "gcc Dialect Options" for more details.

`-f` *type* SunOS

Specify the kind of floating-point code to generate on Sun-2, Sun-3, and Sun-4 systems.

`-Fa` *name* SCO UNIX, XENIX

Write an assembler source listing to *name* (default *file.s*).

`-Fc` *name* SCO UNIX, XENIX

Write a merged assembler and C source listing to *name* (default *file.L*).

`-feedback` *name* SGI

Specify the name of the feedback file used in conjunction with the *–cord* option.

`-Fe` *name* SCO UNIX, XENIX

Specify the name of the executable file.

`-Fl` *name* SCO UNIX, XENIX

Write an assembler listing with assembler source and object code to *name* (default *file.L*).

`-float` SGI

Cause the compiler not to promote `float` to `double`.

`-Fm` *name* SCO UNIX, XENIX

Write a load map to *name* (default *a.map*).

`-Fo` *name* SCO UNIX, XENIX

Specify the name of the object file.

`-Fp` SCO UNIX, XENIX

Specify floating-point arithmetic options for MS-DOS cross-compilation.

`-framepointer` SGI

Use a register other than the stack pointer (sp) for the frame pointers. (See the section called "Stack Frames" in Chapter 21, *Object Files and Friends.*)

`-fullwarn` SGI

Produce all possible warnings.

`-Fs` *name* — SCO UNIX, XENIX

Write a C source listing to *name* (default *file.S*).

`-G` — SVR4

Instruct the linker to create a shared object rather than a dynamically linked executable. This is incompatible with the *–dn* option.

`-G` *`size`* — SGI

Limit items to be placed in the global pointer area to *`size`* bytes.

`-g` — all

Create additional symbolic information in order to support symbolic debuggers. *gcc* has a number of suboptions to specify the amount and the nature of the debugging information—see the section called "gcc Dialect Options" for more details. SGI C specifies a numeric level for the amount of debug information to produce.

`-Gc` — SCO UNIX

Generate code with the alternate calling sequence and naming conventions used in System V 386 Pascal and System V 386 FORTRAN.

`-go` — SunOS

Produce additional symbol table information for *adb*.

`-Gs` — SCO UNIX

Removes stack probe routines. Effective only in non-protected environments.

`-H` — *gcc*, System V

Print the names of header files to the standard output as they are `#included`.

`-H` *num* — SCO UNIX, XENIX

Set the maximum length of external symbols to *num*.

`-help` — SCO UNIX, SunOS

Display help for *cc*.

`-I` *`dir`* — all

Add *`dir`* to a list of pathnames to search for header files included by the `#include` directive.

`-I` — SGI

Remove */usr/include* from the list of paths to search for header files.

`-I-` — *gcc*

Search the list of include pathnames only when the `#include` directive is of the form `#include "header"`. Do not search these directories if the directive is `#include <header>`. In addition, do not search the current directory for header files. If *–I `dir`* options are specified after *–I-*, they apply for all forms of the `#include` directive.

`-i` SCO UNIX, XENIX

Create separate instruction and data spaces for small model programs.

`-J` SCO UNIX

Change the default mode for the `char` type to `unsigned`.

`-J` SunOS, Sun-2, and Sun-3

Generate 32-bit offsets in `switch` statements.

`-J` *`sfm`* SVR4

Specify the pathname of the assembly language source math library *libsfm.sa*. The positioning of this option is important, since the library is searched when the name is encountered.

`-j` SGI

Create a file *file.u* containing intermediate code. Does not create an object file unless used in conjunction with *–c*.

`-KPIC` SGI

Generate position-independent code.

`-imacros` *`file`* *gcc*

Process *`file`* before reading the regular input. Do not produce any output for *`file`*—only the macro definitions will be of use.

`-include` *`file`* *gcc*

Process *`file`* as input before processing the regular input file. The text of the file will be handled exactly like the regular files.

`-K` SVR4

Specify various code generation options.

`-K` SCO UNIX, XENIX

Remove stack probes from a program. Useful only in nonprotected environments.

`-k` *`options`* SGI

Pass *`options`* to the ucode loader.

`-ko` *`name`* SGI

Cause the output of the intermediate code loader to be called *`name`*.

`-L` SCO UNIX, XENIX

Create an assembler listing with assembled code and assembler source instructions with the name *file.L*.

`-L` *`dir`* — all but SCO UNIX, XENIX

Add *`dir`* to the list of directories to search to resolve library references. See the section called "Library Search" in Chapter 18, *Function Libraries* for further details.

`-l` — all but XENIX

Specify a library. The option *–lbaz* searches the library paths specified via *–L* options (see above) for a file typically called *libbaz.a*. See the section called "Library Search" in Chapter 18 for more details.

`-LARGE` — SCO UNIX, XENIX

Invoke the large model compiler to run. Used if heap space problems occur during compilation.

`-link` *`specs`* — SCO UNIX, XENIX

Pass *`specs`* to the linker. All text following up to the end of the command line is passed to the linker, so this command has to be the last one on the line.

`-M` — SVR3

Instruct the linker to output a message for each multiply defined external symbol.

`-M` — *gcc*, SGI, SunOS, Solaris

Instruct the preprocessor to write a list of *Makefile* dependencies to `stdout`. Suppress normal preprocessor output.

`-MM` — *gcc*

Like the *–M* option, but process only `#include "file"` directives—ignore `#include <file>`.

`-MD` — *gcc*

Like the *–M* directive but output to a file whose name is made by replacing the final *.c* with *.d*. This option does not suppress preprocessor output.

`-MDupdate` *`file`* — SGI

While compiling, update *`file`* to contain header, library, and run-time dependency information for the output file.

`-MMD` — *gcc*

Combination of *–MD* and *–MM*. Does not suppress preprocessor output.

`-Ma` — SCO UNIX, XENIX

Compile strict ANSI.

`-M model` SCO UNIX, XENIX
: PSelect model (only 16-bit modes). *model* may be `c` (compact), `s` (small), `m` (medium), `l` (large), or `h` (huge).

`-M num` SCO UNIX, XENIX
: Specify processor model for which code should be generated. `0` specifies 8086, `1` specifies 80186, `2` specifies 80286, and `3` specifies 80386 or later. Sixteen-bit models (`0` to `2`) may be followed by models `s`, `m`, or `l`.

`-Mb` SCO UNIX, XENIX
: Reverse the word order for `long` types.

`-Md` SCO UNIX, XENIX
: Generate code for separate stack and data segments.

`-Me` SCO UNIX, XENIX
: Enable the keywords `far`, `near`, `huge`, `pascal`, and `fortran`.

`-Mf` SCO UNIX, XENIX
: Enable software floating point.

`-Mt num` SCO UNIX, XENIX
: Set the maximum size of data items to *num*. Valid only for large model.

`-m` SVR3
: Write a load map to standard output.

`-m file` SCO UNIX, XENIX
: Write a load map to *file*.

`-mips num` SGI
: Specify the target machine. *num* `1` (default) generates code for R2000/R3000, and `2` generates code for R4000.

`-misalign` SunOS on Sun-4
: Generate code to allow loading and storing misaligned data.

`-mp` SGI
: Enable multiprocessing directives.

`-n` SCO UNIX, XENIX
: Select pure text model (separated text and data).

`-ND name` SCO UNIX, XENIX
: Set the names of each data segment to *name*.

`-nl num` SCO UNIX, XENIX
: Set the maximum length of external symbols to *num*.

`-NM` *name* SCO UNIX, XENIX

Set the names of each module to *name*.

`-nocpp` SGI

Do not run the preprocessor when compiling.

`-nointl` SCO UNIX

Create a binary without international functionality.

`-non_shared` SGI

Produce an executable that does not use shared objects.

`-noprototypes` SGI

Remove prototype error and warning messages when run in *–cckr* mode.

`-nostdinc` *gcc*, SGI

Do not search the standard include file locations (like */usr/include*) for header files. Search only the directories specified with the *–I* option. *gcc* also has a version *–nostdinc*++ for C++ programs.

`-nostdlib` *gcc*

Don't include the standard startup files and library paths when linking. Only files explicitly mentioned on the command line will be included.

`-NT` *name* SCO UNIX, XENIX

Set the names of each text segment to *name*.

`-O` all

Perform optimizations. In some compilers, this option may be followed by a level number (*–O1* normal optimizations, *–O2* additional optimizations, etc.). *–O* means the same as *–O1*. Others, such as the SCO compiler, use letters to specify specific optimizations.

`-o` *file* all

Name the output file *file*. System V compilers use this option only to specify the name of the final executable, whereas other compilers use it to specify the name of the output of the final compiler pass. This can give rise to compatibility problems—see the section called "Choosing a Compiler" in Chapter 20, *Compilers* for further details.

`-oldcpp` SGI

Run with old-style *cpp*.

`-Olimit` *size* SGI

Set the maximum size of a routine to be optimized by the global optimizer to *size* basic blocks.

`-os2` SCO UNIX

Create an executable program for OS/2.

`-P` *gcc*

Instruct the preprocessor not to generate `#line` commands. Used with the *–E* option.

`-P` SunOS, SGI, SVR4, SCO UNIX, XENIX

Use instead of the *–E* option to generate preprocessor output without `#line` directives. The output will be stored in *file.i.*

`-p` all

Generate extra code to aid profiling using the profiling program *prof.*

`-pack` SCO UNIX, XENIX

Ignore alignment considerations in `structs` and pack as tightly as possible.

`-pca` SGI

Run the *pca* processor to discover parallelism in the source code.

`-pedantic` *gcc,* SGI

Be pedantic about syntax checking, issue all required warnings. The variety *–pedantic-errors* treats them as errors instead of warnings.

`-pg` *gcc,* SunOS

Like *–p,* except that the output is suitable for processing by the *gprof* profiler.

`-pic, -PIC` SunOS

Generate position-independent code. The form *–PIC* allows a larger global offset table.

`-pipe` *gcc,* SunOS

Specify that output from one pass should be piped to the next pass, rather than using the more traditional technique of storing it in a temporary file.

`-prototypes` SGI

Output ANSI function prototypes for all functions in the source file when run in *–cckr* mode.

`-qp` System V

A synonym for *–p.*

`-Qn` *gcc* (System V versions), SVR4

Do not output `.ident` directives to the assembler output to identify the versions of each tool used in the output file.

`-Qy` — *gcc* (System V versions), SVR4

Output `.ident` directives to the assembler output to identify the versions of each tool used in the output file.

`-Q` *`prog opt`* — SunOS

Pass option *`opt`* to program *`prog`*. *`prog`* may be `as` (the assembler), `cpp` (the preprocessor), `inline` (the assembly code reorganizer), or `ld` (the loader).

`-Q` *`path`* — SunOS

Specify search paths for compiler passes and other internal files, such as **crt*.o*.

`-Qproduce` *`type`* — SunOS

Produce source code output of type *`type`*. *`type`* specifies the filename extension and may be one of **.c** (C source), **.i** (preprocessor output), **.o** (object output from the assembler) or **.s** (assembler output from the compiler).

`-R` — SunOS

Merge the data segment into text. This creates read-only data.

`-r` — SCO UNIX, XENIX

Invoke the incremental linker */lib/ldr* for the link step.

`-r` — SVR3

Instruct the linker to retain relocation information in the final executable.

`-S` — *gcc*, SGI, SunOS, System V

Stop after compiling the output assembler code, and do not assemble it. Save the results in a file *file.s*.

`-S` — SCO UNIX, XENIX

Create a human-readable assembler source listing in *file.s*. This listing is not suitable for assembly.

`-s` — SCO UNIX, XENIX, SVR3

Strip the final executable.

`-save-temps` — *gcc*

Keep intermediate files even when they are no longer needed.

`-sb` — SunOS

Generate additional symbol table information for the Sun Source Code Browser.

`-SEG` *`num`* — SCO UNIX, XENIX

Set the maximum number of segments that the linker can handle to *`num`*.

`-shared` *gcc*

Produce a shared object that can be linked with other objects to form an executable.

`-show` SGI

Print the names of the passes and their arguments during compilation.

`-signed` SGI

Use signed characters instead of the default unsigned characters.

`-sopt` SGI

Invoke the C source-to-source optimizer. There is nothing corresponding to this on other platforms.

`-Ss` *`subtitle`* SCO UNIX

Sets subtitle of the source listing. This also causes the linker pass to be omitted.

`-St` *`title`* SCO UNIX

Sets title of the source listing. This also causes the linker pass to be omitted.

`-static` *gcc*

Produce a statically linked object. This is of interest only on systems that have shared libraries.

`-systype` MIPS

Specify the name of the compilation environment. Valid names are `bsd4`, `svr3` and `svr4`.

`-t` SVR3

Instruct the linker to suppress warnings about multiply defined symbols that are not the same size.

`-target` *`arch`* SunOS

Specify the target machine. *`arch`* can be one of `sun2`, `sun3`, or `sun4`.

`-Tc` SCO UNIX

Specify that the input file is a C source file. This can be used if the file does not have a standard *.c* filename extension.

`-temp=`*`dir`* SunOS

Store compiler temporary files in *`dir`*.

`-time` SunOS

Print time information for each compiler pass.

`-traditional` *gcc*

Treat the input sources as pre-ANSI-C. There is also an option `-traditional-cpp` that affects only the preprocessor.

`-trigraphs` *gcc*

Enable trigraph processing. By default, trigraphs are disabled unless the `-ansi` option is specified.

`-U` *`macro`* all

Undefine *`macro`*.

`-u` *`symbol`* *gcc*, SVR3

Force the linker to resolve the symbol *`symbol`* by searching additional libraries where specified.

`-u` SCO UNIX

Undefine all predefined macros.

`-undef` *gcc*

Do not predefine standard macros. This includes the macros that define the architecture.

`-use-readonly-const` SGI

Do not allow writing to strings and aggregate constants.

`-use-readwrite-const` SGI

Allow writing to strings and aggregate constants.

`-V` System V

Print version numbers of the compiler passes as they are invoked.

`-V` *`version`* *gcc* 2.X

Tell *gcc* to run version *`version`* of *gcc*.

`-V` *`string`* SCO UNIX

Place *`string`* in the object file, typically for use as a copyright notice or version information.

`-V` *`version`* XENIX

Compile a program compatible with specific versions of UNIX. *`version`* may be 2 (Seventh Edition compatible), 3 (System III compatible), or 5 (System V compatible).

`-v` *gcc*, SGI

Produce verbose output. *gcc* output includes the complete invocation parameters of each pass and the version numbers of the passes.

`-v` SVR4

Perform more and stricter semantic checks.

`-varargs` SGI

Print warnings for lines that may require the *varargs.h* macros.

`-W` *gcc*

Without an argument, print a number of additional warning messages. With an argument, add a specific kind of warning message check—see the section called "gcc Debugging Options" for more details.

`-W` *`num`* SCO UNIX, XENIX

Specify the level of warning messages. If *`num`* is 0, no warnings are produced. A maximum number of warnings is produced by `-W3`.

`-W0,`*`option`* System V

Pass *`option`* to the compiler.

`-W2,`*`option`* System V

Pass *`option`* to the optimizer.

`-Wa,`*`option`* *gcc*, System V

Pass *`option`* to the assembler.

`-Wb,`*`option`* System V

Pass *`option`* to the basic block analyzer.

`-Wl,`*`option`* *gcc*, System V

Pass *`option`* to the linker.

`-Wp,`*`option`* System V

Pass *`option`* to the preprocessor.

`-w` *gcc*, SCO UNIX, SunOS, XENIX

Inhibit warning messages.

`-w` *`num`* SGI

If *`num`* is `0` or `1`, suppress warning messages. If *`num`* is `2`, treat warnings as errors.

`-wline` SGI

Produce *lint*-like warning messages.

`-woff` *`numbers`* SGI

Suppress warning messages corresponding to *`numbers`*.

`-X` SCO UNIX, XENIX

Remove the standard directories from the list of directories to be searched for `#include` files.

`-Xa` SVR4

Compile full ANSI C. Extensions are enabled.

`-Xc` SVR4

Compile strictly conforming ANSI C. Extensions are disabled.

`-Xcpluscomm` SGI

Allow the C++ comment delimiter `//` when processing C code.

`-xansi` SGI

Process ANSI C, but accept the extensions allowed by *-cckr*.

`-xenix` SCO UNIX

Produce XENIX programs using XENIX libraries and include files.

`-xgot` SGI

Compile using a 32-bit offset in the Global Symbol Table. This can be ignored for other systems.

`-x2.3` SCO UNIX

Produce XENIX programs using XENIX libraries and include files. The programs are compatible with release 2.3 of XENIX (the last release, with 80386 capabilities).

`-Xlinker,`*`option`* *gcc*

Pass *`option`* to the linker.

`-Xp` SVR3

Compile for a POSIX.1 environment.

`-Xs` SVR3

Compile for a System V.3 environment (i.e., not POSIX.1).

`-Xt` SVR4

Compile pre-ANSI C, but with compatibility warnings.

`-x` SVR3

Instruct the linker to save space by not preserving local symbols in the final executable.

`-x` *`lang`* *gcc*

Specify the language to be compiled. *`lang`* may be one of `c`, `objective-c`, `c-header`, `c++`, `cpp-output`, `assembler`, or `assembler-with-cpp`. This overrides the filename extensions.

`-Y0,`*`dir`* SVR3

Search for compiler in directory *`dir`*.

`-Y2,`*`dir`* SVR3

Search for optimizer in directory *dir*.

`-Ya,`*`dir`* SVR3

Search for assembler in directory *dir*.

`-Yb,`*`dir`* SVR3

Search for basic block analyzer in directory *dir*.

`-YI,`*`dir`* SVR3

Search for default include directory in directory *dir*.

`-Yl,`*`dir`* SVR3

Search for link editor in directory *dir*.

`-YL,`*`dir`* SVR3

Search for first default library directory in directory *dir*.

`-Ym,`*`dir`* *gcc* (System V versions)

Search for *m4* in directory *dir*.

`-YP,`*`dirs`* SVR3, *gcc* (System V versions)

Tell the compiler to search the directories *dirs* (a colon-separated list, like the PATH environment variable) for libraries specified via the *–l* option. This is an alternative to *–L*. Only the directories specified in the last *–YP* option are searched.

`-Yp,`*`dir`* SVR3

Search for compiler in directory *dir*.

`-YS,`*`dir`* SVR3

Search for startup files *crt1.o* and *crtend.o* in directory *dir*.

`-YU,`*`dir`* SVR3

Search for second default library directory in directory *dir*.

`-z` SCO UNIX, XENIX

Display the passes and arguments, but do not execute them.

`-z` SVR3

Instruct the linker not to bind anything at address 0 so as to aid run-time detection of `NULL` pointers.

`-Za` SCO UNIX, XENIX

Restrict the language to ANSI specifications.

`-Zd` SCO UNIX, XENIX

Include line number information in the object file.

-Ze SCO UNIX

Enables the keywords far, near, huge, pascal, and fortran. The same as the *–Me* option.

-Zi SCO UNIX, XENIX

Include symbolic information in the object file.

-Zl SCO UNIX

Do not include default library information in the object file.

-Zp *align* SCO UNIX, XENIX, SVR3

Force structs to align to the an *align* boundaries. *align* may be 0, 2, or 4, and defaults to 1.

-Zs SCO UNIX, XENIX

Perform syntax check only, do not compile.

gcc Dialect Options

gcc supplies a large number of options to specify what dialect of C should be compiled. In addition, it supplies a further large number of options for C++ dialect. We'll look only at the C dialect options is this section. Check the *gcc* release for the complete documentation.

-ansi

Compile ANSI C. Flag any nonstandard extension as warnings, but do not treat them as errors. This option implies the options *–fn-asm* and *–trigraphs.*

-fno-asm

Do not recognize the keywords asm, inline, or typeof so that they can be used as identifiers. The keywords __asm__, __inline__, and __typeof__ can be used instead.

-fno-builtin

Don't recognize built-in function names that do not begin with two leading underscores.

-trigraphs

Support ANSI C trigraphs.

-traditional

Support pre-ANSI dialects. This also implies *–funsigned-bitfields* and *–fwritable-strings.*

`-traditional-cpp`
: Provide pre-ANSI style preprocessing. This is implied by *-traditional.*

`-fcond-mismatch`
: Allow conditional expressions (such as `a: b? c`) where the second and third arguments have different types.

`-funsigned-char`
: By default, characters are unsigned. This effectively makes the declaration `char` the same as `unsigned char`.

`-fsigned-char`
: By default, characters are signed. This effectively makes the declaration `char` the same as `signed char`.

`-fsigned-bitfields`
: Make bit fields signed by default. This is the default action.

`-funsigned-bitfields`
: Make bit fields unsigned by default.

`-fno-signed-bitfields`
: Make bit fields unsigned by default.

`-fno-unsigned-bitfields`
: Make bit fields signed by default. This is the default action.

`-fwritable-strings`
: Allocate strings in the data segment, so that the program can write to them. See the section called "Kernighan and Ritchie" in Chapter 20 for a discussion of this misfeature.

`-fallow-single-precision`
: Do not perform operations on single precision floating point values with double precision arithmetic. This is needed only if you specify *-traditional.*

gcc Debugging Options

`-g` *`mods`*
: Produce standard debugging information. This can be used in conjunction with *gdb.* It sometimes includes information that can confuse other debuggers.

`-ggdb` *`mods`*
: Produce debugging information in the native format (if that is supported), including *gdb* extensions if at all possible.

`-gstabs` *mods*
: Produce debugging information in stabs format without *gdb* extensions.

`-gcoff` *mods*
: Produce debugging information in the COFF format used by *sdb* on older System V systems.

`-gxcoff` *mods*
: Produce debugging information in the XCOFF format used by *dbs* on IBM RS/6000 systems.

`-gdwarf` *mods*
: Produce debugging information in the DWARF format used by *sdb* on most SVR4 systems.

mods are optional and may take the value `+` or the digits `1` to `3`

- `+` specifies that additional information for *gdb* should be included in the output. This may cause other debuggers to reject the object.
- `1` specifies only that minimal debugging information: include information about function names and external variables, but not about local variables or line numbers.
- `2` (the default): include function names, all variables, and line numbers.
- In addition, `3` includes macro definitions. Not all systems support this feature.

gcc Warning Options

`-W`
: Print a number of "standard" extra warning messages.

`-Wimplicit`
: Warn if functions or parameters are declared implicitly (in other words, if the explicit declaration is missing).

`-Wreturn-type`
: Warn if a function is defined without a return type (in other words, one that defaults to `int`). Also warn if `return` is used without an argument in a non-`void` function.

`-Wunused`
: Warn when local or static variables are not used and if a statement computes a value that is not used.

`-Wswitch`
: Warn if a `switch` statement has an index of an enumeral type and does not cater to all the possible values of the `enum`, or if a `case` value is specified that does not occur in the `enum`.

`-Wcomment`
: Warn if the sequence `/*` is found within a comment. This might mean that a comment end is missing.

`-Wtrigraphs`
: Warn if trigraphs are encountered. Effective only if *–trigraphs* is also specified.

`-Wformat`
: Check the parameters supplied to `printf`, `scanf`, and friends to ensure that they agree with the format string.

`-Wchar-subscripts`
: Warn if an array subscript has type `char`.

`-Wuninitialized`
: Warn if an automatic variable is used before it is initialized. This requires the optimizer to be enabled.

`-Wparentheses`
: Warn if parentheses are omitted in assignments in contexts where truth values are expected—for example, `if (a = foo ())`—or when unusual and possibly confusing sequences of nested operators occur without parentheses.

`-Wenum-clash`
: Warn if `enum` types are mixed. This is issued only for C++ programs. See the section called "UNIX C" in Chapter 20 for further details.

`-Wtemplate-debugging`
: Warn if debugging is not fully available for the platform when using templates in a C++ program.

`-Wall`
: Specify all of the warning options above. The Free Software Foundation (FSF) considers this a good compromise between accuracy and completeness.

`-fsyntax-only`
: Check for syntax errors, but don't compile.

`-pedantic`
: Issue all warnings specified by ANSI C. Reject programs that use extensions not defined in the Standard. The FSF does not consider this to be a useful option, since ANSI C does not specify warnings for all possible situations. It is included because it is required by the ANSI Standard.

`-pedantic-errors`
: The same thing as *–pedantic*, but the warnings are treated as errors.

`-w`
: Inhibit all warning messages.

`-Wno-import`
: Inhibit warning messages about the use of `#import`.

`-Wtraditional`
: Warn about macro parameters in strings, functions declared external within a block and then referenced outside the block, and `switch` statements with `long` indexes. These are treated differently in ANSI and traditional C.

`-Wshadow`
: Warn if a local variable shadows another local variable.

`-Wid-clash-`*`len`*
: Warn whenever two different identifiers match in the first *`len`* characters. To quote the FSF documentation: "This may help you prepare a program that will compile with certain obsolete, brain-damaged compilers."

`-Wpointer-arith`
: Warn about anything that depends on the "size of" a function type or of `void`. GNU C assigns these types a size of `1` for convenience in calculations with `void *` pointers and pointers to functions.

`-Wcast-qual`
: Warn when a cast removes a type qualifier from a pointer; for example, if a `const char *` is cast to a `char *`.

`-Wcast-align`
: Warn if a pointer is cast to a type that has an increased alignment requirement. For example, warn if a `char *` is cast to an `int *` on machines where integers require specific alignments.

`-Wwrite-strings`
: Give string constants the type `const char []`. This causes a warning to be generated if a string address is copied into a non-`const char *` pointer.

`-Wconversion`
: Warn if the existence of a prototype causes a different type conversion from the default, or if a negative integer constant expression is implicitly converted to an unsigned type.

`-Waggregate-return`

Warn when functions that return structures, unions, or arrays are defined or called.

`-Wstrict-prototypes`

Warn if a function is declared or defined without specifying the argument types.

`-Wmissing-prototypes`

Warn if a global function is defined without a previous prototype declaration, even if the definition itself provides the prototype. This warning is intended to help detect missing declarations of global functions in header files.

`-Wredundant-decls`

Warn if anything is declared more than once in the same scope, even in cases where multiple declaration is valid and changes nothing.

`-Wnested-externs`

Warn if an `extern` declaration is encountered within an function.

`-Winline`

Warn if a function was declared as inline, or the C++ option *–finline-functions* was specified, and the function cannot be inlined.

`-Woverloaded-virtual`

C++ only: warn when a derived class function declaration may be an error in defining a virtual function.

`-Werror`

Treat all warnings as errors.

cpp Options

`-$` *gcc*

Disable the use of the character `$` in identifers. This is passed by *gcc* when the *–ansi* option is specified.

`-A` *gcc*

–A`question(answer)` asserts that the answer to `question` is `answer`. This can used with the preprocessor conditional `#if #question (answer)`.

`-A-` *gcc*

Disable standard assertions. In addition, SVR4 *cc* undefines all standard macros except those beginning with `__`.

`-B` SunOS, Solaris

Recognize the C++ comment string //.

`-C` *gcc*, SVR3, SunOS, Solaris, XENIX

Do not strip comments from the preprocessor output.

`-Dname` *gcc*, SVR3, SunOS, Solaris, XENIX

Define *name* as 1. This is the equivalent to specifying *–D*name=1 to *cc* and *not* the same as *–Dname*.

`-Dname=def` *gcc*, SVR3, SunOS, Solaris, XENIX

Define *name*. This is the same as the corresponding *cc* option. This can be overridden by *–Uname* even if the *–U* option appears earlier on the command line.

`-dM` *gcc*

Suppress normal preprocessor output and output `#define` commands for all macros instead. This can also be used with an empty file to show the values of predefined macros.

`-dD` *gcc*

Do not strip `#define` commands from the preprocessor output. This can be useful for debugging preprocessor macros.

`-H` *gcc*, SVR3, SunOS, Solaris

Print the pathnames of included files on `stderr`.

`-Idir` *gcc*, SVR3, SunOS, Solaris

Add *dir* to the path to search for `#include` directives.

`-I-` *gcc*

Search the list of include pathnames only when the `#include` directive is of the form `#include "header"`. Do not search these directories if the directive is `#include<header>`. In addition, do not automatically search the current directory for header files. If *–I dir* options are specified after *–I–*, they apply for all forms of the `#include` directive.

`-imacros file` *gcc*

Process *file* before reading the regular input. Do not produce any output for *file*—only the macro definitions will be of use.

`-include file` *gcc*

Process *file* as input before processing the regular input file. The text of the file will be handled exactly like the regular files.

`-idirafter` *dir* — *gcc*

Add *dir* to the *second include path.* The second include path is an include path that is searched when a file isn't found in the standard include path (the one built by the *–I* option).

`-iprefix` *prefix* — *gcc*

Specify a prefix for the *–iwithprefix* option (see next entry).

`-iwithprefix` *dir* — *gcc*

Add the directory *prefix/dir* to the second include path. *prefix* must previously have been set with the *iprefix* command.

`-lang-`*language* — *gcc*

Specify the source language. *–lang-c++* enables the comment sequence `//`, *–lang-objc* enables the `#import` command, *–lang-objc++* enables both, *–lang-c* disables both.

`-lint` — *gcc*

Replace *lint* commands such as `/*` NOTREACHED `*/` with the corresponding pragma, e.g., `#pragma lint` NOTREACHED.

`-M` — *gcc*, SunOS, Solaris

Write a list of *Makefile* dependencies to `stdout`. Suppress normal preprocessor output.

`-MM` — *gcc*

Like the *–M* option, but process only `#include` *"file" directives—ignore* `#include` *<file>.*

`-MD` — *gcc*

Like the *–M* directive, but output to a file whose name is made by replacing the final *.c* with *.d.* This option does not suppress preprocessor output.

`-MMD` — *gcc*

Combination of *–MD* and *–MM.* Does not suppress preprocessor output.

`-nostdinc` — *gcc*

Do not search the standard include file locations (like */usr/include*) for header files. Search only the directories specified with the *–I* option. A version *–nostdinc++* exists for C++ programs.

`-P` — *gcc*, SVR3, SunOS, Solaris, XENIX

Do not output `#line` directives.

`-p` SunOS, Solaris

Limit the length of preprocessor directives to eight characters.

`-pedantic` *gcc*

Issue the warnings that ANSI C specifies for specific situations. See the section called "C Compiler Options" for more details.

`-pedantic-errors` *gcc*

If the situations specified in the ANSI Standard occur, consider them errors rather than warnings.

`-R` SunOS, Solaris

Allow recursive macros.

`-T` SVR3, SunOS, Solaris

Limit the length of preprocessor directives to eight characters. For backward compatibility only.

`-traditional` *gcc*

Preprocess in the "traditional" (pre-ANSI) manner.

`-trigraphs` *gcc*

Recognize and convert trigraphs.

`-undef` SunOS, Solaris

Undefine all predefined symbols.

`-U`*`name`* SVR3, SunOS, Solaris, XENIX

Remove definition of *name*. This option also overrides *–D* options placed later on the command line.

`-undef` *gcc*

Do not predefine standard macros.

`-Y`*`dir`* SunOS, Solaris

Search only directory *dir* for `#include` files.

`-Wall` *gcc*

Set both *–Wcomment* and *–Wtrigraphs.*

`-Wcomment` *gcc*

Warn if the sequence `/*` is found within a comment. This could imply that a comment end is missing.

`-Wtraditional` *gcc*

Warn about macro parameters in strings. These are treated differently in ANSI and traditional C.

`-Wtrigraphs` *gcc*

Warn if trigraphs are encountered. Effective only if *–trigraphs* is also specified.

In This Appendix:
- *as Options*
- *as Directives*

C

Assembler Directives and Options

as Options

It's particularly evident that *as* seldom sees the light of day when you look at the options, which differ greatly from one system to the next. GNU *as* doesn't even maintain compatibility between versions 1 and 2, as you can see in the following table:

`-a` GNU 2.x

List high-level language, assembly output, and symbols. This is the generic form of the *–a* option; the following variants modify it in some manner. Combinations are possible: for example, *–alh* lists the high-level input and assembly output, but not the symbol table. In order to get the high-level language input, you also need to specify the *–g* option.

`-ad` GNU 2.x

List high-level language, assembly output, and symbols, but omit debugging pseudo-ops from listing.

`-ah` GNU 2.x

List high-level language source.

`-al` GNU 2.x

List assembly output.

`-an` GNU 2.x

Disable forms processing of the listing. This works only in combination with other *–a* options.

`-as` GNU 2.x

List symbols.

`-D` GNU 1.x

Turn on assembler debugging (if available).

`-D` GNU 2.x

No effect—just for compatibility.

`-dl` SVR3

Don't put line number information in object file.

`-f` GNU 2.x

Skip preprocessing (for compiler output).

`-g` GNU 1.x

Generate debugging symbols for source language debugging of assembly programs.

`-I` *path* GNU 2.x

Add *path* to the search list for `.include` directives

`-K` GNU 2.x

Issue warnings when difference tables are altered for long displacements.

`-k` GNU 1.x

Warn about problems with calculating symbol differences.

`-L` GNU

Keep local symbols starting with `L` in the symbol table output to object file.

`-m` System V

Preprocess with *m4*.

`-n` System V

Turn off long/short address optimization.

`-o` GNU 2.x, System V

Specify output filename.

`-Qy` System V

Put assembler version number in object file.

`-R` GNU 1.x

Merge the data segment into the text segment, making it read-only.

`-R` System V

Remove the input file after assembly.

`-W` GNU 1.x

Suppress warnings.

`-f` GNU 1.x

Suppress the preprocessor pass that removes comments and redundant white space from the input. This can also be done with the `#NO_APP` directive.

`-T` System V

Accept (and ignore) obsolete directives without complaining.

`-V` System V

Print the current version number.

`-v` GNU

Print the current version number.

`-W` GNU 2.x

Suppress warning messages

`-Yd` *`dir`* System V

Specify directory *`dir`* for predefined macros.

`-Ym` *`dir`* System V

Specify directory *`dir`* for the *m4* processor.

as Directives

Assembler directives are provided mainly for the convenience of the compiler and are seldom documented. Here is a list of the directives provided by GNU *as*, one of the few that is documented. Many of these directives are provided only on certain platforms—read *Using as*, by Dean Elsner and Jay Fenlason, for specific information.

`.abort`

Abort the assembly. This is obsolete. It was intended to be used by a compiler discovering a fatal error while it piped its output into the assembler.

`.ABORT`

A synonym for `.abort`.

`.align` *`boundary`* `[,` *`content`*`]`

Increment the assembler location counter (the pointer to the location where the next byte will be emitted), to a boundary that has zeros in the last *`boundary`* binary positions. If *`content`* is specified, any bytes skipped are filled with this value.

`.app-file` *`string`*
: Specify the start of a new logical file *`string`*. This is obsolete.

`.ascii` *`string`* ...
: Emit each *`string`* into consecutive addresses. Do not append a trailing `\0` character.

`.asciz` *`string`*
: Emit each *`string`* into consecutive addresses. Append a trailing `\0` character.

`.byte` *`expressions`*
: Emit zero or more *`expressions`* into the next output byte.

`.comm` *`symbol`* , *`length`*
: Declare *`symbol`* a named common area in the bss section. *`length`* is the minimum length—the actual length is determined by the linker as the maximum of the *`length`* fields of all object files that define the symbol.

`.data` *`subsection`*
: Switch to data section *`subsection`* (default zero). All assembled data goes to this section.

`.def` *`name`*
: Begin defining COFF debugging information for a symbol *`name`*. The definition is completed by a `.endef` directive.

`.desc` *`symbol, abs-expression`*
: Set the *`symbol`* descriptor to the low 16 bits of *`abs-expression`*. This is ignored if the assembler is outputting in COFF format.

`.double` *`flonums`*
: Emit `double` floating-point number *`flonums`*.

`.eject`
: Force a page break in the assembly listing at this point.

`.else`
: *else* in conditional assembly—see the `.if` directive.

`.endef`
: End a symbol definition begun with `.def`.

`.endif`
: End a conditional assembly block. See the `.if` directive.

`.equ` *`symbol, expression`*
: Set the value of *`symbol`* to *`expression`*. This is the same thing as `.set`.

`.extern`
: In some assemblers, define a symbol external to the program. This is ignored by GNU *as*, which treats all undefined symbols as external.

`.file` *`string`*
: Specify the start of a new file. This directive is obsolete and may not be available.

`.fill` *`repeat`* , *`size`* , *`value`*
: Create *`repeat`* repeated data blocks consisting of the low-order *`size`* bytes of *`value`*.

`.float` *`flonums`*
: Emit floating-point numbers *`flonums`*.

`.global` *`symbol`*
: Define *`symbol`* as an external symbol.

`.globl` *`symbol`*
: A synonym for `.global`.

`.hword` *`expressions`*
: Emit the values of each *`expression`*, truncated to 16 bits if necessary.

`.ident`
: This directive is used by some assemblers to place tags in object files. GNU *as* ignores it.

`.if` *`expression`*
: If *`expression`* evaluates to nonzero, assemble the following code down to the corresponding `.else` or `.endif` directive. If the next directive is `.else`, do not assemble the code between the `.else` and the `.endif`. If *`expression`* evaluates to 0, do not assemble the code down to the corresponding `.else` or `.endif` directive.

`.ifdef` *`symbol`*
: Like `.if`, but the condition is fulfilled if *`symbol`* is defined.

`.ifndef` *`symbol`*
: Like `.if`, but the condition is fulfilled if *`symbol`* is not defined.

`.ifnotdef` *`symbol`*
: Like `.if`, but the condition is fulfilled if *`symbol`* is not defined.

`.include` *`file`*
: Process the source file *`file`* before continuing this file.

`.int` *`expressions`*
: Emit 32-bit values of each *`expression`*.

`.lcomm` *`symbol`* , *`length`*
: Reserve *`length`* bytes of local common in bss, and give it the name *`symbol`*.

`.ln` *`line-number`*
: Change the logical line number of the next line to *`line-number`*. This corresponds to the C preprocessor `#line` directive.

`.ln` *`line-number`*
: A synonym for `.line`.

`.list`
: Increment the listing counter (initially 0). If the listing counter is > 0, the following lines are listed in the assembly listingp; otherwise, they aren't. `.nolist` decrements the counter.

`.long` *`expressions`*
: A synonym for `.int`.

`.nolist`
: Decrement the listing counter—see `.list`.

`.octa` *`bignums`*
: Evaluate each *`bignum`* as a 16-byte integer, and emit its value.

`.org` *`new-lc, fill`*
: Set the location counter of the current section to *`new-lc`*. *`new-lc`* must be either absolute or an expression in the current subsection: you can't use `.org` to cross sections. `.org` may not decrement the location counter. The intervening bytes are filled with the value *`fill`* (default 0).

`.psize` *`lines, columns`*
: Set the page size for assembly listings to *`lines`* lines (default 60) and *`columns`* columns (default 200). If *`lines`* is set to 0, no automatic pagination occurs.

`.quad` *`bignums`*
: Evaluate each *`bignum`* as an 8-byte integer, and emit its value.

`.sbttl` *`subheading`*
: Set the subtitle of assembly listings to *`subheading`*.

`.section` *`name, subsection`*
: Switch to section called *`name`* (default `.text`), *`subsection`* (default zero). All emitted data goes to this section.

`.set symbol, expression`
Define the value of *symbol* to be *expression*. This may be used more than once to change the value of *symbol* after it is defined. The value of an external symbol is the value of the last `.set` directive.

`.short expressions`
Emit the values of each *expression*, truncated to 16 bits if necessary.

`.single flonums`
Emit floating point numbers *flonums*. This is the same as `.float`.

`.space size, fill`
Emit *size* bytes of value *fill*. *fill* defaults to 0.

`.space`
Usually a synonym for `.block`, but on some hardware platforms, GNU *as* uses it differently.

`.stabd`
Emit debug information. See the section called "Debug Information" for more information.

`.stabn`
Emit debug information. See the section called "Debug Information" for more information.

`.stabs`
Emit debug information. See the section called "Debug Information" for more information.

`.text subsection`
Switch to text section *subsection* (default zero). All assembled data goes to this section.

`.title heading`
Set the title of the assembly listing to *heading*.

`.word expressions`
Emit 32-bit values of each *expression*.

Debug Information

Debug information is very dependent on the kind of object file format in use. In *a.out* format, it is defined by the directives `.stabd`, `.stabn`, and `.stabs`. They can take up to five parameters:

desc
The symbol descriptor. 16 bits wide.

other
The symbol's "other" attribute. Normally not used.

string
The name of the symbol.

type
The symbol type. 8 bits wide.

value
The value of the symbol. Must be absolute.

These symbols are used as follows:

`.stabd` *type*, *other*, *desc*
Define a debugging entry without a name. The value of the symbol is set to the current value of the location counter. This is commonly used for line number information, which is type 68 for line number references in the text segment. For example, `.stabd 68, 0, 27` specifies that the current location is the beginning of line 27.

`.stabn` *type*, *other*, *desc*, *value*
Define a debugging entry without a name. The value of the symbol is set to *value*.

`.stabs` *string*, *type*, *other*, *desc*, *value*
Define a debugging entry with the name *string*. The value of the symbol is set to *value*.

For further information about *stabs* formats and types, see the header file *stab.h* and the man page *stab*(5).

In COFF format, debug information is defined by the directives `.dim`, `.scl`, `.size`, `.tag`, `.type`, and `.val`. They are enclosed in a `.def`/`.endef` pair. For example, to define a symbol `foo`, you would write:

```
.def     foo
.value bar
.size 4
.endef
```

The directives have the following meanings.

`.dim`
Set dimension information.

`.scl` *class*

Set the storage class value of the symbol to *class*.

`.size` *size*

Set the size of the symbol to *size*.

`.tag` *structname*

Specify the `struct` definition of the current symbol.

`.type` *type*

Set the type of the symbol to *type*.

`.val` *addr*

Set the value of the symbol to *addr*.

In ELF format, debug information is output to a special section called `.debug`, so no specific directives are needed.

D

Linker Options

Like the assembler, the linker seldom sees the light of day. You normally start both programs via the C compiler control program *cc*. As with the assembler, the linker can be invoked with a surprising diversity of options, all usually hidden inside the *cc* command. This appendix lists the linker options for the following versions of UNIX:

- the GNU linkers (two of them, with conflicting options)
- SCO UNIX
- Solaris 2
- SunOS 4
- System V.3 (SVR3)
- System V.4 (SVR4)
- SCO XENIX

Currently available BSD systems use one of the GNU linkers. For example, BSD/386 up to version 1.1 uses the old linker, and BSD/OS 2.0 uses the new linker. The Solaris 2 linker is basically the System V.4 linker, but it has a few extra options. Unless otherwise noted, all System V.4 options also apply to Solaris 2. In the list that follows, options that differ between versions of the GNU linker are labeled "old GNU" or "new GNU."

–Aarchitecture GNU

For the Intel 960 family only. *architecture* is a two-letter abbreviation specifying a member of the processor family.

`-A` *`file`* — old GNU

Don't incorporate the text and data from *`file`* into the output file, just use the symbols. This can be used to implement crude dynamic loading.

`-A` *`file`* — SunOS 4

Perform an incremental load: the resultant output file is read in to a process executing from the program *`file`*, which is used to resolve symbolic references.

`-A` *`address`* — XENIX

Produce a standalone program to be loaded at *`address`*.

`-a` — SCO, SVR3, SVR4

Produce an executable file. This is the default behavior and is the opposite of the *−r* option.

`-align` *`datum`* — SunOS 4

Force *`datum`* to be page-aligned. This is typically used for FORTRAN common blocks.

`-assert` *`assertion`* — SunOS 4

Check an assertion. If the assertion fails, print a diagnostic message and abort the link.

`-B`*`binding`* — SunOS 4, Solaris 2

Specify the kind of binding to perform. *`binding`* may be `dynamic` (perform dynamic binding at run time), `nosymbolic` (do not perform symbolic relocation), `static` (perform static binding at link time), or `symbolic` (force symbolic relocation). Solaris 2 does not support the keyword `nosymbolic`.

`-Bstatic` — SunOS 4, GNU

Use static libraries only. GNU *ld* accepts this option but ignores it.

`-B` *`number`* — XENIX

Set the text selector bias to *`number`*.

`-b` — SVR4

When performing dynamic linking, do not perform special processing for relocations to symbols in shared objects.

`-b` *`format`* — new GNU

Specify the binary format of the files whose names follow. This is needed only when linking files with multiple formats.

`-C` new GNU

Ignore the case of the symbols.

`-c` *file* new GNU

Read commands from *file*. These commands override the standard link format.

`-c` *n* XENIX

Specify the target CPU type 80*n*86. *n* defaults to 3.

`-D` *size* old GNU, SunOS 4

Pad the data segment to *size*. The padding may overlap with the bss segment. The SunOS 4 linker interprets *size* in hexadecimal.

`-D` *number* XENIX

Set the data selector bias to *number*.

`-d` *dynlink* SVR4

Specify dynamic (*dynlink* is `y`) or static (*dynlink* is `n`) linking.

`-d` GNU, SunOS 4

When creating a relocatable output file with the *-r* option, convert "common" symbols to bss.

`-dc` SunOS 4

Perform the *-d* option, but also copy initialized data referenced by this program from shared objects.

`-dp` SunOS 4

Force an alias definition of undefined procedure entry points. Used with dynamic binding.

`-defsym` *symbol* = *expression* new GNU

Create the global symbol *symbol* in the output file and assign the value *expression* to it.

`-e` *symbol* all

Set the entry address in the output file to *symbol*.

`-F`*format* new GNU

This is an obsolete option that some older linkers used to specify object file formats. GNU *ld* accepts it but ignores it.

`-F` *name* Solaris 2

Used when building shared objects. The symbol table of the shared object being built is used as a "filter" on the symbol table of the shared object *name*.

`-F` *`size`* XENIX

Reserve *`size`* bytes for the run-time stack.

`-f` *`fill`* SCO, SVR3

Fill unassigned memory (gaps in text and data segments and also the bss segment) with the 16-bit pattern *`fill`*.

`-format` *`format`* new GNU

Specify the binary format of the files whose names follow. This is the same as the *–b* option.

`-G` *`size`* new GNU

Only for MIPS ECOFF format. Set the minimum size of objects to be optimized using the `GP` register.

`-G` Solaris 2

Produce a shared object in dynamic mode.

`-g` new GNU, XENIX

Include symbolic information in the output file. GNU *ld* accepts this option but ignores it because this is the default behavior.

`-h` *`name`* SVR4

When building a dynamic object, record *`name`* as the name of the file to link at run-time.

`-I` *`name`* Solaris 2

Use *`name`* as the path name of the interpreter to be written into the program header. In static mode, *`name`* defaults to no interpreter. In dynamic mode it defaults to */usr/lib/ld.so.1*.

`-i` new GNU

Create a relocatable output file. Same as the *–r* option.

`-i` Solaris 2

Ignore the setting of the `LD_LIBRARY_PATH` environment variable.

`-i` XENIX

Create separate instruction and data spaces for small model programs.

`-L` *`dir`* all

Search the given directory for library archives in addition to the default directories. *ld* searches directories supplied with the *–L* option in the order they appear in the argument list and before the default directories.

`-l` *lib* — all

Search the specified libraries for a library called `lib`*lib*`.a`. This is the same as the C compiler *–l* option. SunOS 4 allows you to write *–l lib.version* to indicate a specific library version number.

`-La` — XENIX

Set advisory file locking.

`-Lm` — XENIX

Set mandatory file locking.

`-LI[NENUMBERS]` — SCO

Create a map file including line number information.

`-M` — GNU, SunOS 4

Print a load map on the standard output.

`-M` *mapfile* — Solaris 2

Read directives to *ld* from *mapfile*.

`-M` — SCO, SVR3

Print warning messages for multiply defined external definitions.

`-m` — SCO, SVR3, SVR4

Print a load map on the standard output.

`-M` *model* — XENIX

Specify the memory model. *model* can be `s` (small), `m` (middle), `l` (large), `h` (huge), or `e` (mixed).

`-m` *emulation* — new GNU

Emulate the *emulation* linker.

`-m` *file* — XENIX

Write a map listing to *file*.

`-M[AP]:`*number* — SCO

Create a map listing with up to *number* symbols. *number* defaults to 2048.

`-Map` *file* — new GNU

Print a load map to *file*.

`-N` — GNU, SunOS 4

Create an OMAGIC format binary. This is the default format for relocatable object files. OMAGIC format binaries have writable text segments. Where appropriate, this option implies *–Bstatic*.

`-N` SVR3

Place the text section at the beginning of the text segment, and the data segment immediately after the text segment.

`-N` *`num`* XENIX

Set the page size to *`num`* bytes.

`-n` GNU, SunOS 4

Create an NMAGIC format shared executable binary. The text segment is read-only. Where appropriate, this option implies *–Bstatic*.

`-n` *`num`* XENIX

Truncate symbol names to *`num`* characters.

`-noinhibit-exec` new GNU

Create an output file even if errors are encountered during linking.

`-o` *`file`* all

Write output to *file* instead of the default *a.out*.

`-oformat` *`format`* new GNU

Write the output file in format *`format`*.

`-P` XENIX

Disable packing of segments.

`-p` SunOS 4

Start the data segment on a page boundary, even if the text segment is not shared.

`-Q`*`identify`* Solaris 2

If *`identify`* is `y`, add an *ident* string to the `.comment` section of the output file identifying the version of the linker used. *cc* does this by default. *–Qn* suppresses this header.

`-q` old GNU on BSD

Create a QMAGIC format demand loaded executable binary.

`-R` *`file`* new GNU

Read symbol information from *`file`*, but do not include it in the output.

`-R` XENIX

Ensure a relocation table of nonzero size.

`-Rd` *`offset`* XENIX

Set the data segment relocation offset to *`offset`*.

`-Rt` *`offset`* XENIX

Set the text segment relocation offset to *`offset`*.

`-R` *`paths`* Solaris 2

Specify *`paths`*, a colon-separated list, as directories to be searched for libraries by the run-time linker.

`-r` all

Generate a relocatable output file.

`-S` GNU, SunOS 4

Strip only stab symbols from the *a.out* files.

`-s` all

Strip all symbols from the output file. This overrides other strip options.

`-SE[GMENTS]:`*`number`* SCO

Allow the program to have *`number`* segments. The default value is 128.

`-sort-common` new GNU

Disable sorting of common blocks by size.

`-ST[ACK]:`*`size`* SCO

Specify that the stack should be *`size`* bytes long.

`-T` *`file`* new GNU

Read commands from *`file`*. These commands override the standard link format. This is the same as the *-c* option.

`-T` *`address`* old GNU, SunOS 4

Start the text segment at *`address`*.

`-Tbss` *`address`* new GNU

Start the bss segment at *`address`*.

`-Tdata` *`address`* GNU, SunOS 4

Start the data segment at *`address`*.

`-Ttext` *`address`* GNU, SunOS 4

Start the text segment at *`address`*. The same as *-T*.

`-t` GNU

Print the names of input files to the standard error file `stderr` as they are processed.

`-t` SCO, SVR3, SVR4

Do not warn about multiply defined symbols of different size.

`-u` *`symbol`* — all

Consider *`symbol`* to be undefined. This can be used to force the extraction of certain files from a library.

`-Ur` — new GNU

Generate relocatable output, like the *-r* option. For C++ programs only, resolve references to constructors.

`-V` — new GNU

Print full version number information, including supported emulations.

`-V` — SCO, SVR3, Solaris 2

Print version number information for *ld*.

`-VS` *`number`* — SCO, SVR3

Store version *`number`* in the optional header of the output file.

`-v` — new GNU

Print version number information for *ld* only.

`--version` — new GNU

Print version number information for *ld* only, then exit.

`-warn-common` — new GNU

Warn when a common symbol is combined with another common symbol or with a symbol definition.

`-X` — GNU, SunOS 4

Strip local symbols that start with the letter *L*. This is the default behavior of the assembler. The new GNU linker performs this operation only if the *-s* or *-S* option is also specified.

`-x` — GNU, SCO, SunOS 4, SVR3

Strip all local symbols. The new GNU linker performs this operation only if the *-s* or *-S* option is also specified.

`-Y [L][U],` *`dir`* — SCO, SVR3, SVR4 in BSD mode

Change the default directory used for finding libraries. If *L* is specified, the standard library directory (`LLIBDIR`, normally */usr/lib*) is replaced with *`dir`*. If *U* is specified and the linker was built with a second library directory (`LLIBDIR`), it is replaced with *`dir`*.

`-YP,` *`dir`* — Solaris 2

Change the default directory used for finding libraries to *`dir`*.

`-y` *`symbol`* — old GNU, SunOS 4

Trace *`symbol`* on the standard error file `stderr` during linking.

`-z` — old GNU, SunOS 4

Create a ZMAGIC format demand loaded executable binary. On SunOS 4, this implies the *–Bdynamic* option.

`-Z` — SCO, SVR3

Do not bind anything at address 0, in order to allow run-time detection of null pointers.

`-z defs` — Solaris 2

Force a fatal error if any undefined symbols remain at the end of a link. This is the default for executables but not for relocatable output.

`-z nodefs` — Solaris 2

Allow undefined symbols in an executable.

`-z text` — Solaris 2

Force a fatal error if any relocations against nonwritable, allocatable sections remain when performing a dynamic link.

In This Appendix:
- *CD-ROM Producers*

E

Where to Get Sources

Throughout this book, I've mentioned lots of freely available software. This appendix contains information on how to get it.

All the software is available on the Internet, and much of it is also available on CD-ROM, sometimes ported to specific platforms. Your choice of where to get it depends a lot on how often you need the software, how fast your connection to the Internet is, and how much you pay to transfer data on the Internet. I personally prefer to obtain and store as many packages as possible on CD-ROM.

CD-ROM Producers

A large number of companies produce CD-ROMs, and the following are of particular interest:

> The Free Software Foundation (FSF)
> 675 Massachusetts Avenue
> Cambridge, MA 02139
> Phone: +1 617 876 3296
> Mail: *gnu@prep.ai.mit.edu*
>
> The producers of GNU software. They sell a CD-ROM with all the GNU software. If you buy your CD-ROM here, you also help support the Free Software Foundation, which is dependent on such income to survive.
>
> The primary Internet site for the Free Software Foundation is *prep@ai.mit.edu*, and you can find the software in the directory */pub/gnu*. This site is frequently overloaded, so please use more local mirrors where possible.
>
> InfoMagic, Inc. (IM)
> P.O. Box 30370
> Flagstaff, AZ 86003-0370

Phone: +1-800-800-6613
+1-602-526-9565
Fax: +1-602-526-9573
Mail: *info@infomagic.com*

They offer a number of UNIX-oriented CDs, including Internet tools, Linux, and standards.

O'Reilly & Associates, Inc. (ORA)
103A Morris Street
Sebastopol, CA 95472
Phone: +1-800-998-9938
+1-707-829-0515
Fax: +1-707-829-0104
Mail: *order@ora.com*

Our favorite source. High-quality, well-thought-out books on UNIX, many with CD-ROMs.

Prime Time Freeware (PTF)
370 Altair Way, Suite 150
Sunnyvale, CA 94086
Phone: +1-408-433-9662
Fax: +1-408-433-0727
Mail: *ptf@cfcl.com*

A small supplier of software of special interest to programmers: well-organized, semi-annual distributions of the latest software packages, source only, including separate editions for TEX and artificial intelligence. In addition, ported software for System V.4 (Intel) and Sun platforms.

Walnut Creek CDROM (WC)
4041 Pike Lane, Suite D-893
Concord, CA 94520
Phone: +1-800-786-9907
+1-510-674-0783
Fax: +1-510-674-0821
Mail: *orders@cdrom.com*

By far the largest choice of CDs, including nearly everything the other companies have to offer. Mainly ported software, including definitive FreeBSD distribution and ported software for System V.4 (Intel), Linux, and Sun.

Table E-1: Software Sources

Package	Internet Site	CD Suppliers
GNU software	prep.ai.mit.edu:*/pub/gnu*	**FSF**, PTF, WC
4.4BSD Lite		IM, **ORA**, WC
ghostscript	in GNU distribution	**FSF**, PTF, WC
jargon file	In GNU distribution	**PTF**, FSF
ncurses	netcom.com:*pub/zmbenhal/ncurses*	
patch	in GNU distribution	PTF, **WC**, FSF
RCS	in GNU distribution	PTF, **WC**, FSF
tcpdump	ftp.ee.lbl.gov	WC[a]
TEX	ftp.shsu.edu:*/tex-archive*	**PTF**, WC
dvips	in TEX distribution	PTF
dviware	in TEX distribution	PTF
ghostview	in TEX distribution	PTF
POSIX.2 regex	zoo.toronto.edu:*/pub*	
SeeTEX	in TEX distribution	PTF
t1ascii	in TEX distribution	PTF
X11	ftp.x.org:*/pub/R6*	PTF, ORA, **WC**
System V shared memory	ftp.ora.com	

[a] *tcpdump* is included in the FreeBSD distribution.

The initials of the CD-ROM publishers in **bold** print indicate, in my opinion, the best choice for the package in question. Your mileage may vary.

Bibliography

Bach, Maurice J. *The Design of the UNIX System.* Englewood Cliffs, NJ: Prentice Hall, 1986.

An in-depth description of an early version of System V.

Berliner, Brian. *CVS II: Parallelizing Software Development.*

In RCS distribution, listed in Appendix E.

Costales, Bryan, et al. *sendmail.* Sebastopol, CA: O'Reilly & Associates, Inc., 1993.

Everything you never wanted to know about *sendmail.*

Cutler, Ellie, et al. *SCO UNIX in a Nutshell.* Sebastopol, CA: O'Reilly & Associates, Inc., 1994.

Darwin, Ian. *Checking C Programs with lint.* Sebastopol, CA: O'Reilly & Associates, Inc., 1988.

A description of the *lint* program checker.

Dougherty, Dale. *sed and awk.* Sebastopol, CA: O'Reilly & Associates, Inc., 1992.

An in-depth treatment of both utilities.

DuBois, Paul. *Software Portability with imake.* Sebastopol, CA: O'Reilly & Associates, Inc., 1993.

A complete manual for *imake* and associated topics.

Ellis, Margaret A., and Stroustrup, Bjarne. *The Annotated C++ Reference Manual.* Reading, MA: Addison-Wesley, 1990.

The definitive reference manual for C++.

Elsner, Dean, and Fenlason, Jay. *Using as.* Cambridge, MA: Free Software Foundation, current.

A detailed description of GNU *as.* Part of the GNU *binutils* distribution.

Estrada, Susan. *Connecting to the Internet.* Sebastopol, CA: O'Reilly & Associates, Inc., 1993.

A buyer's guide to the Internet.

Gilly, Daniel, et al. *UNIX in a Nutshell for System V and Solaris 2.0.* Sebastopol, CA: O'Reilly & Associates, Inc., 1992.

Gircys, Gintaras R. *Understanding and Using COFF.* Sebastopol, CA: O'Reilly & Associates, Inc., 1988.

A description of the Common Object File Format.

Goodheart, Berny. *UNIX curses Explained.* Englewood Cliffs, NJ: Prentice Hall, 1991.

A description of BSD and System V versions of *curses.*

———, and James Cox. *The Magic Garden Explained: The Internals of UNIX System V Release 4.* Englewood Cliffs, NJ: Prentice Hall, 1994.

The definitive guide to the internals of System V Release 4.

Johnson, S. C., and Ritchie, D. M. "Portability of C Programs and the UNIX System." *Bell System Technical Journal.* 2021-48, July/August 1978.

An early description of the portable C compiler.

Kernighan, Brian W., and Ritchie, Dennis M. *The C Programming Language.* Englewood Cliffs, NJ: Prentice Hall, 1978.

The first complete description of the C programming language.

Knuth, Donald E. *The TEXbook.* Reading, MA: Addison Wesley, 1989.

A mystery story about TEX—also the main reference.

Krol, Ed. *The Whole Internet User's Guide and Catalog.* Second edition. Sebastopol, CA: O'Reilly & Associates, Inc., 1994.

The definitive guide to the Internet.

Leffler, Samuel J., et al. *The Design and the Implementation of the 4.3BSD UNIX Operating System.* Reading, MA: Addison-Wesley, 1990.

The definitive description of the 4.3 BSD kernel and communications.

Levine, John R., et al. *lex and yacc.* Second edition. Sebastopol, CA: O'Reilly & Associates, Inc., 1992.

Lewine, Donald A. *POSIX Programmer's Guide.* Sebastopol, CA: O'Reilly & Associates, Inc., 1991.

Loukides, Mike. *Programming with GNU Software.* Sebastopol, CA: O'Reilly & Associates, Inc., 1996.

McGilton, Henry, and McNabb, Mary. *Typesetting Tables on the UNIX System.* Los Altos, CA: Trilithon Press, 1990.

A tutorial introduction to *tbl.*

McKusick, Marshall Kirk, et al. "A Fast File System for UNIX." *4.4BSD System Manager's Manual (SMM)*. Sebastopol, CA: The USENIX Association and O'Reilly & Associates, Inc., 1994.

A description of the Berkeley Fast File System, now known as ufs (UNIX File System).

Mui, Linda, and Pearce, Eric. *X Window System Administrator's Guide. Volume 8 of the X Window System.* Sebastopol, CA: O'Reilly & Associates, Inc., 1993.

Available with companion CD-ROM.

vanRyper, William, and Murray, James D. *Encyclopedia of Graphics File Formats.* Sebastopol, CA: O'Reilly & Associates, Inc.,

A complete description of graphics file formats.

Oualline, Steve. *Practical C Programming.* Sebastopol, CA: O'Reilly & Associates, Inc., 1992.

Oram, Andrew, and Talbott, Steve. *Managing Projects with make.* Second edition. Sebastopol, CA: O'Reilly & Associates, Inc., 1991.

O'Reilly, Tim, and Todino, Grace. *Managing uucp and Usenet.* Sebastopol, CA: O'Reilly & Associates, Inc., 1992.

The definitive guide to uucp management.

Peek, Jerry, O'Reilly, Tim, and Loukides, Mike. *UNIX Power Tools.* Sebastopol, CA: O'Reilly & Associates, Inc., 1993.

Includes CD-ROM. An indispensable collection of tips and tricks.

Plaugher, P. J. *The Standard C Library.* Englewood Cliffs, NJ: Prentice Hall, 1992.

An in-depth description of the standard (i.e., ANSI) C library.

Raymond, Eric, ed. *The New Hacker's Dictionary.* Cambridge, MA: MIT Press, 1991.

Ritchie, Dennis M. "A Stream Input-Output System." *AT&T Bell Laboratories Technical Journal.* 63, pt. 2, 1897,

A description of the original Eighth Edition streams concept.

Rosler, L. "The Evolution of C—Past and Future." *AT&T Bell Laboratories Technical Journal.* 63, pt. 2, 1685,

A description of the state of the C language in 1984.

Seyer, Martin D. *RS-232 Made Easy.* Englewood Cliffs, NJ: Prentice Hall, 1991.

A discussion of the RS-232 standard.

Stevens, W. Richard. *Advanced Programming in the UNIX Environment.* Reading, MA: Addison Wesley, 1992.

An excellent treatise on systems programming under modern UNIX variants.

———. *TCP/IP Illustrated.* Reading, MA: Addison Wesley, 1994.

A description of the IP protocol suite from the viewpoint of the *tcpdump* program.

———. *UNIX Network Programming.* Englewood Cliffs, NJ: Prentice Hall, 1990.

Includes a comparison of sockets and STREAMS.

Strang, John. *Programming with curses.* Sebastopol, CA: O'Reilly & Associates, Inc., 1986.

A description of the BSD version of *curses.*

———, O'Reilly, Tim, and Mui, Linda. *termcap and terminfo.* Sebastopol, CA: O'Reilly & Associates, Inc., 1989.

A description of *termcap* and *terminfo.*

Swift, Jonathan. *Gulliver's Travels.* 1726.

A satire of early eighteenth-century English politics.

Tichy, Walter F. *RCS—A System for Version Control.* 1991.

Part of the RCS distribution.

Todino, Grace, and Dougherty, Dale. *Using uucp and Usenet.* Sebastopol, CA: O'Reilly & Associates, Inc., 1987.

The definitive guide to using *uucp.*

Todino, Grace, Strang, John, and Peek, Jerry. *Learning the UNIX Operating System.* Sebastopol, CA: O'Reilly & Associates, Inc., 1993.

A straightforward introduction to UNIX.

Walsh, Norman. *Making TEX Work.* Sebastopol, CA: O'Reilly & Associates, Inc., 1994.

A useful book on TEX.

UNIX System V Application Binary Interface. Englewood Cliffs, NJ: UNIX Press, 1992.

UNIX Time-Sharing System UNIX Programmer's Manual. New York, NY: Holt, Rinehart, and Winston, 1979.

The original Seventh Edition UNIX documentation (two volumes).

Index

About the Author

Greg Lehey is an independent computer consultant specializing in UNIX. Born in Australia, he was educated in Malaysia and England before studying Chemistry in Germany and Chemical Engineering in England. He has spent his professional career in Germany, where he worked for computer manufacturers such as Univac and Tandem, the German space research agency, nameless software houses, and a large user before deciding to work for himself. In the course of over 20 years in the industry he has performed most jobs you can think of, ranging from kernel support to product marketing, systems programming to operating, processing satellite data to programming gasoline pumps. About the only thing he hasn't done is write commercial software. He is currently engaged in the production of CD-ROMs of ported free software, and this book is one result of his experience in this area. He is available for short-term contracts and can be reached by mail at *grog@lemis.de.*

When he can drag himself away from his collection of UNIX workstations, Greg is involved in performing baroque and classical woodwind music on his collection of original instruments, exploring the German countryside with his family on their Arab horses, and exploring new cookery techniques or ancient and obscure European languages.

Colophon

Our look is the result of reader comments, our own experimentation, and distribution channels. Distinctive covers complement our distinctive approach to technical topics, breathing personality and life into potentially dry subjects. UNIX and its attendant programs can be unruly beasts. Nutshell Handbooks help you tame them.

The animal featured on the cover of *Porting UNIX Software: From Download to Debug* is a South American iguana. This fierce-looking reptile, which can grow up to seven feet in length, can be found in forested areas near rivers throughout South America. Older iguanas feed primarily on plant vegetation, but when younger they prefer to feed on small animals. Iguanas often climb tall trees to bask in their sun-drenched canopies. If disturbed from its rest, an iguana may quickly dive into the river surface below, where it is quite at home. The iguana has developed quick reflex movements to escape impending danger. It will also defend against predators itself using crushing snaps of its long, muscular tail.

Edie Freedman designed the cover of this book, using a 19th-century engraving from the Dover Pictorial Archive. The cover layout was produced with Quark XPress 3.3 using the ITC Garamond font.

The inside layout was designed by Edie Freedman, Jennifer Niederst and, Nancy Priest. Text was prepared in SGML using the DocBook 2.1 DTD. The print version of this book was created by translating the SGML source into a set of gtroff macros using a filter developed at ORA by Norman Walsh. Steve Talbott designed and wrote the underlying macro set on the basis of the GNU troff -gs macros; Lenny Muellner adapted them to SGML and implemented the book design. The GNU groff text formatter version 1.09 was used to generate PostScript output. The text and heading fonts are ITC Garamond Light and Garamond Book. The illustrations that appear in the book were created in Macromedia Freehand 5.0 by Chris Reilley. This colophon was written by Clairemarie Fisher O'Leary.

Programming

UNIX, C and MULTI-PLATFORM

Books from O'Reilly & Associates, Inc.

Fall/Winter 1995-96

C Programming Libraries

Practical C++ Programming

By Steve Oualline
1st Edition September 1995
584 pages, ISBN 1-56592-139-9

Fast becoming the standard language of commercial software development, C++ is an update of the C programming language, adding object-oriented features that are very helpful for today's larger graphical applications.

Practical C++ Programming is a complete introduction to the C++ language for the beginning programmer, and also for C programmers transitioning to C++. Unlike most other C++ books, this book emphasizes a practical, real-world approach, including how to debug, how to make your code understandable to others, and how to understand other people's code. Topics covered include good programming style, C++ syntax (what to use and what not to use), C++ class design, debugging and optimization, and common programming mistakes. At the end of each chapter are a number of exercises you can use to make sure you've grasped the concepts. Solutions to most are provided.

Practical C++ Programming describes standard C++ features that are supported by all UNIX C++ compilers (including *gcc*), DOS/Windows and NT compilers (including Microsoft Visual C++), and Macintosh compilers.

C++: The Core Language

By Gregory Satir & Doug Brown
1st Edition October 1995
228 pages, ISBN 1-56592-116-X

A first book for C programmers transitioning to C++, an object-oriented enhancement of the C programming language. Designed to get readers up to speed quickly, this book thoroughly explains the important concepts and features and gives brief overviews of the rest of the language. Covers features common to all C++ compilers, including those on UNIX, Windows NT, Windows, DOS, and Macs.

Porting UNIX Software

By Greg Lehey
1st Edition November 1995
480 pages (est.), ISBN 1-56592-126-7

This book deals with the whole life cycle of porting, from setting up a source tree on your system to correcting platform differences and even testing the executable after it's built. It exhaustively discusses the differences between versions of UNIX and the areas where porters tend to have problems. The assumption made in this book is that you just want to get a package working on your system; you don't want to become an expert in the details of your hardware or operating system (much less an expert in the system used by the person who wrote the package!).

Programming with Pthreads

By Bradford Nichols
1st Edition February 1996 (est.)
350 pages (est.), ISBN 1-56592-115-1

The idea behind POSIX threads is to have multiple tasks running concurrently within the same program. They can share a single CPU as processes do, or take advantage of multiple CPUs when available. In either case, they provide a clean way to divide the tasks of a program while sharing data. This book features realistic examples, a look behind the scenes at the implementation and performance issues, and chapters on special topics such as DCE, real-time, and multiprocessing.

POSIX.4

By Bill Gallmeister
1st Edition January 1995
570 pages, ISBN 1-56592-074-0

A general introduction to real-time programming and real-time issues, this book covers the POSIX.4 standard and how to use it to solve "real-world" problems. If you're at all interested in real-time applications—which include just about everything from telemetry to transaction processing—this book is for you. An essential reference.

POSIX Programmer's Guide

By Donald Lewine
1st Edition April 1991
640 pages, ISBN 0-937175-73-0

Most UNIX systems today are POSIX compliant because the federal government requires it for its purchases. Given the manufacturer's documentation, however, it can be difficult to distinguish system-specific features from those features defined by POSIX. The *POSIX Programmer's Guide*, intended as an explanation of the POSIX standard and as a reference for the POSIX.1 programming library, helps you write more portable programs.

"If you are an intermediate to advanced C programmer and are interested in having your programs compile first time on anything from a Sun to a VMS system to an MSDOS system, then this book must be thoroughly recommended." —*Sun UK User*

Practical C Programming

By Steve Oualline
2nd Edition January 1993
396 pages, ISBN 1-56592-035-X

C programming is more than just getting the syntax right. Style and debugging also play a tremendous part in creating programs that run well. *Practical C Programming* teaches you not only the mechanics of programming, but also how to create programs that are easy to read, maintain, and debug. There are lots of introductory C books, but this is the Nutshell Handbook®! In this edition, programs conform to ANSI C.

Using C on the UNIX System

By Dave Curry
1st Edition January 1989
250 pages, ISBN 0-937175-23-4

This is the book for intermediate to experienced C programmers who want to become UNIX system programmers. It explains system calls and special library routines available on the UNIX system. It is impossible to write UNIX utilities of any sophistication without understanding the material in this book.

Programming with curses

By John Strang
1st Edition 1986
76 pages, ISBN 0-937175-02-1

Curses is a UNIX library of functions for controlling a terminal's display screen from a C program. This handbook helps you make use of the curses library. Describes the original Berkeley version of curses.

Understanding and Using COFF

By Gintaras R. Gircys
1st Edition November 1988
196 pages, ISBN 0-937175-31-5

COFF—Common Object File Format—is the formal definition for the structure of machine code files in the UNIX System V environment. All machine code files are COFF files. This handbook explains COFF data structure and its manipulation.

C Programming Tools

Microsoft RPC Programming Guide

By John Shirley & Ward Rosenberry, Digital Equipment Corporation
1st Edition March 1995
254 pages, ISBN 1-56592-070-8

Remote Procedure Call (RPC) is the glue that holds together MS-DOS, Windows 3.x, and Windows NT. It is a client-server technology—a way of making programs on two different systems work together like one. The advantage of RPC is that you can link two systems together using simple C calls, as in a single-system program.

Like many aspects of Microsoft programming, RPC forms a small world of its own, with conventions and terms that can be confusing. This book is an introduction to Microsoft RPC concepts combined with a step-by-step guide to programming RPC calls in C. Topics include server registration, interface definitions, arrays and pointers, context handles, and basic administration procedures. This edition covers version 2.0 of Microsoft RPC. Four complete examples are included.

Power Programming with RPC

By John Bloomer
1st Edition February 1992
522 pages, ISBN 0-937175-77-3

RPC, or remote procedure calling, is the ability to distribute the execution of functions on remote computers. Written from a programmer's perspective, this book shows what you can do with RPCs, like Sun RPC, the de facto standard on UNIX systems. It covers related programming topics for Sun and other UNIX systems and teaches through examples.

lex & yacc

By John Levine, Tony Mason & Doug Brown
2nd Edition October 1992
366 pages, ISBN 1-56592-000-7

Shows programmers how to use two UNIX utilities, *lex* and *yacc*, in program development. The second edition contains completely revised tutorial sections for novice users and reference sections for advanced users. This edition is twice the size of the first, has an expanded index, and covers Bison and Flex.

Applying RCS and SCCS

By Don Bolinger & Tan Bronson
1st Edition September 1995
528 pages, ISBN 1-56592-117-8

Applying RCS and SCCS is a thorough introduction to these two systems, viewed as tools for project management. This book takes the reader from basic source control of a single file, through working with multiple releases of a software project, to coordinating multiple developers. It also presents TCCS, a representative "front-end" that addresses problems RCS and SCCS can't handle alone, such as managing groups of files, developing for multiple platforms, and linking public and private development areas.

Programming with GNU Software

By Mike Loukides
1st Edition TBA 1996 (est.)
250 pages (est.), ISBN 1-56592-112-7

This book and CD combination is a complete package for programmers who are new to UNIX or who would like to make better use of the system. The tools come from Cygnus Support, Inc., a well-known company that provides support for free software. Contents include GNU Emacs, *gcc*, C and C++ libraries, *gdb*, RCS, GNATS, and *make*. The book provides an introduction to all these tools for a C programmer.

UNIX Systems Programming for SVR4

By Dave Curry
1st Edition December 1995 (est.)
600 pages (est.), ISBN 1-56592-163-1

Presents a comprehensive look at the nitty gritty details on how UNIX interacts with applications. If you're writing an application from scratch, or if you're porting an application to any System V.4 platform, you need this book. It thoroughly explains all UNIX system calls and library routines related to systems programming, working with I/O, files and directories, processing multiple input streams, file and record locking, and memory-mapped files.

Software Portability with imake

By Paul DuBois
1st Edition July 1993
390 pages, ISBN 1-56592-055-4

imake is a utility that works with ***make*** to enable code to be compiled and installed on different UNIX machines. ***imake*** makes possible the wide portability of the X Window System code and is widely considered an X tool, but it's also useful for any software project that needs to be ported to many UNIX systems.

This Nutshell Handbook®—the only book available on ***imake***—is ideal for X and UNIX programmers who want their software to be portable. The book is divided into two sections. The first section is a general explanation of ***imake***, X configuration files, and how to write and debug an ***Imakefile***. The second section describes how to write configuration files and presents a configuration file architecture that allows development of coexisting sets of configuration files. Several sample sets of configuration files are described and are available free over the Net.

Managing Projects with make

By Andrew Oram & Steve Talbott
2nd Edition October 1991
152 pages, ISBN 0-937175-90-0

make is one of UNIX's greatest contributions to software development, and this book offers the clearest description of ***make*** ever written. It describes all the basic features of ***make*** and provides guidelines on meeting the needs of large, modern projects. Also contains a description of free products that contain major enhancements to ***make***.

Checking C Programs with lint

By Ian F. Darwin
1st Edition October 1988
84 pages, ISBN 0-937175-30-7

The ***lint*** program is one of the best tools for finding portability problems and certain types of coding errors in C programs. This handbook introduces you to ***lint***, guides you through running it on your programs, and helps you interpret ***lint's*** output.

Fortran/Scientific Computing

Migrating to Fortran 90

By James F. Kerrigan
1st Edition November 1993
389 pages, ISBN 1-56592-049-X

This book is a practical guide to Fortran 90 for the current Fortran programmer. It provides a complete overview of the new features that Fortran 90 has brought to the Fortran standard, with examples and suggestions for use. Topics include array sections, modules, file handling, allocatable arrays and pointers, and numeric precision.

"This is a book that all Fortran programmers eager to take advantage of the excellent features of Fortran 90 will want to have on their desk." —*FORTRAN Journal*

High Performance Computing

By Kevin Dowd
1st Edition June 1993
398 pages, ISBN 1-56592-032-5

Even if you never touch a line of code, *High Performance Computing* will help you make sense of the newest generation of workstations. A must for anyone who needs to worry about computer performance, this book covers everything, from the basics of modern workstation architecture, to structuring benchmarks, to squeezing more performance out of critical applications. It also explains what a good compiler can do—and what you have to do yourself. The author also discusses techniques for improving memory access patterns and taking advantage of parallelism.

Another valuable section of the book discusses the benchmarking process, or how to evaluate a computer's performance. Kevin Dowd discusses several of the "standard" industry benchmarks, explaining what they measure and what they don't. He also explains how to set up your own benchmark: how to structure the code, how to measure the results, and how to interpret them.

Database

ORACLE Performance Tuning

By Peter Corrigan & Mark Gurry
1st Edition September 1993
642 pages, ISBN 1-56592-048-1

The Oracle relational database management system is the most popular database system in use today. Oracle offers tremendous power and flexibility, but at some cost. Demands for fast response, particularly in online transaction processing systems, make performance a major issue. With more organizations downsizing and adopting client-server and distributed database approaches, performance tuning has become all the more vital. Whether you're a manager, a designer, a programmer, or an administrator, there's a lot you can do on your own to dramatically increase the performance of your existing Oracle system. Whether you are running RDBMS Version 6 or Version 7, you may find that this book can save you the cost of a new machine; at the very least, it will save you a lot of headaches.

"This book is one of the best books on Oracle that I have ever read.... [It] discloses many Oracle Tips that DBA's and Developers have locked in their brains and in their planners.... I recommend this book for any person who works with Oracle, from managers to developers. In fact, I have to keep [it] under lock and key, because of the popularity of it."
—Mike Gangler

ORACLE PL/SQL Programming

By Steven Feuerstein
1st Edition September 1995
916 pages, Includes diskette, ISBN 1-56592-142-9

PL/SQL is a procedural language that is being used more and more with Oracle, particularly in client-server applications. This book fills a huge gap in the Oracle market by providing developers with a single, comprehensive guide to building applications with PL/SQL—and building them the right way. It's packed with strategies, code architectures, tips, techniques, and fully realized code. Includes a disk containing many examples of PL/SQL programs.

Multi-Platform Programming

DCE Security Programming

By Wei Hu
1st Edition July 1995
386 pages, ISBN 1-56592-134-8

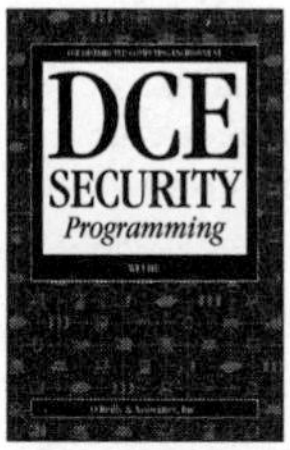

Security is critical in network applications since an outsider can so easily gain network access and pose as a trusted user. Here lies one of the greatest strengths of the Distributed Computing Environment (DCE) from the Open Software Foundation (OSF). DCE offers the most complete, flexible, and well-integrated network security package in the industry. The only problem is learning how to program it.

This book covers DCE security requirements, how the system fits together, what is required of the programmer, and how to figure out what needs protecting in an application. It will help you plan an application and lay the groundwork for Access Control Lists (ACLs), as well as use the calls that come with the DCE security interfaces. Using a sample application, increasingly sophisticated types of security are discussed, including storage of ACLs on disk and the job of writing an ACL manager. This book focuses on version 1.0 of DCE. However, issues in version 1.1 are also discussed so you can migrate to that interface.

Guide to Writing DCE Applications

By John Shirley, Wei Hu & David Magid
2nd Edition May 1994
462 pages, ISBN 1-56592-045-7

A hands-on programming guide to OSF's Distributed Computing Environment (DCE) for first-time DCE application programmers. This book is designed to help new DCE users make the transition from conventional, nondistributed applications programming to distributed DCE programming. In addition to basic RPC (remote procedure calls), this edition covers object UUIDs and basic security (authentication and authorization). Also includes practical programming examples.

"This book will be useful as a ready reference by the side of the novice DCE programmer." —*;login*

Distributing Applications Across DCE and Windows NT

By Ward Rosenberry & Jim Teague
1st Edition November 1993
302 pages, ISBN 1-56592-047-3

This book links together two exciting technologies in distributed computing by showing how to develop an application that simultaneously runs on DCE and Microsoft systems through remote procedure calls (RPC). Covers the writing of portable applications and the complete differences between RPC support in the two environments.

Understanding DCE

By Ward Rosenberry, David Kenney & Gerry Fisher
1st Edition October 1992
266 pages, ISBN 1-56592-005-8

A technical and conceptual overview of OSF's Distributed Computing Environment (DCE) for programmers, technical managers, and marketing and sales people. Unlike many O'Reilly & Associates books, *Understanding DCE* has no hands-on programming elements. Instead, the book focuses on how DCE can be used to accomplish typical programming tasks and provides explanations to help the reader understand all the parts of DCE.

Multi-Platform Code Management

By Kevin Jameson
1st Edition August 1994
354 pages, Includes two diskettes, ISBN 1-56592-059-7

For any programming team that is struggling with build and maintenance problems, this book—and its accompanying software (available for 15 platforms, including MS-DOS and various UNIX systems)—can save dozens of errors and hours of effort. A "one-stop-shopping" solution for code management proplems, this book shows you how to structure a large project and keep your files and builds under control over many releases and platforms. Includes two diskettes that provide a complete system for managing source files and builds.

Encyclopedia of Graphics File Formats

By James D. Murray & William vanRyper
1st Edition July 1994
928 pages, Includes CD-ROM
ISBN 1-56592-058-9

The computer graphics world is a veritable alphabet soup of acronyms; BMP, DXF, EPS, GIF, MPEG, PCX, PIC, RIFF, RTF, TGA, and TIFF are only a few of the many different formats in which graphics images can be stored. *The Encyclopedia of Graphics File Formats* is the definitive work on file formats—the book that will become a classic for graphics programmers and everyone else who deals with the low-level technical details of graphics files. It includes technical information on nearly 100 file formats, as well as chapters on graphics and file format basics, bitmap and vector files, metafiles, scene description, animation and multimedia formats, and file compression methods. Best of all, this book comes with a CD-ROM that collects many hard-to-find resources. We've assembled original vendor file format specification documents, along with test images and code examples, and a variety of software packages for MS-DOS, Windows, OS/2, UNIX, and the Macintosh that will let you convert, view, and manipulate graphics files and images.

Understanding Japanese Information Processing

By Ken Lunde
1st Edition September 1993
470 pages, ISBN 1-56592-043-0

Understanding Japanese Information Processing provides detailed information on all aspects of handling Japanese text on computer systems. It brings all of the relevant information together in a single book and covers everything from the origins of modern-day Japanese to the latest information on specific emerging computer encoding standards. Appendices provide additional reference material, such as a code conversion table, character set tables, mapping tables, an extensive list of software sources, a glossary, and more.

At Your Fingertips—

A COMPLETE GUIDE TO O'REILLY'S ONLINE SERVICES

O'Reilly & Associates offers extensive product and customer service information online. We invite you to come and explore our little neck-of-the-woods.

For product information and insight into new technologies, visit the O'Reilly Resource Center

Most comprehensive among our online offerings is the O'Reilly Resource Center. You'll find detailed information on all O'Reilly products, including titles, prices, tables of contents, indexes, author bios, software contents, and reviews. You can also view images of all our products. In addition, watch for informative articles that provide perspective on the technologies we write about. Interviews, excerpts, and bibliographies are also included.

After browsing online, it's easy to order, too, with GNN Direct or by sending email to **order@ora.com**. The O'Reilly Resource Center shows you how. Here's how to visit us online:

☞ *Via the World Wide Web*

If you are connected to the Internet, point your Web browser (e.g., **mosaic, netscape,** or **lynx**) to:

http://www.ora.com/

For the plaintext version, **telnet** to: **www.ora.com** (login: **oraweb**)

☞ *Via Gopher*

If you have a Gopher program, our Gopher server has information in a menu format that some people prefer to the Web.

Connect your **gopher** to: **gopher.ora.com**
Or, point your Web browser to:
gopher://gopher.ora.com/

Or, you can **telnet** to: **gopher.ora.com** (login: **gopher**)

A convenient way to stay informed: email mailing lists

An easy way to learn of the latest projects and products from O'Reilly & Associates is to subscribe to our mailing lists. We have email announcements and discussions on various topics, for example "ora-news," our electronic news service. Subscribers receive email as soon as the information breaks.

☞ *To join a mailing list:*

Send email to:
listproc@online.ora.com

Leave the message "subject" empty if possible.

If you know the name of the mailing list you want to subscribe to, put the following information on the first line of your message: **subscribe** "listname" "your name" **of** "your company."

For example: **subscribe ora-news**
Kris Webber of Fine Enterprises

If you don't know the name of the mailing list, listproc will send you a listing of all the mailing lists. Put this word on the first line of the body: **lists**

To find out more about a particular list, send a message with this word as the first line of the body: **info** "listname"

For more information and help, send this message: **help**

For specific help, email to: **listmaster@online.ora.com**

The complete O'Reilly catalog is now available via email

You can now receive a text-only version of our complete catalog via email. It contains detailed information about all our products, so it's mighty big: over 200 kbytes, or 200,000 characters.

To get the whole catalog in one message, send an empty email message to: **catalog@online.ora.com**

If your email system can't handle large messages, you can get the catalog split into smaller messages.
Send email to: **catalog-split@online.ora.com**

To receive a print catalog, send your snail mail address to: **catalog@ora.com**

Check out Web Review, our new publication on the Web

Web Review is our new magazine that offers fresh insights into the Web. The editorial mission of Web Review is to answer the question: How and where do you BEST spend your time online? Each issue contains reviews that look at the most interesting and creative sites on the Web.
Visit us at **http://gnn.com/wr/**

Web Review is the product of the recently formed Songline Studios, a venture between O'Reilly and America Online.

Get the files you want with FTP

We have an archive of example files from our books, the covers of our books, and much more available by anonymous FTP.

`ftp` to:

`ftp.ora.com` (login: **`anonymous`** – use your email address as the password.)

Or, if you have a WWW browser, point it to:

`ftp://ftp.ora.com/`

FTPMAIL

The ftpmail service connects to O'Reilly's FTP server and sends the results (the files you want) by email. This service is for people who can't use FTP—but who can use email.

For help and examples, send an email message to:

`ftpmail@online.ora.com`

(In the message body, put the single word: **`help`**)

Helpful information is just an email message away

Many customer services are provided via email. Here are a few of the most popular and useful:

info@online.ora.com
For a list of O'Reilly's online customer services.

info@ora.com
For general questions and information.

bookquestions@ora.com
For technical questions, or corrections, concerning book contents.

order@ora.com
To order books online and for ordering questions.

catalog@online.ora.com
To receive an online copy of our catalog.

catalog@ora.com
To receive a free copy of *ora.com*, our combination magazine and catalog. Please include your snail mail address.

international@ora.com
Comments or questions about international ordering or distribution.

xresource@ora.com
To order or inquire about *The X Resource* journal.

proposals@ora.com
To submit book proposals.

info@gnn.com
To receive information about America Online's GNN (Global Network Navigator).™

O'Reilly & Associates, Inc.

103A Morris Street, Sebastopol, CA 95472

Inquiries: **707-829-0515, 800-998-9938**

Credit card orders: **800-889-8969** (Weekdays 6 A.M.- 5 P.M. PST)

FAX: **707-829-0104**

O'Reilly & Associates—
INTERNATIONAL DISTRIBUTORS

Customers outside North America can now order O'Reilly & Associates books through the following distributors. They offer our international customers faster order processing, more bookstores, increased representation at tradeshows worldwide, and the high-quality, responsive service our customers have come to expect.

EUROPE, MIDDLE EAST, AND AFRICA
(except Germany, Switzerland, and Austria)

INQUIRIES

International Thomson Publishing Europe
Berkshire House
168-173 High Holborn
London WC1V 7AA, United Kingdom
Telephone: 44-71-497-1422
Fax: 44-71-497-1426
Email: itpint@itps.co.uk

ORDERS

International Thomson Publishing Services, Ltd.
Cheriton House, North Way
Andover, Hampshire SP10 5BE, United Kingdom
Telephone: 44-264-342-832 (UK orders)
Telephone: 44-264-342-806 (outside UK)
Fax: 44-264-364418 (UK orders)
Fax: 44-264-342761 (outside UK)

GERMANY, SWITZERLAND, AND AUSTRIA

International Thomson Publishing GmbH
O'Reilly-International Thomson Verlag
Königswinterer Straße 418
53227 Bonn, Germany
Telephone: 49-228-97024 0
Fax: 49-228-441342
Email: anfragen@ora.de

ASIA *(except Japan)*

INQUIRIES

International Thomson Publishing Asia
221 Henderson Road
#08-03 Henderson Industrial Park
Singapore 0315
Telephone: 65-272-6496
Fax: 65-272-6498

ORDERS

Telephone: 65-268-7867
Fax: 65-268-6727

JAPAN

O'Reilly & Associates, Inc.
103A Morris Street
Sebastopol, CA 95472 U.S.A.
Telephone: 707-829-0515
Telephone: 800-998-9938 (U.S. & Canada)
Fax: 707-829-0104
Email: order@ora.com

AUSTRALIA

WoodsLane Pty. Ltd.
7/5 Vuko Place, Warriewood NSW 2102
P.O. Box 935, Mona Vale NSW 2103
Australia
Telephone: 02-970-5111
Fax: 02-970-5002
Email: woods@tmx.mhs.oz.au

NEW ZEALAND

WoodsLane New Zealand Ltd.
21 Cooks Street (P.O. Box 575)
Wanganui, New Zealand
Telephone: 64-6-347-6543
Fax: 64-6-345-4840
Email: woods@tmx.mhs.oz.au

THE AMERICAS

O'Reilly & Associates, Inc.
103A Morris Street
Sebastopol, CA 95472 U.S.A.
Telephone: 707-829-0515
Telephone: 800-998-9938 (U.S. & Canada)
Fax: 707-829-0104
Email: order@ora.com

Here's a page we encourage readers to tear out...

O'REILLY WOULD LIKE TO HEAR FROM YOU

Please send me the following:

❑ *ora.com*
O'Reilly's magazine/catalog, containing behind-the-scenes articles and interviews on the technology we write about, and a complete listing of O'Reilly books and products.

Which book did this card come from?

____

Where did you buy this book?
❑ Bookstore ❑ Direct from O'Reilly
❑ Bundled with hardware/software ❑ Class/seminar

Your job description: ❑ SysAdmin ❑ Programmer
❑ Other ________________________________

Describe your operating system: ________________

____

Please print legibly

Name ________________ Company/Organization Name ________________

Address ________________________________

City ________________ State ________________ Zip/Postal Code ________________ Country ________________

Telephone ________________ Internet or other email address (specify network) ________________

Nineteenth century wood engraving of raccoons from the O'Reilly & Associates Nutshell Handbook® *Applying RCS and SCCS.*

POST CARD

PLACE STAMP HERE

O'Reilly & Associates, Inc., 103A Morris Street, Sebastopol, CA 95472-9902

NO POSTAGE NECESSARY IF MAILED IN THE UNITED STATES

BUSINESS REPLY MAIL

FIRST CLASS MAIL PERMIT NO. 80 SEBASTOPOL, CA

Postage will be paid by addressee

O'Reilly & Associates, Inc.
103A Morris Street
Sebastopol, CA 95472-9902